by G. Goos, J. Hartmanis and J. van Leeuwen

Springer
Berlin
Heidelberg
New York
Barcelona
Hong Kong
London
Milan
Paris
Singapore
Tokyo

oordination
anguages and Models

nternational Conference, COORDINATION 2000
ssol, Cyprus, September 11-13, 2000
eedings

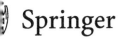 Springer

rhard Goos, Karlsruhe University, Germany
ris Hartmanis, Cornell University, NY, USA
n van Leeuwen, Utrecht University, The Netherlands

lume Editors

tónio Porto
iversidade Nova de Lisboa, Departamento de Informática
onte de Caparica, 2825-114 Caparica, Portugal
mail: ap@di.fct.unl.pt

uia-Catalin Roman
ashington University in St. Louis, Department of Computer Science
x 1045, One Brookings Drive, St. Louis, MO 63130, USA
mail: roman@cs.wustl.edu

taloging-in-Publication Data applied for

e Deutsche Bibliothek - CIP-Einheitsaufnahme

ordination languages and models : 4th international conference,
ordination 2000, Limassol, Cyprus, September 11 - 13, 2000 ;
oceedings / António Porto ; Gruia-Catalin Roman (ed.). - Berlin ;
eidelberg ; New York ; Barcelona ; Hong Kong ; London ; Milan ;
ris ; Singapore ; Tokyo : Springer, 2000
Lecture notes in computer science ; Vol. 1906)
SBN 3-540-41020-1

R Subject Classification (1998): D.1.3, C.2.4, F.1.2, D.2.4, I.2.11

SN 0302-9743
BN 3-540-41020-1 Springer-Verlag Berlin Heidelberg New York

ringer-Verlag Berlin Heidelberg New York
member of BertelsmannSpringer Science+Business Media GmbH
 Springer-Verlag Berlin Heidelberg 2000
nted in Germany

pesetting: Camera-ready by author, data conversion by Steingräber Satztechnik GmbH, Heidelberg
nted on acid-free paper   SPIN: 10722670   06/3142   5 4 3 2 1 0

Preface

This volume contains the *Proceedings of the Fourth International Conference on Coordination Models and Languages*, **Coordination 2000**. It was held in the wake of three successful earlier conferences whose proceedings were also published in this series, in volumes 1061, 1282 and 1594. The need for increased programmer productivity and rapid development of complex systems provides pragmatic motivation for the development of coordination languages and models. The intellectual excitement associated with such endeavors is rooted in the decades-old desire to cope with increasingly higher levels of abstraction. Coordination-based methods provide a clean separation between individual software components and their interactions within the overall software organization. This separation promises to make application development more tractable, to support global analysis, and to enhance software reuse. These are indeed major concerns in the information age, at a time when all aspects of society are relying, to an ever increasing degree, on software systems of unprecedented complexity. Research on coordination methods is likely to play a central role in addressing these technological concerns by changing the software culture around us and by leading to the development of effective technical solutions for a broad range of important problems.

Following a tradition of careful selection of high-quality contributions, 18 regular papers were chosen out of 52 submissions. Another nine were selected for presentation as short papers. The papers included in this volume reflect some of the new directions coordination research is pursuing (e.g., mobility, coordination styles, open systems, etc.) as well as continued study of established problem areas (e.g., semantic models, software architecture, dependability, etc.). The volume exhibits intellectual breadth, a great deal of diversity in views and pursuits, but also a surprising degree of cohesion. This enabled us to group papers by subject matter into sessions that are reflected in the organization of this volume. It is our hope that these papers will become a useful reference for many researchers worldwide and will stimulate further advances in coordination-centered technologies, methods, and formal studies.

The conference and this volume would not have been possible without the intellectual contributions of all the authors, the advice and careful reviews by members of the program committee, and the additional referees who helped us complete the paper evaluations. Special thanks go to Amy L. Murphy for helping with the administration of the submission and review process and to George Papadopoulos for chairing the local organization in Cyprus. Finally, we acknowledge the support from the University of Cyprus and the sponsorship and support from the Esprit Working Group 24512 "Coordina".

July 2000   António Porto
Gruia-Catalin Roman

Steering Committee

Paolo Ciancarini   U. Bologna, Italy
Roberto Gorrieri   U. Bologna, Italy
Chris Hankin   Imperial College, London, UK
Daniel Le Métayer   IRISA/INRIA, Rennes, France
António Porto   New U. Lisbon, Portugal
Robert Tolksdorf   T.U. Berlin, Germany

Program Committee

Co-chairs   António Porto   New U. of Lisbon, Portugal
           Gruia-Catalin Roman   Washington U. in St. Louis, USA

Members   Gul Agha   U. Illinois, Urbana-Champaign, USA
          Farhad Arbab   CWI, Amsterdam, The Netherlands
          Lubomir Bic   U. California, Irvine, USA
          GianLuigi Ferrari   U. Pisa, Italy
          Jose Luiz Fiadeiro   U. Lisbon, Portugal
          Roberto Gorrieri   U. Bologna, Italy
          Paola Inverardi   U. l'Aquila, Italy
          Jean-Marie Jacquet   U. Namur, Belgium
          Edwin de Jong   Silicon Graphics, De Meern,
                       The Netherlands
          Joost Kok   U. Leiden, The Netherlands
          Jose Meseguer   SRI, Menlo Park, USA
          Naftaly Minsky   Rutgers U., Piscataway, NJ, USA
          Antonio Natali   U. Bologna, Italy
          Rocco De Nicola   U. Firenze, Italy
          George Papadopoulos   U. Cyprus, Cyprus
          Rick Schlichting   U. Arizona, USA
          Katia Sycara   Carnegie Mellon U., Pittsburg, USA
          John Thomas   IBM Almaden, USA
          Robert Tolksdorf   T.U. Berlin, Germany
          Alan Wood   U. York, UK
          Daniel Yankelevich   Pragma Consultores, Buenos Aires,
                       Argentina

Organizing Chair

George Papadopoulos   U. Cyprus, Cyprus

Additional Reviewers

Lorenzo Bettini   Maurizio Gabrielli   Henry Muccini   Davide Rossi
Monica Bobrowski   Mauro Gaspari   Amy Murphy   Laura Semini
Victor Braberman   Dan Hirsch   Enrico Nardelli   Sebastian Uchitel
Nadia Busi   Michele Loreti   Alfredo Olivero   Betti Venneri
Enrico Denti   Chiara Meo   Rosario Pugliese   Gianluigi Zavattaro
Miguel Felder   Michela Milano

Table of Contents

Mobility

Semantic Models

Short papers

Shifting Linda Perspectives

Directions in Software Architecture

Achieving Software Dependability

Author Index 353

OpenSpaces: An Object-Oriented Framework for Reconfigurable Coordination Spaces *

Stéphane Ducasse, Thomas Hofmann, and Oscar Nierstrasz

Software Composition Group, Institut für Informatik (IAM), Universität Bern
{ducasse,hofmann,oscar}@iam.unibe.ch
http://www.iam.unibe.ch/~(ducasse,hofmann,oscar)/

Abstract. Tuple spaces have turned out to be one of the most fundamental abstractions for coordinating communicating agents. At the same time, researchers continue to propose new variants of tuple spaces, since no one approach seems to be universally applicable to all problem domains. Some models offer a certain configurability, but existing approaches generally stop at a fixed set of configuration options and static configuration at instantiation time. We argue that a more open approach is needed, and present OPENSPACES, an object-oriented framework that supports static configurability through subclassing across several dimensions, as well as dynamic configurability of policies through run-time composition. We introduce OPENSPACES by showing how it can be used to instantiate a typical application, and we present an overview of the framework, implemented in Smalltalk, detailing the various degrees of configurability.

Keywords: Object-Oriented Languages, Frameworks, White Box Reuse, Black Box Reuse, Dynamic Reconfiguration

1   Introduction

Tuple spaces have proven to be among the most fundamental and successful abstractions for coordinating concurrent activities. There are numerous reasons why this should be so, both technical and pragmatic.

On the technical side, tuple spaces have the advantage of capturing both communication and synchronisation in a simple and natural way. Tuples themselves represent resources that can be communicated, shared and exchanged, without the need to use additional synchronisation mechanisms. Furthermore, associative lookup obviates the need for communicating agents to be explicitly aware of one another's "identity."

On the pragmatic side, there are many kinds of problems that map naturally to the tuple space view of the world, namely, that there are many different kinds of concurrent "agents" that want to exchange "stuff" with one another. Tuples, in a sense, represent the least common denominator of data structures, and can therefore be used to easily model almost any kind of "stuff."

Why, then, have so many different variants of tuple spaces appeared over the years? Numerous variations on tuple spaces have been proposed, and it does not seem as though this proliferation will end soon [PA98]. Again, there are numerous reasons why this should be so, both technical and pragmatic.

---

* This research is funded by the Swiss Government under Project no. NFS-2000-46947.96.

A. Porto and G.-C. Roman (Eds.): COORDINATION 2000, LNCS 1906, pp. 1–18, 2000.
© Springer-Verlag Berlin Heidelberg 2000

On the pragmatic side, applications requirements impose different policies governing what kinds of "stuff" are exchanged, which agents have access to which resources, how resources are matched against queries, and what kinds of actions may be triggered upon exchanges of resources. On the technical side, tuple spaces say nothing about how such policies may be introduced as higher-level abstractions. (Linda, for example, provides no abstraction mechanisms whatsoever, considering that to be a matter for the host language.)

To alleviate this problem, some researchers have proposed tuple spaces with various configurable parameters [Tol97]. Still, the degree of configurability in these approaches tends to be limited, and any configuration parameters must be fixed when the tuple space is instantiated. Even approaches that allow different matching algorithms to be employed do not allow these to be changed at run-time. For application domains in which the policies under which agents exchange information and resources may be dynamically negotiated, this is not enough.

We propose OPENSPACES, an object-oriented framework which offers the core services of tuple spaces as standard features, and at the same time allows the policies in place to be arbitrarily tailored, and set in place at run-time. OPENSPACES is both a white-box and black-box framework. Individual tuple space abstractions can be specialised by subclassing, and their instances can be dynamically configured and composed at run-time.

OPENSPACES can be tailored in the following ways: (1) Different kinds of entities to be stored in an OpenSpace are defined by subclassing Entry. (2) Different matching policies are defined by subclassing ConfigurationPolicy. (3) Methods to be triggered before and after every access to a space can be specialized. This is useful for validating, modifying or rejecting entries, or for triggering any useful side effect. (4) These hook methods and the matching algorithms can be plugged in dynamically in a black-box fashion and take effect without restarting the system. (5) A special update method can be triggered to automatically adapt affected entries whenever the policy in place is dynamically changed.

In section 2 we introduce a motivating example that illustrates several of the kinds of configurability typical of coordination applications. In section 3 we introduce OPEN-SPACES by showing how it can be used to tackle the motivating example. Sections 4 and 5 present the OPENSPACES framework in more detail and illustrate how the framework supports variation. In the last two sections we present related work and conclusions.

2   Example: An Electronic Market Place

We will motivate OPENSPACES with a running example that exhibits not only a classical set of coordination requirements, but also common forms of variability. In the following section we will see how OPENSPACES can fulfill both sets of needs.

2.1   Scenario

Let us consider a typical trading situation: a buyer agent (i.e., someone representing a client) is looking for some goods or services. He wants to inform potential sellers of his needs and publishes his request e.g. as an advertisement in a newspaper. The sellers see the request and may react by offering a concrete bid for it. The buyer agent can choose amongst all received offers and may accept the one that meets his needs best.

This simple scenario exhibits several classical coordination requirements: the buyer doesn't know the sellers in advance; multiple potential sellers should be informed of the request; neither simultaneous nor synchronous communication between the buyer and sellers is needed; instead, the request should be *published* in some suitable medium; the request can be withdrawn once it is fulfilled (or expires); multiple buyers may wish to publish requests in thematically related media. This negotiation protocol therefore perfectly matches the characteristics of a blackboard-style architecture. Every step can be performed by posting a corresponding entry to the blackboard. It can be read or taken (consumed) by the receiver. Participants don't have to know each others' location or name, they just need to know where to find the blackboard.

2.2   Analysis

Even this simple scenario poses special requirements for the *policies* in place for the blackboard. A minimal implementation would require the following setup: (1) There are two kinds of agents to represent the buyers and the sellers. (2) The agents exchange entries (possibly, but not necessarily tuples) representing requests, offers and deals. *Requests* describe the desired product and maximum price. *Offers* describe the offered product and price. A *Deal* finally is written to accept a received Offer. (3) An offer must reference the request it responds to. A deal must reference the offer it accepts. (4) Requests must be readable by anyone interested, but they may only be withdrawn by the issuing buyer, when he is no longer interested in receiving more offers. (5) Offers referencing a request may only be read and removed by the initiating *Buyer*. (6) Deals may be read and removed by the seller who has issued the referenced offer. (7) To divide the market into multiple thematic sections, all entries must have a label with the name of the section they belong to.

3   The Market Place Using OPENSPACES

We will now introduce OPENSPACES by showing how it can be used to implement the market place scenario. We start with the simplest solution that works and incrementally show how we can specialize and extend the framework to provide new features or more refined solutions. First we present an overview of the framework to introduce the different entities involved.

3.1   OPENSPACES in a Nutshell

Our framework is tailored to instantiate data-driven coordination languages. The core defines a blackboard style medium, an OpenSpace, which allows agents to interact by exchanging data that are encapsulated as Entry objects. The agents are specializations of SpaceAgent. To get a reference to an OpenSpace, the agent calls the globally accessible SpaceServer, a name server that holds a SpaceAdministrator maintaining a collection of currently registered spaces.

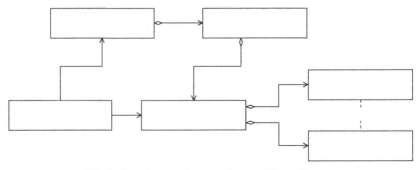

Fig. 1. Overview on the core classes of OPENSPACES.

The space offers the standard accessing primitives: write: anEntry puts the entry into the space, read: aTemplateEntry and take: aTemplateEntry retrieves an entry by associative lookup. The *template* is an entry that is used as a mask to select an entry from the space. The *matching algorithm* determines whether or not an actual entry matches the template and may be returned for it.

In OPENSPACES the matching algorithm is variable. It can be specified as needed for an application. Every used subclass of Entry may have its own strategy, which is defined in an associated ConfigurationPolicy. In addition the policy object *controls the access to the space* for entries of its associated class. This is realized with validating methods that are applied before and after all accesses. These methods may basically trigger any action on attempts to access the space (cf. section 4.3).

3.2   Market Place V.1: Standard Implementation

Instead of communicating tuples, we will use Form as a concrete subclass of Entry. It has as its sole attribute a dictionary, called bindings, which is used to store associations of any keys and values. This is a flexible approach since additionally needed values may be added without the need to define new subclasses.

A template matches a Form: (1) if the form is an instance of the same class as the template or of a subclass, and if (2) the form's bindings contains all the keys of the template's bindings and (3) their respective values are equal. Additional keys of the form are not considered.

The definition of the matching strategy is a responsibility of configuration policy objects. Figure 2 shows the implementation of the matching algorithm for the used forms. It is defined in class FormPolicy, extending ConfigurationPolicy.

Using the Market Place Forms. In the forms' bindings we enter the needed data for the trade communication and the name of the section of the market the form belongs to. As mentioned, a Form may be a request, an offer or a deal. Therefore it gets a value denoting its type. A request form can have bindings for a product name, for a description of the product, and for the maximum price the buyer is willing to pay for it. An offer form may describe a concrete product and price, and holds a reference to the request. A deal form has a reference to the offer it accepts.

```
FormPolicy >> does: aForm matchWith: aTemplate
  "Answer true if aForm contains all keys of aTemplate and all
  respective values are equal."
  |ok|
  ok := (aForm isKindOf: aTemplate class)
          and: [aTemplate bindings notNil].
  ok ifTrue:
      [aTemplate bindings keys
        do: [:key |
          (aForm bindings includesKey: key)
            ifFalse: [ok := false]
            ifTrue:
              [ok := (aForm bindings at: key)
                    = (aTemplate bindings at: key)]]].
  ^ ok
```

Fig. 2. The matching algorithm for forms defined in class `FormPolicy`.

3.3 Uniquely Identifiable Entries

To have a uniquely referenceable index for each form, we add a binding for the index and its value to every form when writing the form to the space. To remember the highest index used so far, there is a `Tail` entry to hold its current value. A `MarketAgent` – a specialized `SpaceAgent` – who wishes to append a new form to the market place, takes the tail entry, increments its index value, puts it back to the space and writes the form with the new index to the space (See figure 3). Beside remembering the last used index, the `Tail` entry – actually a counter – acts also as a semaphore, ensuring that only one form is written per index.

```
MarketAgent >> append: aForm
  "Get a new index, add it to aForm and write aForm to the space"
  |template tail|
  template := TailEntry new.
  template section: (aForm bindings at: #section)).
  tail := self hostSpace take: template.
  tail index: tail index + 1.
  self hostSpace write: tail.
  aForm bindings at: #index put: tail index.
  self hostSpace write: aForm
```

Fig. 3. The MarketAgent's appending method.

A `MarketAgent` who wants to read all present requests would have to iterate over all indices up to the last one denoted by the tail. As a simplification the agent may use the `readAll` operation provided by OPENSPACES, which is similar to `read`, but returns a collection with ALL entries from the space that match the template.

3.4 Stepping through a Trade

As actual participants we specialize `MarketAgent` to `Buyer` and `Seller`. Their respective protocols support the role specific actions of their respective parts. These are as follows: (1) The buyer makes a request by appending a new request form to the market space. (2) Sellers get the request when scanning for newly arrived requests. (3) Each seller may make an offer for it by appending an offer form that references the request with its index. (4) The buyer scans for offers to her request and takes them from the market. (5) When detecting a valuable offer, the buyer accepts it by appending a deal form with a reference to the offer and also the initial request to avoid differences. She then removes referenced requests. (6) The seller detects the deal form by scanning for any reactions to its own offers and removes it.

For each participant we have built a simple user interface. The `BuyerUI` allows a user to specify a requested product and send a request form to the space. The UI shows the received index for the request. The UI shows the collected offers and lets the user select the best and send a deal form. The seller has a similar UI for her counterpart.

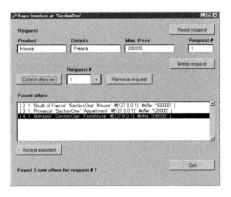

Fig. 4. The user interface for the buyer.

3.5 Market Place V.2: Consistency Assertions

In the first version of the market place, we defined a special matching algorithm for our market forms. In addition to the specific form matching algorithm we now define *access control assertions* in the configuration policy, which are applied at each attempt to read, take or write certain entries. We thereby check the forms for completeness and correctness.

This checking is made in subclasses of `ConfigurationPolicy`. To become effective the policies must be registered with the class of entries it will be affecting. We therefore subclassed `Form` to `Request`, `Offer` and `Deal` (without any changes in the implementation). The corresponding policies each override the `preWriteCheck:` method to specify the needed checks on the used forms before they are written to the space. The forms are accepted only if they are correct, otherwise they are rejected. (In section 4.3 is a more detailed discussion of these hook methods).

```
RequestPolicy >> preWriteCheck: aForm
 "Check aForm for necessary keys, if its index is equal to the
 tail's and if there is no other form present with this index."
 |ok|
 "... ok := aForm includes keys #section, #product, and #index"
 ok ifTrue:
     [ |template tail|
     template := TailEntry new.
     template section: (aForm bindings at: #section).
     tail := self hostSpace read: template.
     ok := (aForm bindings at: #index) = tail index ].
 ok ifTrue:
     [ template := Form new.
     template bindings
       at: #section put: (aForm bindings at: #section).
     (hostSpace readAll: template)
       do: [:each |
         (each bindings at: #index)=(aForm bindings at: #index)
            ifTrue: [ok := false]]].
 ^ok
   ifTrue: [aForm]      "passed"
   ifFalse: [nil]       "reject"
```

Fig. 5. The preWriteCheck: method of the RequestPolicy for consistency assertion.

The RequestPolicy checks if the request form is complete and if its index actually is unique and equal to the tail entry's index. Figure 5 shows this consistency check. The OfferPolicy checks if the offer includes a reference to a request that is actually (still) present at the space. The DealPolicy checks if the deal includes references to an offer and a request. If the referenced forms are still at the space they are removed (space clean up).

With the same approach we may increase consistency of the system more by e.g. not allowing an agent to write the same form twice, etc. Note that the form and policy classes can be used with the new policies as soon as they are defined and registered at the space.

3.6 Market Place V.3: Automatic Index Handling

The index incrementing procedure for writing market forms is somewhat awkward. We want to reduce the workload and the responsibility of the market agents - and also the network traffic(!) - by doing this at the space.

We specialize the configuration policies to handle the indices automatically. The agents append forms without checking for a correct index. The policy takes care of the tail business and sets the index of the form accordingly. Since the write operation of the space returns the actually written entry, the agent checks this for the received index.

In Figure 6 the preWriteCheck: method passes the validated form back to the space's writing operation where it will be used instead of the original form. Since the

```
AutomaticIndexPolicy >> preWriteCheck: aForm
  "Take the tail entry, increment its index and put it back.
  Enter the new tail index to the form"
  |checkedForm|
  checkedForm := (aForm bindings includesKey: #section)
                  ifTrue: [aForm]
                  ifFalse: [nil].
  checkedForm notNil
    ifTrue:
      [ |template tail newIndex|
      template := TailEntry new.
      template section: (aForm bindings at: #section).
      tail := self hostSpace take: template.
      newIndex := tail index + 1.
      tail index: newIndex.
      self hostSpace write: tail.
      aForm bindings at: #index put: newIndex.
      self hostSpace write: aForm
      checkedForm bindings at: #index put: newIndex].
  ^checkedForm      "return form with new index"
```

Fig. 6. The automatic index handling at the configuration policy.

configuration policy is local to the space, this is quickly done and causes less network traffic. It allows us to reduce the responsibilities the agent has to fulfill, allowing it to be 'thinner'. Altogether this modification reduces the risk of errors, improves consistency of the market, and thereby assures even better performance.

3.7   Reconfiguration

As soon as a new configuration policy class is defined and is associated with an entry class, it will be used. I.e. the next space operation with an affected entry will be ruled by the policy's matching algorithm and access checking methods. The important implication here is that the space can be *dynamically* reconfigured. In section 5.4 we present how the framework lets the programmer define the needed procedure to adapt entries that are in the space at the moment the reconfiguration becomes effective.

   After these examples of using our framework, we continue with a more detailed description of the classes and contracts in OPENSPACES.

4   The OPENSPACES **Framework**

OPENSPACES is an object-oriented framework implemented in Smalltalk. It offers the possibility to implement a variety of different data-driven coordination languages to be used in distributed environments. Instantiations may have the characteristics of the original LINDA [GC85] model, of object-oriented approaches like proposed by JAVA-SPACES [FHA99] and TSPACES [WMLF99]. The novelty of OPENSPACES is that it offers fine-grained configuration options which may also be dynamically changed.

We now present the core classes and their structural relationships, collaborations and the key contracts between these classes.

4.1 Core Classes and Their Relationships

The core of OPENSPACES consists of the following six classes:

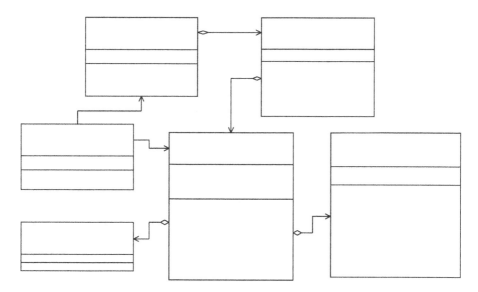

Fig. 7. Structural Relationships of the core of OPENSPACES.

Entries. contain the data which space agents may exchange via a space. Entry is the abstract root class for all space entries. It has no attributes, applications must define subclasses with the necessary instance variables to hold the exchanged data. There is no restriction concerning number or kind of objects to be held.

The class of a concrete Entry descendant forms also the key which is used to associate the class with a ConfigurationPolicy. This association governs the behaviour of the Space concerning all operations with instances of the specified entry class. Actually every entry subclass has to be registered at the space with a corresponding configuration policy. Unregistered entry types are rejected.

Configuration Policies. represent the semantics of the space's access operations affecting certain classes of entries. Subclasses of ConfigurationPolicy define the matching algorithm to be used for retrieving operations and a set of access controlling methods which are applied at each access with the involved entry types.

Open Space. is the abstraction representing the blackboard medium. It holds a collection of entries and offers several ways of accessing it. The standard primitives adapted from

LINDA are supported: `write`, `read` and `take`. [1] The two retrieving operations `read:` `aTemplateEntry` and `take: aTemplateEntry` use their parameters as a mask to do an associative lookup of a matching entry. The template is an `Entry` which may have some of its data fields defined and some not. In a general matching strategy the undefined fields act as wildcards for the lookup. Those with actual values restrict the selection of entries that have equal values. The lookup in general is nondeterministic.

The simple `read` and `take` operations are non-blocking, i.e. the calls return immediately, either with a found entry or a null-value, if nothing was detected. OPEN-SPACES also supports the blocking variants: `blockingRead` and `blockingTake`. These cause the calling client process to suspend until a matching entry is available.

Two additional bulk-retrieving operations are supported. `readAll` and `takeAll` act the same as the simple ones with the exception that they return collections with *all* currently available matching entries. All space access operations are atomic.

The exact behaviour of an `OpenSpace` may be different for any class of used entries, depending on the *configuration policy* objects they are associated with. Therefore `OpenSpace` provides the functionality to manage the *mapping* between entry classes and configuration policies.

Space Agent. is the standard user abstraction for the space. It holds a reference to its current space which it gets from the globally accessible `SpaceServer`. The class `SpaceAgent` is often subclassed to add application specific behavior and hide the underlying communication structures.

The Space Server. is used by all space agents to access a space. `SpaceServer` is a singleton object that acts as a name server. Spaces are looked up by their name, they must be registered to become available. If a request is made specifying an unknown space name, the space server may act as a factory. It can create and register a new space with the given name. The space server delegates the actual managing of the space references to the `SpaceAdministrator` and redirects the allowed requests to it.

The Space Administrator. is the actual manager of `OpenSpaces`. The `SpaceAdministrator` holds a collection with references to all currently registered Spaces and implements their accessing by name. It offers the methods to register (and unregister) any local or remote Spaces.

4.2   CORBA **as an Implementation Layer**

OPENSPACES uses Cincom DST (Distributed Smalltalk) for the distribution. DST is CORBA 2.0 compliant and offers in addition a special feature called 'Implicit Invocation Interface' (I3) which is an extension to the CORBA facilities that provides remote communication between Smalltalk applications without explicit IDL definitions.

---

[1] The naming convention was borrowed from JAVASPACES, since it seems more natural and clear to "write" an entry instead of "out-ing" it.

Connecting to a Space. To get an initial reference to the SpaceServer OPEN-
SPACES offers two options for a client. The first is to set its ORB as client to the
corresponding address and port number of the server ORB. Like that the naming service
of the server ORB can be used to resolve a reference to the space server. The second
option is to write an IOR file with the stringified object reference of the space server to
an accessible location where the agents may read it and connect themselfes.

Distributed Event Service. DST provides an implementation of the CORBA event
service protocol. In OPENSPACES this is used for a notification option: a SpaceAgent
may subscribe to be notified by the space when an entry is written that matches a
given template. The subscription is terminated when a match is found. For continuing
notification it can repeatedly be renewed.

Market Place V.4: Automatic Notification. As example of notification mechanism,
we implemented an automated variant of the Market Place. Buyers would like to be
informed of newly arriving Offers the reference their own Requests. Sellers would like
to be notified of new Requests and also of Deals for their own Offers.

  This variant is easily realized by extending the two agent classes to Notified-
Buyer and NotifiedSeller. Upon every request the buyer makes, he subscribes
at the space with a template of an offer holding the corresponding request number.
When notified, he automatically takes the newly arrived offer from ths space. The seller
subscribes for requests at initialisation time and for the accepting deals at each offer she
issues.

4.3   Framework Contracts

After having briefly described the core classes, we now present how they interact. An
important part of the framework's flexibility originates from the contracts of the different
access methods available to clients of an OpenSpace. We describe in detail the read
contract. The take contract is analogous. The write contract differs in some parts.

Read Contract. An attempt to perform a read operation by an agent initiates the
following interactions between the participating entities (cf. figure 8):

1. An agent creates a *template* representing the kind of information he wants to retrieve
   from the space.
2. The agent calls the space's read: method with the template.
3. The space looks up the configuration policy associated with the template class.
4. The space calls the cpolicy's preReadCheck: method with the template.
5. The policy creates a *checked template* and returns it.
6. The space iterates over its entries asking the policy for each if it matches with the
   checked template.
7. The space passes the first *found entry* to the policy's postReadCheck: method.
8. The policy creates a *checked entry* and returns it.
9. The space returns the checked entry to the agent.

All read variants (read, blockingRead, readAll) apply the same pre- and post-
hooks before and after the retrieving, the same holds for the variants of take.

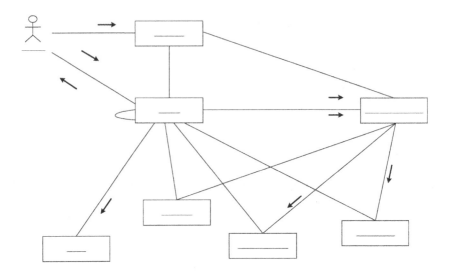

Fig. 8. The read contract: instead of directly accessing the space's entries, the presented template and the found entry are controlled by the configuration policy.

Take and Write Contracts. The take contract is analogous to the one for read accesses. The difference is that the called hook methods are `preTakeCheck:` and `postTakeCheck:` and a successful lookup results in the removal of the matching entry from the space. The write contract again differs in using its own hook methods. Additionally the write operation has to check the lists with reservations for reading or taking which are maintained for the blocking accesses. This means that it has to scan these two lists to check if the written entry matches with a template used for the blocking accesses. If so the waiting process has to be resumed. The same with all notification handlers. If the new entry matches one of the event handler's templates it has to issue the corresponding event. These checks are performed after the postWriteChecks.

Discussion. With the described contract, the hook methods allows a user to specify many useful variants of a space's behaviour. This offer advantages like:

- *Protection* The space can ensure that the entry put in the space holds certain properties and the space agent is ensured that the retrieved entry is coherent.
- *Shifting Responsibility* Instead of requiring the space agents to be responsible for consistency of the space, it is the space itself that does so by invoking the configuration policy that controls its state.
- Reduction of the *network traffic*.
- *Hiding space administration* The space can perform administrative tasks that are hidden from the space agent.
- Basically *any action* may be triggered if needed.

5   Extensions, Configurations and Reconfigurations

The OPENSPACES framework provides three main axes of variability. First, simple subclassing of the core classes allows *white-box extension* and reuse [JF88]. Second, the specialisation of *configuration policy* objects offers *black-box extension*. Moreover, besides compile-time extension, the configuration policy objects allows the runtime *reconfiguration* of a given system. The following sections present these three aspects of the framework extension.

5.1   White-Box Extensions

Subclassing `Entry` **Class.** serves two purposes: (1) to define application specific data fields and (2) to map the considered entry type to a specific configuration policy as shown in the assertions example in section 3.5.

The baseclass `Entry` doesn't have any predefined data fields. Subclasses define any kind of attributes: arrays like in LINDA, named instance variables like e.g. in JAVA-SPACES, or any mixed strategies.

Subclassing `SpaceAgent` **Class.** will be used for any application-specific adaption of space-using. E.g. summarizing several single accesses like the `append` method in the Market Place example in figure 3. Other examples that motivate specialization include handling of multiple space references or automatic subscription for notification.

Subclassing `OpenSpace` **Class.** allows one to introduce new or specialised operations like e.g. an update method which allows an agent to modify an entry at the space in one step, instead of having to read, modify and rewrite it. Or a direct exchange method, allowing to agents exchange their entries atomically, as realized in TSPACES with the `rhonda` operation. Many extensions however can be realized with suitably choosen configuration policies, as shown with the index handling example in 3.6.

5.2   Black-Box Extension: Configuration Policies

As we already mentioned, each space maintains a *mapping* between entry classes and their associated configuration policies. These policies determine the way the space controls accesses of entries. We discuss the detailed mechanism how this is organized. Then we present another variation of our market promoting an automatic garbage collection at the space.

Matching Algorithm. The basic strategy for the associative lookup of entries at retrieving operations is simple: the space scans its entries collection for an entry that matches the given template. The ConfigurationPolicy provides the boolean function `does: anEntry matchWith: aTemplate` which is used for this scan (cf. form matching in figure 2). The state of the template may be controlled, special values may be required, a keyed matching may be performed. Any condition may be tested.

Pre- and Post-access Hooks. For each access operation, the Configuration-Policy class defines two *hook* methods. preReadCheck: aTemplate is called before the space's scan for a matching entry. It returns a validated version of the template that will be used for the lookup. To reject a template the method returns nil which causes the read operation method to abort and also return nil. After a successful lookup of a matching entry this is validated in the same manner by the postReadCheck: hook. This validated entry finally will be returned to the calling space agent. The take and write operations each employ an analogous pair of validators.

These hooks may be used for entry verification, modification, exchange or access refusal. Moreover, any additional actions can be triggered, like accessing the space to check for consistency, for doubles, perform some logging activity, etc.

5.3   Market Place V.5: Automatically Discarding Outdated Forms

Some automatic handling of outdated forms is a realistic requirement. Without such support, obsolete Requests and forgotten Offers can easily start to clutter a space. One possible solution for this is to add a timestamp to every entry being written to the space. After the expiry of the lifetime of the entry it will be discarded, this may be after a collectively defined duration for all entries or after an individually amount that is specified in the entry's fields.

The task of adding the arrival time at the space can be done by the preWriteCheck: method, by adding a key #entryTime with the current time to the form's bindings before writing it to the Space.

The check for expiration can be done periodically or triggered by the space accessing operations. Each of the hook methods of the configuration policy may call a garbage collection method that scans through all entries and discards the expired ones. This is sufficient for consistency since every access 'sees' a freshly updated view of the Space.

We implemented a Market Place variant with a default expiration time for all forms, using the policy's pre-operation hooks to trigger the cleanup. The following code extends the FormPolicy by creating a new subclass LeasingPolicy on which the hooks methods are specialized. Figure 9 shows the specification of preReadCheck:. The boolean variable isCleaning is used to distinguish if the hook method is triggered by a client or by the configuration policy itself in the course of cleaning up.

5.4   Run-Time Configuration

Beside the static extension of the framework, OPENSPACES provides dynamic configuration of the spaces. Indeed, changing requirements of any kind can necessitate a reconfiguration of the used mapping. With OPENSPACES, an application can change the policies on a running system.

Dynamic Configurations. To define a configuration mapping, the space offers a registering method register: anEntryClass withPolicy: #aConfigurationPolicy that associates entry classes with specific policies. Since the needed configuration policy is looked up for every access of the space, a modification of the

```
FormPolicy subclass: #LeasingPolicy
  instance variables: 'defaultLeasingTime isCleaning'.

LeasingPolicy >> preWriteCheck: aTemplate
  |checkedTemplate|
  checkedTemplate := super preWriteCheck: aTemplate.
  checkedTemplate notNil
    ifTrue: [aForm bindings at: #arrivingTime put: Time now].
  ^checkedTemplate

LeasingPolicy >> preReadCheck: aTemplate
  |checkedTemplate|
  ^ self isCleaning    "Is the method initiated by the receiver?"
    ifTrue:
      [aTemplate]       "Do not cause a loop"
    ifFalse:
      [checkedTemplate := super preReadCheck: aTemplate.
       self cleanupSectionOfTemplate: checkedTemplate]

LeasingPolicy >> preTakeCheck: aTemplate
  "... same as preReadCheck: "

LeasingPolicy >> cleanupSectionOfTemplate: aTemplate
  "Enter 'cleaning-mode', perform cleanup and exit again"
  |section|
  self isCleaning: true.
  section := aTemplate bindings at: #section.
  self throwAwayOutdatedFormsAtSection: section.
  self isCleaning: false.
  ^aTemplate

LeasingPolicy >> throwAwayOutdatedFormsAtSection: aSectionName
  |template forms arrived|
  template := Form new.
  template bindings at: #section put: aSectionName.
  forms := hostSpace readAll: template.
  forms do: [:each |
    (each bindings includesKey: #arrivingTime)
      ifTrue:
        [arrived := each bindings at: #arrivingTime.
         ((arrived addTime: defaultLeasingTime) < Time now)
          ifFalse: [hostSpace take: each]]
```

Fig. 9. The configuration policy for automatic garbage collection.

mapping automatically becomes effective. Therefore, it is easy to apply a new configuration on the fly. It is actually the standard procedure to register all needed entries after the creation of the space.

Note that the registration methods use the same mechanism for mutual exclusion as the basic operations. This guarantees that no running execution is interrupted.

Reconfigurations. There are situations that may require policies to be changed without restarting and resetting the entire system. New requirements or temporary changes may call for restrictions or modifications of the parameters.

To change the policy of an entry class we just unregister the old association before registering the new one. This is easily done with OPENSPACES. Dynamically changing the configuration mapping however can have an impact on the entries that are already present in the space, having been written under the previous policy. The OPENSPACES approach to this delicate problem is to give the programmer the possibility to specify necessary actions to be applied when a new policy is activated. To do so the space's method to register a new configuration calls a hook method of the new configuration policy, called `updateOldEntriesOfClass: anEntry`. It is executed after the new policies are activated, before any client may access the space thereafter. Any actions can be triggered for a clean transition. (It's the responsibility of the programmer to implement them!)

In Figure 10 we show the code used to dynamically introduce the lease time extension of the previous example. Any forms already present at the space should be supplied with an arrival time binding. The easiest way to do this is to take them all from the space and write them again, letting the new policy take care of it.

```
LeasingPolicy >> updateOldEntriesOfClass: anEntryClass
   "Take all present forms from the space and rewrite them. Like
   that they are supplied by the policy with a binding denoting
   they had just arrived."
   | template forms |
   template := Form new.
   forms := hostSpace readAll: template.
   forms
      do: [:each | hostSpace write: each]   "adds arriving time"
```

Fig. 10. The update method for the dynamic introduction of the lease time policy.

Caveats. The triggered actions in all of these hooks methods of the configuration policies may easily cause loops. When e.g. a `preReadCheck:` method of a configuration policy calls the read method with an entry of the same class as the policy is registered for, some precautions must be taken to prevent infinite loops. A solution can be to distinguish between the first call to the method (by the client) and the following calls (by the policy itself) with a flag that is set before the policy does its accesses and unset afterwards. Like that the hook is bypassed for 'internal use' (cf. figure 9).

It is also not recommendable to use the blocking variants of the retrieving operations because they would cause the main space process to block.

6   Related Work

There are several parameters regarding configurability of a data-space framework: is it object-oriented, does it support white-box extensions, are there options for pluggable configurations in the black-box style? We will focus on three implementations promoting configurability options.

R.Tolksdorf's BERLINDA [Tol97] is a object-oriented framework similar to OPEN-SPACES. It has a set of basic abstractions for a space, entries, agents. It can be extended in a white-box style. In BERLINDA, a concrete entry class has to implement the matching function, which can be defined as desired. Like in OPENSPACES, this feature is remarkable, since all other known implementations use a fixed algorithm, which cannot be modified. Note however that in OPENSPACES the matching algorithm is decoupled from the entries and then can be changed dynamically.

Concerning access control, the work of Minsky and Leichter [ML95] on LAW--GOVERNED LINDA is of great interest. In this model a *Law* rules the reactions of the tuple space to events occurring on attempts to use the access operations or when a successful matching has been performed. These events may trigger actions that are defined in the global law. [MMU00] introduces controller-processes for each agent using a space which enforce the application of the law.

OPENSPACES has a similar reaction model. The events are all types of access operations at the space, the reactions are the different hooks methods that are applied before and after each of them. By modifying or exchanging a used template or a found entry in the hook methods we can model LAW-GOVERNED LINDA's variants of operation completions. The two different post-retrieving hooks allow one additionally to distinguish between a matching of a read or of a take operation. The enforcing of the rules in OPEN-SPACES is encapsulated in the configuration policies of which are local to the space. This has the advantage that a reconfiguration does not have to modify multiple copies of a law that are spread amongst the controllers. Moreover, OPENSPACES does not restrict the space operations that may be used as reactions, but it is left to the framework user to be aware of potentially blocking methods or loops.

In "Programmable Coordination Media" Denti et al. show well the principal benefits of a space with programmable behaviour [DNO97]. Indeed, their specialization of the space behaviour to enforce resource accessing strategies inspired us for searching ways to let a space take care of additional responsibilities. This helps to free the agents from unnecessary responsibilities and adds control to the space.

Two popular tuple space frameworks in Java have been released in '99: Sun Soft's JAVASPACES [FHA99] and IBM's TSPACES [WMLF99]. Both use subclassing of a general entry (resp. tuple) abstraction for the exchanged data. The matching algorithm is fixed for both of the systems. TSPACES provides some interesting extensions like the mentioned rhonda operator, or a set of query-like range matching options and set-retrieval operations.

In summary, while LAW-GOVERNED LINDA offers a fine grained access control at the space, most implementations provide at most extension through subclassing. The matching algorithm is definable in BERLINDA, in all other works it is fixed. Moreover, dynamic reconfiguration of the space behaviour is not addressed.

7   Conclusion

In this paper we have presented OPENSPACES, an object-oriented framework for building applications with architectures in a blackboard style. The kernel of OPENSPACES is based on six entities: *Space agents* access *spaces* to store or retrieve *entries*. *Configuration policy* objects are responsible for the matching strategy and for a complete set of access controlling methods. The *space server* provides access for the space agents and the *space administrator* manages creation and lifecycle of the spaces.

We have presented several extensions to show how the design of the framework allows the developer to control all the important parameters of space manipulations. Beside *white-box extension* based on the specialization of the core entities, OPEN-SPACES allows us to extend it in a *black-box* style by defining new policy objects that can be plugged to configure the space's behavior. This reconfiguration may be done *dynamically* during runtime. OPENSPACES offers support to handle the transition between two consecutive configurations.

For the future we plan to extend our prototypical framework with support for pure CORBA using IDL. This will allow clients agent written in other languages to use OPENSPACES for coordination.

Acknowledgements. The authors would like to thank Juan-Carlos Cruz for his constant and competent support.

References

CR96.   P. Ciancarini and D. Rossi. Jada: Coordination and communication for java agents. In *MOS'96: Towards the Programmable Internet*, LNCS 1222, pp. 213–228, Linz, Austria, July 1996. Springer-Verlag.

DNO97.   E. Denti, A. Natali, and A. Omicini. Programmable coordination medium. In D. Garlan and D. Le Métayer, editors, *Proceedings of COORDINATION'97 (Coordination Languages and Models*, LNCS 1282, pp. 274–288. Springer-Verlag, 1997.

FHA99.   E. Freeman, S. Hupfer, and K. Arnold. *JavaSpaces Principles, Patterns and Practice*. Addison-Wesley, 1999. ISBN: 0201309556.

GC85.   D. Gelernter and N. Carriero. Generative communication in linda. *ACM TOPLAS*, 7(1), January 1985.

JF88.   R. E. Johnson and B. Foote. Designing reusable classes. *Journal of Object-Oriented Programming*, 1(2):22–35, 1988.

ML95.   N. H. Minsky and J. Leichter. Law-governed linda as a coordination model. In P. Ciancarini, O. Nierstrasz, and A. Yonezawa, editors, *Object-Based Models and Languages for Concurrent Systems*, LNCS 924, pp. 125–146. Springer-Verlag, 1995.

MMU00.   N. H. Minsky, Y. M. Minksy, and V. Ungureanu. Making tuple space safe for heterogeneous distributed systems. In *Proceedings of SAC'2000*, pp. 218–226, 2000.

PA98.   G. A. Papadopoulos and F. Arbab. Coordination Models and Languages. In *The Engineering of Large Systems*, volume 46 of *Advances in Computers*. Academic Press, August 1998.

Tol97.   R. Tolksdorf. Berlinda: An object-oriented platform for implementing coordination languages in java. In *Proceedings of COORDINATION'97 (Coordination Languages and Models*, LNCS 1282, pp. 430–433. Springer-Verlag, 1997.

WMLF99.   P. Wyckoff, S.W. McLaughry, T.J. Lehman, and D.A. Ford. T spaces. *IBM Systems Journal*, 37(3), 1999.

Scripting Coordination Styles

Franz Achermann, Stefan Kneubuehl, and Oscar Nierstrasz

Software Composition Group, University of Bern[1]

Abstract. The fact that so many different kinds of coordination models and languages have been proposed suggests that no one single approach will be the best for all coordination problems. Different *coordination styles* exhibiting different properties may be more suitable for some problems than others. Like other architectural styles, coordination styles can be expressed in terms of components, connectors and composition rules. We propose an approach in which coordination styles are expressed as "component algebras": components of various sorts can be combined using operators that realize their coordination, yielding other sorts of components. We show how several coordination styles can be defined and applied using Piccola, a small language for composing software components. We furthermore show how *glue abstractions* can be used to bridge coordination styles when more than one style is needed for a single application.

1   Introduction

We are rapidly moving towards a world of spontaneously networked, multi-platform applications in which people, companies, web servers and mobile devices interact and exchange services with the help of software agents and components. Components will help to separate the stable from the evolving aspects of application domains, and to provide standardized interfaces and protocols for common services. Agents will help to represent both clients and service providers, negotiate terms of cooperation (both functional and non-functional aspects), manage aspects of concurrency (e.g., synchronization policies) and distribution (e.g., failure and recovery policies), and bridge differences in platform and protocol, in short, to *coordinate* the components.

Building such applications will not be trivial, even with the help of components, because too many low-level aspects come into play at once in the logic of the coordination code. There have been many proposals for high-level coordination models and languages, such as tuple spaces or the IWIM model [7], each of which proposes a way to separate coordination from computation. We believe that this is not enough, and take our cue from three other domains: *software architecture*, *scripting* and *object-orientation*. First, it is now well-established that different architectural styles exhibit different properties [10][27], and may be more or less well-suited to a given problem or problem domain. (For example, pipes and filters are great for text

---

[1] *Authors' address:* Institut für Informatik (IAM), Universität Bern, Neubrückstrasse 10, CH-3012 Berne, Switzerland. *Tel:* +41 (31) 631.4618. *Fax:* +41 (31) 631.3965. *E-mail:* {acherman,kneubuhl,oscar}@iam.unibe.ch.   http://www.iam.unibe.ch/~scg.

A. Porto and G.-C. Roman (Eds.): COORDINATION 2000, LNCS 1906, pp. 19-35, 2000.

processing, but unsuitable for specifying GUI interaction.) Second, scripts and scripting languages can be very good at specifying how an application is constructed from external components and services according to a given architectural or compositional "style". Finally, object-oriented development encourages the programmer to develop his own model of the application and its domain using the abstraction facilities of object-oriented languages, rather than forcing the problem to fit a pre-packaged paradigm.

We propose an approach to composing and coordinating software components in which different high-level, algebraic *coordination styles* may be defined, and agents *script* components according to these styles. Furthermore, multiple styles may be required to address more complex problems and problem domains, since each style will exhibit different strengths and weaknesses. In this case, high-level *glue abstractions* may be needed to bridge the different styles.

Piccola is a small "composition language" designed to support this mode of software development. The core abstractions of Piccola are *forms* (immutable, extensible records), *agents* (communicating processes), and *channels* (locations where agents asynchronously exchange forms). The semantics of Piccola is given in terms of the ! L-calculus, a variant of the ! -calculus where agents exchange forms instead of tuples [20][21]. On top of this simple model, forms are used to build higher-level abstractions. Forms can be seen as "primitive objects", whose fields can store not only values but also abstractions, and they allow us to define styles of composition much in the same way that object-oriented languages are used to defined black-box frameworks of composable abstractions [18]. This encourages an *algebraic* view of styles, in which one defines different sorts of objects (forms) for a given style, each of which implements a given protocol, and algebraic operators (i.e., *connectors*, defined as fields of the forms) can be used to write expressions that compose objects and yield instances, possible of other sorts. For example, a stream (a kind of form) can be connected to a filter (another kind of form) by means of a pipe (a connector provided by the stream), yielding a new stream.

Basic services and components are written in conventional programming languages (presently Java, Squeak or Object Pascal), and appear to Piccola agents as native forms. Agents are *scripted* using forms that implement the coordination and composition abstractions of a particular style. Finally, styles may be combined if the appropriate glue abstractions have been defined in Piccola to bridge the styles.

In section 2 we introduce algebraic coordination styles in Piccola using the conventional example of streams and filters. In section 3 we show how Piccola can be used to develop very different coordination styles. We illustrate styles for event handling, grouped actors, and regulated coordination, each with their own compositional properties. In section 4 we show how glue abstractions can be used to bridge different styles. In section 5 we draw some observations from these experiments, and in section 6 we place our work in relation to others and outline future and ongoing work. Section 7 concludes the paper.

2 Component Algebras — Plugging vs Wiring

Software components are black-box abstractions that not only provide services, but may also require services in order to function correctly. Building an application from components, then, should be a *simple matter of wiring* these services together.

The problem is that wiring is the wrong paradigm for component-based development: wiring is an inherently low-level activity that can easily lead to configuration errors. Instead, it is more natural to *plug* components together. A *connector* captures a set of provided and required services that can be connected to a compatible socket in a single step. Furthermore, components that are plugged together hide their connected interfaces, *thus forming a larger component.*

We argue that this view of plugging components is the right way to think about coordination: components are computational elements that can be coordinated by plugging them into other components. The plugs and sockets represent not only services, but also the logic required to coordinate these services. Different kinds of components and connectors correspond to different coordination styles, and special adaptors will act as bridges between these styles.

We furthermore argue that coordination styles are most naturally implemented as *component algebras*, which define sets of components with similar plugs as the *sorts* of the algebra, and coordination abstractions as the *operators* of the algebra. A script, then, is an expression of the algebra that specifies how the components are plugged together. This immediately yields two important properties:

1. Scripts are *high-level specifications* that make the coordination of components explicit.
2. Scripts are *syntactically constrained* to generate only certain kinds of compositions, making it easier to reason about properties of the resulting configurations.

Note that we do not define an algebra in the mathematical sense, since the objects of our "algebra" may have mutable state. Thus, we don't necessarily have referential transparency and therefore cannot use the classical proof techniques. We mainly borrow the notation of signatures to achieve a declarative style of composition.

In the rest of this section we introduce the notion of expressing a coordination style as a component algebra with the familiar example of streams and filters. In section 3 we will see how this idea can be generalized to other coordination styles.

2.1 A Push-Flow Coordination Style

Let us consider a push-flow coordination style [19]. In this style, an individual component pushes data downstream to another component to which it is connected. There are three kinds of components: A source produces data and pushes it downstream. A filter allows an upstream component to push data towards it, process it, and pushes the result further downstream. Finally, a sink accepts data pushed towards it, and represents the end of the stream.

Sources, filters and sinks can be distinguished by the different basic services they provide and require (see Table 1).

	Provided services	**Required services**
Source		put (X): write element downstream close (): signal end of stream
Filter	put (X): accept a data element close (): close the input stream	put (X): write element downstream close (): signal end of stream
Sink	put (X): accept a data element close (): close input stream	

Basically, filters and sinks provide put and close services to upstream components which use them to push data and signal the end of the stream. Sources and filters require these same services from downstream components to which they are connected.

Now, we can easily *wire* such components together by, for example, binding the provided services put and close of a filter to the corresponding required services of a source. Using a binding-oriented notation, as for instance in Darwin [13], this could be written as:

```
filter.put = source.put
```

There are two limitations to this approach: First it does not scale up, since we may only wire one connection at the time. Second, the composite is not a component.

Using an algebraic notation, on the other hand, we can define an operator to connect a filter to a data source and we can demand that the composite is again an instance with provided and required services. The composition rule *Source | Filter ∀ Source* specifies:

• that the expression "source | filter" is again a *Source*.
• that the required put and close services of the source are bound by the provided services of the filter.

Following this approach, we can use the composite source as a first class value. It is important to notice that this is not only a question of syntax. Using the algebraic notation, connecting two components yields a composite instance, whereas the binding notation only binds services.

The set of composition rules of the stream style defines a *signature*, which is shown in Table 2. Connecting a source to a sink is the essential operation of this style. The data of the source is written to the sink and then the sink is closed. The *()* denotes the empty form, i.e. a component with no provided and required services.

*Source	Sink*	∀	*()*	Connect stream *s* to the sink
*Source	Filter*	∀	*Source*	manipulate streams *s* using filter
*Filter	Filter*	∀	*Filter*	composition two filters
*Filter	Sink*	∀	*Sink*	build a new sink using the filter
Source + Source	∀	*Source*	concatenate streams (sequential composition)
Source & Source	∀	*Source*	merge streams (parallel composition)
Sink + Sink	∀	*Sink*	multiplex a stream to two sinks

The signature of a style is a level of abstraction above the notion of provided and required services. Instead of low-level wiring of provided and required services, we have defined a small language (an algebra) to work with. In this language we can compose streams without paying too much attention to the individual services of the components. The high level operators of the stream-language ensure that the services are bound correctly.

2.2   Implementing the Operators

How do we implement the operators in our stream style? In Piccola, forms represent interfaces to components. The component may be external to Piccola or it may be scripted entirely in Piccola. In the latter case the behaviour of a the component is implemented by a Piccola agent [1][20].

A *form* is an extensible record, given as a set of bindings. A binding maps a label to a value, which may be a nested form or a service. Thus a form is a kind of primitive object, providing public services. It is feasible to model advanced object-oriented features, such as inheritance using forms [25]. The required services are represented as *slots*, which are implemented as Piccola objects. Slots are analogous to futures: invoking a bound slot invokes the service it has been bound to; invoking an unbound slot delays the client until the slot is bound.

The following script defines a trivial example of a source:

```
mySource =
    reqPut = newSlot()          # required put service
    reqClose = newSlot()        # required close service
    run(do: (reqPut("Hello"), reqClose()))
```

A source does not provide any services. The service `run` is predefined in Piccola. It executes a block in a new agent and returns the empty form. Thus, the value of the form `mySource` contains two bindings, one called `reqPut` one called `reqClose`. These slots need to be bound by a client of the component. What is the behaviour of this component? The agent representing it is given as a `do` block and passed to `run`. It calls `reqPut` to invoke the required `put` service. But this service blocks, unless the slot has been filled. Thus, the agent representing the behaviour of `mySource` blocks until a sink or a filter is connected to it. Once connected, the agent writes "Hello" to the stream and closes the stream.

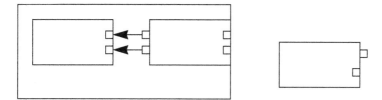

Wiring this source to a filter in Piccola means binding the provided services to the slots of the source:

```
mySource.reqPut.bind(filter.put)
mySource.reqClose.bind(filter.close)
```

The projection `filter.put` denotes the provided `put` service of the filter. Note that services are first class values in Piccola.

We would like to abstract from this low-level wiring by providing a high-level *connector* that treats the set of required or provided services as a plug. The extensibility of forms makes it possible to add such a connector to any source component. This connector will bind the services and return a form giving access to a new source component or the empty form. We can make an abstraction `asSource` that adds such a connector to any form:

```
asSource(S):
    S
    __|(Right):                                   # define the | connector
        S.reqPut.bind(Right.put)
        S.reqClose.bind(Right.close)
        return asEmptyOrSource(Right)
```

The result of applying `asSource` to a form `S` is the form `S` extended with a `__|` service, representing the | infix operator. The right hand argument to the | operator may be either a sink or a filter, thus the form `Right` must provide the `put` and `close` plug. The connector binds these services and either returns the empty form if `Right` is a sink or it returns a new source with the required services of the filter (see Fig. 1). The service `asSource` raises the level of abstraction by hiding the wiring behind connectors.

In order to plug `mySource` into a filter we apply `asSource` to it:

```
s = asSource(mySource)
s | filter | ...
```

The Piccola term `s | filter` is just syntactic sugar for `s.__|(filter)`, thus `s | filter` evaluates to a source, with the required services `put` and `close` of the filter.

The coordination between the two components, respectively the agents providing the behaviour for them is performed as procedure calls. Sinks and filters in the push flow style are always willing to accept data elements. An invocation of `put` on such instances is not allowed to block. In the case of the sequential composition of two streams (*Source + Source ∀ Source*), the connector instantiates a pipe to buffer the data elements pushed by the second source. These elements are flushed when the first source calls `close`.

Connecting a source changes the state of the non-connected instance (with unbound slots) to a connected one. It is important to understand that individual *instances* are composed. Thus a source can only be connected to a single sink. The fact that we compose instances becomes essential when we glue components from different styles in section 4.

3   Coordination Styles as Component Algebras

Streams and filters are perhaps the most obvious coordination style that can be naturally expressed as a component algebra. What is less obvious is that other, very different coordination styles may benefit from an algebraic notation.

In this section we intend to demonstrate, by a series of examples, that other coordination styles can indeed be expressed in this way. In each case, the main advantages gained are that (i) coordination is expressed at the higher level of *plugging*, which abstracts from the lower level of wiring, (ii) coordination is expressed as a declarative *composition* of components, thereby exposing the pertinent dependencies, and hiding irrelevant detail.

We do not claim that the styles we present are ideal! They are intended rather as a proof of concept and as an indication that much richer and more expressive styles could be formulated in a similar way.

3.1   Event Style

This style uses event notification [9] as its wiring mechanism. Event types are composed with Piccola services to yield event handlers. An event handler is attached to one or more event producers, which are components that can raise events. When an event occurs inside the component it notifies all its attached handlers. Table 3 contains the signature for the event style.

Event(do: Service) ∀ *Handler*	compose event handlers
Producer ? Handler ∀ *Producer*	attach handler to event producer

Event styles are of particular interest in building graphical user interfaces. For instance, parts of the Java AWT framework can be wrapped so that they conform to the event style (see [1] for more details). The following example creates a button using the factory `newButton` and attaches an action event handler to this button:

```
myButton = newButton()
myButton.set(Label = "sayHello")
myButton ? Action(do: println("Hello"))
```

Contrast this code with the more typical event wiring, expressed directly in terms of an API. In Java, for example, an listener object must be explicitly instantiated and connected (i.e. wired) to a button using a particular binding method (`addActionListener`). The situation is pretty much the same using other frameworks, such as Tcl/Tk.

3.2   Grouped Actors (GA) Style

Actors constitute one of the foundational models of communicating agents [4][15]. Actors are autonomous entities that exchange asynchronous messages with each other. An actor has a queue of pending messages. It can accept the next message in the queue, create new actors, send messages to other actors, or *become* a new actor (i.e., replace its behaviour by a continuation).

	provided services	required services
Actor	receive(M)	send(M) broadcast(M)
Bus	send(M) broadcast(M)	receive(M)

Here we are not interested in specifying the actors themselves, but in expressing *groups* of actors that can share communications that are broadcasted to the group. In such approaches, each actor can typically participate in multiple groups [8][12].

Groups exchange messages by means of a *software bus* [6]. The component types of the grouped style are given in Table 4. An actor can send a message to a single recipient (send) or broadcast it to all actors in the group (broadcast). Actors also provide a service to accept a message (receive). Accepted messages are kept in a queue. Observe that the provided and required services of the bus are matched by those of the actors. Figure 3 graphically illustrates the grouping of multiple actor into a set of actors and the connection with a bus, yielding a *group*. The signature for the grouped actors is given in Table 5. It is separated into four parts:

- Actors form sets of actors using the operator ^ to create a singleton from an actor and + to extend sets.
- A bus is parameterized by a set of message types.
- A bus is combined with a set of actors to yield a group. A group represents a configuration of actors connected through a message bus. A group provides services like join and leave to dynamically add and remove actors.
- A reactive actor is a specific case of an actor. A reactive actor reacts to a given message by executing a service. The scope of this reaction may be restricted by requiring that the message come from a specific actor. Multiple reactive actors can be composed.

^Actor	∀	*Actors*	create a set containing one actor
Actor + Actor	∀	*Actors*	combine two actors
Actors + Actor	∀	*Actors*	extend the set with an actor
emptyActors	∀	*Actors*	empty set
Msg + Msg	∀	*Bus*	define messages of a message bus
Bus + Msg	∀	*Bus*	extend bus with message
Bus ‖ Actors	∀	*Group*	combine bus with a set, yielding a group
Msg -> Service	∀	*RActor*	run service S on behalf of message M
Msg / Actor -> Service	∀	*RActor*	run S on behalf of message M from A
RActor & RActor	∀	*RActor*	compose reactive actors
RActor	∀	*Actor*	a reactive actor is also an actor

An example application to coordinate actors for a vote is given in Figure 2. It contains four parts:

```
StartVote = newMessageType                      # define message type
    contents(init): topic = init.topic
...
bus = StartVote + CastVote + EndVote + VoteResults

chair = newActor                                # define a chair actor
    do(self):
        StartVote.broadcast(topic = "Join EU?")
        sleep(10000)
        EndVote.broadcast(topic = "Join EU?")
        self.stop()

secretary = ...                                 # collect and count votes

newEcoVoter():
    onStartVote(msg):
        CastVote.send
            destination = msg.sender
            vote = if (msg.topic.contains("car"))(then: "no", else: "yes")
    onVoteResults(msg):
        if (msg.result == "yes" && (msg.topic.contains("car"))
            then: demonstrate()
            else: smile()
    return                                      # return a reactive actor
        StartVote / chair -> onStartVote &
        VoteResults -> onVoteResults

members = chair + secretary + newEcoVoter() + ...
parliament = bus || members
```

1. First the message types are created and composed into a bus. The example contains the StartVote message type. A message of this type will contain a topic label. Several message types are connected to a bus component using the + operator.

2. Next, the chair actor is created using newActor. The behaviour of the chair agent is given in the do service. The chair initiates a vote by broadcasting a topic, waits some time, broadcasts the end of the vote, and then stops.

3. An ecoVoter is created as a reactive actor. Observe that this voter only reacts on startVote messages that come from the chair actor.

4. Finally, voting actors are collected into a member set and connected with the message bus to form the parliament group.

Note the expressive power of the || operator. It connects all the provided and required services of the actors with the bus (see Figure 3). Using an explicit binding notation, we would have had to establish separately the bindings (send, broadcast and receive) for each actor in the group.

3.3   Regulated Coordination (RC) Style

Now we consider a style for expressing *regulated coordination* [23]. According to Minsky, a coordination policy P is a triple (*M, G, L*) where

- *M* is a set of messages
- *G* is a group of agents that are permitted to exchange messages in *M*.

- *L* is a set of rules (law) regulating the exchange of messages between the agents of *G*.

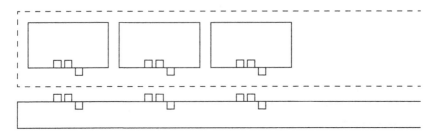

The agents participating in a policy exchange messages with each other. This suggests that the actors of the previously described GA style can be used as our agents.

	provided service	**required service**
Actor	`receive(M)`	`send(M)` `broadcast(M)`
Law	`send(M)` `broadcast(M)`	`apply(M)` `receive(M)`
Rule	`apply(M)`	

The basic component types in the this style are actors, messages, rules, and two predefined event types. Actors and messages have been described in the GA style. A law is a set of rules. Rules regulate the sending and receiving of messages. The event types *Sent* and *Arrived* are used to instantiate rules.

The signature for the RC style is given in Table 7. We reuse the signature to define and group actors from the GA style. A law regulates message passing, thus it subsumes the bus of the GA style. The connection of a law and a set of actors is a policy that enforces the law on all its actors.

^Rule	∀	*Law*	create a law with one rule
Rule + Rule	∀	*Law*	combine two rules
Law + Rule	∀	*Law*	extend law with a rule
emptyLaw	∀	*Law*	the empty law
Event 'of' Msg(Action)	∀	*Rule*	compose rule
Event 'of' Msg(CondAction)	∀	*Rule*	compose conditional rule
Law ‖ Actors	∀	*Policy*	bind actors to a law

To enforce the law, a *controller* is placed between each actor and the communication network. The controller triggers the rules (i.e. calls `apply`) on sending and receiving messages. In the body of a rule, we can access and modify the state of the controller, deliver messages to the controlled actor, and forward messages to the network [23].

We illustrate how rules are scripted in Piccola using the voting example. A flaw of the example is that a malicious voter could cast multiple votes on the same topic. This is not the case if we use the regulated coordination style, since the RC style enforces rules on the actors. The following two rules ensure that a voter can cast at most one vote on each topic:

```
R1 = Arrived 'of' StartVote
     action(msg):
          state().put(key = msg.voteId)   # store identifier
          deliver()                        # and deliver msg
R2 = Sent 'of' CastVote
     cond(msg): state().containsKey(msg.voteId)
     action(msg):
          state().remove(msg.voteId)       # remove identifier
          forward()                        # forward message
```

The rule `R1` triggers when a `StartVote` message arrives at an actor. The body of the rule stores the vote identifier in the controller's state and delivers the message. Rule `R2` is triggered when an actor sends a `CastVote` message. The action is only executed provided the condition (`cond`) holds — that is only if the state contains the vote identifier. In that case the identifier is removed from the state, thus preventing further casts on the same vote.

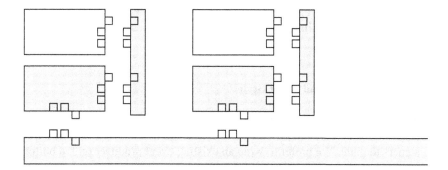

The RC style is built on top of the GA style rather than implementing it from scratch. The controller is a special actor that guards every participating actor. The controller communicates with the actor over a local bus (unregulated communication) and with other controllers over the policy bus (regulated communication). Figure 4 shows the architecture of the RA style expressed in the GA style. The dotted components are hidden in the RC style.

Note that although the same actors can participate in an actor group as well as in a policy, it is impossible for an actor to avoid the enforcement of the law.

4   Combining Styles

So far, we only used a single coordination style within an application. However, there are at least two reasons why we need to be able to combine multiple styles, and therefore to bridge between styles:

- Different parts of an application are naturally expressed in different styles. Consider a 3-tier business application. The user interface part is composed using an event style, the business layer is expressed by a set of business rules, whereas the persistency layer is implemented in a database style using transactions. Such an application will contain components that participate in more than one style, e.g. in the event style as well as in the business rule style.
- Legacy components may be designed and developed for a different style than that required by the application in which we intend to deploy them. An example is the case where we deploy a pull-stream filter in a push-stream style [17].

Glue code is used to wrap components so that they can work in a context they have not been designed for. *Glue abstractions* provide generic glue to ease the generation of glue code. For example, a service may wrap a given component from one style to fit another.

Glue code can be tedious to write — for instance when we have to rename some services or add default arguments to functions calls. But bridging between styles is normally not only a question of renaming. Consider wrapping a pull-stream filter to a push-stream style. To resolve these kinds of compositional mismatch [28], we need to introduce glue code that bridges the gap between push and pull streams. The glue code consists of a coordinator and a pipe. The proceeding push stream then writes into the pipe where the data elements can be fetched by the pull stream filter. The responsibility of the coordinator is to terminate the pull-stream when the push stream gets closed [2].

4.1   Bridging Event and Actor Style

Assume we need a visual interface for our voting application. It would be a nightmare to entangle all the actors with statements to create and layout visual components and add listeners to them. We prefer to wrap an existing event producer (e.g. a button) as an actor that broadcasts an action message. Here is a generic glue abstraction to do this:

```
eventToActor(GuiInst)(Event):
    actor = asActor         # wrap GuiInst as an actor
        GuiInst
        reqBroadcast = newMultiSlot()
        ...
    GuiInst ? Event
        do(event): actor.reqBroadcast(event)    # wire !
    return actor
```

This service wraps a GUI element as an actor and attaches to it an event handler. The handler is wired to the actor using the required `broadcast` service of the actor. Observe that the glue abstraction is responsible for both wrapping and wiring. The following code uses the glue abstraction to embed a button into the actor style:

```
yesButton = newButton(Label = "Say Yes")
...
GuiBus || eventToActor(yesButton)(Action) + ...
```

When the button is pressed, the wrapped actor broadcasts an action message on the `GuiBus`.

4.2   Multistyle Programming

Combining the actor style and the push-flow style, we wrap a source as an actor. This source pushes an element downstream each time it receives a message. The actor is used, for instance, as an archiver in the voting application, storing each vote together with its result. The resulting data flow is further processed by some filters and finally written to a log file. Using algebraic styles, we can directly express the architecture of the resulting application:

```
votingLaw || voter1 + sourceAsActor(archiver) + ...
archiver | filter | ... | logFile
```

The application is now easier to maintain because the architecture is clearly visible in the code. It is obvious how to change the code to achieve a different formatting or which component to replace in order to send the voting results directly to a printer. The low-level coordination aspect of such an application is hidden to the application developer. The chosen coordination styles ensure the correct wiring of the components.

5   Lessons Learned

What are the lessons learned from the experiment implementing coordination styles as many-sorted algebras? On one side, we made the experiments to validate the expressiveness of Piccola. On the other side, we want to see how coordination models should be implemented using existing languages. For instance, Jada is a object oriented framework providing tuple spaces in Java [11].

Validating Piccola, we conclude that the formal basis of Piccola of agents, forms, and channels turned out to be the right core abstractions. In particular the fact that everything is a form and that it is possible to abstract over arbitrary forms give Piccola high expressive power. This is demonstrated by the fact that many higher level coordination abstractions can be reused. Coordination abstractions use various containers such as slots, blackboards, sets, buffers and queues. They also include generic synchronization policies. We have argued elsewhere how abstraction over forms is the key to implement, for instance, exception handling mechanisms [3].

Implementing coordination styles as algebras makes it possible to reuse the actor style for the regulated coordination style. In fact, the controllers are also actors and the actual actor together with its controller form a local group. Reusing a coordination style would be of particular interest in languages like Java. In Java, one often has to implement certain synchronization and coordination aspects at the lowest level the language offers: the final and native `wait` and `notify` methods and the keyword `synchronized`. This is not due to the chosen coordination primitives but to missing abstraction expressiveness. For instance it is not possible to abstract over the methods of an object, which would be necessary to implement certain generic coordination policies.

Representing a coordination style as an algebra considerably reduces the steep learning curve traditionally associated with object-oriented frameworks. For instance, using the actor style, it took one of the authors only half an hour to implement a bidding example. To a large extent, this is due to the compact representation of composition. In contrast to an object oriented framework which is normally presented as inheritance tree and API, the algebraic notation helps one to identify the components, the connectors, and the rules.

6   Related and Future Work

This work is related to two distinct areas of research. The first area is the growing field of architectural description languages (ADLs) and tools to support their use (see for instance [26]). While ADLs are not yet in widespread use in industry, there have been several examples of their application to realistic case studies. ADLs support specification and reasoning about software at a very high level, but are not necessarily executable. Many ADLs provide a fixed set of predefined connectors to use and they do not support the definition of user-defined connectors at a higher level. They model architecture up to a certain abstraction level using predefined connectors. One of the few ADLs supporting user-defined connectors is Wright. It uses CSP as a formal basis to specify the roles of the connectors [5]. Studying the nature of connectors is an area of intense research. A recent paper by Mehta et al. [22] proposes a taxonomy of software connectors.

The other area that influenced our work is the algebraic specification approach (see for example [29]). In this approach, the behaviour of objects is specified using equational algebraic theories. We plan to further investigate how to formally analyse configurations using algebraic techniques. A challenging question is how to deal with mutable instances in a configuration. Is it possible to develop a type system to reason about immutable (i.e. algebraic) configurations? An interesting proposal deserving further investigation is the hidden order sorted approach of Goguen et al. [14].

We have only presented a limited number of coordination models as algebraic styles. Future work is needed to cover more coordination styles. We also want to investigate bridging between data and control driven coordination [24]. It is intriguing to explore whether we can use the formal foundation of Piccola to derive the operational semantics of coordination models. An earlier version of Piccola describes the mapping to the ! L-calculus [21]. Implementing a model in Piccola gives us the denotational semantics in terms of the ! -calculus almost for free. We further plan to develop a type system for the connectors and components in a style. A type checker might then be used to statically identify invalid configurations.

More work needs to be done in formally expressing the properties of components. The semantics of Piccola in terms of the ! L-calculus serves as a starting point. Interesting work in that area is done by Issarny on the Aster environment. She uses pre and post predicates to describe the non-functional properties for connectors [16].

We are also working on a enhanced and distributed version of Piccola that will include syntactical elements for user defined collections. So far, we used infix operators to sum up sets and lists.

7   Conclusion

We have presented an approach to composing and coordinating software components in terms of high-level, algebraic coordination styles. User defined connectors hide the low-level wiring of provided and required services. Programming at the higher abstraction level leads to more flexible applications, since unnecessary coordination details are hidden. The connectors are responsible for plugging components. They ensure valid configurations and provide the coordination.

Using Piccola, a small composition language, we have demonstrated how connectors can be implemented, how an application can be scripted using a given style, and how styles are bridged. Since each style has its own strengths and weaknesses, glue abstraction help to combine styles and to get the best out of each style.

Acknowledgements

We thank the members of the SCG for stimulating discussions on this topic, in particular Jean-Guy Schneider and Sander Tichelaar for helpful comments on a draft of this paper. We also thank the anonymous reviewers for their constructive critic. This work has been funded by the Swiss National Science Foundation under Project No. 20-53711.98, "A framework approach to composing heterogeneous applications" and the ESPRIT working group "COORDINA" under BBW No. 96.0335-1.

References

[1]   Franz Achermann and Oscar Nierstrasz, "Applications = Components + Scripts — A tour of Piccola," *Software Architectures and Component Technology*, Mehmet Aksit (Ed.), Kluwer, 2000, to appear.

[2]   Franz Achermann, Markus Lumpe, Jean-Guy Schneider and Oscar Nierstrasz, "Piccola — a Small Composition Language," *Formal Methods for Distributed Processing, an Object Oriented Approach*, Howard Bowman and John Derrick. (Eds.), Cambridge University Press., 2000, to appear.

[3]   Franz Achermann and Oscar Nierstrasz, "Explicit Namespaces", *Proceedings of JMLC* 2000, to appear.

[4]   Gul Agha, *ACTORS: A Model of Concurrent Computation in Distributed Systems*, MIT Press, Cambridge, Mass., 1986.

[5]   Robert Allen and David Garlan, "The Wright Architectural Specification Language," Technical Report, September 1996, Technical Report CMU-CS-96-TB, School of Computer Science, Carnegie Mellon University, Pittsburgh.

[6]   Marcel Altherr, Martin Erzberger and Silvano Maffeis, "SoftWired iBus - Middleware for the Java Platform," *Java Report*, 4(12), December 1999.

[7]   Farhad Arbab, "The IWIM Model for Coordination of Concurrent Activities," *Proceedings of COORDINATION'96*, P. Ciancarini and Chris Hankin (Eds.), LNCS 1061, Springer-Verlag, Cesena, Italy, 1996, pp. 34-55.

[8]   Fernanda Barbosa and José C. Cunha, "A Coordination Language for Collective Agent Based Systems: GroupLog," *Proceedings of SAC'00*, ACM, Como, Italy, March 2000.

[9]   Daniel J. Barrett, Lori A. Clarke, Peri L. Tarr and Alexander Wise, "A Framework for Event-Based Software Integration," *IEEE Transactions on Software Engineering*, vol. 5(4), October 1996, pp. 378-421.

[10]   Len Bass, Paul Clements and Rick Kazman, *Software Architecture in Practice*, Addison-Wesley, 1998.

[11]   Paolo Ciancarini and Davide Rossi, "Jada: Coordination and Communication for Java Agents," *MOS'96: Towards the Programmable Internet*, LNCS 1222, Springer-Verlag, Linz, Austria, July 1996, pp. 213-228.

[12]   Juan-Carlos Cruz and Stéphane Ducasse, "A Group Based Approach for Coordinating Active Objects," *Proceedings of Coordination'99, LNCS 1594*, 1999, pp. 355-371.

[13]   Susan Eisenbach and Ross Paterson, "Pi-Calculus Semantics of the Concurrent Configuration Language Darwin," *Proceedings of the 26th Annual Hawaii International Conference on System Sciences*, vol. 2, IEEE Computer Society Press, 1993.

[14]   Joseph Goguen, "Hidden Algebra for Software Engineering," *Proceedings Combinatorics, Computation and Logic*, 21(3), Springer Verlag, New Zealand, January 1999.

[15]   Carl Hewitt, "Viewing Control Structures as Patterns of Passing Messages," *Artificial Intelligence,* 8(3), June 1977, pp. 323-364.

[16]   Valérie Issarny, Christophe Bidan and Titos Saridakis, "Characterizing Coordination Architectures According to their Non-Functional Execution Properties," *Proceedings of the 31st Annual Hawaii International Conference on System Sciences*, 1998, pp. 275-283.

[17]   Paola Inverardi, Alexander L. Wolf and Daniel Yankelevich, "Checking Assumptions in Component Dynamics at the Architectural Level," *Proceedings of COORDINATION'97*, LNCS 1282, Springer-Verlag, September 1997, pp. 46-63.

[18]   Ralph E. Johnson and Brian Foote, "Designing Reusable Classes," *Journal of Object-Oriented Programming*, 1(2), 1988, pp. 22-35.

[19]   Doug Lea, *Concurrent Programming in Java[tm], Second Edition: Design principles and Patterns* (2nd edition), Addison-Wesley, The Java Series, 1999.

[20]   Markus Lumpe, "A Pi-Calculus Based Approach to Software Composition," Ph.D. thesis, University of Bern, January 1999.

[21]   Markus Lumpe, Franz Achermann and Oscar Nierstrasz, "A Formal Language for Composition," *Foundations of Component Based Systems,* Gary Leavens and Murali Sitaraman (Eds.), pp. 69-90, Cambridge University Press, 2000.

[22]   Nikunj R. Mehta, Nenad Medvidovic and Sandeep Phadke, "Towards a Taxonomy of Software Connectors," *Proceedings ICSE'00*, Limerick, Ireland, June 2000, pp. 178-187.

[23]   Naftaly Minsky and Victoria Ungureanu, "Regulated Coordination in Open Distributed Systems," *Proceedings COORDINATION'97*, David Garlan and Daniel Le Mètayer (Eds.), LNCS 1282, Springer-Verlag, Berlin, Germany, September 1997, pp. 81-97.

[24] George A. Papadopoulos and Farhad Arbab, "Coordination Models and Languages," *The Engineering of Large Systems*, Academic Press, August 1998.

[25] Jean-Guy Schneider and Markus Lumpe, "A Metamodel for Concurrent, Object-based Programming," Proceedings of LMO'00, Québec, January 2000, pp. 149-165.

[26] Mary Shaw, R. DeLine, D. V. Klein, T. L. Ross, D. M. Young and G. Zelesnik, "Abstractions for software and architecture and tools to support them," *IEEE Transactionss on Software Engineering*, April 1995.

[27] Mary Shaw and David Garlan, *Software Architecture: Perspectives on an Emerging Discipline*, Prentice-Hall, 1996.

[28] Clemens A. Szyperski, *Component Software*, Addison-Wesley, 1998.

[29] Wolfgang Wechler, *Universal Algerbra for Computer Scientists*, Springer-Verlag, vol. 25, EATCS, 1991.

Coordination Technology for Workflows on the Web: Workspaces

Robert Tolksdorf

Technische Universität Berlin, Fachbereich Informatik, FLP/KIT,
Sekr. FR 6–10, Franklinstr. 28/29, D-10587 Berlin, Germany,
tolk@cs.tu-berlin.de, http://www.cs.tu-berlin.de/~tolk

Abstract. The need for coordination technology in Web applications is evident. It has been shown that Linda-like systems are a suited to facilitate the interaction amongst agents and processes over the Internet. Workspaces is the application of Linda-like coordination technology to the domain of Internet-based workflow management systems.

The Workspaces architecture is based on workflows as coordinated transformations of documents. A set of basic steps transform XML documents under the control of an XSL engine. Coordination operations affect the order of execution in the workflow. A meta step compiles a workflow graph from the XML-based Workspaces Coordination Language into a set of XSL rules for single transformation steps.

The Workspaces architecture uses a Linda-like data space for coordination by XML documents. This XMLSpace contains documents describing the steps in a workflow and application specific documents to be transformed in the course of work. It involves multiple matching relations on XML documents.

The combination of standard Internet technology with coordination technology exhibits various benefits of explicit procedure representation, distributed and uncoupled architecture and ease of access.

1   Workflow and the World Wide Web

With the advent of active processing on the World Wide Web with languages like Java, the need for coordinating distributed applications over the Web has been evident. Several projects explored the use of coordination technology à la Linda to provide a general coordination platform for such systems. While systems like PageSpace ([CTV+98]) are limited by being a research project, a commercial product like JavaSpaces ([FHA99]) shows serious confidence in uncoupled coordination technologies.

While such efforts aim at a general platform, the work presented here focuses on one application domain, that of workflow management. The necessity of integrating workflow and Internet technologies has been widely accepted and discussed in depth by the industry consortium of the major workflow management system vendors, the Workflow Management Coalition WfMC [Wor98b]. Workflow systems and the Internet are recognized as complementary technologies whose combination could lead to tremendous changes in the workplace.

A. Porto and G.-C. Roman (Eds.): COORDINATION 2000, LNCS 1906, pp. 36–50, 2000.
© Springer-Verlag Berlin Heidelberg 2000

According to the paper, the Internet brings to workflow technology zero application deployment costs, ubiquity, integration tools, distribution and virtual enterprise, and electronic data interchange. On the other hand, workflow is expected to enhance the Internet with functions like procedure representation and interpretation, dispatching work to the right participant at the right time, integration of existing applications, assistance with activity execution, monitoring and alerting, and statistics. In sum the WfMC expects the following benefits of the Internet from workflow technologies: increased security, enhanced reactivity, clear progress reports, productivity, and quality and cost control.

In this paper, we discuss, how coordination technology in the Linda style [GC92] can be efficiently combined with recent Internet standards by the World Wide Web Consortium (W3C) – namely XML [Wor98c] and XSL [Wor99,Wor00] – to implement a workflow management system that provides the expected benefits of Internet based workflow systems.

The paper is organized as follows. First, we describe the underlying approach to workflow management in Workspaces by understanding a workflow as a series of document transformations. We then present the XML-based Workspaces coordination language used to describe workflow models. We show how the various kinds of steps in such a workflow are implemented and describe the use of Linda-like coordination technology in Workspaces. We finally look at the Workspaces implementation and present conclusions and future directions.

2 Coordination by Transforming Documents

In this section we describe the approach of Workspaces for workflow management. This application domain is interesting from a coordination viewpoint, as it represents coordination systems in which both humans and system components interact. The coordination options are slightly more general as those in a pure computing system because of the human involvement and the commonly sub-formal work specifications.

Our design – called *Workspaces* – is based on the notion of a *step* as the basic kind of activity. As depicted in figure 1(a), each step is the transformation of one or more documents by an activity into a number of other documents which can,

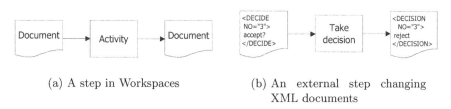

(a) A step in Workspaces   (b) An external step changing XML documents

Fig. 1. Transformed documents

in turn, cause further activities to start. We distinguish several *kinds* of steps as follows:

- *Automatic steps* are pure document transformations and require only activity of some transformation component within the system. An example is a text formatter that transforms a document from some markup language into a formatted and printable representation.
- *External steps* involve applications that take a document as input, let the user perform some activity on it, and finally generate an output document. An example is an editor used on some text.
- *User steps* are performed by a user without any support by a computing system. An example is the activity to read a conference submission, or to develop an opinion towards it. The user has to report the completion of such a step at a GUI.
- *Coordination steps* coordinate the flow of work only. In the process model put forth by the WfMC [Wor98a] we find examples of explicit coordination steps with the ROUTE, LOOP and SUBFLOW activities. In addition, JOIN and SPLIT activities are implicitly embedded in the topology of the workflow graph. We consider these also as explicit steps. Together, these coordination activities play the role of the coordination language of the workflow, as opposed to the set of automatic, external, and user steps that represent the actual work performed.
- *Meta steps* change or generate the structure of the workflow. An example is the generation of a set of individual steps from a process description.

In the following, we will refer to automatic, external and user steps as *basic steps*.

An *engine* is responsible for the execution of the respective activity upon the presence of an input document and the generation of output. In the Workspaces implementation, it consists of several processes that can be distributed.

The dominant format for marking up documents on the Internet will be the *Extensible Markup Language* XML [Wor98c]. XML is a language to describe the grammar of application specific markup languages. For Workspaces, all documents on which work is performed are XML documents that follow application specific grammars depending on the domain in which the workflow happens.

For the example domain of managing the reviewing process for a scientific conference ([CNT98]), we can envision a special markup language for reviews. Open decisions shall me marked up with <DECIDE> and judgments shall be marked as <DECISION>. Figure 1(b) shows the step of actually taking the decision about a paper. It is an external step by a reviewer, because some editor is used to type the answer.

Above we listed five kinds of steps and introduced the engine responsible to perform a step. However, we want a *generic* engine, not one for calling an editor and another one for asking the user to read a book. Thus, *activity descriptions* define the specific kind of step and are interpreted by the engine. An activity description itself is a document as shown in figure 2(a).

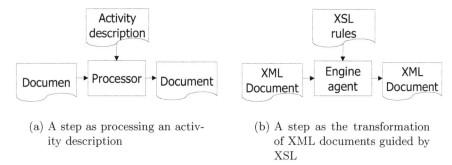

(a) A step as processing an activ-
ity description

(b) A step as the transformation
of XML documents guided by
XSL

Fig. 2. Steps with descriptions

The task of transforming an XML document into another one is the very subject of the *Extensible Stylesheet Language* XSL technology currently developed by the W3C [Wor99,Wor00]. An XSL processor takes an XSL rule set which contains patterns and transformations. It tries to match patterns in the input document and to apply transformations on the match that generate fragments in the output document. In Workspaces activity descriptions are represented as an XSL rule set and the engine is implemented with an XSL processor, as depicted in figure 2(b).

3   The Workspaces Coordination Language

A workflow in Workspaces is described by a graph of activities and represented as an XML document following the DTD of the *Workspaces Coordination Language*, WSCL. WSCL is based on the Workflow Process Description Language (WPDL) as defined by the WfMC. Changes to the WPDL concern:

1. The alignment of the syntax to the rules of XML and the appropriate definitions of tags and their attributes.
2. The usage of references in the workflow definition. In the Web context, any reference is a global URI resolvable by network access.

Figure 3 shows an example workflow and its markup as a graph. The workflow is an excerpt from peer reviewing of conference papers. It involves reviewing forms and the papers as data manipulated. We model two activities, reading the paper and sending the review form to some program committee chair. Reading is marked up as being not supported by a tool and will be implemented as a user step in Workspaces. Sending the form is an external step that uses a browser application to fill out and send it. The only dependency marked up by a transition amongst activities is that the paper has to be read before the form is sent.

```
<WORKFLOW ID="review">
  <DESCRIPTION>This describes the workflow from the
  reviewers perspective.</DESCRIPTION>
  <DATA ID="form" TYPE="Reviewform"/>
  <DATA ID="paper" TYPE="Paper"/>
  <ACTIVITY ID="read">
    <DESCRIPTION>Read the paper, check its contents and
      get an opinion</DESCRIPTION>
    <NOIMPLEMENTATION PERFORMER="pcmember"/>
  </ACTIVITY>
  <ACTIVITY ID="sendreview">
    <APPLICATIONS>
        <TOOL NAME="browser"/>
    </APPLICATIONS>
  </ACTIVITY>
  <TRANSITION ID="paperread" FROM="read" TO="sendreview"/>
</WORKFLOW>
```

Fig. 3. An example workflow in WSCL

Figure 4 shows an excerpt from the XML-DTD that defines the grammar of WSCL with tags and their attributes derived from the WSCL definition.

An editor as in figure 5 with a graphical interface to model such workflows and to automatically generate the respective WSCL representation is implemented as part of the master thesis of TU-Berlin student Amarilis Macedo-Aranya.

4   The Steps and Their Implementation

In this section we describe the implementation of steps based on XSL technology.

```
<!ELEMENT WORKFLOW (DESCRIPTION?,
 %ParticipantsApplicationsData;,
 (ACTIVITY|TRANSITION)*)>
<!ATTLIST WORKFLOW
    ID              %ProcessId;      %Required;
    NAME            %Name;           %Optional;
    CREATED         %Date;           %Optional;
    DURATION-UNIT   (Y|M|D|h|m|s)    %Optional;
    PRIORITY        %Priority;       %Optional;
    LIMIT           %Duration;       %Optional;
    VALID-FROM      %Date;           %Optional;
    VALID-TO        %Date;           %Optional;
```

Fig. 4. An excerpt from the WSCL-DTD

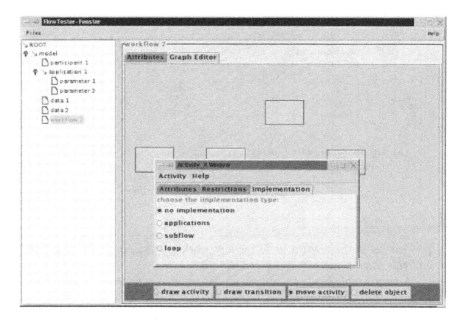

Fig. 5. Editing a Workspaces graph

4.1 Basic Steps

With activity descriptions as XSL rules, the implementation of the basic steps mentioned above is provided by an XSL engine as follows:

- *Automatic steps* are the very normal XSL processing that takes a document and outputs another one.
- *External steps* lead to the invocation of an external application by the XSL engine as depicted in figure 6(a). There are several options for implementing this behavior, such as to use a standardized scripting language within XSL, by a processing instruction built into the Workspaces XSL engine to perform the invocation, of by wrapping the engine with component that either calls an application or the XSL-engine.
- *User steps* result in an invocation of a GUI as depicted in figure 6(b). This can be implemented as a function built into out XSL engine, by a scripting function, or unified with external steps by invocation of an external program that only displays a small GUI.

4.2 Coordination Steps

The kind of steps that affect the order of execution in the workflow are called *coordination steps*. Workflow procedures describe temporal and causal dependencies amongst activities represented as steps. The management of these de-

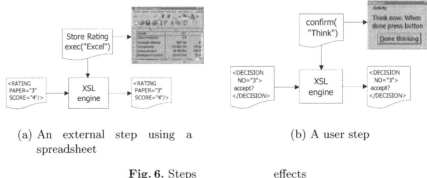

(a) An external step using a   (b) A user step
    spreadsheet

Fig. 6. Steps   effects

pendencies is the central issue for any workflow system. Following [MC94], we with external call this management activity *coordination*.

A very simple kind of managing a dependency amongst two activities is their sequential execution which is represented in a workflow graph by one activity being the direct or indirect successor of the activity on which it depends, as shown in figure 7.

More complex coordination operations are ones that change the direction of threads of work such as OR-JOIN, start multiple such threads (SPLIT), or synchronize them with a single successor activity (JOIN).

In Workspaces, special XSL rules implement these steps. As all activities are started by the presence of some document, a SPLIT simply generates a number of identical documents that start a set of threads as in figure 8(a). JOIN is a step that consumes several documents, processes them and outputs a single document as in figure 8(b).

4.3   Meta Steps

Basic steps together with coordination steps form complete workflow graphs. Figure 9 shows such a graph where review forms on a paper submission are distributed, answered, and finally collected and merged.

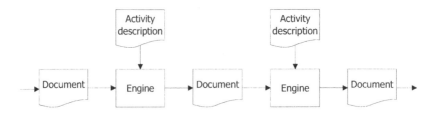

Fig. 7. Two steps in sequence

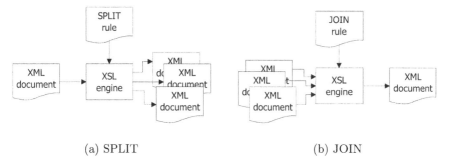

(a) SPLIT   (b) JOIN

Fig. 8. Coordination steps in Workspaces

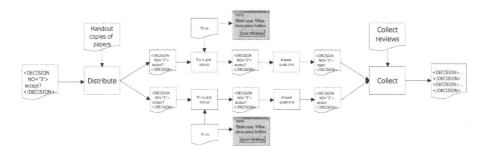

Fig. 9. A complete workflow graph

The graph is represented as an XML document following the grammar of WSCL. The execution of a workflow is the execution of individual steps by the respective XSL engines. This resembles the notion of an "instruction" in microprocessors. The workflow graph can be considered the "program" written in a higher level language.

The remaining step, that of "compiling" is performed by *meta steps* in Workspaces. The workflow graph is represented as an XML document following the grammar of WSCL. XSL rule sets are by definition also represented as XML documents following a syntax defined in the XSL standard. Thus, the compilation of the graph into steps is the transformation of one XML document into a set of XML documents, each containing an XSL rule for one step, as depicted in figure 10.

As the transformation of XML documents is performed by an XSL engine, the compilation can be described by a set of *meta rules* that describe the respective meta step.

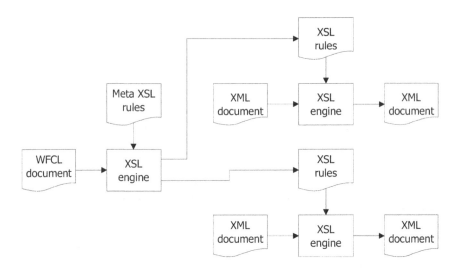

Fig. 10. Compiling a workflow graph into steps

The "compiler" is implemented as a complex set of XSL rules that take the graph document and generate a set of step documents. The initial implementation of this process has been the subject of a master thesis by TU-Berlin student Marc Stauch (see figure 11).

5   The Coordination Medium XMLSpace

In this section we describe the use of Linda-like coordination technologies in Workspaces.

While workflow usually facilitates *control-driven* coordination of activities, Workspaces uses a *data-driven* coordination medium to implement the enactment of the workflow (see [PA98]). The coordination language Linda [GC92] introduced the notion of a tuplespace and that of a *coordination language* as a set of primitive operations manipulating that space. The tuplespace uncouples the coordinated entities in time and space as they communicate indirectly, anonymous, undirected and asynchronous by one process placing some data into the space (using the out primitive) and another retrieving it from there using the in primitive with a template describing the desired data. in blocks until a matching tuple is present.

Our Workspaces model is very close to that abstraction: One activity generates a document that is taken by another step for further transformation. That other step has to wait for the presence of a matching document. Thus, the central coordination medium for documents and steps in our architecture is a Linda-like coordination kernel, *XMLSpace*. While tuples were the elements contained in

Fig. 11. Compilation of a graph

the coordination medium for Linda, they are XML documents for XMLSpace. XMLSpace is being implemented on top of TSpaces [WMLF98].

Linda is based on matching tuples – lists of typed values – associatively with some template based on a single given matching rule. For Workspaces, the concept has to be extended:

– There is a varying degree of associativity in a workflow. For example, a reviewer who is assigned a set of papers starts a sub-workflow "read paper – judge – fill out review form – send form to PC" for *any* paper from that set. Within that instance of the workflow model, the form sent to the chair is the *specific* one which has been filled out in the prior step. Documents involved with an instance of a workflow have to be made unique by some identification and their retrieval from some space will be non-associatively performed. Documents that start a workflow are in part associatively retrieved.
– The data structure involved – XML documents – is much richer than lists of typed values. XML documents are trees in which the nodes are elements defined in the DTD or text. Elements can carry attributes that have values.

From the requirement on different degrees of associativity and the opportunities given by the richer data structure XML document, we can deduce a set of useful relations amongst XML documents to be used for matching in XMLSpace. Some of these are:

- An XML document can be matched to another one which validates against the same given grammar, ie. DTD.
- An XML document can be matched to another one which validates against the same minimal grammar.
- An XML document can be matched to another one which validates against the same minimal grammar with renaming of element- and attribute-names.
- An XML document can be matched to a query expression following the syntax and semantics of those, for example XML-QL, XQL, or XPath/Pointer.
- An XML document can be matched to another based on equality of contents.
- An XML document can be matched to another based on equality of attributes in elements.

Each of these relations can be implemented by a specific matching-function in XMLSpace. For Workspaces, we match specific documents in a workflow instance by using a unique identifier kept in an attribute of the root-element. XSL engines retrieve step descriptions by matching on the PERFORMER attribute of steps. To start a workflow, a step description with the unique identifier _start is sought. The initial application specific document on which a workflow instance will work, is retrieved based on the DTD used.

6   Implementation

The Workspaces implementation is based on Java. It uses the XT XSL engine ([Cla]) at its core to implement the document transformations and TSpaces for the coordination medium.

At the users machine, a Workspaces client component consists of some Workspaces specific communication component, a GUI component (see figure 12) and a varying set of platform specific applications.

The Workspaces server component embodies the XSL engine. It communicates via an in/out protocol with TSpaces server components that keep the documents and the rules for the steps that drive the workflow coordination.

Multiple Workspaces engines can be located on different machines. As depicted in figure 13, each of them retrieves some step to coordinate from the XMLSpace. Based on that, it waits for the necessary document by issuing an in operation to the XMLSpace. Upon receipt of a matching document, it performs the XSL-based transformation and finally outputs the result with out. The engine then can terminate or retrieve another step description.

With that, the individual engines benefit from the application of coordination technology in the Linda style. They are completely uncoupled and can be distributed and mobile. Their number does not have to fixed at any time. The engine that will process future steps does not necessarily have to run when the workflow starts being run. These attractive advantages of our architecture are due to the use of coordination technology and indicate its usefulness.

The Workspaces architecture tries to decompose the workflow in its atomic parts – the steps. Thereby the execution of the steps becomes more independent

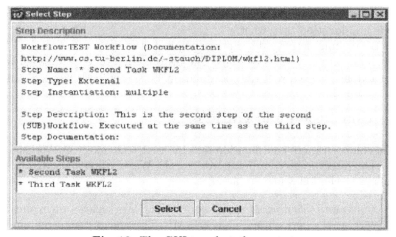

Fig. 12. The GUI to select the next step

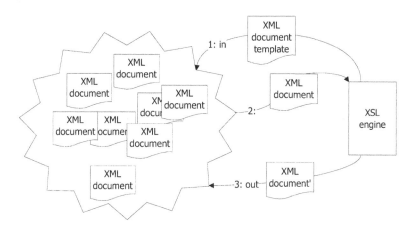

Fig. 13. An XMLSpace

of the execution of others. The condition for a step to be executed is a local one: There has to be a document to be transformed. There is no need to have a global control over the complete workflow.

This decomposition is enabling for the distributed execution of steps. It enables mobility of the actors in workflows: As there is no central control, no connection to some server has to be kept established. The decomposition allows for the delegation of steps. The decomposition leads to a higher autonomy of the people that execute parts of the workflow.

The decoupled coordination style, indirected by a coordination medium that masks any issues of distribution and synchronization, gives the technical freedom for a distributed and open implementation. The number of engines participating in the system can be dynamic as new engines can join and leave at whatever time and location they want.

By making activity descriptions explicit, the system is open and flexible to accommodate new kinds of steps. The introduction of meta steps makes the system extensible even wrt. the coordination steps used and their implementations.

7   Conclusion and Outlook

The composition of coordination and Internet technology in Workspaces results in an architecture to coordinate work on the Web with various attractive benefits caused by the following characteristics:

1. *Communicable procedures* All workflows in Workspaces are explicitly notated with a standard syntax, namely XML. This makes them communicable just as normal Web pages. Several scenarios are implied by this:
   - "Standard procedures" can be used as such. There could be a standard ACM approved workflow for reviewing papers. It could be put online and used by reviewers for any ACM conference.
   - One can delegate a task plus a possible workflow of how to perform it to some other person by passing the Workspaces workflow.

   All of these are implied by the specific representation of workflows, as anticipated in the WfMC white paper mentioned in the beginning. Moreover, we use a standard, machine readable and machine processable representation with XML and introduce meta steps in which the procedure representation is taken as data.
2. *Decomposition and decoupling* With this, we provide a platform that supports especially the distribution of workflows as mentioned as an Internet contribution in the WfMC white paper.
3. *Using standard technologies* The Workspaces architecture incorporates standard components and standard formats only. We build on XSL, XML and the Java platform – each of which is available without license costs and each of which will be standard components of near future Web systems. Thus, Workspaces does in fact provide zero application deployment costs and ubiquity, as required in the WfMC white paper mentioned initially,

While the initial implementation of the Workspaces concepts presented here is currently underway, several further issues are not yet dealt with in a sufficient manner. Most important are:

- *Exceptions* that naturally occur in workflows – for example, a reviewer could become ill, or some network connection breaks. The reference model by the WfMC does not provide means to model exceptions and reactions on them. It is unclear, how coordination technology can deal with exceptions. a major problem is the lack of adequate support for fault-tolerance ([TR00]) and the missing of concepts to "undo" interactions over a Linda-like coordination medium.

- *Adaption* of workflows are necessary because of changes in organizations and procedures. Such adaptions are often performed by graph-transformations of the complete workflow (eg. in [Nar00]). In Workspaces, the compilation of the graph into individual steps rules out this approach. It is not clear, how a decomposed workflow that runs distributedly, can be stopped and changed. It also has to be explored, what notion of consistency for the XMLSpace then has to be obeyed.
- *Disconnected operation* in workflows is quite common – a reviewer could review a paper while in a plane on a notebook. So far, it is unclear, what parts of the XMLSpace have to be packaged for the sub-workflow and how reconnection should take place.
- *Integration in Web browsers* can conceptually follow a clear path. However, a seamless integration of Workspaces clients with future versions of Web browsers with embedded XSL engines will have to overcome a number of compatibility issues.

Further information about the current status of Workspaces is available on the Web at *www.cs.tu-berlin.de/~tolk/workspaces*.

References

Cla.   James Clark. XT. http://www.jclark.com/xml/xt.html.

CNT98.   P. Ciancarini, O. Niestrasz, and R. Tolksdorf.   A case study in coordination: Conference   Management   on   the   Internet. ftp://cs.unibo.it/pub/cianca/coordina.ps.gz, 1998.

CTV$^+$98. Paolo Ciancarini, Robert Tolksdorf, Fabio Vitali, Davide Rossi, and Andreas Knoche. Coordinating Multiagent Applications on the WWW: A Reference Architecture. *IEEE Transactions on Software Engineering*, 24(5):362–375, May 1998.

FHA99.   Eric Freeman, Susanne Hupfer, and Ken Arnold. *JavaSpaces principles, patterns, and practice*. Addison-Wesley, Reading, MA, USA, 1999.

GC92.   David Gelernter and Nicholas Carriero. Coordination Languages and their Significance. *Communications of the ACM*, 35(2):97–107, 1992.

MC94.   T.W. Malone and K. Crowston. The Interdisciplinary Study of Coordination. *ACM Computing Surveys*, 26(1):87–119, 1994.

Nar00.   N.C. Narendra. Adaptive Workflow Management - An Integrated Approach and System Architecture. In *Proceedings of the 15th Sympoium on Applied Computing (SAC 2000)*, 2000.

PA98.   G. Papadopoulos and F. Arbab. Coordination models and languages. In *Advances in Computers*, volume 46: The Engineering of Large Systems. Academic Press, 1998.

TR00.   R. Tolksdorf and A. Rowstron. Evaluating Fault Tolerance Methods for Large-Scale Linda-Like Systems. In *Proceedings of the 2000 International Conference on Parallel and Distributed Processing Techniques and Applications (PDPTA'2000)*, 2000.

WMLF98.   P. Wyckoff, S. McLaughry, T. Lehman, and D. Ford. T Spaces. *IBM Systems Journal*, 37(3):454–474, 1998.

Wor98a. Workflow Management Coalition. Interface 1: Process Definition Interchange Process Model, 1998. http://www.wfmc.org.

Wor98b. Workflow Management Coalition. Workflow and Internet: Catalysts for Radical Change. WfMC White Paper, 1998. http://www.wfmc.org.

Wor98c. World Wide Web Consortium. Extensible Markup Language (XML) 1.0. W3C Recommendation, 1998. http://www.w3.org/TR/REC-xml.

Wor99.   World Wide Web Consortium. XSL Transformations (XSLT). W3C Recommendation, 1999. http://www.w3.org/TR/xslt.

Wor00.   World Wide Web Consortium. Extensible Stylesheet Language (XSL) Version 1.0. W3C Working Draft, 2000. http://www.w3.org/TR/xsl.

A Principled Semantics for inp

Jeremy L. Jacob[1] and Alan M. Wood[2]

[1] Department of Computer Science, University of York, UK
Jeremy.Jacob@cs.york.ac.uk
[2] Department of Computer Science, University of York, UK
Alan.Wood@cs.york.ac.uk

Abstract. The 'predicated' forms of the LINDA in and rd primitives have given problems for both kernel implementors and LINDA formalists. This paper firstly analyses these problems and then proposes a precise semantics for inp which is both *reasonable*, in that it does not admit unexpected or useless implementations, and *implementable* for open distributed tuple-space systems.

The semantics is given in a CSP style by the introduction of several new operators including *kick-start*, and *deadlock-breaking concurrency* which together enable a variety of well-defined, and feasibly implementable interpretations.

The paper includes a discussion of the implementation of these operators, and examples of the use of the resulting inp in practical coordination applications.

1 Introduction

Why is there a debate about the pros and cons of inp? It would seem that there is a fairly deep-seated need in programmers for such an operation — it feels somehow 'wrong' to write code that can block forever. This psychological imperative could be discounted as a consequence of the fact that every programmer has, unfortunately, learned his/her trade in a firmly sequential environment, and thus cannot intuitively deal with concurrent processes. This is especially true of open LINDA-like systems in which the process coordination is fundamentally asynchronous and non-deterministic. However, although in a LINDA context it is often possible to program around the lack of an inp, it still feels more 'natural' to have a retrieval operation whose informal meaning is: "... give me a matching tuple, or tell me if you can't".

The problems arise with the use of the word "can't". There can be many interpretations of this, ranging from "provably cannot for all possible future process behaviours" to "are not willing to supply a tuple at the moment". These two extremes are both unacceptable in practice since the first case is uncomputable (at least for open systems), and the second conveys no useful information — they will be referred to as the 'impossible', and 'useless' semantics of inp in this paper. Presumably, programmers have neither of these interpretations in mind when they feel the need to use an inp — they must believe that some useful information can be gained from its use.

A. Porto and G.-C. Roman (Eds.): COORDINATION 2000, LNCS 1906, pp. 51–65, 2000.

Consequently, rather than dismiss the desire for inp as aberrant, and indicating the need for re-education, it is worth trying to overcome the problems with the operation and provide a principled version which goes some way to meet the programmer's requirements.

There are two possible cases when using an inp in place of an in might be felt necessary:

Avoiding Blocking: some computation is to be performed which is independent of any tuple that might be returned from the in, and thus can be performed while the tuple is being retrieved. An inp enables this — in essence the programmer implements a polling loop in which the 'other' computation is progressed.

Termination detection: a process consumes tuples iteratively, with no prior knowledge of how many will be available. The use of an inp in a while loop seems the natural solution.

The first case is better solved using two threads, the first doing the 'other' computation, and the second executing, and possibly blocking on, an in. In fact, the programmer, in making use of inp, is merely simulating some aspects of multi-threading. Consequently an inp is not required in this situation — one might argue that under these circumstances, the perceived need for inp arises from a lack of thread support in the host language, which is a *calculational* rather than a *coordinative* problem and so should not be part of LINDA [8]. An intermediate solution, which would be applicable for host languages which do not explicitly provide support for multiple threads, would be to use the Bonita [24] primitives in which the request for a tuple is dissociated from the (local) test for its reception. However, this still requires a potential 'busy-wait' at the point that the tuple is required.

The second case is difficult to get to work, due to the fundamental properties of the LINDA model: there is no way to tell whether the lack of a matching tuple is because there are none available at the moment, or because no more will be produced. To get round this, a producing process must out a distinct 'termination' tuple into tuple-space when it has finished producing the work tuples, and the consumer then uses inp to watch for *that*. However, this requires that the LINDA system supports out-ordering [7,2], which is possible, although it isn't clear that many LINDA-like kernel implementations are aware of this fact. In any case, for this technique to be used again requires host language support for multiple threads, and so reduces to the first case.

This paper is concerned with proposing a 'sane' formal semantics for inp, which matches the above informal meaning *as far as is reasonable*, and which is *feasibly implementable*. These two properties are essential, and are related — the first implies that there are *unreasonable* semantics relative to practical implementation. To justify this statement, and to demonstrate the problems with an informal semantics, consider the following descriptions/definitions of inp (or rdp), or equivalent operation:

How to Write Parallel Programs (1990) "If and only if it can be shown that, irrespective of relative process speeds, a matching tuple must have been added to tuple space before the execution of `inp`, and cannot have been withdrawn by any other process until the `inp` is complete, the predicate operations are *guaranteed* to find a matching tuple." [5, p.47]

How to Write Parallel Programs (1990) "The only difference between `in` and `inp` is that the predicates will not block if no matching tuple is found." [5, p.207]

C-Linda Programmers Manual (1995) "If no matching tuple is available, they will not block." [26, p.2-25][1]

C-Linda Programmers Manual (1995) "They do not block if no matching tuple exists." [26, p.7-1]

TSpaces Programmer's Guide (1999) "Retrieves a tuple. Does not block." [11]

TSpaces Specification (javadoc) (1999) "When found the tuple is removed and returned. If none is found, returns null." [12]

JavaSpaces Specification (1999) "...If no match is found, null is returned." [27, §2.4]

It can be seen from these that there is a variety of informal specifications for `inp`. However, we suggest that all but the first fall into the 'useless' category mentioned above — since there is no guarantee as to the circumstances under which a 'match' will occur, then no information can be derived from the `inp` returning false (or null etc.).

The first specification, although not quite consistent with the second, is the closest to being a precise and reasonable, if rather contorted, definition. The problem is that it gives a firm guarantee of the behaviour of `inp` when a match is found, but leaves loose the conditions under which an indication of *failure* is to be returned, and this is exactly the point at issue.[2]

Part of the difficulty with the above definitions lies in their informality — natural language is not the most appropriate means for conveying intricate and precise technical meaning. However, apart from the first, they also under-specify the behaviour in the open concurrent systems context which is precisely the domain in which the LINDA-like coordination is being applied. The following sections address both these problems by developing a formal algebraic semantics for `inp` (§ 2.2), which approaches the 'impossible' semantics by identifying situations in which it *is* possible to prove that an `in` would never find a matching tuple. This version of `inp` is then shown to be feasibly implementable given the properties of any 'reasonable' LINDA kernel (§ 3.1), and an example application is sketched demonstrating its use (§ 3.2).

---

[1] Interestingly, programmers are discouraged from using `inp` by the manual stating that "Using `inp` and `rdp` can complicate your program, because they tend to introduce timing dependencies and non-deterministic behavior that may not have been intended."

[2] It also appears to give all `in`s a higher priority for retrieving matching tuples than any pending `inp`s — this is probably not expected by LINDA programmers.

2   Sane Predicated Input

2.1   Formal Models

There are two principal ways of giving the semantics of a LINDA construct. One is to produce a formal model of the tuple space itself, reflecting the way it responds to, say, an `inp` request depending on its current state. Another way, which we do here, is to abstract away virtually everything but the behaviour of note and codify it in an operator.

The semantics of an operator can be given in several ways: operational, denotational, axiomatic and algebraic semantics are all possible. The commonest method in the coordination community seems to be an operational semantics, after Milner's style of definition of the Calculus of Communicating Processes (CCS) and the π-calculus [19,20]. However, as Hoare and He point out operational semantics are more fragile than algebraic semantics [10, Section 10.5, Page 277]. Hence we choose an algebraic semantics, and we do so in the style of Hoare's Communicating Sequential Processes (CSP) [9,22,25].

Our semantics gives enough rules to eliminate the operator. The elimination rules have four parts:

- eliminating recursion;
- eliminating the operator applied to a non-deterministic choice;
- eliminating the operator applied to a divergent argument; and
- eliminating the operator applied to a general deterministic choice.

Elimination of recursion is achieved by the general fixed point law:

$$E = FE \implies E = \mu F$$

(where E is an expression over CSP processes, F is a function of processes to processes, and μF is the least fixed point of F under the determinism ordering). Hence an occurrence of an operator $\_\oplus\_$ can be eliminated in a recursive context if we can show:

$$P \oplus Q = F(P \oplus Q)$$

for some F .

The only sensible elimination rule for non-determinism is *distributivity* in each argument:

$$P \oplus (Q \sqcap R) = (P \oplus Q) \sqcap (P \oplus R)$$

$$(P \sqcap Q) \oplus R = (P \oplus R) \sqcap (Q \oplus R)$$

(Here $\_\sqcap\_$ is the CSP operator that describes a non-deterministic choice between its arguments.) Distributive operators are not sensitive to the order in which non-determinism is resolved.

We must also give rules for when one of the arguments is **div** , the divergent process which only engages in infinite internal chatter.[3] In most circumstances,

---

[3] The process **div** , due to Roscoe [22, p83], is of the same spirit as Hoare's *CHAOS* [9, p126] but differs in that it only has infinite internal behaviour.

including those of interest in this paper, **div** is taken to be a zero of any operator.[4]

All that remains is to give elimination rules for the case of deterministic choice. Here is where the differences between operators show up. A deterministic choice has two aspects:

- the enabled events; and
- the behaviours (processes) that follow the occurrence of each event.

We use the following syntax for deterministic choices:[5]

$$E \rightarrow f$$

where E is the set of *enabled events* and f is a process-valued function with domain at least E .

As an example, the definition of *environmental choice* for initially deterministic processes is:

$$D \rightarrow f \,\square\, E \rightarrow g = (D \cup E) \rightarrow \lambda x \bullet \textbf{if } x \in D \setminus E \textbf{ then } fx$$
$$\textbf{elif } x \in E \setminus D \textbf{ then } gx$$
$$\textbf{elif } x \in D \cap E \textbf{ then } gx \sqcap fx$$
$$\textbf{fi}$$

If $D \cap E = \emptyset$ this is a deterministic choice. Otherwise, on the shared enabled events, the behaviour is demonically non-deterministic.

Another example, *alphabetised synchronous concurrency*, is:

$$D \rightarrow f \,_A\|_B\, E \rightarrow g = (D \setminus B) \rightarrow (\lambda x \bullet fx \,_A\|_B\, E \rightarrow g)$$
$$\square\, (E \setminus A) \rightarrow (\lambda x \bullet D \rightarrow f \,_A\|_B\, gx)$$
$$\square\, (E \cap D) \rightarrow (\lambda x \bullet fx \,_A\|_B\, gx)$$

This operator is given in the style of Roscoe, with explicit alphabets [22]. The process $D \rightarrow f$ is constrained to communicate only events in the set A and the process $E \rightarrow g$ is constrained to communicate only events in the set B . When either process wishes to engage in an event that is not also in the other process's alphabet (either $B \setminus D$ or $A \setminus E$ as appropriate) the communication may take place and just the communicating process moves into the next state (either fx or gx as appropriate). When a process wishes to communicate an event in the shared alphabet (that is, in $A \cap B$) then both processes must agree, and both progress to their next state following the occurrence of x .

---

[4] The main exception is in a sequential construct where **div** is the postponed argument.
[5] This syntax is based on the more usual syntax $x : E \rightarrow P$ where x is a binding occurrence of a variable name, E the set of enabled events which does *not* depend on x and P a process expression which may depend on the value x . We have

$$x : E \rightarrow P \equiv E \rightarrow \lambda x \bullet P \qquad .$$

A similar operator is *independent concurrency*. It is defined for deterministic choice by:

$$D \rightarrow f \parallel E \rightarrow g = D \rightarrow \lambda x \bullet fx \parallel (E \rightarrow g)$$
$$\square \, E \rightarrow \lambda x \bullet (E \rightarrow f) \parallel gx$$

Both arguments evolve through communication with the environment and are completely independent of each other.

We can use the above operators to describe the architecture of LINDA systems. Suppose that T is a description of a tuple space, and that P_i, for i in the finite range $0..n-1$, describe agents communicating through the tuple space. The system architecture can be described:

$$T \, _A\|_B \, (P_0 \parallel \ldots \parallel P_{n-1})$$

where $A \subseteq B$. Such an approach is taken by Magee and Kramer [14]. An out operation is represented by a single event. An in operation could be represented in the agents by a pair of events: output of a request followed immediately by input of the response:

$$i.\text{req\_in}!p \rightarrow i.\text{res\_in}?t : U \rightarrow \ldots$$

Here U is the set of all tuples, i is the name of the agent (it is possible to write the text of the agents independent of their names: we ignore this for simplicity), $i.\text{req\_in}.p$ is the event of Agent i requesting a tuple matching pattern value p, and $i.\text{res\_in}?t : U \rightarrow \ldots$ is a general choice of events of the form $i.\text{res\_in}.t$ where t ranges over the set U. The choice will be resolved by the tuple space, T.

An alternative is to use a single event:

$$i.\text{in}?t : p \rightarrow \ldots$$

Here $p \subseteq U$ is a pattern represented as the set of all matching tuples.

Either of these forms can be extended to represent inp. The input is extended to allow a 'no such tuple' event as well as any (matching) tuple. For example,

$$i.\text{req\_inp}!p \rightarrow (i.\text{res\_in}?t : U \rightarrow \ldots \, \square \, i.\text{inp\_false} \rightarrow \ldots)$$

In this style the new version of inp could be described by modifying T. However, we take a different tack. We choose to modify the concurrency operator between the tuple space and its using agents. This is akin to putting the functionality in the kernel (although it need not be implemented this way). Another way of looking at our approach is that it introduces a program 'by super-position' [6].

This approach allows us to concentrate on the issue at hand without having to worry about any other features of LINDA. It thus allows us to suggest subtle variants without confounding the issues. This we do in Section 2.2.

2.2 A Model of Sane Predicated Input

We identify a special set of events, F to represent calls of inp returning *false*. (The above suggestion is that these would be of the form $i.\text{inp\_false}$, for each index i , but other representations are possible.)

We now define the *kick-start* operator, $\hookrightarrow_F P$. It represents what happens after deadlock has been detected and a non-empty but non-deterministic set of processes waiting on an inp are chosen to receive the 'false' result. The operator is distributive and has **div** as zero.

To define the elimination rule for general choice we first define the set of non-empty sequences of enabled F events.[6]

$$\tau(D \rightarrow f) = \{\, t \in (D \cap F)^* | 0 < \#t = \#(\text{elems}\, t)\, \}$$

This operator is not defined if $D \cap F = \emptyset$.

The generalised choice case of kick-start is then:[7]

$$\hookrightarrow_F (D \rightarrow f) = \prod_{t \in \tau(D \rightarrow f)} (D \rightarrow f)/t$$

That is, the process continues in a state that has occurred after a non-empty but nondeterministic set of 'inp false's are returned.

Note that $\hookrightarrow_F (D \rightarrow f)$ is only defined if $(D \rightarrow f)/t$ is defined for every $t \in \tau(D \rightarrow f)$. This obtains if the occurrence of an event in $D \cap F$ does not disable any other event in $D \cap F$. One way of ensuring this is to insist that each blocked inp represents *a separate thread of control independent of other blocked threads*; this is the way we expect LINDA to be used. A more liberal behaviour is permitted: the order in which the elements of F are released may affect future behaviour.

We are now in a position to define a version of concurrent composition that releases blocked processes when it detects deadlock. *Deadlock breaking concurrency* is written $P \;_A\|_B Q$, where the alphabets must satisfy $A \cap F = \emptyset \wedge F \subseteq B$. As usual it distributes over nondeterministic choice in both arguments and has **div** as a zero in both arguments. Unusually it is an asymmetric concurrency operator (compare with *subordination* [9, pp161–170] and *enslavement* [22, pp105–109], which are also asymmetric).

---

[6] If t is a sequence we define elems t to be the *set* of elements appearing in t . Also, $\#w$ gives the size of w whether it is a set or a sequence. If a sequence and its set of elements have the same size then each element can only occur once in the sequence.

[7] The *after* operator P/t generalises the application of a function to an event. It satisfies:

$$D \rightarrow f/\langle\rangle = D \rightarrow f$$
$$D \rightarrow f/\langle e\rangle \frown t = fe/t$$

The second equation is only defined if $e \in D$.

We split the elimination rules for deadlock breaking concurrency in two, for ease of presentation. First, when there is no deadlock:

$$D \to f \;_{A}\wr\wr_B E \to g = (D \setminus B) \setminus F \to (\lambda x \bullet fx \;_{A}\wr\wr_B E \to g)$$
$$\square\, (E \setminus A) \setminus F \to (\lambda x \bullet D \to f \;_{A}\wr\wr_B gx)$$
$$\square\, (E \cap D) \setminus F \to (\lambda x \bullet fx \;_{A}\wr\wr_B gx)$$

whenever

$$(D \setminus B) \cup (E \setminus A) \cup (E \cap D) \not\subseteq F$$

The condition is the test for absence of deadlock, abstracted: *some* (non-F) event is enabled. In that case the operator is very like alphabetised concurrency.

The more interesting case is when deadlock is present:

$$D \to f \;_{A}\wr\wr_B E \to g = D \to f \;_{A}\wr\wr_B \hookrightarrow_F (E \to g)$$

whenever

$$(D \setminus B) \cup (E \setminus A) \cup (E \cap D) \subseteq F$$

Deadlock-breaking concurrency is 'associative' in the following sense:

$$T \;_{A}\wr\wr_{B\cup C} (P \;_B\|_C Q) = (T \;_{A}\wr\wr_B P) \;_{A\cup B}\wr\wr_C Q$$

when $B \cap C = \emptyset$. We expect LINDA systems to obey this condition.

2.3   Alternative Definitions

Above we noted that the informal definitions of inp admitted unpleasant implementations. Here are (sketches of) formalisations of two.

The useless implementation differs from $\_\_\wr\wr\_\_$ in that the useless implementation *always* kick-starts a process that has an element of F enabled. Such an operator may be defined in two clauses. First when neither argument has an element of F enabled:

$$D \to f \;_{A}!!_B E \to g = (D \setminus B) \to (\lambda x \bullet fx \;_{A}!!_B E \to g)$$
$$\square\, (E \setminus A) \to (\lambda x \bullet D \to f \;_{A}!!_B gx)$$
$$\square\, (E \cap D) \to (\lambda x \bullet fx \;_{A}!!_B gx)$$

whenever

$$E \cap F = \emptyset$$

If the right argument is waiting on a predicated input:

$$D \to f \;_{A}!!_B E \to g = D \to f \;_{A}!!_B \hookrightarrow_F (E \to g)$$

whenever

$$E \cap F \neq \emptyset$$

The impossible implementations are those in which the conditions are not computable. An example is the condition

$$e \notin \beta(D \to f \;_{A}\mathord{\mathrm{ii}}_B E \to g)$$

where e is an event of an out of a tuple matching the pattern of a waiting inp and the function β gives the set of elements appearing in any behaviour of its argument process.

2.4   Turing Equivalence

Busi and others have considered how alternative semantics for the LINDA primitives impact on the ability of tuple spaces to simulate a Turing machine [2,3]; they did this by showing how to simulate register machines (which are Turing-equipotent). Brogi and Jacquet have also looked at the expressiveness obtained by varying the semantics of the primitives [1].

The question arises as to what expressiveness our version of inp gives. Our definition of inp simulates[8] that given by Busi and Zavattaro [3]. Hence our version of inp gives a Turing-equipotent system in the presence of *ordered outs* and in the presence of *unordered outs* with *notify*.

3   Pragmatics

The previous sections have developed the formal properties of the 'principled' semantics for inp. In the introduction it was emphasised that an essential part of the semantics is that it must be feasibly implementable. We have discussed one part of that ... that it must not admit 'useless' or 'impossible' implementations. This much is obvious! However, it remains to demonstrate that the inp as we have defined it can be implemented to a reasonable degree of efficiency. In addition we shall want to show that the principled inp is also *useful*. Since, as was argued in the introduction, programmers often see inp as an essential part of their tool kit, perhaps it shouldn't be necessary to argue for the principled version's utility. However, there are some significant differences between the properties of the earlier versions of inp,[9] and those of the principled inp, and so some examples will be given.

3.1   Implementation Issues

The formal semantics says that to implement a sane inp, the kernel must maintain enough information about the state of LINDA processes to be able to

1. detect when a group of processes (call it a *process clique*) becomes deadlocked, and
2. know which processes in the clique are blocked on an inp.

The kernel is then free to select a non-empty subset of the inp-blocked processes and to unblock them by returning false. Since the kernel is the agent which is *maintaining* the block on the processes, any LINDA kernel will have the information required for 2. Consequently, the crucial point is how to detect a deadlocked process clique.[10]

---

[8] In the sense that it gives more guarantees.

[9] Whatever they may be — since we are arguing that these properties are ill-defined for the earlier versions, it's difficult to be certain what programmers thought these properties were.

[10] In essence, any kernel will already have the ability to execute $\hookrightarrow_F$, but it must be shown that it can implement $\_\mathcal{U}\_$.

A process will be deadlocked if the primitive it is using to access a tuple-space T is blocked, and all other processes which 'know about' T are deadlocked. Since there can be many tuple-spaces in a LINDA system, it can be seen that deadlock might involve a chain of tuple-space blocks, and so the kernel must be able to detect the existence of such chains. A crucial property for a kernel is, therefore, to be have information about which processes 'know about' each tuple-space. Given a 'strict' LINDA system, in which processes can only communicate via tuple-space, there are three ways in which a process can have knowledge of a tuple-space:

1. The process *creates* the tuple-space with a LINDA primitive,
2. The process has retrieved a tuple (using in etc.) which *contains* the tuple-space reference.
3. The process has been spawned by a parent process, and the tuple-space reference has been passed as a parameter of the spawning mechanism.

In case 1, the kernel can record that the process knows about the tuple-space that it has created.

Case 2 is similar to case 1. As part of the tuple matching mechanism, the kernel will see that one of the tuple's elements is a tuple-space reference, and so can note that the recipient has knowledge of that tuple-space. This therefore requires that the kernel implements *tuple monitoring* [17].

The final case is potentially more of a problem, since whether the kernel can or cannot find out about the spawned process's tuple-space knowledge depends on the spawning mechanism . . . and this might be part of the host language and not part of the LINDA implementation. There are, however, several solutions which cover the main mechanisms, and they all rely on the necessity for processes to 'register' with a LINDA kernel.

In order that a process can 'join' an open distributed LINDA system, some sort of registration protocol [17] must occur — typically a process will send a message to a 'known' location indicating its existence and intention to use LINDA. Thus, an independent process will always be 'known' to the kernel before using LINDA primitives. This 'knowledge' will be in the form of some process identifier supplied by the underlying operating system, When a process (locally) executes a LINDA primitive, the process id will be sent to the kernel together with the request.

If a process has been spawned in such a way that that it has been passed tuple-space references, it must be required to 'admit' this during the registration procedure. This is an extreme case, but could easily occur in a UNIX environment in which a (UNIX) process can fork/exec another while passing arbitrary data (such as a tuple-space reference) to the child.

The other common way of spawning concurrent processes is via *threads*. Under this mechanism, it is normal that at least some of the address space of the parent thread is accessible to the child, and so it is possible that the child will have the same tuple-space knowledge as the parent. The question then is whether it is necessary for the child thread to register with the kernel. Often this will not be the case, since in a typical threading environment, the fact that a thread is related to a particular parent is often coded in a thread's 'process' id — for instance, in some systems a thread has the *same* process id as all the others in its 'thread group' since, as far as the operating system is concerned, there is only a single *process* which might consist of multiple threads. Again, UNIX is an example. In these circumstances, the kernel implementor can take a conservative approach and maintain tuple-space reference data on a per-*process* basis.

Finally, there must be a mechanism for the kernel to know when a process will no longer use a reference to a tuple-space. This can be achieved by providing a 'deregister' primitive or, for finer control, a tuple-space 'free' operation. It would then be required that processes at least 'deregister' prior to terminating. Although it is important for the correct operation of a group of coordinating processes that all processes obey this rule, if an errant program did not, this would only affect other processes with knowledge of the tuple-spaces in the errant process's scope.

These considerations show that it is possible for a kernel to maintain sufficient information about the tuple-space references that processes hold to enable it to identify deadlock cliques. The actual detection can be costly, however. The target LINDA environment is a fully-distributed, open, wide-area system, which implies that 'the' kernel may be implemented as a number distributed peer-kernels running on networked nodes, the tuple-spaces will in general be partitioned across these kernels, and the processes will be running on a multitude of machines. Consequently, any task which requires that these sub-kernels cooperate in a global sense will be a significant system overhead. So, is it worth it? The answer is 'yes', on two counts:

- Firstly, it is *useful* — as sketched in the next section, there are algorithms which require the principled `inp`'s particular properties, and which would have to be expressed in an unnatural way without it. This in itself would not be a sufficient reason for including the overhead in a LINDA implementation, however ...
- There is almost no additional overhead in a practical distributed LINDA kernel. Most of the information, and much of the processing cost must already be accounted for by the *garbage collection* mechanism that is required in a robust open LINDA implementation. The deadlock detection mechanism is very similar in nature to the garbage detection mechanism, and the associated data structures maintain both registration and tuple-monitoring information in order for the garbage collector to work [16,15]. Therefore the 'overhead' must be taken relative to a kernel incorporating garbage-collection, which is *essential* for any practical implementation.

3.2   Example: Stable Marriages

The Stable Marriages algorithm is a well-known [13] solution to the problem of pairing the members of two sets according to the participants' ranked preferences for members of the opposite set. The algorithm derives from a constructive proof [21] of the existence of a stable assignment (set of pairings) for any two sets of preference rankings. The concept of 'stability' is precise, but its definition and the proof of the algorithm's correctness are beyond the scope if this paper. However, the algorithm is extremely easily expressed as a collection of LINDA processes, and is sketched in Figure 1,[11] where it can be seen that the com-

```
        ┌─────┐                                    ┌─────┐
        │ m_j │                                    │ w_i │
        └─────┘                                    └─────┘
fiancee = FirstChoice();             fiance = null;
while(true) {                        while(true) {
out( <'propose', m_j, fiancee> );      if( !inp( <'propose', ?suitor, w_i> )
                                       break;
                                       fiance = BestOf(fiance, suitor);
                                       reject = WorstOf(fiance, suitor);
if( !inp( <'reject', m_j, ?fiancee> ) out( <'reject', reject, w_i> );
break;
fiancee = NextChoice();                }
}
```

Fig. 1. Processes modeling 'Men' and 'Women' in a LINDA Stable Marriages solution

putation reaches the solution (a stable set of pairings) precisely when deadlock occurs. Consequently, with a kernel capable of deadlock-breaking concurrency, this implementation of the algorithm will terminate with a correct result. It is likely that this is the simplest implementation of the algorithm.

Without a deadlock-breaking kernel, it is necessary to have an additional process — the Broker — which determines when the stable assignment has been reached. This can be done using *Scope*-based coordination [18], or with an operation such as copy-collect [23], but this involves iteratively examining the tuple-space until the correct number of 'accept' tuples are seen, and then checking that these tuples constitute a one-one assignment. Using the principled inp dispenses with the Broker, with the participant processes distributively determining when the assignment has resulted.

Although this implementation of the participant processes using the deadlock-detecting inp is extremely simple and elegantly parallels the problem's solution, some care has to be taken when considering how the system of processes are created, and how the resulting assignments are obtained.

In order that the inps can be kick-started, the kernel has to detect deadlock. This can only happen if no process other than those in the figure have references to the tuple-space being used to coordinate the participants. Therefore, the process which spawned the participants, and which must therefore have a reference to the coordination tuple-space, must deregister its knowledge of that tuple-space before the participants can terminate. This implies that the participants must return their assignments via a tuple-space distinct from the coordination space.

---

[11] For simplicity, the tuple-space being used to coordinate the processes is left implicit — in practice its reference would appear as a parameter of the LINDA primitives.

4   Conclusion

A version of the LINDA `inp` operation has been proposed which overcomes many of the difficulties, both semantic and pragmatic, of the loosely defined earlier versions. The properties of this primitive have been expressed algebraically and it has been indicated how this definition can be implemented in a practical LINDA kernel, and that the implementation is likely to cause little extra overhead when added to any practical open-system LINDA kernel which includes garbage collection (which it must).

Further work will be carried out in both the practical and theoretical directions. Practically, we shall incorporate the primitive in our latest kernel, with a view to verifying the predictions on overhead. Theoretically, we wish to investigate the relationships between the new CSP operations and the bulk primitives previously developed [23,4].

In addition, we expect that useful information can be derived from the use of 'attributes' [28] to refine the kernel's deadlock detection. For example, if is known that a process can only *read* from a tuple-space, then it could not unblock any process, and so the kernel could discount it from parts of its deadlock calculation. Thus deadlock could be detected, and processes kick-started, earlier.

Finally, it is important to note the following health warnings:

- `inp` is *not* a 'non-blocking' version of `in` — it will block, as `in`, until a matching tuple is retrieved, *or* until deadlock is detected.
- `inp` is an *expensive* primitive — it is slightly more expensive (in terms of kernel load) than an `in` that retrieves a tuple, since the kernel must *also* engage in deadlock-breaking when necessary. The effects of this costly operation will not only be felt by the process executing the `inp`, but might propagate throughout the whole of the open LINDA system, degrading every participant's performance.

We have attempted to develop a version of `inp` which is *useful, implementable,* and which provides simple, well-defined *guarantees* about its behaviour. Programmers should use `inp` only when its specific properties are essential — as they sometime *are* — and not as a quick fix for the perceived 'costs' of waiting for an `in` to return.

References

1. Antonio Brogi and Jean-Marie Jacquet. On the expressiveness of coordination models. In Paolo Ciancarini and Alexander L. Wolf, editors, *Coordination Languages and Models: Third International Conference, COORDINATION '99*, number 1594 in Lecture Notes in Computer Science, pages 134–149, Berlin, April 1999. Springer.
2. N. Busi, R. Gorrieri, and G. Zavattaro. Three Semantics for the Output Operation for Generative Communication. In D. Garlan and D. Le Métayer, editors, *Coordination Langauges and Models: Proceedings of the Second International Conference COORDINATION '97*, volume LNCS 1282, pages 205–21. Springer, 1997.

3. Nadia Busi and Gianluigi Zavattaro. Event notification in data-driven coordination languages: Comparing the ordered and unordered interpretations. In Janice Carroll, Ernesto Damiani, Hisham Haddad, and Dave Oppenheim, editors, *Applied Computing 2000: Proceedings of the 2000 ACM Symposium on Applied Computing*, volume 1, pages 233–239. ACM Press, March 2000.

4. Paul Butcher, Alan Wood, and Martin Atkins. Global Synchronisation in Linda. *Concurrency: Practice and Experience*, 6(6):505–516, 1994.

5. N. Carriero and D. Gelernter. *How to Write Parallel Programs: a First Course*. MIT Press, 1990.

6. K. Mani Chandy and Jayadev Misra. *Parallel Program Design: A Foundation*. Addison-Wesley, Reading, MA, 1988.

7. Andrew Douglas, Alan Wood, and Antony Rowstron. Linda Implementation Revisited. In *Transputer and occam Developments*, pages 125–138. IOS Press, 1995.

8. David Gelernter and Nicholas Carriero. Coordination Languages and their Significance. *Communications of the ACM*, 35(2):97–107, 1992.

9. C. A. R. Hoare. *Communicating Sequential Processes*. Series in Computer Science. Prentice Hall International, Hemel Hempstead, 1985.

10. C. A. R. Hoare and Jifeng He. *Unifying Theories of Programming*. Series in Computer Science. Prentice Hall, London, 1998.

11. IBM. *IBM TSpaces Programmer's Guide*.
http://www.almaden.ibm.com/cs/TSpaces/html/ProgrGuide.html, 1999.

12. IBM. *Untitled (TSpaces specification)*.
http://www.almaden.ibm.com/cs/TSpaces/html/javadoc/index.html, 1999.

13. D. E. Knuth. *Stable Marriage and its Relation to Other Combinatorial Problems: an introduction to the mathematical analysis of algorithms*. American Mathematical Society, 1997.

14. Jeff Magee and Jeff Kramer. *Concurrency: State models and Java programs*. Worldwide Series in Computer Science. Wiley, Chichester, UK, 1999.

15. Ronaldo Menezes. Ligia: Incorporating Garbage Collection in a Java based Linda-like Run-Time System. In *Proceedings of the 2nd Workshop on Distributed Systems (WOSID'98)*, pages 81–88, 1998.

16. Ronaldo Menezes and Alan Wood. Garbage Collection in Open Distributed Tuple Space Systems. In *Proc. 15th Brazilian Computer Networks Symposium - SBRC '97*, pages 525–543, 1997.

17. Ronaldo Menezes and Alan Wood. Using Tuple Monitoring and Process Registration on the Implementation of Garbage Collection in open Linda-like Systems. In *Proceedings of the Tenth IASTED International Conference: PDCS'98*, pages 490–495. IASTED/Acta Press, 1998.

18. I. Merrick and A. M. Wood. Coordination with Scopes. *Proc. ACM Symposium on Applied Computing*, pages 210–217, 2000.

19. R. Milner. *Communications and Concurrency*. Series in Computer Science. Prentice-Hall International, Hemel Hempstead, 1989.

20. Robin Milner. *Communicating and Mobile Systems: the π-calculus*. Cambridge University Press, Cambridge, UK, 1999.

21. E.S. Page and L.B. Wilson. *An Introduction to Computational Combinatorics*. Cambridge University Press, 1979.

22. A. W. Roscoe. *The Theory and Practice of Concurrency*. Series in Computer Science. Prentice Hall Europe, 1998.

23. A. Rowstron and A. M. Wood. Solving the Multiple-**rd** Problem. *Science of Computer Programming*, 31:335–358, July 1998.

24. Antony Rowstron and Alan Wood. BONITA: A Set of Tuple Space Primitives for Distributed Coordination. In Hesham El-Rewini and Yale N. Patt, editors, *Proc. of the 30th Hawaii International Conference on System Sciences*, volume 1, pages 379–388. IEEE Computer Society Press, January 1997.

25. Steve A. Schneider. *Concurrent and Real-time Systems: The CSP approach*. Worldwide Series in Computer Science. Wiley, Chichester, UK, 2000.

26. Scientific Computing Associates. *Linda User's Guide & Reference Manual*, 1995.

27. Sun Microsystems. *JavaSpaces Specification*, 1999.

28. Alan Wood. Coordination with Attributes. In P. Ciancarini and A.L. Wolf, editors, *Coordinatiion Languages and Models: Proceedings of the Third International Conference COORDINATION '99*, volume LNCS-1594, pages 21–36. Springer, 1999.

Proving the Correctness of Optimising Destructive and Non-destructive Reads over Tuple Spaces

Rocco De Nicola[1], Rosario Pugliese[1], and Antony Rowstron[2]

[1] Dipartimento di Sistemi ed Informatica, Università di Firenze,
Via C. Lombroso, 6/17 50135 Firenze, Italy.
{denicola, pugliese}@dsi.unifi.it
[2] Microsoft Research Ltd, St. George House,
1 Guildhall Street, Cambridge, CB2 3NH, UK.
antr@microsoft.com

Abstract. In this paper we describe the proof of an optimisation that can be applied to tuple space based run-time systems (as used in Linda). The optimisation allows, under certain circumstances, for a tuple that has been destructively removed from a shared tuple space (for example, by a Linda in) to be returned as the result for a non-destructive read (for example, a Linda rd) for a different process. The optimisation has been successfully used in a prototype run-time system.

1 Introduction

In this paper we present the proof of an optimisation that can be applied to tuple space based run-time systems, which was first presented in Rowstron [1]. Examples of tuple space based systems are JavaSpaces [2], KLAIM [3], Linda [4], PageSpace [5], TSpaces [6], TuCSoN [7] and WCL [8] to name just a few.

Throughout this paper we will just use the three standard Linda tuple space access primitives:

out(tuple) Insert a tuple into a tuple space.

in(template) If a tuple exists that matches the template then remove the tuple and return it to the process performing the in. If no matching tuple is available then the process blocks until a matching tuple is available.

rd(template) If a tuple exists that matches the template then return a copy of the tuple to the process that performed the rd. If there is no matching tuple then the process blocks until a matching tuple is available.

Moreover, we shall assume that a single global tuple space is being used by all processes.

The optimisation proved in this paper is referred to as *tuple ghosting*. The (informal) semantics of the in primitive leads implementers to remove the tuple that is returned to a process from the tuple space as soon as the in primitive is completed. Tuple ghosting allows the tuple to potentially remain as a valid

A. Porto and G.-C. Roman (Eds.): COORDINATION 2000, LNCS 1906, pp. 66–80, 2000.

result tuple for a non-destructive read performed by another process whilst a set of assumptions holds.

Studying the soundness of the optimisation has been highly valuable; it showed that the original algorithm [1] was too optimistic and allowed the result to remain visible for too long. In certain circumstances, the original rules used for the optimisation altered the semantics of the access primitives. We are confident now that the actual optimisation, modified to use the semantics given in Section 3, is sound.

1.1 Motivation for the Optimisation

Optimisation of tuple removal is useful because often tuples are used to store shared state between processes. For instance, a list is usually stored in a tuple space so that the items of the list are stored in separate tuples, with each tuple containing a unique number as the first field, representing its position in the list. A single tuple is required that contains a shared counter indicating the number of the next element that can be added. In order to add an element to the list, the shared counter is removed using an in, the value of the counter increased and the tuple is re-inserted, and then a new tuple is inserted containing the number of the counter and the data as an element in the list. This is a common operation and there have been proposals for the addition of new primitives to help performing the update of the shared counter (see e.g. Eilean [9]), and, when using compile-time analysis, to convert the counter updating into a single operation [10]. The proposals were made with the intention of increasing concurrency. Additionally, in high performance servers the cost of managing a primitive blocked waiting for a matching tuple is greater than finding a matching tuple and not blocking. One of the new challenges for tuple space implementers is to create large-scale high throughput servers, and therefore optimisations that reduce the server load are important.

1.2 Implementation

Tuple ghosting has been implemented in a Java run-time environment and it has proved to be clean and efficient. To provide tuple ghosting the implementation uses the following informal rules. When a tuple is returned as the result of an in:

1. the same tuple cannot be returned as a result of another in;
2. the process which performed the in cannot access the tuple anymore;
3. whenever the process which performed the in performs any tuple space access or terminates, the tuple is removed.

The kernel works by marking tuples as ghosted once they have been returned by an in primitive. Every process using the kernel has a Globally Unique Identifier (GUID) created dynamically as it starts to execute. When the process registers with the run-time system, the process GUID is passed to the run-time system that creates a primitive counter associated with the process. Each time a process performs a tuple space access, the counter associated with the process is incremented by one (before the primitive is performed). When a process requests a tuple using an in, the matched tuple is marked as "ghosted" and tagged with the GUID of the process that removed the tuple and with the current value of the primitive counter associated with the process. Any other process can then perform a rd and have this tuple as the result. However, whenever the tuple is matched, the system compares on-the-fly the current value of the primitive counter associated with the GUID attached to the tuple with the counter value attached to the tuple. If the primitive counters differ or if the process has terminated then the tuple is discarded, and not used as a result for the rd.

All communication between the processes must occur through the shared tuple space. Hidden communication between the processes would allow the processes to determine that one had read a tuple after it had been destructively removed by another. Process termination is an example of hidden communication (where, for example, one process is started after another process terminates). The starting process can deduce that any tuples removed by the terminated process should not exist. Therefore, accounting for termination is important.

The rules that the kernel uses are described in detail in Section 3.

1.3   Performance

Table 1 shows some experimental results which, by means of the example of a list stored in a tuple space, demonstrate the advantages of using tuple ghosting using. In our scenario, the list is accessed by two reader processes that read the counter 20 times, and a writer process that appends 40 elements to the end of the list (updates the counter and adds new element).

The experimental run-time was written in Java, with the reader and writer processes running as Java threads. The results were gathered on a Pentium II 400 MHz PC. The results shown in Table 1 are the average times of 20 executions with tuple ghosting both enabled and disabled. The execution times (with standard deviations) are shown for the three processes. For the reader processes, the number of blocked and ghosted rd primitives are also shown. A ghosted rd is one that would have blocked if tuple ghosting was not enabled.

The results show (as expected) that no rd primitive leads to blocking when tuple ghosting is enabled, but when ghosting is disabled we have that 70% of the rd primitives do lead to a block. Tuple ghosting has therefore increased the level of concurrency achieved in the system. In addition, the execution times are reduced when the tuple ghosting is enabled. This is due to the overhead associated with managing a rd that is blocked because no tuple is available.

The rest of the paper is structured as follows. In the next section the structural operational semantics for a traditional Linda implementation is outlined, then in Section 3 the optimisation is outlined in more detail, and the structural operational semantics for the optimised Linda implementation is presented. The proof of correctness of the optimised version is then given in Section 4.

Table 1. Performance of the implementation with tuple ghosting enabled and disabled.

		Ghosting disabled		Ghosting enabled	
		Value	St. Dev.	Value	St. Dev.
Reader 1	Time (ms)	**4367**	566	**185**	39
	No. of blocking **rd**	**15.75**	1.37	**0**	0
	No. of ghosted **rd**	0	0	9.75	0.64
Reader 2	Time (ms)	**4281**	743	**194**	37
	No. of blocking **rd**	**15.35**	1.81	**0**	0
	No. of ghosted **rd**	0	0	9.9	0.85
Writer	Time (ms)	**4886**	670	**590**	71

2   Structural Operational Semantics for a Linda Kernel

2.1   Syntax

We assume the existence of some predefined syntactic categories that processes can use. EXP, the category of *value expressions*, which is ranged over by e, contains a set of *variable symbols*, VAR, ranged over by x, y and z, and a non-empty countable set of value symbols, VAL, ranged over by v.

The three standard Linda tuple space primitives are the elementary actions that processes can perform. Processes are constructed by using three composition operators: the *null* process nil is a process constant that denotes a terminated process, the *action prefix* operator $a.\_$ is a unary operator that denotes a process that first executes action a and then behaves as its process argument, and the *parallel composition* operator $\_ \parallel \_$ is a binary operator that denotes the concurrent execution of its two arguments. Processes can also consist of *evaluated* tuples (they are a separate syntactic category), that represent tuples that have been added to the tuple space (as in [11]). An evaluated tuple is denoted by $\underline{out}(v)$ with $v \in VAL$.

To give a simpler presentation of our formal framework, we make a few simplifying assumptions. We assume that tuples and templates consists of just one field. The only difference between tuples and templates is that the formers can only contain expressions (or values) while the latters can also contain formal parameters (i.e. variables to be assigned). A parameter x is denoted by $\underline{x}$, the set of all parameters $\{\underline{x} \mid x \in VAR\}$ is denoted by $\underline{VAR}$.

By summarizing, the syntax of the language is

$P, Q \ ::= \ nil \mid a.P \mid P \parallel Q \mid P \parallel O \mid O \parallel P$

$O \ ::= \ \underline{out}(v) \mid O_1 \parallel O_2$

$a \ ::= \ out(e) \mid rd(t) \mid in(t)$

$t \ ::= \ e \mid \underline{x}$

Variables which occur in formal parameters of a template t are *bound* by $rd(t).\_$ and $in(t).\_$. If P is a process, we let $bv(P)$ denote the set of bound variables in P and $fv(P)$ denote that of free variables in P. If $bv(P) = \emptyset$ we say that process P is *closed*. Sets $bv(\_)$ and $fv(\_)$ can be inductively defined as follows:

$$fv(nil) \stackrel{\text{def}}{=} \emptyset \qquad\qquad\qquad bv(nil) \stackrel{\text{def}}{=} \emptyset$$

$$fv(a.P) \stackrel{\text{def}}{=} fv(P) \setminus bv(a) \qquad\qquad bv(a.P) \stackrel{\text{def}}{=} bv(P) \cup bv(a)$$

$$fv(P \parallel Q) \stackrel{\text{def}}{=} fv(P) \cup fv(Q) \qquad\qquad bv(P \parallel Q) \stackrel{\text{def}}{=} bv(P) \cup bv(Q)$$

$$fv(P \parallel O) \stackrel{\text{def}}{=} fv(P) \qquad\qquad\qquad bv(P \parallel O) \stackrel{\text{def}}{=} bv(P)$$

$$fv(O \parallel P) \stackrel{\text{def}}{=} fv(P) \qquad\qquad\qquad bv(O \parallel P) \stackrel{\text{def}}{=} bv(P)$$

$$fv(out(e)) \stackrel{\text{def}}{=} \begin{cases} \{e\} & \text{if } e \in VAR \\ \emptyset & \text{otherwise} \end{cases} \qquad bv(out(e)) \stackrel{\text{def}}{=} \emptyset$$

$$fv(in(t)) \stackrel{\text{def}}{=} \begin{cases} \{t\} & \text{if } t \in VAR \\ \emptyset & \text{otherwise} \end{cases} \qquad bv(in(t)) \stackrel{\text{def}}{=} \begin{cases} \{x\} & \text{if } t = \underline{x} \\ \emptyset & \text{otherwise} \end{cases}$$

$$fv(rd(t)) \stackrel{\text{def}}{=} \begin{cases} \{t\} & \text{if } t \in VAR \\ \emptyset & \text{otherwise} \end{cases} \qquad bv(rd(t)) \stackrel{\text{def}}{=} \begin{cases} \{x\} & \text{if } t = \underline{x} \\ \emptyset & \text{otherwise} \end{cases}$$

As usual, we write $P[v/t]$ to denote the term obtained by substituting each free occurrence of t in P with v, whenever $t \in VAR$, and to denote P, otherwise.

2.2   Operational Semantics

The operational semantics assumes the existence of a function for evaluating value expressions; $[\![\cdot]\!] : EXP \longrightarrow VAL$. So, $[\![e]\!]$ will denote the value of expression e, provided that it does not contain variables. $[\![\cdot]\!]$ is extended to templates in the obvious way (i.e. $[\![\underline{x}]\!] = \underline{x}$).

The operational semantics of the language is defined in the SOS style [12] by means of a *Labelled Transition System* (LTS). This LTS is the triple $(\mathcal{P}_1, \mathcal{L}_1, \longrightarrow_1)$ where:

- $\mathcal{P}_1$, ranged over by P and Q, is the set of closed processes generated by the syntax given in Section 2.1.
- $\mathcal{L}_1 \stackrel{\text{def}}{=} \{out(v), rd(v), in(v) | v \in VAL\}$ is the set of *labels* (we shall use a to range over $\mathcal{L}_1$ and s over $\mathcal{L}_1^*$).
- $\longrightarrow_1 \subseteq \mathcal{P}_1 \times \mathcal{L}_1 \times \mathcal{P}_1$, called the *transition relation*, is the least relation induced by the operational rules in Table 2 (to give a simpler presentation of the rules, we rely on a *structural relation* defined as the least equivalence relation closed under parallel composition that satisfies the structural rules in Table 2). We shall write $P \stackrel{a}{\longrightarrow} Q$ instead of $(P, a, Q) \in \longrightarrow_1$.

For $s \in \mathcal{L}_1^*$ and $P, Q \in \mathcal{P}_1$, we shall write $P \stackrel{s}{\longrightarrow} Q$ to denote that $P = Q$, if $s = \epsilon$, and that $\exists P_1, \ldots, P_{n-1} \in \mathcal{P}_1 : P \stackrel{a_1}{\longrightarrow} P_1 \stackrel{a_2}{\longrightarrow} \ldots P_{n-1} \stackrel{a_n}{\longrightarrow} Q$, if $s = a_1 a_2 \ldots a_n$.

Let us briefly comment on the rules in Table 2. The structural laws simply say that, as expected, parallel composition is commutative, associative and has *nil* as the identity element. The operational rules S1-S5 should be self-explanatory. Rules S1 and S2 just account for the intentions of processes to perform operations. They define an auxiliary transition relation whose states are (not necessarily closed) processes and whose set of labels is $\{\underline{out(e)}, \underline{rd(t)}, \underline{in(t)} | e \in EXP, t \in$

Table 2. Linda Operational Semantics

Structural Rules

$$P \parallel nil \equiv P \qquad P \parallel Q \equiv Q \parallel P \qquad P \parallel (Q \parallel R) \equiv (P \parallel Q) \parallel R$$

Operational Rules

S1 $\quad a.P \xrightarrow{a} P$

S2 $\quad \dfrac{P \xrightarrow{a} P'}{P \parallel Q \xrightarrow{a} P' \parallel Q}$

S3 $\quad \dfrac{P \xrightarrow{out(e)} P' \quad \wedge \quad [\![\, e \,]\!] = v}{P \xrightarrow{out(v)} P' \parallel \underline{out}(v)}$

S4 $\quad \dfrac{P \xrightarrow{rd(t)} P' \quad \wedge \quad ([\![\, t \,]\!] = v \vee t \in \underline{VAR})}{P \parallel \underline{out}(v) \xrightarrow{rd(v)} P'[v/t] \parallel \underline{out}(v)}$

S5 $\quad \dfrac{P \xrightarrow{in(t)} P' \quad \wedge \quad ([\![\, t \,]\!] = v \vee t \in \underline{VAR})}{P \parallel \underline{out}(v) \xrightarrow{in(v)} P'[v/t]}$

S6 $\quad \dfrac{P \equiv Q \quad \wedge \quad Q \xrightarrow{a} Q' \quad \wedge \quad Q' \equiv P'}{P \xrightarrow{a} P'}$

$EXP \cup \underline{VAR}\}$. The remaining rules build upon them. Rule S3 says that an output operation is always non blocking, provided that the argument tuple can be evaluated. Rule S4 says that a read operation can be performed only if there is a tuple matching the template used by the operation. To check pattern-matching, condition "$[\![\, t \,]\!] = v \vee t \in \underline{VAR}$" is used; it is satisfied when either t is an expression that evaluates to v (the value stored in the tuple) or t is a parameter (a parameter matches any value). Rule S5 differs from S4 just for the management of the accessed tuple: indeed, in S5, the tuple is consumed, while, in S4, the tuple is left untouched. Finally, rule S6 ensures that the structural relation does not modify the behaviour of processes.

3   Structural Semantics for Optimised Linda

Having described the basic Linda structural semantics, we now consider the structural semantics for the optimised Linda implementation that uses tuple ghosting. In order to illustrate tuple ghosting in more detail, let us consider two very simple processes that interact through the tuple space. Their actions are shown in Table 3.

Table 3. Two simple example processes.

Process A	Process B
A_1 out(a)	B_1 in(a)
A_2 rd(a)	B_2 out(b)
A_3 rd(b)	B_3 out(a)

We shall use Petri Nets and their unfoldings as case graphs to describe the difference between the "classical" and the "optimized" semantics. In a Petri net the circles represent places, and the squares represent transitions. A transition can fire only when all the places that are preconditions for that transition contain tokens. When a transition fires it consumes the tokens in its preconditions and places a token in each of the output places that are linked to it by arcs.

The Petri net and the case graph showing the parallel composition of our two processes can be seen in Figure 1. If one ignores the dotted links in the figure, then the Petri net and the case graph are those created according to the semantics for the primitives as given in the previous section.

In Figure 1 the token starts in the initial place, and the only transition that can fire is A1:out(a). When this fires, a token is placed in the three output places connected to the transition. This means that either the transitions A2:rd(a) or

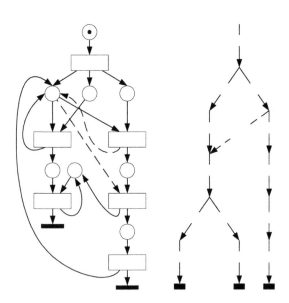

Fig. 1. A Petri Net and case graph for processes A and B.

`B1:in(a)` can fire. If `B1:in(a)` fires then the other cannot fire, because the token is removed from one of its preconditions. This token is replaced when the transition `B3:out(a)` is fired. If `A2:rd(a)` fires, then the precondition tokens are consumed, but the transition is linked to one of its own preconditions. So, a token is reinserted in that place. However, the same rule cannot re-fire because the other precondition does not contain a token any longer. This means that the transition `B1:in(a)` is the only one that can fire, as it is the only transition that has all precondition places filled with a token. The case graph shown in the same figure shows the different ordering of the possible transition firings (of course, the dotted arc has to be ignored).

In Figure 1 the dotted arcs represent the tuple ghosting optimisation. We allow the transition `A2:rd(a)` to fire after the transition `B1:in(a)` fires. This means that the manipulation of a tuple has been suspended in the middle of the operation; Process B has performed the in operation and has received the tuple and can continue, but the tuple is not actually removed whilst Process A cannot know that process B has received the tuple. This only occurs when there is the possibility of a synchronisation between the two processes, which happens using the tuple b, when Process B inserts it.

From the global perspective, this appears to be incorrect; it allows the reading of a tuple that should have been removed. We will now present the formal semantics of the optimised version, and then show the proof that the two semantics are equivalent.

3.1   Optimized Operational Semantics

The *optimized* operational semantics of the language is defined by means of another LTS. To this aim, we assume the existence of a set of process *locations*, Loc, ranged over by ℓ, where the parallel components of processes can be allocated, and of a distinct location, τ, where evaluated tuples are placed. We denote by $\underline{Loc}$ a disjoint set of *ghost* locations (where *ghost* tuples can be placed) which is in bijection with Loc via the operation $\underline{\cdot}$. Finally, we let $LOC = Loc \cup \underline{Loc} \cup \{\tau\}$, ranged over by λ, be the set of all locations. Locations shall be used to model the GUID assigned to processes in the implementation.

The idea is that Linda processes are statically allocated, e.g. distributed over a net of processors, once and for all. The names of locations and the distribution of processes over locations can be arbitrarily chosen. Hence, for any given process P, its distribution is determined by the number of its parallel components, i.e. by the number of occurrences of the parallel operator which are not guarded by any action. For instance, the process $\underline{out}(1) \parallel \underline{out}(2).(\underline{out}(3) \parallel \underline{out}(4))$ has initially two parallel components (although, after the execution of the $\underline{out}(2)$ operation, it is composed of three parallel processes) and can be allocated over, at most, two processors. This means that, as far as distribution is concerned, we have conceptually two different parallel operators and it is convenient to use different notations for them: we shall use $\mid$ to denote the occurrences of the parallel operator that do not cause distribution of their components, e.g. those occurrences guarded by some action, and shall still use $\parallel$ for the other occurrences, e.g. (some of) the unguarded occurrences. Obviously, the semantics of | is defined by rules analogues to S2 and to the structural ones.

To manage locations we introduce two new operators: an *allocator* operator $\lambda :: P$, that says that process P is allocated at location λ, and a *location remover* operator $P \setminus \lambda$, that says that location λ (and the process located there) must be removed from P.

The optimized LTS is the triple $(\mathcal{P}_2, \mathcal{L}_2, \longrightarrow_2)$ where:

-   $\mathcal{P}_2$, ranged over by P and Q, is the set of closed processes generated by the syntax given in Section 2.1 extended with the following productions

    $$P, Q ::= \ \dots \ | \ P \ | \ Q \ | \ \lambda :: P \ | \ P \setminus \lambda$$

    Hence, $\mathcal{P}_2$ also contains the *distributed* versions of processes from $\mathcal{P}_1$.
-   $\mathcal{L}_2 \stackrel{\text{def}}{=} \{out(v)@\lambda, rd(v)@\lambda, in(v)@\lambda, stop@\lambda | v \in VAL, \lambda \in LOC\}$ is the set of *labels* (we shall use $a@\lambda$ to range over $\mathcal{L}_2$ and σ over $\mathcal{L}_2^*$).
-   $\longrightarrow_2 \subseteq \mathcal{P}_2 \times \mathcal{L}_2 \times \mathcal{P}_2$, called the *transition relation*, is the least relation closed under parallel composition that satisfies the operational rules in Table 4 (again, to give a simpler presentation of the rules, we rely on a *structural relation* defined as the least equivalence relation closed under parallel composition that satisfies the structural rules in Table 4). We shall write $P \xrightarrow{a@\lambda} Q$ instead of $(P, a@\lambda, Q) \in \longrightarrow_2$.

For $\sigma \in \mathcal{L}_2^*$ and $P, Q \in \mathcal{P}_2$, we shall write $P \xrightarrow{\sigma} Q$ to denote that $P = Q$, if $\sigma = \epsilon$, and that $\exists P_1, \dots, P_{n-1} \in \mathcal{P}_2 : P \xrightarrow{\alpha_1@\lambda_1} P_1 \xrightarrow{\alpha_2@\lambda_2} \dots P_{n-1} \xrightarrow{\alpha_n@\lambda_n} Q$, if $\sigma = \alpha_1@\lambda_1 \cdot \alpha_2@\lambda_2 \cdot \dots \cdot \alpha_n@\lambda_n$.

Let us briefly comment on the rules in Table 4. The additional structural laws say that the location remover distributes with respect to parallel composition and that the removal just concerns the location (and the process located there) explicitly named by the operator. The operational rules should be quite explicative. The general idea is as follows. Tuples are initially allocated at location τ. When a tuple located at τ is accessed by an **in** action performed by a process located at ℓ, the tuple becomes a ghost tuple and is relocated at the ghost location $\underline{\ell}$. Whenever a process located at ℓ performs an action or terminates, removal of the ghost tuple that could have been allocated at $\underline{\ell}$ takes place. In particular, rules OS1-OS3 just account for the intentions of processes to perform operations. They define an auxiliary transition relation whose states are (not necessarily closed) processes generated by the extended syntax and whose set of labels is $\{out(e)@\ell, rd(t)@\ell, in(t)@\ell, stop@\ell \ | \ e \in EXP, t \in EXP \cup VAR, \ell \in Loc\}$. The remaining rules build upon them. Process termination is modelled by letting $\ell :: nil$ perform the action $stop@\ell$ (rule OS2), and, in the presence of a $stop@\ell$ action, requiring the removal of ghost tuples at $\underline{\ell}$ (rule OS4). Rule OS5 deals with addition of tuples to the tuple space (located at τ). Rule OS6 says that a **rd** operation can access both tuples in the tuple space and ghost tuples that are not allocated at the location of the process that performs the operation. Rule OS7 says that an **in** operation can access just tuples in the tuple space (i.e., it cannot access ghost tuples). Location removal is actually performed into

Table 4. Optimized Linda Operational Semantics

Structural Rules

$$P \parallel nil \equiv P \qquad\qquad P \parallel Q \equiv Q \parallel P$$

$$P \parallel (Q \parallel R) \equiv (P \parallel Q) \parallel R \qquad (P \parallel Q) \setminus \ell \equiv P \setminus \ell \parallel Q \setminus \ell$$

$$(\underline{\ell} :: P) \setminus \ell \equiv nil \qquad (\lambda :: P) \setminus \ell \equiv \lambda :: P \quad \text{if } \lambda \neq \underline{\ell}$$

Operational Rules

OS1
$$\dfrac{P \xrightarrow{a} P'}{\ell :: P \xrightarrow{a@\ell} \ell :: P'}$$

OS2 $\quad \ell :: nil \xrightarrow{stop@\ell} nil$

OS3
$$\dfrac{P \xrightarrow{\alpha@\ell} P'}{P \parallel Q \xrightarrow{\alpha@\ell} P' \parallel Q}$$

OS4
$$\dfrac{P \xrightarrow{stop@\ell} P'}{P \xrightarrow{stop@\ell} P' \setminus \ell}$$

OS5
$$\dfrac{P \xrightarrow{out(e)@\ell} P' \quad \wedge \quad [\![e]\!] = v}{P \xrightarrow{out(v)@\ell} P' \setminus \ell \parallel \tau :: \underline{out}(v)}$$

OS6
$$\dfrac{P \xrightarrow{rd(t)@\ell} P' \quad \wedge \quad ([\![t]\!] = v \vee t \in \underline{VAR}) \quad \wedge \quad \lambda \neq \underline{\ell}}{P \parallel \lambda :: \underline{out}(v) \xrightarrow{rd(v)@\lambda'} P'[v/t] \setminus \ell \parallel \lambda :: \underline{out}(v)} \quad \text{where } \lambda' = \begin{cases} \ell \text{ if } \lambda = \tau \\ \lambda \text{ otherwise} \end{cases}$$

OS7
$$\dfrac{P \xrightarrow{in(t)@\ell} P' \quad \wedge \quad ([\![t]\!] = v \vee t \in \underline{VAR})}{P \parallel \tau :: \underline{out}(v) \xrightarrow{in(v)@\ell} P'[v/t] \setminus \ell \parallel \underline{\ell} :: \underline{out}(v)}$$

OS8
$$\dfrac{P \equiv Q \quad \wedge \quad Q \xrightarrow{\alpha@\lambda} Q' \quad \wedge \quad Q' \equiv P'}{P \xrightarrow{\alpha@\lambda} P'}$$

---

two steps: first, a location restriction is put and, then, when applying rule OS8, the removal actually takes place by means of the structural relation. The transition labels always refer the location of the process that performs the operation, apart for the label in the conclusion of rule OS6 that, whenever a ghost tuple is accessed, refers the location of such a tuple.

4   Proof of Correctness

The actual proof is technically involved, although not conceptually difficult, and can be found in the full paper [13]. In this section, we only provide a sketch.

The two main results can be informally stated as follows:

- each computation from a distributed version of a process P allowed by the optimized semantics can be simulated by a computation from P within the original semantics (Theorem 1);
- each computation from a process P allowed by the original semantics can be simulated by a computation from a distributed version of P within the optimized semantics (Theorem 2).

To simplify the statement of properties, in the rest of this section we shall use P, Q and R to range over $\mathcal{P}_1$ and P_o, Q_o and R_o to range over $\mathcal{P}_2$.

First, it is convenient to fix the allocation function used to distribute the parallel components of processes. To this aim, we assume that $\{l,r\}^* \subseteq Loc$ and use ρ to range over $\{l,r\}^*$. Hence, strings of the form llr and $rllrl$ are valid locations. Now, by relying on locations of the form $\{l,r\}^*$ that can be easily "duplicated" (given a ρ, ρl and ρr are two new different locations), we define an allocation function that, intuitively, for any process $P \in \mathcal{P}_1$ returns its "maximal" distribution: each parallel component is allocated over a different location.

Definition 1. The *allocation function* $\mathcal{L}_\rho : \mathcal{P}_1 \longrightarrow \mathcal{P}_2$ is defined as follows:

$$\mathcal{L}_\rho(nil) \stackrel{\mathrm{def}}{=} \rho :: nil \qquad\qquad \mathcal{L}_\rho(a.P) \stackrel{\mathrm{def}}{=} \rho :: a.P$$

$$\mathcal{L}_\rho(P \mid Q) \stackrel{\mathrm{def}}{=} \rho :: (P \mid Q) \qquad\qquad \mathcal{L}_\rho(P \parallel Q) \stackrel{\mathrm{def}}{=} \mathcal{L}_{\rho l}(P) \parallel \mathcal{L}_{\rho r}(Q)$$

$$\mathcal{L}_\rho(P \parallel O) \stackrel{\mathrm{def}}{=} \mathcal{L}_\rho(P) \parallel \mathcal{T}(O) \qquad\qquad \mathcal{L}_\rho(O \parallel P) \stackrel{\mathrm{def}}{=} \mathcal{T}(O) \parallel \mathcal{L}_\rho(P)$$

$$\mathcal{T}(O_1 \parallel O_2) \stackrel{\mathrm{def}}{=} \mathcal{T}(O_1) \parallel \mathcal{T}(O_2) \qquad\qquad \mathcal{T}(\underline{out}(v)) \stackrel{\mathrm{def}}{=} \tau :: \underline{out}(v)$$

where function $\mathcal{T}$ separately allocates all evaluated tuples at location τ.

Correctness will be sketched in the case function $\mathcal{L}_\rho$ (hence, maximal distribution) is used for allocating processes. The proof would proceed similarly also if a different allocation function was used to initially allocate processes from $\mathcal{P}_1$.

We will also use an "inverse" function $\mathcal{C}$ that relates the states of $\mathcal{P}_2$ to those of $\mathcal{P}_1$.

Definition 2. The *cleaning function* $\mathcal{C} : \mathcal{P}_2 \longrightarrow \mathcal{P}_1$ is defined as follows:

$$\mathcal{C}(\ell :: P) \stackrel{\mathrm{def}}{=} P \qquad\qquad \mathcal{C}(\tau :: \underline{out}(v)) \stackrel{\mathrm{def}}{=} \underline{out}(v)$$

$$\mathcal{C}(\underline{\ell} :: P) \stackrel{\mathrm{def}}{=} nil \qquad\qquad \mathcal{C}(P \mid Q) \stackrel{\mathrm{def}}{=} P \mid Q$$

$$\mathcal{C}(P_o \parallel Q_o) \stackrel{\mathrm{def}}{=} \mathcal{C}(P_o) \parallel \mathcal{C}(Q_o)$$

With abuse of notation, given a label $\alpha@\lambda \in \mathcal{L}_2$ we write $\mathcal{C}(\alpha@\lambda)$ to denote the action part α whenever $\alpha \in \mathcal{L}_1$, and the empty action ϵ otherwise (i.e. whenever $\alpha = stop$). A similar notation shall be used for sequences of labels from $\mathcal{L}_2^*$.

We shall use $\Lambda(P)$ to denote the set of locations occurring in P_o. Formally, function $\Lambda : \mathcal{P}_2 \longrightarrow LOC$ is defined inductively as follows:

$$\Lambda(nil) = \Lambda(a.P) = \Lambda(\underline{out}(v)) = \Lambda(P_o \mid Q_o) = \emptyset, \quad \Lambda(P_o \parallel Q_o) = \Lambda(P_o) \cup \Lambda(Q_o),$$
$$\Lambda(\lambda :: P) = \{\lambda\}, \qquad\qquad\qquad\qquad\qquad \Lambda(P_o \setminus \lambda) = \Lambda(P_o) \setminus \{\lambda\}.$$

As a matter of notation, we shall use $P_o[\ell'/\ell]$ to denote the term obtained by substituting each occurrence of ℓ in P_o with ℓ'. Finally, we use the notation $\Pi_{\ell_i \in L} \ell_i :: \underline{out}(v_i)$ as a shorthand for $\ell_1 :: \underline{out}(v_1) \parallel \ldots \parallel \ell_n :: \underline{out}(v_n)$ (the order in which the operands $\ell_i :: \underline{out}(v_i)$ are arranged is unimportant, as $\parallel$ is associative and commutative in both the two operational semantics considered in the paper); and when $n = 0$, this term will by convention indicate nil.

We first outline the proof that the original semantics can simulate the optimized one. To this aim, we introduce the following preorder over traces (i.e. sequences of actions) in $\mathcal{L}_2^*$.

Definition 3. Let $\prec$ be the least preorder relation over $\mathcal{L}_2^*$ induced by the two following laws:

$$\text{TP1} \quad \sigma' \cdot rd(v)@\tau \cdot in(v)@\ell \cdot \sigma \prec \sigma' \cdot in(v)@\ell \cdot rd(v)@\ell \cdot \sigma$$
$$\text{TP2} \quad \sigma' \cdot \alpha@\lambda \cdot in(v)@\ell \cdot \sigma \prec \sigma' \cdot in(v)@\ell \cdot \alpha@\lambda \cdot \sigma \quad \text{if } \lambda \neq \ell, \ell$$

The intuition behind the trace preorder $\prec$ is that if $P_o \overset{\sigma}{\longrightarrow} Q_o$ and $\sigma' \prec \sigma$ then it also holds that $P_o \overset{\sigma'}{\longrightarrow} Q_o$, hence σ' can simulate σ. Law TP1 permits exchanging the execution order of two operations accessing the same evaluated tuple in order to avoid accessing ghost tuples. Law TP2 permits exchanging the execution order of operations that are not causally related. Its simple presentation relies on the observation that there cannot be two ghost tuples at the same location, hence if $\mathcal{L}_\rho(P) \overset{\sigma}{\longrightarrow} \overset{in(v)@\ell}{\longrightarrow} \overset{\alpha@\ell}{\longrightarrow} Q_o$ then it should be $\alpha = rd(v)$ and we would fall in the case dealt with by law TP1. Note that operations that take place at the same location can never be swapped because there is no way to ascertain when they are causally independent.

Let us now introduce some useful notations. We shall write $a \notin s$ to denote that there are not s_1, s_2 such that $s = s_1 a s_2$ ($\alpha@\lambda \notin \sigma$ has a similar meaning). Moreover, we write $g(\sigma)$ to denote the number of occurrences in σ of locations of $\underline{Loc}$ ('g' stands for 'ghost').

Intuitively, sequences of labels $\sigma \in \mathcal{L}_2^*$ such that $g(\sigma) > 0$ are obtained from sequences of operations that also access ghost tuples and, hence, cannot be mimicked in the original semantics. We will show that, however, for each σ with $g(\sigma) > 0$ it is possible to find a σ' such that (i) $g(\sigma') = 0$, hence σ' is obtained from a sequence of operations that can also be performed according to the original semantics, and (ii) $\sigma' \prec \sigma$, hence σ' simulates σ according to the optimized semantics.

The laws of the trace preorder can be used to reduce the number of ghost tuples accessed during a computation. The following crucial property gives a method for transforming a generic computation in an equivalent one (i.e. with the same final state) that corresponds to a sequence of operations that never access ghost tuples.

Proposition 1. $\mathcal{L}_\rho(P) \xrightarrow{\sigma} Q_o \xrightarrow{rd(v)@\ell} R_o$ implies that there are σ_1 and σ_2 such that $\sigma = \sigma_1 \cdot in(v)@\ell \cdot \sigma_2$ and $a@\ell \notin \sigma_2$. Moreover, if $a@\ell \notin \sigma_2$ then there is ℓ' such that $\mathcal{L}_\rho(P) \xrightarrow{\sigma_1} \xrightarrow{\sigma_2} \xrightarrow{rd(v)@\ell'} \xrightarrow{in(v)@\ell} R_o$.

By repeatedly applying the previous property we have that

Proposition 2. $\mathcal{L}_\rho(P) \xrightarrow{\sigma} Q_o$ implies that there is $\sigma' \prec \sigma$ such that $\mathcal{L}_\rho(P) \xrightarrow{\sigma'} Q_o$ and $g(\sigma') = 0$.

We now relate the single transitions of the optimized semantics that do not access ghost tuples to the transitions of the original semantics. Notice that the states of the optimized semantics may contain ghost tuples.

Proposition 3. For all $L \subseteq \Lambda(\mathcal{L}_\rho(P))$, $\mathcal{L}_\rho(P) \parallel \Pi_{\ell_i \in L}\underline{\ell_i} :: \underline{out}(v_i) \xrightarrow{a@\ell} Q_o$ implies that there are R, ρ' and $L' \subseteq \Lambda(\mathcal{L}_{\rho'}(R))$ such that $P \xrightarrow{a} R$ and $Q_o \equiv \mathcal{L}_{\rho'}(R) \parallel \Pi_{\ell_i \in L'}\underline{\ell_i} :: \underline{out}(v_i)$.

Proposition 4. For all $L \subseteq \Lambda(\mathcal{L}_\rho(P))$, $\mathcal{L}_\rho(P) \parallel \Pi_{\ell_i \in L}\underline{\ell_i} :: \underline{out}(v_i) \xrightarrow{stop@\ell} Q_o$ implies that there is R such that $P \equiv R$ and $Q_o \equiv \mathcal{L}_\rho(R) \parallel \Pi_{\ell_i \in L \setminus \{\ell\}}\underline{\ell_i} :: \underline{out}(v_i)$.

We can generalize the previous two properties to sequences of transitions.

Proposition 5. $\mathcal{L}_\rho(P) \xrightarrow{\sigma} Q_o$ and $g(\sigma) = 0$ imply that there are P', ρ', $L \subseteq \Lambda(\mathcal{L}_{\rho'}(P'))$ and v_i such that $P \xrightarrow{\mathcal{C}(\sigma)} P'$ and $Q_o \equiv \mathcal{L}_{\rho'}(P') \parallel \Pi_{\ell_i \in L}\underline{\ell_i} :: \underline{out}(v_i)$.

Finally, from Propositions 2 and 5, we get that the original semantics can simulate the optimized one. Formally,

Theorem 1. $\mathcal{L}_\rho(P) \xrightarrow{\sigma} Q_o$ implies that there are $\sigma' \prec \sigma$ and P' such that $P \xrightarrow{\mathcal{C}(\sigma')} P'$ and $\mathcal{C}(Q_o) \equiv P'$.

Now, we outline the proof that the optimized semantics can simulate the original one (Theorem 2). First, we need to formalize the idea that locations can be arbitrarily chosen and that distributed processes that only differ for the names of their locations behave similarly. The important point here is that the allocation function does not preserve the structural equivalence. Indeed, the allocation of two structurally equivalent processes gives rise to two new processes that are not structurally equivalent. However, structural equivalence can be recovered by appropriately renaming the locations of one of the two processes by means of a one-to-one function. The crucial properties are

Proposition 6. If $P \equiv P'$ can be proved without using the first structural law, then there is a one-to-one function $\phi : \Lambda(\mathcal{L}_{\rho'}(P')) \longrightarrow \Lambda(\mathcal{L}_\rho(P))$ such that $\mathcal{L}_\rho(P) \equiv \phi(\mathcal{L}_{\rho'}(P'))$.

Proposition 7. Let $\phi : \Lambda(\mathcal{L}_{\rho'}(P')) \longrightarrow \Lambda(\mathcal{L}_\rho(P))$ be a one-to-one function. If $P \equiv P'$ can be proved without using the first structural law, $\phi(\mathcal{L}_{\rho'}(P')) \equiv \mathcal{L}_\rho(P)$ and $\Lambda(\mathcal{L}_{\rho'}(P')) = \Lambda(\mathcal{L}_{\rho'}(Q'))$, then there is Q such that $Q \equiv Q'$ and $\phi(\mathcal{L}_{\rho'}(Q')) \equiv \mathcal{L}_\rho(Q)$.

Now, by exploiting the above properties, we are able to relate the transitions of the original semantics to those of the optimized one. Notice that the states of the optimized semantics may contain ghost tuples.

Proposition 8. For all $L \subseteq \Lambda(\mathcal{L}_\rho(P))$, $P \xrightarrow{a} Q$ implies that there are R, ℓ and $L' \subseteq \Lambda(\mathcal{L}_\rho(R))$ such that $\mathcal{L}_\rho(P) \parallel \Pi_{\ell_i \in L}\underline{\ell_i} :: \underline{out}(v_i) \xrightarrow{a@\ell} \mathcal{L}_\rho(R) \parallel \Pi_{\ell_i \in L'}\underline{\ell_i} :: \underline{out}(v_i)$ and $R \equiv Q$.

By generalizing the previous property to nonempty sequences of transitions, we get that the optimized semantics can simulate the original one. Formally,

Theorem 2. $P \xrightarrow{s} Q$ implies that there are R_o and σ such that $\mathcal{L}_\rho(P) \xrightarrow{\sigma} R_o$, $s = \mathcal{C}(\sigma)$ and $\mathcal{C}(R_o) \equiv Q$.

5   Conclusion

We have described a tuple ghosting optimisation that allows tuples to be still used as the results of non-destructive tuple space accesses once they have been destructively removed. The motivation for tuple ghosting has been briefly outlined, as have some practical results from a prototype system demonstrating the advantage of the approach.

The operational semantics of the original Linda and of the version with the optimisation are illustrated. Using these operational semantics, we have presented a sketch of the formal proof of the tuple ghosting optimisation, and shown that the optimisation does not alter the semantics of the primitives from a programmers' perspective. This has been achieved by proving that the optimised semantics can simulate the original semantics, and that a sequence of transitions from the optimised semantics can be mimicked by a sequence of transitions from the original semantics.

Acknowledgements

This work has been partially supported by MURST projects SALADIN and TOSCA.

References

1. A. Rowstron. Optimising the Linda in primitive: Understanding tuple-space runtimes. In J. Carroll, E. Damiani, H. Haddad, and D. Oppenheim, editors, *Proceedings of the 2000 ACM Symposium on Applied Computing*, volume 1, pages 227–232. ACM Press, March 2000.

2. Sun Microsystems. Javaspace specification. available at: http://java.sun.com/, 1999.

3. R. De Nicola, G. Ferrari, and R. Pugliese. KLAIM: A kernel language for agents interaction and mobility. *IEEE Transactions on Software Engineering*, 24(5):315–330, 1998.

4. N. Carriero and D. Gelernter. Linda in context. *Communications of the ACM*, 32(4):444–458, 1989.

5. P. Ciancarini, R. Tolksdorf, F. Vitali, D. Rossi, and A. Knoche. Coordinating multiagent applications on the WWW: A reference architecture. *IEEE Transactions on Software Engineering*, 24(5):362–366, 1998.

6. P. Wyckoff, S. McLaughry, T. Lehman, and D. Ford. TSpaces. *IBM Systems Journal*, 37(3):454–474, 1998.

7. A. Omicini and F. Zambonelli. Coordination for internet application development. *Autonomous Agents and Multi-agent Systems*, 2(3):251–269, 1999. Special Issue on Coordination Mechanisms and Patterns for Web Agents.

8. A. Rowstron. WCL: A web co-ordination language. *World Wide Web Journal*, 1(3):167–179, 1998.

9. J. Carreria, L. Silva, and J. Silva. On the design of Eilean: A Linda-like library for MPI. Technical report, Universidade de Coimbra, 1994.

10. N. Carriero and D. Gelernter. Tuple analysis and partial evaluation strategies in the Linda precompiler. In D. Gelernter, A. Nicolau, and D. Padua, editors, *Languages and Compilers for Parallel Computing*, Research Monographs in Parallel and Distributed Computing, pages 114–125. MIT Press, 1990.

11. R. De Nicola and R. Pugliese. Linda based applicative and imperative process algebras. *Theoretical Computer Science*, 238(1-2):389–437, 2000.

12. G.D. Plotkin. A structural approach to operational semantics. Technical Report DAIMI FN-19, Dep. of Computer Science, Aarhus University, Denmark, 1981.

13. R. De Nicola, R. Pugliese, and A. Rowstron. Proving the correctness of optimising destructive and non-destructive reads over tuple spaces. Technical Report available at: http://music.dsi.unifi.it/, Dipartimento di Sistemi e Informatica, Univ. Firenze, 2000.

On Timed Coordination Languages

J.-M. Jacquet[1], K. De Bosschere[2], and A. Brogi[3]

[1] Department of Computer Science, University of Namur
[2] Department of Electronics and Information Systems, Ghent University
[3] Department of Computer Science, University of Pisa

Abstract. Although very simple and elegant, Linda-style coordination models lack the notion of time, and are therefore not able to precisely model real-life coordination applications, featuring time-outs and soft real-time constraints. This paper aims at introducing time in these models. To that end, we consider two notions of time, relative time and absolute time, and, for each notion, two types of features. On the one hand, with respect to relative time, we describe two extensions: (i) a delay mechanism to postpone the execution of communication primitives, and (ii) explicit deadlines on the validity of tuples and on the duration of suspension of communication operations. On the other hand, for absolute time, we introduce: (iii) a wait primitive capable of waiting till an absolute point of time, and (iv) time intervals, both on tuples in the data store and on communication operations.

The resulting four coordination models are analyzed and compared both from the semantics viewpoint and from the implementation viewpoint. Moreover, a few programming examples suggest their practical interest.

1 Introduction

As motivated by the constant expansion of computer networks and illustrated by the development of distributed applications, the design of modern software systems centers on re-using and integrating software components. This induces a paradigm shift from stand-alone applications to interacting distributed systems, which, in turn, naturally calls for well-defined methodologies and tools aiming at integrating heterogeneous software components.

In this context, a clear separation between the *interactional* and the *computational* aspects of software components has been advocated by Gelernter and Carriero in [15]. Their claim has been supported by the design of a model, Linda ([8]), originally presented as a set of inter-agent communication primitives which may be added to almost any programming language. Besides process creation, this set includes primitives for adding, deleting, and testing the presence/absence of data in a shared dataspace.

A number of other models, now referred to as coordination models, have been proposed afterwards. Some of them extend Linda in different ways, for instance by introducing multiple dataspaces and meta-level control rules (e.g., Bauhaus Linda [20], Bonita [23], μLog [18], PoliS [10], Shared Prolog [6]), by addressing open distributed systems (e.g., Laura [30]), middleware web-based

A. Porto and G.-C. Roman (Eds.): COORDINATION 2000, LNCS 1906, pp. 81–98, 2000.

environments (e.g., Jada [11]), or mobility (e.g., KLAIM [21]). A number of other coordination models rely on a notion of shared dataspace, e.g., Concurrent Constraint Programming [26], Gamma [3], Linear Objects [1] and Manifold [2], to cite only a few. A comprehensive survey of these and other coordination models and languages has been recently reported in [22].

However, the coding of applications evidence the fact that data rarely has an eternal life. For instance, a request for information on the web has to be satisfied in a reasonable amount of time. More crucial is even the request for an ambulance which, not only has to be answered eventually but within a critical period of time. The list could also be continued with software in the areas of air-traffic control, manufacturing plants and telecommunication switches, which are inherently reactive and, for which, interaction must occur in "real-time".

Although there is an obvious application need, the introduction of time has not been deeply studied in the context of coordination languages and models, the notable exceptions being [5,24,25], but have been proposed in the context of concurrent constraint programming.

We turn in this paper to the study of the introduction of time in coordination languages. As evidenced by research in other communities, the design space is huge so that, due to lack of space in this paper, we will stick to two principles. On the one hand, we will be concerned only with extensions of the Linda model. On the other hand, we will adopt the classical *two-phase functioning* approach to real-time systems illustrated by languages such as Lustre ([9]), Esterel ([4]) and Statecharts ([16]). This approach may be described as follows. In a first phase, elementary actions of statements are executed. They are assumed to be atomic in the sense that they take no time. Similarly, composition operators are assumed to be executed at no cost. In a second phase, when no actions can be reduced or when all the components encounter a special timed action, time progresses by one unit.

Although simple, this approach has been proved to be effective for modelling reactive systems. For instance, in many reactive systems, time actions determine instants at which inputs are sampled and from which output is processed. In the coordination context, it still leaves room for several variants:

1. time may be introduced in the form of delays, stating that a communication primitives should only be processed after some units of time or at some particular point in time;
2. time may also be introduced by stating that tuples on the tuple space are only valid for some units of time; similarly, request for tuples cannot be postponed infinitely;
3. time may finally be introduced by specifying absolute intervals of time in which actions should be processed.

All these possibilities are explored subsequently, from the viewpoints of the expressiveness of the resulting languages, of their use for coding several timing mechanisms and of their implementation. This is operated as follows. Section 2 introduces the families of languages. All of them rest on common sequential,

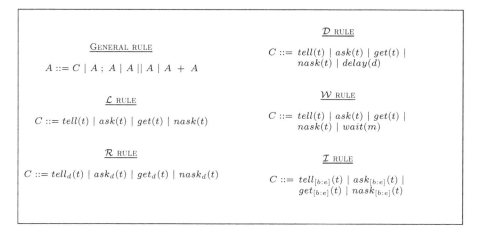

Fig. 1. Comparative syntax of the languages.

parallel and choice operators which are specified in subsection 2.1. The Linda-like languages are modelled as the $\mathcal{L}$ family in subsection 2.2. Relative delays are introduced in subsection 2.3 and relative timing primitives are defined in subsection 2.4. Their absolute counterparts are presented in subsections 2.5 and 2.6, respectively.

The expressiveness of these families of languages is studied in section 3 and their interest in practice is argued through examples in section 4. A prototype implementation under construction is explained in section 5. Finally, section 6 draws our conclusion and discuss related work.

2   The Families of Languages

2.1   Common Syntax and Rules

All the languages considered in this paper contain sequential, parallel and choice operators. They only differ in the set of communication primitives they embody. As a result, assuming such a set, the syntax of a statement, called agent subsequently, is defined by the "general rule" of figure 1 and its semantics is provided by rules (S), (P), and (C) of figure 2. There, configurations are of the form $\langle A \mid \sigma \rangle$ where A represents the agent under consideration and σ represents a memory, to be specified for each family of languages.

Note that, for simplicity of the presentation, only finite processes are treated here, under the observation that infinite processes can be handled by extending the results of this paper in the classical way, as exemplified for instance in [17].

2.2   The Family of Linda-Like Concurrent Languages

To start with, let us consider the family of languages $\mathcal{L}(\mathcal{X})$, parameterized on the set of Linda-like communication primitives $\mathcal{X}$. This set $\mathcal{X}$ consists of the

GENERAL RULES

L RULES

$$(S) \quad \frac{\langle A \mid \sigma \rangle \longrightarrow \langle A' \mid \sigma' \rangle}{\langle A \; ; \; B \mid \sigma \rangle \longrightarrow \langle A' \; ; \; B \mid \sigma' \rangle}$$

$$(T) \quad \langle tell(t) \mid \sigma \rangle \longrightarrow \langle E \mid \sigma \cup \{t\} \rangle$$

$$(A) \quad \langle ask(t) \mid \sigma \cup \{t\} \rangle \longrightarrow \langle E \mid \sigma \cup \{t\} \rangle$$

$$(P) \quad \frac{\langle A \mid \sigma \rangle \longrightarrow \langle A' \mid \sigma' \rangle}{\substack{\langle A \parallel B \mid \sigma \rangle \longrightarrow \langle A' \parallel B \mid \sigma' \rangle \\ \langle B \parallel A \mid \sigma \rangle \longrightarrow \langle B \parallel A' \mid \sigma' \rangle}}$$

$$(N) \quad \frac{t \notin \sigma}{\langle nask(t) \mid \sigma \rangle \longrightarrow \langle E \mid \sigma \rangle}$$

$$(C) \quad \frac{\langle A \mid \sigma \rangle \longrightarrow \langle A' \mid \sigma' \rangle}{\substack{\langle A + B \mid \sigma \rangle \longrightarrow \langle A' \mid \sigma' \rangle \\ \langle B + A \mid \sigma \rangle \longrightarrow \langle A' \mid \sigma' \rangle}}$$

$$(G) \quad \langle get(t) \mid \sigma \cup \{t\} \rangle \longrightarrow \langle E \mid \sigma \rangle$$

W RULE

D RULE

$$(W1) \quad \frac{A \neq E, A \gg u, \langle A \mid \sigma \rangle_u \not\rightarrow}{\langle A \mid \sigma \rangle_u \rightsquigarrow \langle A \mid \sigma \rangle_{u+1}}$$

$$(D1) \quad \frac{A \neq E, A \neq A^-, \langle A \mid \sigma \rangle \not\rightarrow}{\langle A \mid \sigma \rangle \rightsquigarrow \langle A^- \mid \sigma \rangle}$$

$$(W2) \quad \frac{u \geq v}{\langle wait(v) \mid \sigma \rangle_u \longrightarrow \langle E \mid \sigma \rangle_u}$$

$$(D2) \quad \langle delay(0) \mid \sigma \rangle \longrightarrow \langle E \mid \sigma \rangle$$

I RULE

R RULE

$$(T0) \quad \langle tell_0(t) \mid \sigma \rangle \longrightarrow \langle E \mid \sigma \rangle$$

$$(Ta) \quad \frac{b \leq u \leq e}{\langle tell_{[b:e]}(t) \mid \sigma \rangle_u \longrightarrow \langle E \mid \sigma \cup \{t_{[u:e]}\} \rangle_u}$$

$$(Tr) \quad \frac{d > 0}{\langle tell_d(t) \mid \sigma \rangle \longrightarrow \langle E \mid \sigma \cup \{t_d\} \rangle}$$

$$(Aa) \quad \frac{b \leq u \leq e, b' \leq u \leq e'}{\langle ask_{[b:e]}(t) \mid \sigma \cup \{t_{[b':e']}\} \rangle_u \longrightarrow \langle E \mid \sigma \cup \{t_{[b':e']}\} \rangle_u}$$

$$(Ar) \quad \frac{d > 0}{\langle ask_d(t) \mid \sigma \cup \{t_k\} \rangle \longrightarrow \langle E \mid \sigma \cup \{t_k\} \rangle}$$

$$(Nr) \quad \frac{d > 0, \nexists k : t_k \in \sigma}{\langle nask_d(t) \mid \sigma \rangle \longrightarrow \langle E \mid \sigma \rangle}$$

$$(Na) \quad \frac{b \leq u \leq e,}{\nexists b', e' : b' \leq u \leq e' \wedge t_{[b':e']} \in \sigma} \frac{}{\langle nask_{[b:e]}(t) \mid \sigma \rangle_u \longrightarrow \langle E \mid \sigma \rangle_u}$$

$$(Gr) \quad \frac{d > 0}{\langle get_d(t) \mid \sigma \cup \{t_k\} \rangle \longrightarrow \langle E \mid \sigma \rangle}$$

$$(Ga) \quad \frac{b \leq u \leq e, b' \leq u \leq e'}{\langle get_{[b:e]}(t) \mid \sigma \cup \{t_{[b':e']}\} \rangle_u \longrightarrow \langle E \mid \sigma \rangle}$$

$$(Wr) \quad \frac{A \neq E, A \neq A^- \text{ or } \sigma \neq \sigma^-, \langle A \mid \sigma \rangle \not\rightarrow}{\langle A \mid \sigma \rangle \rightsquigarrow \langle A^- \mid \sigma^- \rangle}$$

$$(Wa) \quad \frac{A \neq E, A \gg u \text{ or } \sigma \gg u, \langle A \mid \sigma \rangle \not\rightarrow}{\langle A \mid \sigma \rangle_u \rightsquigarrow \langle A \mid \sigma^{+u} \rangle_{u+1}}$$

Fig. 2. Comparative semantics of the languages.

basic Linda primitives out, in, and rd primitives, for putting an object in a shared dataspace, getting it and checking for its presence, respectively, together with a primitive testing the absence of an object from the dataspace. Formally, the language is defined as follows.

Definition 1. *Let Stoken be a denumerable set, the elements of which are subsequently called* tokens *and are typically represented by the letters* t *and* u. *Define the set of communication actions Scom as the set generated by the* L *rule of figure 1. Moreover, for any subset* X *of Scom, define the language* $L(X)$ *as the set of agents* A *generated by the general rule of figure 1.*

For any X, computations in $L(X)$ may be modelled by a transition system written in Plotkin's style. Following the intuition, most of the configurations consist of an agent together with a multi-set of tokens denoting the tokens currently available for the computation. To easily express termination, we shall introduce particular configurations composed of a special terminating symbol E together with a multi-set of tokens. For uniformity purposes, we shall abuse language and qualify E as an agent. However, to meet the intuition, we shall always rewrite agents of the form $(E \; ; \; A)$, $(E \parallel A)$, and $(A \parallel E)$ as A. This is technically achieved by defining the extended set of agents as follows, and by operating simplifications by imposing a bimonoid structure.

Definition 2. *Define the extended set of agents Seagent by the following grammar*

$$Ae ::= E \mid C \mid A \; ; \; A \mid A \parallel A \mid A + A$$

Moreover, we shall subsequently assert that the structure $(Seagent, E, \; ; \; , \parallel)$ is a bimonoid and simplify elements of Seagent accordingly.

Definition 3. *Define the set of stores Sstore as the set of finite multisets with elements from Stoken.*

Definition 4. *Define the set of configurations Sconf as $Seagent \times Sstore$. Configurations are denoted as $\langle A \mid \sigma \rangle$, where A is an (extended) agent and σ is a multi-set of tokens.*

Definition 5. *The transition rules for the $\mathcal{L}$ agents are the general ones of figure 2 together with rules (T), (A), (N), (G) of that figure, where σ denotes a multi-set of tokens.*

Rule (T) states that an atomic agent $tell(t)$ can be executed in any store σ, and that its execution results in adding the token t to the store σ. Rules (A) and (N) state respectively that the atomic agents $ask(t)$ and $nask(t)$ can be executed in any store containing the token t and not containing t, and that their execution does not modify the current store. Rule (G) also states that an atomic agent $get(t)$ can be executed in any store containing an occurrence of t, but in the resulting store the occurrence of t has been deleted. Note that the symbol $\cup$ actually denotes multiset union.

We are now in a position to define the operational semantics.

Definition 6.

1. *Let δ^+ and δ^- be two fresh symbols denoting respectively success and failure. Define the set of final states Sfstate as the set $Sstore \times \{\delta^+, \delta^-\}$.*
2. *Define the operational semantics $\mathcal{O} : Sagent \to \mathcal{P}(Sfstate)$ as the following function: For any agent A,*

$$\mathcal{O}(A) = \{(\sigma, \delta^+) : \langle A \mid \emptyset \rangle \to^* \langle E \mid \sigma \rangle\}$$
$$\cup \{(\sigma, \delta^-) : \langle A \mid \emptyset \rangle \to^* \langle B \mid \sigma \rangle \not\to, B \neq E\}$$

2.3 The Family of Linda-Like Concurrent Languages with Delay

One way of introducing time in coordination languages is to postpone the execution of the primitives for some period of time. This amounts to introducing a special delay primitive.

Definition 7. *Let Stime be the set of positive integers. Define the set Sdcom as the set generated by the $\mathcal{D}$ rule of figure 1, where $t \in Stoken$ and $d \in Stime$. Moreover, for any subset $\mathcal{X}$ of Sdcom, define the language $\mathcal{D}(\mathcal{X})$ as the set of agents generated by the general rule of figure 1.*

The configurations to be considered here are similar to those used for the $\mathcal{L}$ family. However, time needs to be taken into account explicitly in the transitions. This is operated in two ways. First, by the introduction of a new rule (D1), which defines a new transition relation $\rightsquigarrow$ to express the progress of time by one unit. In fact, the $\rightarrow$ reduction is used to model the first phase of the two-phase functioning approach to real-time while the $\rightsquigarrow$ relation is used to model the second phase of this approach.

Second, as a result of time progress, delays under reduction, must be decreased by one unit. This is achieved by the A^- construct. Note that, to avoid that the computation infinitely tries to decrease blocked non-delay primitives, rule (D1) requires A^- to be make some progress, namely to be different from A.

Finally, rule (D2) is introduced to reduce a delay of 0 unit of time to E.

Summing up, the transitions to be considered are defined as follows.

Definition 8. *Define the set of configurations Sdconf as Seagent' $\times$ Sstore, where Seagent' is the set of extended agents defined as in definition 2 but by taking $C \in Sdcom$ instead of $C \in Scom$.*

Definition 9. *Given an agent $A \in \mathcal{D}(\mathcal{X})$, we denote by A^- the agent defined inductively as follows where $d > 0$*

$$
\begin{array}{lll}
tell(t)^- = tell(t) & get(t)^- = get(t) & (B \; ; \; C)^- = B^- \; ; \; C \\
ask(t)^- = ask(t) & delay(0)^- = delay(0) & (B \; || \; C)^- = B^- \; || \; C^- \\
nask(t)^- = nask(t) & delay(d)^- = delay(d-1) & (B + C)^- = B^- + C^-
\end{array}
$$

Definition 10. *Define the transition rules for the $\mathcal{D}$ agents as the general ones of figure 2 and rules (T), (A), (N), (G), (D1) and (D2) of that figure.*

The operational semantics is defined by integrating the two phase-relations in one relation.

Definition 11.

1. *Let $\longmapsto$ be the relation defined by $\langle A \mid \sigma \rangle \longmapsto \langle B \mid \tau \rangle$ iff $\langle A \mid \sigma \rangle \rightarrow \langle B \mid \tau \rangle$ or $\langle A \mid \sigma \rangle \rightsquigarrow \langle B \mid \tau \rangle$.*
2. *Define the operational semantics $\mathcal{O}_d : \mathcal{D}(Sdcom) \rightarrow \mathcal{P}(Sfstate)$ as the following function: For any timed agent A,*

$$
\begin{aligned}
\mathcal{O}_d(A) = \; & \{(\sigma, \delta^+) : \langle A \mid \emptyset \rangle \longmapsto^* \langle E \mid \sigma \rangle\} \\
& \cup \{(\sigma, \delta^-) : \langle A \mid \emptyset \rangle \longmapsto^* \langle B \mid \sigma \rangle \not\longmapsto, B \neq E\}
\end{aligned}
$$

2.4 The Family of Linda-Like Concurrent Languages with Relative Durations

Another way of introducing time in the family $\mathcal{L}(\mathcal{X})$ consists of enriching the primitives ask, nask, get, and tell themselves by durations. Formally, the new family of languages $\mathcal{R}(\mathcal{X})$ is defined as follows.

Definition 12. *Define the set Stcom of timed communication primitives as the one generated by the $\mathcal{R}$ rule of figure 1, where $t \in Stoken$ and $d \in Stime \cup \{\infty\}$. For any subset $\mathcal{X}$ of Stcom, define the language $\mathcal{R}(\mathcal{X})$ as the set of agents generated by the general rule of figure 1.*

The configurations to be considered for the family $\mathcal{R}(\mathcal{X})$ are similar to those used for the family $\mathcal{L}(\mathcal{X})$. The introduction of time induces here the following adaptations:

1. The intuition behind the construct $tell_d(t)$ is that t is added to the store but for d units of time only. To capture this fact, the tokens of the store have to be associated with a duration.
2. As another consequence, this duration has to be updated after each tick of the clock. This motivates the introduction of the $-$ operator acting on the store.
3. Similarly, the intuition behind the $ask_d(t)$, $nask_d(t)$, and $get_d(t)$ primitives is that, if needed, suspension may only occur during d units of time. As a result, a similar operator, also denoted $-$, has to be introduced to decrease the period of suspension after each tick of the clock.

This intuition leads to the following definitions.

Definition 13.

1. *Given an agent $A \in \mathcal{R}(\mathcal{X})$, we denote by A^- the agent defined inductively as follows:[1]*

$$tell_d(t)^- = tell_d(t)$$
$$ask_d(t)^- = ask_{max\{0,d-1\}}(t) \qquad (B \; ; \; C)^- = B^- \; ; \; C$$
$$nask_d(t)^- = nask_{max\{0,d-1\}}(t) \qquad (B \parallel C)^- = B^- \parallel C^-$$
$$get_d(t)^- = get_{max\{0,d-1\}}(t) \qquad (B + C)^- = B^- + C^-$$

2. *Define the set of timed stores Ststore as the set of multisets of elements of the form t_d where t is a token and d is a duration. Given a timed store σ, we denote by σ^- the new store obtained by decreasing the duration associated with the tokens by one unit and by removing those associated in σ with 1 unit of time: precisely, if all the notations are understood to relate to multi-sets:*

$$\sigma^- = \{t_{d-1} : t_d \in \sigma, d > 1\}$$

---

[1] We extend classical arithmetic on natural numbers by $\infty - 1 = \infty$.

3. *Define the set of configurations $Sconf$ as $Seagent \times Ststore$. Configurations are denoted as $\langle A \mid \sigma \rangle$, where A is an (extended) timed agent and σ is a timed store.*

Due to the introduction of time, the operational semantics is defined by means of the transition relations $\rightarrow$ and $\rightsquigarrow$ describing the two phases approach. They basically adapt the relations defined for the $\mathcal{L}$ family. Accordingly, rules (Tr), (Ar), (Nr), and (Gr) adapt respectively rules (T), (A), (N), (G) in the obvious way by requiring that that communication primitives be only executed for a strictly positive duration. Moreover, rule (T0) states that telling a token for a zero duration succeeds by not updating the store. Rule (Wr) is the analogue of rule (D1).

Definition 14. *Define the transition rules for the $\mathcal{R}$ agents as rules (S), (P), (C), (T0), (Tr), (Ar), (Nr), (Gr), (Wr) of figure 2.*

The operational semantics is defined by using an auxiliary relation $\longmapsto$, defined in a similar way as in the previous subsection. We shall subsequently write this semantics as $\mathcal{O}_r$.

2.5   The Family of Linda-Like Concurrent Languages with Wait Declarations

A third way of introducing time in coordination languages consists of delaying the execution of the communication primitives after a precise point of time. This is obtained by introducing a primitive $wait(m)$ which forces suspension until time m has been reached. Formally, the resulting family of languages is defined as follows.

Definition 15. *Define the set $Swcom$ as the set generated by the $\mathcal{W}$ rule of figure 1, where $t \in Stoken$ and $m \in Stime$. Moreover, for any subset $\mathcal{X}$ of $Swcom$, define the language $\mathcal{W}(\mathcal{X})$ as the set of agents generated by the general rule of figure 1.*

The configurations to be used here are similar to those used for the $\mathcal{L}$ family of languages. Time introduced here in an absolute way induces just one adaptation: to explicitly introduce time in the configurations. We are thus lead to configurations of the form $\langle A \mid \sigma \rangle_u$ where u represents the current time. The general rules (S), (P), (C) need then to be rephrased to this new notation. Of course, they leave the u subscript unchanged. Rule (W1) is introduced to make time progress and rule (W2) is used to reduce a wait declaration. As in rule (D1), time is allowed to progress if the new situation differs from the old one. This is expressed by the relation $A \gg u$, which states that A contains a $wait(m)$ operation with $m > u$.

Definition 16. *Define the set of configuration $Swconf$ as the set $Seagent \times Sstore \times Stime$. Define the transition rules for the $\mathcal{W}$ agents as the general ones of figure 2 and rules (T), (A), (N), (G), (W1) and (W2) of that figure.*

With the slight adaptation of the subscripts, the operational semantics is defined in a way similar to the semantics $\mathcal{O}_d$. It is subsequently noted as $\mathcal{O}_w$.

2.6   The Family of Linda-Like Concurrent Languages with Time Intervals

Finally, we extend the Linda primitives with time interval during which the reduction should take. We are thus lead to communication primitives of the form $tell_{[b:e]}(t)$, $ask_{[b:e]}(t)$, $nask_{[b:e]}(t)$, $get_{[b:e]}(t)$. These notations assume that $0 \leq b \leq e$. The resulting family of languages is referred to as $\mathcal{I}(\mathcal{X})$.

Definition 17. *Define Sicom as the set generated by the $\mathcal{I}$ rule of figure 1, where $t \in Stoken$ and $b \in Stime$, $e \in Stime \cup \{\infty\}$ with $b \leq e$. Moreover, for any subset $\mathcal{X}$ of Sicom, define $\mathcal{I}(\mathcal{X})$ as the set of agents generated from Sicom by the general rule of figure 1.*

The transition relations are defined as the extension of those of the $\mathcal{W}$ family according to the lines of subsection 2.4.

Definition 18.

1. *Define the set of interval stores Sistore as the set of multisets of elements of the form $t_{[b:e]}$ where $t \in Stoken$, $b \in Stime$, $e \in Stime \cup \{\infty\}$ are such that $b \leq e$.*
2. *Define the set of configuration Siconf as the set $(\mathcal{I}(Sicom) \cup \{E\}) \times Sistore \times Stime$.*
3. *For any agent A of $\mathcal{I}$ and time u, define $A \gg u$ to hold if A contains at least one primitive $tell_{[b:e]}(t)$, $ask_{[b:e]}(t)$, $nask_{[b:e]}(t)$, $get_{[b:e]}(t)$, with $b > u$.*
4. *For any interval store σ and time u, define $\sigma \gg u$ to hold if there is $t_{[b:e]} \in \sigma$ such that $e \neq \infty$ and $e > u$. Moreover, define σ^{+u} as*

$$\sigma^{+u} = \{t_{[max\{b,u+1\}:e]} : t_{[b:e]} \in \sigma, u+1 \leq e\}.$$

5. *Define the set of transition rules for the $\mathcal{I}$ agents as rules (S), (P), (C) rewritten so as to include the u subscript and rules (Ta), (Aa), (Na), (Ga), and (Wa) of figure 2.*

The operational semantics is adapted from that of the previous section. It is subsequently written as $\mathcal{O}_i$.

3   Language Comparison

3.1   Introduction

A natural question to ask is whether the time extensions we just introduced strictly increase the expressivity of the Linda language and, if so, whether some of the timed primitives may be expressed in terms of others.

A basic approach to answer that question has been given by Shapiro in [27] as follows. Consider two languages L and L'. Assume given the semantics mappings (*observation criteria*) $\mathcal{S} : L \rightarrow \mathcal{O}$ and $\mathcal{S}' : L' \rightarrow \mathcal{O}'$, where $\mathcal{O}$ and $\mathcal{O}'$ are some suitable domains. Then, according to [27], L can *embed* L' if there exists a mapping $\mathcal{C}o$ (*coder*) from the statements of L' to the statements of L, and a mapping $\mathcal{D}e$ (*decoder*) from $\mathcal{O}$ to $\mathcal{O}'$, such that $\mathcal{D}e(\mathcal{S}(\mathcal{C}o(A))) = \mathcal{S}'(A)$, for every statement $A \in L'$.

This approach is however too weak since, for instance, the above equation is satisfied by any pair of Turing-complete languages. To circumvent this problem, De Boer and Palamidessi have proposed in [12] to add three constraints on the coder $\mathcal{C}o$ and on the decoder $\mathcal{D}e$. First, $\mathcal{D}e$ should be defined in an element-wise way w.r.t. $\mathcal{O}$:

$$\forall X \in \mathcal{O} : \ \mathcal{D}e(X) = \{\mathcal{D}e_{el}(x) \mid x \in X\} \tag{P_1}$$

for some appropriate mapping $\mathcal{D}e_{el}$. Second, the coder $\mathcal{C}o$ should be defined in a compositional way w.r.t. the sequential, parallel and choice operators:[2]

$$\begin{aligned} \mathcal{C}o(A \ ; \ B) &= \mathcal{C}o(A) \ ; \ \mathcal{C}o(B) \\ \mathcal{C}o(A \ || \ B) &= \mathcal{C}o(A) \ || \ \mathcal{C}o(B) \\ \mathcal{C}o(A \ + \ B) &= \mathcal{C}o(A) \ + \ \mathcal{C}o(B) \end{aligned} \tag{P_2}$$

Finally, the embedding should preserve the behavior of the original processes w.r.t. deadlock, failure and success (*termination invariance*):

$$\forall X \in \mathcal{O}, \forall x \in X : \ tm'(\mathcal{D}e_{el}(x)) = tm(x) \tag{P_3}$$

where tm and tm' extract the information on termination from the observables of L and L', respectively. An embedding satisfying these properties (P_1, P_2, P_3) is said to be *modular*.

The existence of a modular embedding from L' into L is subsequently denoted by $L' \leq L$. It is easy to see that $\leq$ is a pre-order relation. Moreover if $L' \subseteq L$ then $L' \leq L$, that is, any language embeds all its sublanguages. This property descends immediately from the definition of embedding, by setting $\mathcal{C}o$ and $\mathcal{D}e$ equal to the identity function.

3.2 Comparing the $\mathcal{L}$ and $\mathcal{D}$ Families

A first result is that introducing time is a safe and necessary extension to the Linda family. Rephrased in more formal terms, the $\mathcal{L}$ family of languages can be embedded in the $\mathcal{D}$ and $\mathcal{W}$ families but not conversely. The property for the other families holds as well; it will be established as a consequence of propositions 5 and 8.

Proposition 1. *For any* $\mathcal{X} \subseteq \{ask, nask, get, tell\}$, *one has* $\mathcal{L}(\mathcal{X}) \leq \mathcal{D}(\mathcal{X} \cup \{delay\})$.

Proof. Indeed, for any such $\mathcal{X}$, the language $\mathcal{L}(\mathcal{X})$ is a sublanguage of the language $\mathcal{D}(\mathcal{X} \cup \{delay\})$.

---

[2] Actually, this is only required for the parallel and choice operators in [12].

Proposition 2. *For any* $\mathcal{X} \subseteq \{ask, nask, get, tell\}$ *containing at least, on the one hand, tell and, on the other hand, ask or get, one has* $\mathcal{D}(\mathcal{X} \cup \{delay\}) \nleq \mathcal{L}(\mathcal{X})$.

Proof. Let us assume that $\mathcal{X}$ contains both *tell* and *ask* primitives; the proof for $\mathcal{X}$ including both *tell* and *get* primitives is conducted similarly.

Let us proceed by contradiction. Assume that $\mathcal{D}(\mathcal{X} \cup \{delay\}) \leq \mathcal{L}(\mathcal{X})$ and, in particular, that there is a coder $\mathcal{C}o$ from agents of $\mathcal{D}(\mathcal{X} \cup \{delay\})$ to agents of $\mathcal{L}(\mathcal{X})$. Then, consider the following agents

$$A = ask(a) \ ; \ tell(c)$$
$$B = delay(1) \ ; \ tell(b)$$
$$C = tell(a) \ ; \ ask(c)$$

Obviously, $\mathcal{O}_d((A + B) \parallel C) = \{(\{a, c\}, \delta^+)\}$. To conclude, we shall establish that $\mathcal{O}_l(\mathcal{C}o((A + B) \parallel C))$ contains a failing computation, which is impossible in view of property (P_3).

Indeed, by property (P_2), one has $\mathcal{C}o((A + B) \parallel C) = (\mathcal{C}o(A) + \mathcal{C}o(B)) \parallel \mathcal{C}o(C)$. As $\mathcal{O}_d(A) = \{(\emptyset, \delta^-)\}$ and $\mathcal{O}_d(A + B) = \{(\{b\}, \delta^+)\}$ one should have $\langle \mathcal{C}o(B) \mid \emptyset \rangle \rightarrow \langle T \mid \tau \rangle$, for some agent $T \in \mathcal{L}(\mathcal{X})$ and store τ, with $\langle T \mid \tau \rangle$ leading to one successful computation. However, as $\mathcal{O}_d(B \parallel C) = \{(\{a, b\}, \delta^-)\}$ and $\langle \mathcal{C}o(B) \parallel \mathcal{C}o(C) \mid \emptyset \rangle \rightarrow \langle T \parallel \mathcal{C}o(C) \mid \tau \rangle$ is a valid prefix of a computation of $\mathcal{C}o(B \parallel C)$, any continuation from $\langle T \parallel \mathcal{C}o(C) \mid \tau \rangle$ should fail. The thesis results then from the fact that $\langle (\mathcal{C}o(A) + \mathcal{C}o(B)) \parallel \mathcal{C}o(C) \mid \emptyset \rangle \rightarrow \langle T \parallel \mathcal{C}o(C) \mid \tau \rangle$ is a valid computation prefix of $\mathcal{C}o((A + B) \parallel C)$ which leads to a failing computation.

3.3   Comparing the $\mathcal{L}$ and $\mathcal{W}$ Families

The two proofs can be directly rephrased for absolute time. We can thus state the following proposition for the $\mathcal{W}$ family of languages.

Proposition 3.

1. *For any* $\mathcal{X} \subseteq \{ask, nask, get, tell\}$, *one has* $\mathcal{L}(\mathcal{X}) \leq \mathcal{W}(\mathcal{X} \cup \{wait\})$.
2. *For any* $\mathcal{X} \subseteq \{ask, nask, get, tell\}$ *containing at least, on the one hand, tell and, on the other hand, ask or get, one has* $\mathcal{W}(\mathcal{X} \cup \{wait\}) \nleq \mathcal{L}(\mathcal{X})$.

3.4   Comparing the $\mathcal{D}$ and $\mathcal{R}$ Families

Let us now compare the $\mathcal{D}$ and $\mathcal{R}$ families.

Proposition 4. *For any* $\mathcal{X} \subseteq \{ask, nask, get, tell\}$, *one has* $\mathcal{L}(\mathcal{X}) \leq \mathcal{R}(\mathcal{X})$

Proof. Indeed, it is sufficient to code any communication primitive $C(t)$ as $C_\infty(t)$, with $C = ask, nask, get, tell$.

Proposition 5. *For any $\mathcal{X} \subseteq \{ask, nask, get, tell\}$ containing at least, on the one hand, tell, nask and, on the other hand, ask or get, one has $\mathcal{R}(\mathcal{X}) \not\leq \mathcal{L}(\mathcal{X})$.*

Proof. The proof amounts to rephrasing that of proposition 2 for the agents $A = ask_1(a); tell_2(c)$, $B = tell_1(d); nask_2(d); tell_2(b)$ and $C = tell_2(a); ask_2(c)$.

The main idea of the proof consists of coding the $delay(1)$ primitive of the proof of proposition 2 in terms of the combination $tell_1(d)$; $nask_2(d)$. At first sight, it seems that this idea can be reused to embed the $\mathcal{D}$ family in the $\mathcal{R}$ family. However, different occurrences of the same delay d would share the same token which would possibly lead one delay to fail waiting simply because another concurrent delay, slightly desynchronized, would have occurred. This problem disappears under the reasonable hypothesis that the language contains a form of local declaration. This is what is done in the following proposition where $\mathcal{D}_l$ denotes the extension of the $\mathcal{D}$ family with the operator $local\ d \in D\ in\ A$ which forces d to be replaced by a fresh token of the infinite set D in A.

Proposition 6. *For any $\mathcal{X} \subseteq \{ask, nask, get, tell\}$ containing at least tell and nask primitives, one has $\mathcal{D}_l(\mathcal{X} \cup \{delay\}) \leq \mathcal{R}(\mathcal{X})$*

Proof. Since the set of tokens is denumerable, let us code the tokens and the durations alternatively by the tokens themselves thanks to some numbering function. For each token t and duration d, we denote by t' and d' the resulting token. One may furthermore assume that the first token t_0 in this numbering function is the image of no token or duration. Moreover, let D be the set of tokens d'.
     The coder $\mathcal{C}o$ is then defined as follows:

$$\mathcal{C}o(C(t)) = C_\infty(t') \text{ for } C = ask, nask, get, tell$$
$$\mathcal{C}o(delay(d)) = local\ d' \in D\ in\ (tell_d(d')\ ;\ nask_{d+1}(d'))$$

3.5   Relating the $\mathcal{W}$ and $\mathcal{I}$ Families

The relations between the $\mathcal{W}$ and $\mathcal{I}$ families of languages consist of a transposition of those of the previous section to an absolute context. Note that the problem of the translation of *delay* in terms of timed primitive does not occur here due to the absolute nature of the timing primitives.

Proposition 7. *For any $\mathcal{X} \subseteq \{ask, nask, get, tell\}$, one has $\mathcal{L}(\mathcal{X}) \leq \mathcal{I}(\mathcal{X})$*

Proposition 8. *For any $\mathcal{X} \subseteq \{ask, nask, get, tell\}$ containing at least, on the one hand, tell, nask and, on the other hand, ask or get, one has $\mathcal{I}(\mathcal{X}) \not\leq \mathcal{L}(\mathcal{X})$.*

Proposition 9. *For any $\mathcal{X} \subseteq \{ask, nask, get, tell\}$ containing at least tell and nask primitives, one has $\mathcal{W}(\mathcal{X} \cup \{wait\}) \leq \mathcal{I}(\mathcal{X})$*

3.6 Relating the $\mathcal{D}$ and $\mathcal{W}$ Families

The $\mathcal{D}$ and $\mathcal{W}$ families of languages are very different in nature. The former family refers to a relative notion of time while the latter uses an absolute notion of time. As a result, it is not possible to express one family in terms of the other in a compositional way. However, a positive result is that it is possible to do so with the help of an auxiliary function returning the current time. This function is subsequently called ν. The families extended with it are respectively denoted as $\mathcal{D}_\nu$ and $\mathcal{W}_\nu$.

Proposition 10. *For any subset $\mathcal{X}$ of $\{ask, nask, get, tell\}$, one has $\mathcal{D}_\nu(\mathcal{X} \cup \{delay\}) = \mathcal{W}_\nu(\mathcal{X} \cup \{wait\})$.*

Proof. Since ask, nask, get, tell primitives can be translated into themselves, the proof amounts to describing the coding of wait primitives in terms of delay primitives and vice-versa. This is operated according to the following equalities:

$$wait(m) = delay(max\{0, m - \nu\})$$
$$delay(d) = wait(\nu + d)$$

3.7 Relating the $\mathcal{R}$ and $\mathcal{I}$ Families

Similarly, due to their different nature of time they embody, the $\mathcal{R}$ and $\mathcal{I}$ families cannot be expressed one another in a compositional way. It is however possible to express the $\mathcal{R}$ family extended with the ν function in terms of the corresponding extension of the $\mathcal{I}$ family. The families extended with ν are respectively denoted as $\mathcal{R}_\nu$ and $\mathcal{I}_\nu$.

Proposition 11. *For any subset $\mathcal{X}$ of $\{ask, nask, get, tell\}$, one has $\mathcal{R}_\nu(\mathcal{X} \cup \{delay\}) \leq \mathcal{I}_\nu(\mathcal{X} \cup \{wait\})$.*

Proof. The coding of the $\mathcal{R}_\nu(\mathcal{X} \cup \{delay\})$ family of languages in term of the $\mathcal{I}_\nu$ family results from the following equalities:

$$ask_d(t) = ask_{[\nu:\nu+d]}(t)$$
$$nask_d(t) = nask_{[\nu:\nu+d]}(t)$$
$$get_d(t) = get_{[\nu:\nu+d]}(t)$$
$$tell_d(t) = tell_{[\nu:\nu+d]}(t)$$

The decoding of a store maps each timed token $t_{[b:e]}$ to t_{e-b+1}.

4 Programming Examples

The interest of the timed mechanisms introduced may be evidenced through the coding of the following examples.

Abstracting the web as a tuple space, a request for information on the web may be typically programmed as follows:

$$tell_d(request) ; (get_d(answer) + (delay(d) ; tell_\infty(no\_answer))).$$

Indeed, this agent first posts a request and then performs a choice consisting, on the one hand, of waiting at most d units of time for the answer, and, on the other hand, wait for d units of time before reporting the absence of answer. Consequently, if an answer is produced within d units of time, then the get action of the choice is enabled whereas the $delay$ operation is not. Alternatively, if an answer is not produced within d units of time, then the get operation is not enabled while the $delay$ operation is. Note that because of the $tell_d$ primitive, the request will stay for d units of time only.

This example naturally generalizes to prove that exceptions resulting from the expiration of time can be captured in our framework. Suppose we would like to define constructs of the form $ask_d(t) \square A$, $get_d(t) \square A$, $nask_d(t) \square A$ with the semantics that, if after d units of time the corresponding primitive has not succeeded, then the agent A should be executed. This behavior can be programmed by the following translations:

$$ask_d(t) \square A \equiv ask_d(t) + (delay(d) ; A)$$
$$get_d(t) \square A \equiv get_d(t) + (delay(d) ; A)$$
$$nask_d(t) \square A \equiv nask_d(t) + (delay(d) ; A)$$

5   Implementation Issues

In order to argue the feasibility of the $\mathcal{D}$, $\mathcal{R}$, $\mathcal{W}$ and $\mathcal{I}$ families of languages, let us now sketch how they can be implemented. This section actually reports on a prototype under development. It builds upon previous work made in order to implement the $\mathcal{L}$ family of languages (see e.g., [13]).

5.1   Implementation of the Linda Primitives

The implementation of the Linda primitives has been done by using the threads library of Solaris. The tuple space is implemented as a token-indexed list. Per list element (token), we keep track of the number of identical tokens (*token counter*), and of the input primitives that are suspended on this token. The token list is stored in shared memory. The list is directly updated by the communication primitives. In order to guarantee exclusive access, the individual list elements are protected with a lock, which means that operations on different tokens can execute in parallel. Only adding or removing list elements to the global list requires the complete tuple space to be locked. The following algorithms are employed for the primitives.

Performing an *nask* primitive first checks whether the associated token is known to the tuple space (already has an element in the list of tokens). If not, the tuple space is locked, and a list element for the token is created. If the token counter equals zero, the *nask*-primitive succeeds. If not, it suspends, and is added to the list of suspended primitives, until the token counter reaches zero.

Asking a token t first checks whether at least one occurrence of t is present in the tuple space. If so, the primitive succeeds. Otherwise, the ask primitive is put in the associated list of waiting processes, until the token counter is positive.

Getting a token t proceeds similarly but decrements the token counter for t. If the token counter reaches zero, we check whether there are suspended $nask(t)$-primitives. If so, the process associated with the *nask* primitive is resumed and is removed from the list of waiting primitives.

Finally, telling a token t proceeds dually. The list of waiting processes is first inspected to discover an *ask* or *get* primitive waiting for t. In case an *ask* primitive is discovered, it is resumed and the search continues. In case a *get* primitive is discovered the token t is consumed by that primitive and the corresponding process is resumed. If no waiting *get* primitives are encountered, then the token counter for t is incremented.

5.2   Implementing Time

The implementation of the timed primitives is simplified by the observation that, thanks to the results of section 3, it is sufficient to implement the primitives dealing with absolute time, provided that the kernel keeps track of the current time. Note that any operating system provides a means to deliver to its processes the current time as well as to awake suspended processes after a given interval.

Consequently, with respect to the untimed implementation, the basic adaptations are, on the one hand, to associate a period of validity with the tokens and processes of the waiting lists, and, on the other hand, to use the waking-up facilities provided by the operating system kernel to force *wait* primitives to succeed when the specified waiting time has been reached, to force timed *ask*, *nask*, and *get* primitives to fail when their period of validity is over, and to remove tokens whose period of validity is over.

5.3   Correctness Issues

It is here worth stressing that such an implementation rests on the hypothesis that the number of operations actually performed per time unit is small enough or, restated in other terms, that the granularity of the time unit is big enough. Indeed, although the theoretical model of section 2 allows an unlimited number of operations to take place at the same moment, in practice any operation takes some time, even if it is very small. If the amount of work to be done in one time unit exceeds the available time, the model must be adapted by introducing additional wait primitives which means that some operations are effectively delayed to the following time units.

6   Conclusion

The paper has presented four extensions of Linda in order to introduce time in coordination languages. All of them are based on the two-phase functioning approach to real-time systems already employed by languages such as Lustre ([9]) and Esterel ([4]).

The resulting families of languages have been described by means of transition systems written in Plotkin's style. Their expressiveness has been studied by means of the concept of modular embedding introduced in [12]. Several typical real-time mechanisms have been coded in order to suggest the interest of the languages in practice. Finally, the design of a prototype implementation has been sketched in order to argue the feasibility of our approach.

The most related proposals for the introduction of time in coordination-like languages are [24] and [25]. Both pieces of work concern concurrent constraint languages ([26]), which may be viewed as a variant of Linda restricted to two communication primitives putting information of a tuple space and checking the presence of information on it. Technically, concurrent constraint languages can thus be viewed as the language $\mathcal{L}(\{ask, tell\})$. The paper [24] introduces time in this context by identifying quiescent points in the computation where no new information is introduced and by providing an operator for delaying computations by one unit. At each quiescent point of time, the tuple space is reinitialized to an empty content. The paper [25] extends this framework, on the one hand, by introducing a primitive for checking the absence of information and reacting on this absence during the same unit of time and, on the other hand, by generalizing the $delay(1)$ mechanism in an $hence\ A$ construct which states that A holds at every instant after the considered time. The resulting languages are called tcc and $tdcc$. In fact, rephrased in our framework, these languages correspond respectively to restricted variants of our $\mathcal{D}(\{ask, tell, nask, delay\})$ with delays of one units only and to $\mathcal{D}(\{ask, tell, nask, delay\}) \cup \{tell_\infty\}$. Although weaker than, for instance, the whole $\mathcal{R}$ language, the paper [29] has shown that the language tcc can embed one classical representative of the state oriented synchronous languages, namely Argos ([19]), and one representative of the declarative class of dataflow synchronous languages, namely Lustre ([9]). It follows from section 3 that the same result hold for most of the languages we have proposed.

De Boer, Gabbrielli, and Meo have presented in [5] a timed interpretation of concurrent languages by fixing the time needed for the execution of parallel tell and ask operations as one unit and by interpreting action prefixing as the next operator. A delay mechanism is presented in Oz ([28]), a language which combines object oriented features with symbolic computation and constraints, and, (relative) time-outs have been introduced in TSpaces ([31]) and JavaSpaces ([14]). A formal semantics of these time-outs and other mechanisms – not related to our concerns – is presented in [7].

We have proposed similar but also quite different features and studies. First, all the above work deal with relative time whereas we have described two families of languages – the $\mathcal{W}$ and $\mathcal{I}$ families of languages – which incorporate absolute time. There is also no counterpart for the complete language

$\mathcal{R}(\{ask, nask, get, tell\})$. As a result, the expressiveness of our four families of languages has not been studied in these pieces of work. Finally, except for Oz, TSpaces and JavaSpaces, no real implementation has been realized.

Our proposals share the synchronous hypothesis with the languages Lustre and Esterel. Lustre ([9]) is a language based on dataflow whereas Esterel ([4]) is a language of an imperative style. Our contribution with respect to these languages is to have adapted this hypothesis to the coordination context. Delays have counterparts in Lustre and Esterel but no counterpart is proposed in these languages for the primitives of the $\mathcal{R}$ and $\mathcal{I}$ families.

Acknowledgements

Koen De Bosschere is research associate with the Fund for Scientific Research – Flanders.

References

1. J.-M. Andreoli and R. Pareschi. Linear Objects: Logical Processes with Built-in Inheritance. *New Generation Computing*, 9(3-4):445–473, 1991.
2. F. Arbab, I. Herman, and P. Spilling. An Overview of Manifold and its Implementation. *Concurrency: practice and experience*, 5(1):23–70, 1993.
3. J. Banatre and D. LeMetayer. Programming by Multiset Transformation. *Communications of the ACM*, 36(1):98–111, 1991.
4. G. Berry and G. Gonthier. The Esterel Synchronous Programming Language: Design, Semantics, Implementation. *Science of Computer Programming*, 19, 1992.
5. F.S. De Boer, M. Gabbrielli, and M.C. Meo. A Timed Concurrent Constraint Language. *Information and Computation*, pages 47–61, 2000. To appear.
6. A. Brogi and P. Ciancarini. The Concurrent Language Shared Prolog. *ACM Transactions on Programming Languages and Systems*, 13(1):99–123, January 1991.
7. N. Busi, R. Gorrieri, and G. Zavattaro. Process Calculi for Coordination: from Linda to JavaSpaces. In *Proc. AMAST*, Lecture Notes in Computer Science. Springer Verlag, 2000. To appear.
8. N. Carriero and D. Gelernter. Linda in Context. *Communications of the ACM*, 32(4):444–458, 1989.
9. P. Caspi, N. Halbwachs, P. Pilaud, and J. Plaice. Lustre: a Declarative Language for Programming Synchronous Systems. In *Proc. POPL'87*. ACM Press, 1987.
10. P. Ciancarini. Distributed Programming with Logic Tuple Spaces. *New Generation Computing*, 12(3):251–284, 1994.
11. P. Ciancarini and D. Rossi. Jada: Coordination and Communication for Java Agents. In *Proc. 2nd International Workshop on Mobile Object Systems*, volume 1222 of *Lecture Notes in Computer Science*, pages 213–228. Springer-Verlag, 1996.
12. F.S. de Boer and C. Palamidessi. Embedding as a Tool for Language Comparison. *Information and Computation*, 108(1):128–157, 1994.
13. K. de Bosschere and J.-M. Jacquet. $\mu^2 Log$: Towards Remote Coordination. In P. Ciancarini and C. Hankin, editors, *Proceedings of the Coordination Conference*, volume 1061 of *Lecture Notes in Computer Science*, pages 142–159. Springer-Verlag, April 1996.

14. E. Freeman, S. Hupfer, and K. Arnold. *JavaSpaces: Principles, Patterns, and Practice*. Addison-Wesley, 1999.
15. D. Gelernter and N. Carriero. Coordination Languages and Their Significance. *Communications of the ACM*, 35(2):97–107, 1992.
16. D. Harel. Statecharts: a Visual Formalism for Complex Systems. *Science of Computer Programming*, 8, 1987.
17. E. Horita, J.W. de Bakker, and J.J.M.M. Rutten. Fully abstract denotational models for nonuniform concurrent languages. *Information and computation*, 115(1):125–178, 1994.
18. J.-M. Jacquet and K. De Bosschere. On the Semantics of μLog. *Future Generation Computer Systems*, 10:93–135, 1994.
19. F. Maraninchi. Operational and Compositional Semantics of Synchronous Automaton Composition. In *Proc. Concurr'92*, volume 630 of *Lecture Notes in Computer Science*. Springer, 1992.
20. D. Gelernter N. Carriero and L. Zuck. Bauhaus Linda. In In P. Ciancarini, O. Nierstrasz, and A. Yonezawa, editors, *Object based models and languages for concurrent systems*, volume 924 of *Lecture Notes in Computer Science*, pages 66–76. Springer-Verlag, 1994.
21. R. De Nicola, G. Ferrari, and R. Pugliese. KLAIM: a Kernel Language for Agents Interaction and Mobility. *IEEE Transactions on Software Engineering*, 1998.
22. G.A. Papadopolous and F. Arbab. Coordination Models and Languages. *Advances in Computers*, 48, 1998.
23. A. Rowstron and A. Wood. A Set of Tuple Space Primitives for Distributed Coordination. In *Proc. 30th Hawaii International Conference on System Sciences*, volume 1, pages 379–388. IEEE Press, 1997.
24. V. Saraswat, R. Jagadeesan, and V. Gupta. Programming in Timed Concurrent Constraint Languages. In B. Mayoh, E. Tougu, and J. Penjam, editors, *Computer and System Sciences*, volume ASI-131 of *NATO*. Springer Verlag, 1994.
25. V. Saraswat, R. Jagadeesan, and V. Gupta. Timed Default Concurrent Constraint Programming. *Journal of Symbolic Computation*, 11, 1996.
26. V.A. Saraswat. *Concurrent Constraint Programming Languages*. The MIT Press, 1993.
27. E.Y. Shapiro. Embeddings among Concurrent Programming Languages. In W.R. Cleaveland, editor, *Proceedings of CONCUR'92*, pages 486–503. Springer-Verlag, 1992.
28. G. Smolka. The Oz Programming Model. In J. Van Leuwen, editor, *Computer Science Today*, volume 1000 of *Lecture Notes in Computer Science*, pages 324–343. Springer Verlag, 1995.
29. S. Tini. On the Expressiveness of Timed Concurrent Constraint Programming. *Electronics Notes in Theoretical Computer Science*, 1999.
30. R. Tolksdorf. Coordinating Services in Open Distributed Systems with LAURA. In P. Ciancarini and C. Hankin, editors, *Coordination'96: First International Conference on Coordination Models and Languages*, volume 1061 of *Lecture Notes in Computer Science*. Springer-Verlag, 1996.
31. P. Wyckoff, S.W. McLaughry, T.J. Lehman, and D.A. Ford. TSpaces. *IBM Systems Journal*, 37(3), 1998.

Coordination and Access Control in Open Distributed Agent Systems: The   Approach

Marco Cremonini[1], Andrea Omicini[1], and Franco Zambonelli[2]

[1] – DEIS – Università di Bologna Viale Risorgimento 2
40126 Bologna, Italy
{mcremonini, aomicini}@deis.unibo.it

[2] DSI – Università di Modena e Reggio Emilia Via Campi 213/b
41100 Modena, Italy
franco.zambonelli@unimo.it

Abstract. Coordination and access control are related issues in open distributed agent systems, being both concerned with governing interaction between agents and resources. In particular, while coordination deals with enabling interaction and making it fruitful, access control is meant to control interaction to make it harmless. We argue that this twofold facet has to be supported by a system in a uniform and decentralised manner. To this end, we describe how the application of the   tuple-based coordination model over a hierarchical topology is well-suited in this context. On the one hand, policies can be enforced by means of a single mechanism based on tuples and can be scoped to manage access to groups of distributed resources. On the other hand, agents can interact along a hierarchical infrastructure by applying a standard tuple-based communication template. This makes   a single coherent framework for the design and development of Internet-based multiagent systems, which takes coordination as the basis for dealing with network topology and access control in a uniform way.

1 Introduction

Open distributed multiagent systems (*MAS*s, henceforth) have gained sheer interest due to their suitability to the Internet scenario. Their best property is to cope well with the *unpredictability* and the *dynamics* of the environment. The lack of a global state of the Internet can be addressed by exploiting the agent autonomy and flexibility. In addition, the openness and the spatial distribution of systems make the ability to deal with *heterogeneous* environments and *decentralised* forms of control an issue. In particular, systems are likely to be composed of several heterogeneous subsystems managed by *independent authorities*, where heterogeneity refers both to their design and implementation [9, 16].

In such a context, the ability to coordinate the agents [1] coupled with the possibility to control the operations they perform is important, so we argue that *coordination* and *access control* should be regarded as tightly connected issues [3, 4, 14].

A. Porto and G.-C. Roman (Eds.): COORDINATION 2000, LNCS 1906, pp. 99-114, 2000.

Furthermore, the openness and the distribution of the environment make traditional centralised solutions no longer effective. Architectures with a central coordinator, which supervises to the whole activity of a system, are not applicable in many contexts. In open distributed systems is convenient to employ components in charge of coordinating tasks and active entities, but they should be decentralised and managed by local authorities. Consequently, the relationships among subsystems, local authorities and decentralised coordinators should be explicitly represented in the design of a system infrastructure. This leads to design system topologies for modelling the distribution of the components and their interconnection. Both the coordination and the access control issue should be addressed in such a decentralised, unpredictable and dynamic environment.

The aim of this paper is to present how the   system faces to and manages such a complexity of open distributed agent systems. The essential components of   are:

- a coordination model based on multiple programmable tuple spaces that mediates all communications among active entities;
- a distributed infrastructure, modelling a system, upon which tuple spaces are deployed;
- the integration of mechanisms for the access control within the tuple-based environment and their application to the hierarchical infrastructure.

In particular, the paper shows that implementing access control mechanisms in   is worthwhile and may provide for a relevant benefit: agents could be supported along their interaction without a static knowledge of the environment.

In Section 2 we discuss the relationship between coordination and access control. Section 3 describes the   coordination model and its application to a hierarchical infrastructure. Section 4 presents how access control techniques have been applied and fully integrated with the coordination model. In Section 5, the case study considered throughout the paper is presented in its entirety. Finally, in Section 6, some related systems are analysed and conclusions drawn.

2   Coordination and Access Control

In general, coordination technology for the Internet is typically concerned with enabling interaction and making it fruitful, while access control technology is typically meant to bound interaction to make it harmless. Then, access control could be regarded as the conceptual security counterpart of coordination. This makes coordination and access control two strictly related topics, and their combination allows to fully characterising the interaction between agents and resources in an Internet-based environment.

In addition, both coordination and access control policies (i.e., sets of rules) have to be defined and enforced. *Enforcement of policies*, that is agents being compelled to act according to preset policies, should occur in a decentralised manner, with a single and uniform mechanism, and be applied with different granularity, i.e., to individual agents or to entire multiagent systems.

Decentralisation is necessary because agent systems need to be scalable, possibly spread over a wide area network and have no single point of failure.

A *single and uniform mechanism* for the enforcement of policies is required for managing the heterogeneity of the overall system. In an organisation, many different MASs could be deployed, each one with a specific policy to be supported.

Finally, also the *granularity* of access control policies should be considered: whether rights are granted to single agents or to entire MASs. New MASs could be dynamically added in the organisation, and new agents could be dynamically created within each MAS. Thus, it is often convenient to be able to define policies first in term of MASs, so as to bound the interaction space of a system within the organisation, and then in term of agents belonging to MASs.

Before discussing in more detail the   's coordination and access control models, which are the subjects of next two sections, we first introduce an underlying assumption that holds throughout this paper. The pre-condition for each system in order to establish what an entity is allowed to do is to recognise whom the interacting entity is. This leads to the *authentication* issue: each execution environment holding protected resources should determine which agent is requiring the execution of an action before allowing it to be done [11]. A coordination framework should then endorse an agent naming scheme and support an authentication protocol, univocally mapping agents onto names. Coherently, a coordination model should embody a suitable notion of *agent identity*, by allowing any communication operation to be associated to an agent identifier. This way, given that policies have to be also defined in terms of MASs and not only in terms of single agents, a broader notion of identity should be supported, which enables a MAS to be denoted as a whole.   defines a global agent naming scheme by combining a *MAS identity* and an *agent individual identity*, where the latter is determined within the scope of the former. Hence, when we refer to agent identities, we intend composite objects having the form $MAS_{ID}{:}Agent_{ID}$, where the first is a global name referring a specific MAS and the second is the relative name for the single agent.

Throughout this paper, we always assume that whether an agent interacts with an execution environment and access a tuple space, its global name, composed by a MAS and an individual identity, has been already verified by the system.

3   Coordination Model

In   [13], agents interact through a multiplicity of independent coordination media, called *tuple centres*, spread over Internet nodes. Agents exchange tuples by means of standard Linda primitives [2, 6, 7].

Each tuple centre is associated to a node and has a unique name: in particular, a tuple centre can be denoted either by its full Internet (*absolute*) name or by its local (*relative*) name. By means of the absolute name *tc@node*, tuple centre *tc* provided by the Internet node *node* is referred to from everywhere in the Internet, and by means of its relative name *tc* in the context of node *node*. The general form for any admissible communication operation performed by an agent is *tc@node?op(tuple)* asking tuple centre *tc* of node *node* to perform operation *op* using *tuple*.

tuple centres are tuple spaces enhanced with the notion of *behaviour specification*: the behaviour in response to communication events of every tuple centre can be defined according to the system requirements as the observable state transition following a communication event. Correspondingly, the definition of a new behaviour for a tuple centre basically amounts to specifying a new state transition in response to a standard communication event. This is achieved by allowing any communication event to be associated to specific computations, called *reactions*. In particular, a *specification tuple*, stated by *reaction(Op,R)*, associates the event generated by an incoming communication operation *Op* to the reaction *R*.

A reaction is defined as a sequence of *reaction goals*, which may access the properties of the communication event triggering the reaction, perform simple term operations, and manipulate tuples in the tuple centre. Each reaction is executed with a transactional semantics: a successful reaction can atomically modify the tuple centre state, while a failed reaction yields no result at all. In particular, operations on the tuple space (*out_r, in_r, rd_r, no_r*) work similarly to communication operations, and can trigger further reactions in a chain. Reaction goals are executed sequentially and a chain of reactions is either a *successful* or a *failed* atomic operation depending on whether or not all its reactions succeed [5].

Then, from the agent's viewpoint, the result of the invocation of a communication primitive is the sum of the effects of the primitive itself and of all the reactions it has triggered, perceived altogether as a single-step transition of the tuple centre state. This makes it possible to uncouple the agent's view of the tuple centre, viewed as a standard tuple space, from the tuple centre actual state, and to connect them so as to embed the laws of coordination and access control.

3.1   Tree-Like Infrastructure

The interaction space provided by a   system relies on a multiplicity of distributed tuple centres. This way,   shares the advantages of models based on multiple tuple spaces and goes beyond, since different coordination media can encapsulate different coordination and access control laws. This leads to introduce the relationship between a coordination model and its distributed topology, and to discuss two main problems: *(i)* how the space where agents live is modelled (*network modelling*), and *(ii)* how the knowledge about the structure of that space is made available to the agents (*network knowledge*).

The problem of network modelling is particularly evident when dealing with intrinsically structured domains, as Internet-based organisations frequently are. In fact, Internet nodes are often grouped in clusters, subject to highly coordinated management policies and possibly protected by firewalls. Moreover, large clusters can be further characterised by the presence of enclosed sub-clusters, often arranged as a (logical or physical) hierarchical structure of protected organisational domains. Different enclosed clusters provide protected domains of shared resources and are largely independent from the rest of the organisation in the definition of policies concerning their resources. For example, most academic environments or medium- and large-sized companies have infrastructures that suit this hierarchical model.

As far as network knowledge is concerned, it is, at least, unrealistic to assume that agents could have a complete knowledge of the whole network topology, as well as of resources availability. In fact, Internet-based domains are typically dynamic and unpredictable, due to their complex structure where many decentralised authorities are present and no central repository of information is available. Therefore, knowledge about the environment should be acquired dynamically and incrementally by agents through their interaction. This actually affects the coordination protocol, since part of the agent interaction concerns the acquisition of information about topology, and makes network knowledge a coordination-related issue.

In   the *gateway* locality abstraction has been specifically introduced to enable the modelling of an Internet-based agent system as a hierarchical infrastructure. A *gateway* is a node augmented with the ability of authenticating (although we do not address this issue in the present paper) and of authorising agents to access some other nodes and their tuple centres. By connecting gateways in a tree-like topology, the definition of nested protection domains is natural: for each possible sub-tree, the root gateway may hold the policy for managing the access to the corresponding children. Ordinary nodes are the leaves of the tree, while intermediate nodes could act also as gateways. Fig. 1 provides an example for a case study. This way, the collection of the Internet nodes hosting a MAS can be conveniently represented. A hierarchical structure is well-suited in many real-world cases and the root of the hierarchy, that is the most external gateway, may work as a bridge with the Internet so as to permit the connection among different systems and infrastructures.

Considering the coordination model, each node and each gateway of a infrastructure implements its own set of tuple centres. In particular, one or more *application* tuple centres can be defined to coordinate and authorise the agent access to the local resources of a node. Each *gateway*, in addition, is supposed to provide for a unique *default* tuple centre, which represents the standard communication media that agents access to get information about other available tuple centres of nodes and gateways.

3.2 The Journal Review Case Study: A First Glance

As our case study, we consider a reviewing process of a scientific journal, as depicted in Fig. 1: the hierarchical topology represents the relationships among the *Publisher*, the *Editors*, the *Area Editors* and the *Reviewers* agents, showed as ovals. The system is configured with several distributed tuple centres, drawn as boxes: each member of the system exchanges papers and reviews through tuple centres called *papers*. Differently from Reviewers, the Publisher, Editors and Area Editors also act as gateways, thus exploiting a *default* tuple centre to exchange information with agents. Relationships among the components of the reviewing process are represented with arrows. The Authors are the external entities interacting with the Publisher gateway to submit papers and receive reviews. The Publisher receives submitted papers from Authors, allocates them to the Editors and should be enabled to manage both papers and re-

views (i.e., check the status of a paper under review, collect reviews, re-allocate papers, etc.). Editors act as the Publisher with respect to their corresponding Area Editors, although they can not interfere with each other or with Publisher's actions. Area
Editors may work for different Editors (see Area Editor2 in Fig. 1), allocate papers to
Reviewers and collect reviews. Reviewers may receive papers from different Area
Editors. Finally, consider agent identities, which have the form $MAS_{ID}:Agent_{ID}$. We
assume to distinguish between two systems (MAS_{ID}), one managing the first issue of
the journal (*issue1*) and another managing the second issue (*issue2*). The Publisher
deals with both issues, as Area Editor2 that can receive papers from both editors.
Editor1 and Area Editor1 deals with the first issue only, while Editor2 and Area Edi-
tor3 deals only with the second. Reviewers can deal with both issues.

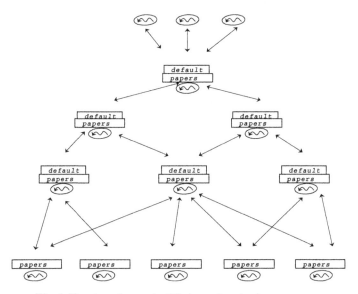

Fig. 1. Topology for a scientific journal reviewing process

4   Protection in

As far as agent interaction through tuple centres is concerned, the control of agent
access and authorisation can be achieved only by handling *all* the communication
events performed in tuple centres. Each communication event should be carried out
according to *access control policies*. In   , tuple centres could be made visible
or invisible to agents under the control of a gateway and the access to the tuples can
be controlled for each agent by tuple centres reactions. The programmability of reactions in response to each communication event allows serving differently any operation performed in a tuple centre, according to the rights granted to agents.

4.1 Access Control Matrix

In   , the different behaviours of gateways and nodes are exploited in order to control agent access to tuple centres.

Firstly, nodes are the natural location for the definition and the enforcement of authorisation policies, because resources are located in nodes, tuple centres mediate all interactions, and each node might be independently managed. Considering that a node may implement several independent tuple centres, the global security policy supported by a node can be formalised by an *access matrix* in terms of both agent identities, tuple centres and permissions [10].

$$[i,j] ::= \quad_{i,j}, \forall\, i \in \quad, \forall\, j \in \qquad (1)$$

where
- is a set of different *agent identifiers*.
- is the set of different *tuple centres* implemented by that node.
- $_{i,j}$ is the access permission granted to the i-th identity by the j-th tuple centre of the given node.

Since   is sparse, in practice, it is never stored in its tabular form. Instead, two implementations have been traditionally derived [10].

From the *rows* of   , a policy could be represented as a collection of *capabilities*:

$$[i] ::= <j, \quad_{i,j}>\, , \forall\, j \in \quad | i \in \qquad (2)$$

where   , and   are defined as in (1).

From the *columns* of   , instead, *access control lists* have been defined as list of pairs:

$$[j] ::= <i, \quad_{i,j}>, \forall\, i \in \quad | j \in \qquad (3)$$

where   is the set of agent identifiers defined in the policy of a given tuple centre. and   are defined as in (1).

Let us show an example of these access control mechanisms applied to our case study. Consider, for instance, the Area Editor1. He should permit Editor1 to insert papers and withdraw reviews concerning the first issue of the journal, and the Publisher to do every desired action. In terms of capabilities and access control lists, the following could be defined:

$$[issue1:editor1] ::= <\{default@areaed1, \textit{insert papers}\},$$
$$\{default@areaed1, \textit{withdraw reviews}\}>$$
$$[publisher] ::= <default@areaed1, \textit{everything}>$$

$$[default@areaed1] ::= <\{issue1:editor1, \textit{insert papers}\},$$
$$\{issue1:editor1, \textit{withdraw reviews}\},$$
$$\{publisher, \textit{everything}\}>$$

The two mechanisms are managed differently: capabilities are meant to be physically held by interacting entities, i.e., Editor1 and the Publisher, while the   is meant to be stored by the resource holder, i.e., Area Editor1.

For sake of completeness, however, if the administrator of a tuple centre needs to allow *anonymous accesses* (i.e. agents having unknown identities), the *anonymous* pseudo-identity must be defined in the access control policy. In   tuple centres, agents with an identifier not listed in the policy succeed in matching against the *anonymous* one, if specified, thus gaining the permission assigned to it.

In the following, we focus on the case of   s, although the analysis could be easily generalised to the case of capabilities as well.

4.2 Enhanced Access Control Matrix

In the previous subsection, we have described the most traditional mechanisms for protecting shared resources, and their integration with the   coordination model. Conversely, when the distribution of the system is considered, some particularities arise and traditional protection models need to be enhanced. This, in   impacts on the hierarchy of gateways.

On the one hand, a gateway is queried by all agents willing to access the tuple centres implemented by the nodes of its associated domain, thus it is well-suited to enforce access control policies on the behalf of those nodes. Furthermore, the hierarchical topology of the infrastructure lets gateways control both the accesses to nodes' tuple centres and the ability of agents to further interact with sub-gateways. This permits gateways to decide which agents could be allowed to explore different sub-trees of an infrastructure.

On the other hand, for the characteristics of open distributed systems, local administrators have the authority over their resources, thus policies still have to be locally defined in nodes, not in gateways.

Then, to make gateways able to enforce access control policies, the *default* tuple centre implemented by each gateway must hold a combination of the access control policies defined by tuple centres located in domain's nodes and sub-gateways. More precisely, nodes and sub-gateways must partially *delegate* their authority to an upper gateway. *Delegation*, in this context, is an action performed by nodes and gateways, whose effect is to invest another gateway with the onus of matching agents identities against their access control policies and thus granting some permissions to agents. The authority is only partially delegated since gateways can not modify the delegated policies on their own.

In practice, the result of delegation actions is that the delegated gateway receives from some nodes and/or sub-gateways, a number of tuples representing entries of their   [i,j] (1). The combination of those policies in the default tuple centre can be formalised with the *3-dimensions Access Control Matrix*.

$$[i,j,k] ::= \quad_{i,j,k}, \forall\, i \in \quad, \forall\, j \in \quad, \forall\, k \in \qquad (4)$$

where

*   is the set of different *identifiers* stated by all the access control policies delegated to the gateway.

-      is the set of different *tuple centres* from which the default tuple centre has been delegated.
-      is the set of *nodes* (nodes and sub-gateways) hosting the   tuple centres.
-     $_{i,j,k}$ is the access permission granted to the i-th identifier by the j-th tuple centre of the k-th node of the matrix.

Again, in real contexts the access matrix tends to be highly sparse, being many $_{i,j,k}$ possibly left unspecified. The reason is twofold: *(i)* agent identifiers relevant for a MAS occur only in policies defined by nodes interacting with that MAS; *(ii)* not all tuple centres are implemented by every node. Hence, in   , an   is represented by a table listing only the elements that exhibit legal values of $_{i,j,k}$. The semantic of an unspecified element of   - and then of an empty value of $_{i,j,k}$ - is that no right should be granted.

Differently from the traditional case discussed in the previous subsection, in this one it is useful to maintain the access matrix as a global table held by gateways. This permits to inspect the matrix along all the three dimensions, making possible both the enforcement of access policies and the control of agent interaction along the hierarchy.

Let us show what discussed above with an example. Consider Area Editor2 gateway in Fig.1. Agents that interact with it want information and permissions to further interact with tuple centres of lower nodes, not with its local resources. Hence, it is in charge of enforcing access policies for its protection domain. In this case, its domain is composed by Reviewers' nodes Rev1, Rev3, Rev4 and Rev5. Agents interacting with him could be the ones of the Publisher and those of the two Editors. In the case of Publisher's agents, they must be allowed to further access whatever Reviewer's *papers* tuple centre they want among the ones of the domain. In the case of an Editor's agent, it must be allowed to access only reviews concerning its corresponding journal issue, not the ones of the other. An example of access control matrix of Area Editor2 might be:

$$[issue1:editor1, papers, \{rev1, rev4\}] ::= <withdraw\ reviews>,$$
$$[issue2:editor2, papers, \{rev3, rev5\}] ::= <withdraw\ reviews>,$$
$$[publisher, papers, \{rev1, rev3, rev4, rev5\}] ::= <everything>$$

where Editor1, for example, receives, from the *default* tuple centre of Area Editor2, permissions to withdraw tuples from *papers* tuple centres of Reviewers Rev1 and Rev4. This way, Editor1's agents are unaware of — and have no rights on — both other Reviewers and other tuple centres apart the *papers* one.

4.3 Standard Tuple-Based Communication Template

As we have seen so far, in a   infrastructure policies could be uniformly defined and enforced in a decentralised manner. We move now to consider how agents may interact with such an infrastructure. We first recall the two basic features: *(i)*   tuple-based interaction has the standard form *tc@node?op(tuple)*, and *(ii)* all the default tuple centres of an infrastructure hold a standard name, e.g., *default*.

From this, a *standard tuple-based communication template* can be applied to the interaction of agents with *default* tuple centres:

```
default@gateway?in(standard domain tuple template)
```

where the standard domain tuple template is:

```
domain(Id, info(Tc, Node, Permission), InfoList))
```

and

- the `Id` parameter holds the actual value of the identifier of the interacting agent, which has, in general, a form like $MAS_{ID}{:}Agent_{ID}$;
- `info(Tc, Node, Permission)` is the template for the expected tuples carrying the information about the domain policy. Each `info` tuple carries an access permission (`Permission`) that is granted to the agent identifier `Id` by the tuple centre `Tc` of the node `Node`;
- `InfoList` is the variable that will hold the resulting list of `info` tuples by unifying with the `domain/3` answer tuple produced by the reaction(s).

This way, all agents accessing a   environment are able to interact with the hierarchy of gateways without any previous knowledge of its structure – a part the firstly accessed gateway, which is supposed to be statically known. Then they could explore the infrastructure in a controlled fashion, because they only rely on the information acquired dynamically and incrementally from gateways.

Therefore, a querying agent is enabled to specify which information and permissions it needs by setting in different manners the attributes of the standard tuple template. Let us show an example, in our case study, by supposing that Editor1 and Editor2 agents want to check the status of two papers that they have allocated to Area Editor2. The partial knowledge that agents own can be represented as: *(i)* both editors do not know who are the actual reviewers of their papers (the Area Editor2 itself might be as well) and *(ii)* Editor2 knows that papers, reviews and status information are stored in tuple centres called *papers*. Consequently, their queries for the default tuple centre of Area Editor2 might be:

From editor1

```
default@areaed2?in(domain(editor1, info(_, _, _),
InfoList))
```

From editor2

```
default@areaed2?in(domain(editor2, info(papers, _, _),
InfoList))

default@areaed2?in(domain(editor2, info(default, _, _),
InfoList))
```

In the former, Editor1 agent generically queries for all tuple centres, local or remote, application-based or *default*, that it is allowed to access, having no additional information. Differently, in the latter, Editor2 agent can make a more specific search by querying only for *papers* tuple centres, but must also specify a second tuple for retrieving accessible sub-gateways. Tuples *out*'ed in response to the previous templates may be:

```
domain(editor1, info(_, _, _), [info(papers, rev1,
withdraw reviews), info(papers, rev3, withdraw re-
views)])

domain(editor2, info(papers, _, _), [info(papers, rev2,
withdraw reviews), info(papers, rev5, withdraw re-
views)])

domain(editor2, info(default, _, _), [])
```

the first matched by Editor1, while the others matched by Editor2.

In Table 1 the possible configuration of info(Tc, Node, Permission) are shown and explained.

Table 1. Main instances of the info tuple parameter

info(_,_,_)	All possible info *tuples are out'ed. This way, the agent has a complete knowledge about tuple centres, nodes and permission in that domain, according with the rights granted to its identity.*
info(tc,_,_)	*This way, the agent requests only those nodes that hold a certain* tc *tuple centre, if accessible.*
info(_,node,_)	*The agent requests only tuple centres hold by the node* node, *if accessible*
info(_,_,perm)	*The agent requests all the tuple centres of the domain where it could act with the access right* perm.

4.4 Delegated Access Control Policies

The application of our security model needs to be further elaborated when policies are propagated along a hierarchy of gateways, i.e., some nodes delegate policies to a gateway, this one, in turn, delegates another upper gateway and so on. This because, whether the process of delegating tuples that compose a policy is applied *as-is* also to access matrixes delegated from gateway to gateway, the system consistency would be hard to be kept. All distributed access matrixes should be *synchronised* when application tuple centres modify their local policies. Local modifications would be propagated to every gateway's *default* tuple centre that was previously delegated with the changed policy.

The time frame from one consistent state of the configuration of delegated access control policies to another one could vary according to the depth of the tree, the network latency, and the size of the access matrixes. We have focused in particular the latter aspect for improving the system scalability. The idea is that recording in a gateway the combination of the access matrixes held by all its sub-gateways is not strictly necessary. Instead, a gateway should simply establish whether a certain agent could be permitted to interact with nodes and sub-gateways directly connected with it in the hierarchical model, and not be concerned with nodes and sub-gateways of lower levels. To this end, the knowledge of the complete sub-gateway's access matrix is not required. Hence, the complexity of policies delegated from gateway to gateway could be reduced by establishing that delegation along the gateway tree should proceed in the following way:

- when delegation is performed *from a node to a gateway*, the delegated policies are the ones effectively defined by application tuple centres as   s;
- when delegation is performed along the gateway tree, *from gateway to gateway*, the delegated policies should depend only from the multiagent system to which an agent belongs (MAS_{ID}) and not from its individual identifier ($Agent_{ID}$).

Hence, delegation between gateways can be realised by delegating tuples as:

$$< \quad *, default, \quad *, explore> \qquad (5)$$

where

- \quad * is the set of different *MAS identifiers* exhibited by the access matrixes of the * sub-gateways. This parameter has the form $MAS_{ID}:\_$.
- *default* is the standard name of all the tuple centres providing for the gateway facility.
- \quad * is the set of sub-gateways that delegate a policy.
- *explore* is a new access mode that we have introduced, which captures the fact that a gateway may allow agents simply to interact with a sub-gateways, being unaware of the exact sub-gateways' access matrixes.

As an example, consider the delegation from Editor1 and Editor2 to the Publisher. Its resulting access control matrix is:

[issue1:_, default, editor1] ::= *<explore>*
[issue2:_, default, editor2] ::= *<explore>*

which is meant to provide each agent interacting with the Publisher with the minimum set of information and rights needed to deal with the review process. In this case, for instance, agents related to the first issue of the journal are authorised to interact with Editor1, which holds its own   , built up by entries from Area Editors.

From the scalability viewpoint, this solution has some benefits: when some modifications occur in local policies of a node but no MASs is removed or created, the access matrix to be synchronised is only the one of the gateway delegated by that node. A distributed synchronisation along the hierarchy is required only when MASs are created or deleted from the system, because only in this case the   * parameter of (5) should be changed.

5   The Journal Review Process Case Study

In this section, the Journal Review Process case study is drawn out for showing how it works in the   framework, including the implications of the hierarchy and the tuple-based interactions. To this end, first consider an outlook of the system's local and delegated policies, as depicted in Fig.2. Access matrixes have been determined following the rules defined in the previous section. For sake of simplicity, we have kept at the minimum the information presented, thus the example is not completely specified, even though its generalisation has no difficulties. The elements for which details are not provided (AreaEd3, Rev2, Rev4 and Rev5) are left unspecified.

Firstly, consider identities: we have supposed that two systems exist for managing different issues of the journal, marked with *issue1* and *issue2* identifiers. This would make clear how different systems could co-exist and be separately managed in

. For example, in Rev3 the access control policy states that: *(i)* agents belonging to the *issue2* system and holding the *areaed2* identifier could access the local *papers* tuple centre *out'*ing papers and *in'*ing reviews; *(ii)* the belonging to the system that manage the *issue2* permits agents to read the status of a paper to be reviewed; and *(iii)* any other agent is rejected. Policies defined by other nodes follows the same schema.

Secondly, consider the delegation performed by the Rev1's and the Rev3's *papers* tuple centres towards Area Editor2's *default* tuple centre. The access matrix is the combination of all Rev1's and the Rev3's access control policies.

Finally, consider what happens when delegation proceeds through the hierarchy. The access matrix of the Publisher gateway is build up only by considering journal issues' identifiers and its policy depends only from the number of different MASs.

Given the above configuration of policies, agents can interact with the hierarchy by using the communication template described in Subsection 4.3 to explore the whole infrastructure. In this way, they are unaware of the physical structure of the environment and are granted with the permissions corresponding to their behaviour. For instance, assume to let Author's agents check their paper's status. To this extent, Author's agents can interact with the Publisher's gateway, they can be assigned with a journal issue identifiers and can be informed about the corresponding editor. In its turn, the editor may advise them who is the area editor to contact, which, finally, can provide author's agents with the required information.

6. Conclusions and Related Work

In this paper, we have discussed the relation between coordination and access control in open, distributed agent systems and argued that the two issues are tightly connected. We have then presented how these issues have been integrated in the design of the   framework and how the resulting features have been exploited for supporting a well-known case study in the area of tuple-based coordination. As far as the relationship between coordination and access control is concerned, we highlight how this aspect still lacks an extensive analysis, and this underestimation might slow-down the adoption of coordination models in open environments. The aim of this work, hence, has been to approach this important facet, presenting a solution that is applicable to a variety of application contexts. Further works will be devoted to improve and extend the integration of access control and coordination. For instance,

other models for the access control seems well-suited for   , the role-based
one in particular [14].

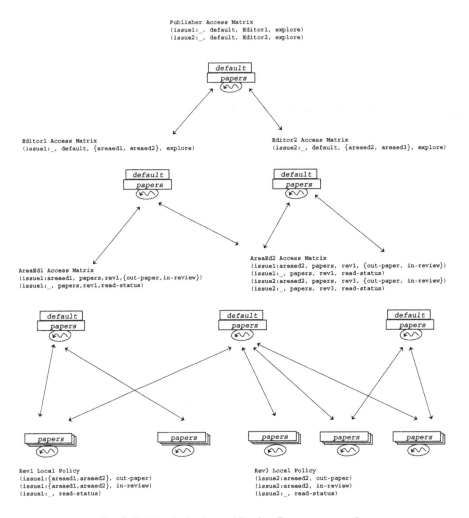

Fig. 2. Policies in the Journal Review Process case study

However, other works have addressed issues similar to the ones of this paper, Law-
Governed Interaction, SecOS and ActorSpace in particular.

Law-Governed Interactions (LGI) [12] is a coordination mechanism that allows an
open group of distributed active entities (agents, processes) to interact with each
other, under an explicitly specified policy – called the *law* of the group. A peculiar
feature of LGI is that for each member of a group, a *controller* is defined. A controller is a specific system component that holds the law governing an agent (i.e., the
security and coordination policy) and its control state. In this way a controller totally
mediates each event involving the associated entity and has complete knowledge and

authority over it. This is a different design choice with respect to   , which, in turn, embeds laws into the behaviour specification of tuple centres and does not need to associate external components to agents or spaces. In the context of LGI, various access control policies have been modelled, but differently from   , issues concerning network modelling, partial knowledge and delegation of policies are not considered.

The *SecOS* model [15] is a different example of integration between a Linda-like coordination model and security-related issues. In this case, the problem been tackled is to protect the access to tuples and tuple's attributes by means of cryptographic mechanisms. Its basic idea is to associate cryptographic keys with attributes in tuples. An agent needs to furnish a matching key before it can access the corresponding tuple's object. What is more interesting to highlight about SecOS is that the use of cryptography in the access to tuple's data is in some way complementary with respect to the subject of this paper. It represents in fact another possible direction for future developments of   .

ActorSpace [8] provides an underlying platform for agent systems that enables to control the access to, and the management of resources, but does not adopt coordination models based on tuples. ActorSpace explicitly models the location of agents on particular hosts and the amount of computational resources that an agent is allowed to consume. Resource interaction is mediated by means of proxies, which are components of the agent's behaviour specifically customised to interact with a certain type of resource. Differently from ActorSpace, in   agents interact in a standard way with resources and have no need to embed components (i.e. proxies) specifically tailored for the different resource types. This better management of the heterogeneity of the interaction space is one of the main benefits derived from the adoption of a tuple-based coordination model. Moreover, also issues related to the structure of the environment are not explicitly addressed in ActorSpace.

References

[1]   Cabri, G., Leonardi, L., Zambonelli, F., Mobile-Agent Coordination Models for Internet Applications. IEEE Computer, 33(2): 52-58, Feb.2000.

[2]   Carriero, N. and Gelernter, D., Linda in context. Communications of the ACM, 32(4): 444-458, 1989.

[3]   Ciancarini, P., Tolksdorf, R., Vitali, F., Rossi, D., Knoche, A., Coordinating Multiagent Applications on the WWW: A Reference Architecture. IEEE Transactions on Software Engineering, 24(5): 362-375, May 1998.

[4]   Cremonini, M., Omicini, A., Zambonelli, F., Multi-agent systems on the Internet: Extending the scope of coordination towards security and topology. In Proc. of the 9th European Workshop on Modelling Autonomous Agents in a Multi-Agent World (MA-MAAW'99), LNAI no. 1647, pages 77-88, Springer-Verlag, 1999.

[5]   Denti, E., Natali, A., Omicini, A., On the expressive power of a language for programming coordination media. In Proceedings of the 1998 ACM Symposium on Applied Computing (SAC'98), pages 169-177, Atlanta (GA), 1998.

[6]   Gelernter, D., Generative Communications in Linda. ACM Transactions on Programming Languages and Systems, 7(1), January 1985.

[7]   Gelernter, D., Carriero, N., Coordination languages and their significance, Communications of the ACM, 35(2): 97-107, Feb. 1992.

[8]   Jamali, N., Thati, P., Agha, G. A., An Actor-based Architecture for Customising and Controlling Agent Ensembles. IEEE Intelligent Systems, Special Issue on Intelligent Agents, 38-44, March-April 1999.

[9]   Jennings, N. R., Sycara, K., and Wooldridge, M., A Roadmap of Agent Research and Development. International Journal of Autonomous Agents and Multi-Agent Systems 1(1): 7-38, 1998.

[10] Lampson, B., Protection. ACM Operating Systems Review, 8(1), 1974.

[11] Lampson, B., Abadi, M., Burrows M., Wobber, E. P., Authentication in distributed systems: Theory and Practice. ACM Transactions on Computer Systems, 10(4): 265-310, November 1992.

[12] Minsky, N., Ungureanu, V. Unified support for heterogeneous security policies in distributed systems. In Proc. of the 7th USENIX Security Symposium, San Antonio, Tx, USA, 1998.

[13] Omicini, A. and Zambonelli, F., Coordination for Internet Application Development. Journal of Autonomous Agents and Multi-Agent Systems, Special Issue: Coordination Mechanisms for Web Agents, Kluwer Academic Press, 2(3), September 1999.

[14] Sandhu, R. (editor), ACM Transactions on Information and System Security, 2(1):1-135, 1999.

[15] Vitek, J., Bryce, C., Oriol, M., Coordinating Agents with Secure Spaces, In Proceedings of Coordination '99, Amsterdam, The Netherlands, May 1999.

[16] Weiss, G., Multiagent Systems: A Modern Approach to Distributed Artificial Intelligence. The MIT Press, June 1999.

Distributed Splitting
of Constraint Satisfaction Problems

Farhad Arbab and Eric Monfroy

CWI
Kruislaan 413, 1098 SJ Amsterdam, the Netherlands
{Farhad.Arbab,Eric.Monfroy}@cwi.nl

Abstract. Constraint propagation aims to reduce a constraint satisfaction problem into an equivalent but simpler one. However, constraint propagation must be interleaved with a splitting mechanism in order to compose a complete solver. In [13] a framework for constraint propagation based on a control-driven coordination model was presented.
In this paper we extend this framework in order to integrate a distributed splitting mechanism. This technique has three main advantages: 1) in a single distributed and generic framework, propagation and splitting can be interleaved in order to realize complete distributed solvers, 2) by changing only one agent, we can perform different kinds of search, and 3) splitting of variables can be dynamically triggered before the fixed point of a propagation is reached.

1 Introduction

Constraint propagation aims to reduce a constraint satisfaction problem (CSP) into an equivalent but simpler one by narrowing domains of variables until a fixed-point is reached. However, constraint propagation must be interleaved with a splitting mechanism in order to compose a complete solver. This mechanism works by splitting the domain of a variable (i.e., the values the variable can assume) into (sub)domains, creating in this way sub-CSP's. After several splittings, we obtain a tree of sub-CSP's.

In [13] a framework for constraint propagation based on a control-driven coordination model was presented. In this paper we extend this framework in order to integrate a distributed splitting mechanism.

Intuitively, with every split, we would like to duplicate the entire network of agents in a CSP, one replica dedicated to each resulting sub-CSP. However, this idea is not conceivable in practice because the resulting network replicas quickly exhaust any reasonable amount of resources. Thus, by correctly indexing domains of variables in sub-CSP's, and by adding some more control agents, we perform a distributed splitting, preserving the same original network of agents, their connections, and their control for propagation.

At every moment in time, each variable agent has several domains corresponding to several sub-CSP's, and each function agent can compute in several domains, reducing several sub-CSP's. Using domain indices, we can associate

A. Porto and G.-C. Roman (Eds.): COORDINATION 2000, LNCS 1906, pp. 115–132, 2000.

variable values in each domain with its respective sub-CSP, and thus we are able to select which sub-CSP is reduced. The search agent aims to coordinate function and variable agents in order to guide the search in the search space: if variables send both domains after a split and functions compute with all the domains they receive, then we obtain a breadth first search; if variables and functions focus on certain indexed domains coordinated by the search agent, then we perform a depth first search in the branch selected by the search agent.

In our framework, communication (for constraint propagation, splitting, and search) is totally asynchronous. Contrary to other methods, the split of a variable is not broadcast to all variables, but only to the concerned variable. Subsequently, the result of this split is propagated to other agents through computation of domain reduction functions.

This technique has three main advantages. First, in a single distributed and generic framework, propagation and splitting can be interleaved, and thus, complete distributed solvers can be realized. Second, by changing only the search agent, we can perform different kinds of search. Finally, splitting of variables can be dynamically triggered before the fixed point of a propagation is reached, and thus, in many cases (e.g., when reductions are not strong enough) computation of solutions can be more efficient.

2   Constraint Solving and Coordination Languages

2.1   Constraint Solving

As claimed in [1], many algorithms for constraint solving can be described using a simple component-based framework based on two main interleaving processes: constraint propagation and splitting (i.e., a kind of enumeration mechanism).

Constraint propagation is one of the most important techniques for solving constraint satisfaction problems (CSP's). It attempts to reduce a CSP into an equivalent but simpler one, i.e., the solution space is preserved while the search space is reduced. A CSP is given as a set of constraints, and for each variable that occurs in each constraint, a domain of values that the variable can assume, e.g., $\langle\{X + Y = Z, Z < 5\}, \{X \in [0..10], Y \in [2..8], Z \in [1..17]\}\rangle$ is a CSP.

Constraint propagation algorithms usually aim at computing some form of "local consistency" described as a common fixed point of some *domain reduction functions*. These algorithms are instances of a more general mathematical framework: the framework of *chaotic iterations* (CI) [2]. CI is a basic technique used for computing limits of iterations of finite sets of functions. By "feeding" domain reduction functions into a chaotic iteration algorithm, we generate an algorithm that enforces a local consistency.

Domain reduction functions (drf's) are related to domains of constraints (see Section 5 for examples of drf's for the *and* and *not* Boolean constraints), and they have been widely studied for standard domains (e.g., Boolean constraints [9], integers, interval arithmetic [8,12]). When considering less usual domains, these functions must either be hand-crafted, or, for finite domains, techniques such as in [4] can automate generation of the reduction functions.

However, constraint propagation is generally not strong enough to provide the user with convenient solutions. Thus, a CSP can be split into sub-CSP's (whose union contains all the solutions of the original CSP) by splitting the domain d of a variable X into several (sub)domains $d_1, \ldots, d_n$ such that $\bigcup_i d_i = d$. Thus, instead of searching for solutions in the initial CSP with d as the domain of X, we now search in n CSP's, each with its respective sub-domain for X. Since in each sub-CSP the domain of X is smaller, propagation is generally applicable again. Each of these sub-CSP's is then reduced again using propagation, split again, and so on, until convenient solutions are found. Different splitting techniques exist, such as splitting into domains of similar sizes, or labeling (i.e., enumeration) which splits the domain into a singleton, and the rest of the domain. Consider the abovementioned CSP. We can split it into the two following CSP's: $\langle \{X+Y = Z, Z < 5\}, \{X \in [0..10], Y \in [2..5], Z \in [1..17]\} \rangle$ and $\langle \{X+Y = Z, Z < 5\}, \{X \in [0..10], Y \in [6..8], Z \in [1..17]\} \rangle$

As soon as a CSP is split, the issue of search arises, i.e., how to explore the resulting search sub-spaces (or branches). Standard methods either explore one branch at a time (depth-first search), or all branches (breadth-first search).

Thus, by combining constraint propagation and splitting, one obtains a complete solver. In [13], a distributed version of the CDA algorithm (i.e., one algorithm for computing chaotic iterations [3]) is presented. We now extend this framework in order to integrate a distributed splitting mechanism into it.

2.2   Coordination Model and Language

To realize constraint propagation using a data-driven coordination model, we can consider a shared data-space (representing the variables and their values) used by agents (the reduction functions) that asynchronously post and retrieve values until they reach a fixed-point. However, we have chosen a control-driven coordination model to realize chaotic iteration techniques. Here, variables become coordinators that request computing agents to perform reductions. The reasons are quite simple. First, this allows us to easily change strategies by just changing coordinators. Second, splitting and search will become just two extra agents coordinating the variables. For more details about this choice, see [14].

Hence, we have chosen the IWIM (Ideal Worker Ideal Manager) model [5,6] to realize our framework. The IWIM model is based on a complete symmetry between and decoupling of producers and consumers, as well as a clear distinction between the computational and the coordination/communication work performed by each process. A direct realization of the IWIM model in terms of a concrete coordination language, namely **MANIFOLD** [7], already exists.

MANIFOLD is a language for managing complex, dynamically changing interconnections among sets of independent, concurrent, cooperative processes [5]. The basics concepts in the IWIM model (thus also in **MANIFOLD**) are *processes*, *events*, *ports*, and *channels*. A **MANIFOLD** application consists of a (potentially very large) number of processes running on a network of heterogeneous hosts, some of which may be parallel systems. Processes in the same application may be written in different programming languages. **MANIFOLD** has been successfully used in a number of applications.

3   The Framework

We now explain constraint propagation, splitting mechanisms, and search techniques as coordination of cooperative agents. In this section, we thus map the main components of constraint propagation to specific IWIM processes (see [13] for more details). Splitting mechanisms and search techniques are realized by certain specific agents that either observe computation, or are queried by agents involved in propagation. The task of these two agents is thus to coordinate global computation, and to manage exploration of the search space.

3.1   Overview

We consider two types of agents and a special agent to perform constraint propagation: variables, drf's, and a Master agent. The general skeleton of the coordination-based constraint propagation framework is as follows. Each variable of the CDA algorithm is represented by one coordination variable, and each drf is represented by one worker. The Master agent builds the network of variables and drf's, and collects solutions. We do not detail the termination agent in this paper: we assume that termination of a set of agents is detected by using a standard coordination pattern of **MANIFOLD**.

The splitting mechanism is embodied in one agent which observes the states of variables (using an inquiry protocol). This agent decides which variable must be split, and how. It then communicates to the splitting variable all of its new sub-domains. Contrary to [13], a variable now has several domains, corresponding to several sub-CSP's.

In order to guide the search for solution, we consider a Search agent. Its task is to select the order for exploring sub-CSP's. An example of a network is illustrated in Figure 3.

3.2   Behavior of the Network

Let us detail the process. A variable X is modified when it receives a new value for a given sub-CSP $\mathcal{P}$ whose intersection with its current domain in $\mathcal{P}$ (or in a compatible sub-CSP) is smaller than the current domain in $\mathcal{P}$. Each time a variable X is modified, it requests the drf's $F_1, \ldots, F_n$ (all the drf's containing x in their input) to work with its new domain value. $F_1, \ldots, F_n$ have thus new tasks to perform. When done, they send their results to each of the variables $X_1 \ldots, X_m$ of their output. $X_1, \ldots, X_m$ can eventually be modified by these values, and this will iterate the process.

In parallel, the Split agent observes the computation by observing the states of the variables, and may split one or more variables. In this case, a split variable is informed of its new domains corresponding to the new sub-CSP's. It is not necessary to broadcast these new CSP's to all agents in the network: the split is propagated through all the network by successive applications of drf's and modifications of variables.

When a variable X gets a value for a new sub-CSP (i.e., either X was split, or another variable was split and the split was subsequently propagated to X), it requests the Search agent to define which sub-domains must be explored first.

The process terminates when all solutions have been extracted.

3.3   Worlds and MCSP

Contrary to [13], at a given moment in time, the network of agents represents and solves several CSP's that are sub-CSP's of the initial CSP. Thus, we now solve a Multiple Constraint Satisfaction Problem (MCSP), i.e., a union of CSP's derived by splitting and constraint propagation from the original CSP that was to be solved. Note that the set of solutions of the union of such CSP's is equal to the solutions of the original CSP. Intuitively, we change the domain of computation. Previously, we had a single domain for each variable. Now we have a set of *indexed domains* for each variable. An indexed domain *(domain, world)* for a variable represents the *domain* of the variable in the sub-CSP denoted *world*.

The notion of *world* is equivalent to the notion of sub-CSP. The name of a world is a string of symbols. We denote by $\top$ the initial world, i.e., the initial CSP (before any splitting). Consider a world w. When a variable x is split into n sub-domains, w gives rise to n sub-worlds denoted respectively as $w.x_1, \ldots, w.x_n$. Furthermore, we can compare such worlds in order to perform correct reductions. Consider the world w, and the worlds $w.x_1, \ldots, w.x_n$ derived from w after the split of the variable x. We say that w is compatible with each $w.x_i$, and we denote it as $w.x_i \preceq w$. The relation $\preceq$ is a partial order: $w.x_i.y_j \preceq w$ since $w.x_i.y_j$ is derived from $w.x_i$ after the split of y, but we cannot compare $w.x_i$ with $w.x_j$, nor $w.x_i$ with $w.y_j$. We can thus easily compare worlds:

$$w' \preceq w \ \text{ iff } \ w' = w.w''$$

In a world w such that $w' \preceq w$, the domain of a variable X is larger than or equal to the domain of X in the world w'. This is obvious: the difference between w and w', if any, is because at least either X or some other variable has been split, and this may have resulted in a reduction of X in the sub-CSP w'.

Since we do not require domain reduction functions to be contracting, and that we do not enforce synchronization of reductions (a drf can send a new domain to a variable which is larger than the current domain already reduced by another function), a variable must always intersect its current domain with the new domain it receives from a drf. For this reason, two cases can arise:

– The received domain is in a world w not yet known by the variable X (the set of worlds X knows about is denoted as *Worlds*). Then, X intersects this new domain with a domain in the smallest world w' greater than w known to X, i.e., $w' = min_{\preceq}\{w'' \in \textit{Worlds} \mid w \preceq w''\}$. The intersection is then the domain of X in the world w.

- The received domain is in a world w already known to the variable X. Then, for each worlds w' such that $w' \preceq w$, X must intersect this new domain with the domain in w'. Hence, we update the domain in each w' with the intersection of the domain in w and the domain in w'.

This computation is correct, because we always update a domain in a world w by intersecting it with a domain in a world w' such that $w \preceq w'$. Thus, we can be sure that we do not lose a solution. In this way, some computation may be useless (e.g., if the Search agent directs variables to different branches), but this is the price we pay to avoid a costly synchronization of all reductions performed by drf's (which would also lead to sequential reduction of the CSP). Moreover, considering a correct Search agent, all variables will work on the same world, and such useless work will not happen.

4   The Agents

We now describe the different agents, their connections, their tasks, and their coordination. Tasks of agents are guarded actions of the following form:

name: guard
        actions_1, ..., action_n.

where a guard is an event, such as the reception of a message on an input port, or a notification by another agent. When the agent is in its waiting state (i.e., not executing a task), as soon as the guard guard is satisfied, the guarded action name is triggered and action_1, ..., action_n are executed sequentially to the end without interruption. The process then returns to its waiting state.

4.1   Variables

Each variable in a CSP is implemented by a *generalized variable* of **MANIFOLD** (i.e., extensions of variables with call back functions) whose possible domains in each world are updated via an assignment operation, i.e., one of its call back functions.

Assume a CSP $\mathcal{P}$ over a set of variables $\mathcal{X}$, and a set $\mathcal{F}$ of r domain reduction functions $f_1, \ldots, f_r$. Consider x a variable in $\mathcal{X}$. Hence, the generalized variable X implementing x has the following features and connections (see Figure 1):

- one output port Out connected via channels to the implementations $F_{i_1}, \ldots, F_{i_m}$ of $f_{i_1}, \ldots, f_{i_m}$, i.e., the drf's that accept x as an input variable;
- one input port In connected via channels to the implementations $F_{o_1}, \ldots, F_{o_l}$ of $f_{o_1}, \ldots, f_{o_l}$ (i.e., the drf's that accept x as an output variable), and connected to the Split agent;
- one output port $OutSplit$ connected via a channel to the Split agent in order to send it the current state of the variable;
- an output port $OutMaster$ for forwarding to the Master agent the indexed domains of the variable when a solution is computed;

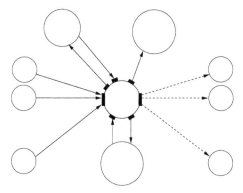

Fig. 1. A variable agent

- an output port *OutSearch* to query the Search agent to select which current worlds (i.e., branches of the search space) must be explored;
- a set *Domains* of indexed domains to keep current domains and the worlds they are associated with;
- a set *Worlds* to store the worlds known by X. This set is used by the Search agent to select on which world X must concentrate;
- a set *Splits* to store the worlds known by X, and resulting after a split of X. This store is used for detecting when all solutions have been computed;
- a set *SearchWorlds* to store the worlds that are currently being explored (i.e., worlds that have been selected by the Search agent); and
- three call back functions: a domain intersection function, a domain comparison function, and an assignment function.

We now describe the guarded actions of X. Note that when sending a message on a port with multiple connections, the message is replicated into each connected channel.

Updating domains When the variable X gets an indexed domain (v', w') from one of the DRF's $F_{o_1}, \ldots, F_{o_l}$, the world w' may be unknown for X. This happens if the indexed domain (v', w') for X was computed in a DRF using other variables known in w' (i.e., w' results from the split of variables other than X).

When X encounters w' for the first time, it adds w' in its set *Worlds* of known worlds, and requests the Search agent to select which set of worlds (i.e., branches of the search space) must be explored. Note that X does not wait for the new decision of the Search agent before continuing. This can lead to useless work, e.g., when looking for a single solution. Nevertheless, this scheme avoids a costly synchronization with the Search agent (we can however consider this synchronization when looking for a single solution). Then, the new indexed domain must be integrated in the set of indexed domains of X after intersecting the domain with the domain of the "smallest" world "bigger" than w'.

When w' is already known, the domain of each world that is "smaller" than or "equal" to w' must be updated. For each such world w, X intersects the current domain with v'. When the result is different than the current domain, the current domain in the world w is updated, and consequently, X requests all the DRF's $F_{i_1}, \ldots, F_{i_m}$ to execute again.

These tasks are realized by the following guarded action:

update: (v',w') on input port Inp
    if $w' \notin Worlds$
        % the world w' is unknown to X
        then $Worlds := Worlds \cup \{w'\}$
            % request **Search** to define the search
            send $Worlds$ on output port $OutSearch$
            % intersects the domain v' in w' with the domain of the
            % "smallest" world known by X strictly "greater" than w'
            (v, w) **s.t.** $w = min_{\preceq}\{w'' \in Worlds \mid w' \preceq w''\}$
            $Domains := Domains \cup \{ (v' \cap v, w') \}$

        % the world w' is already known by X
        else % eventually modifies domains of worlds known by X "smaller"
            % than or "equal" to w' using new domain in w'
            foreach $(v,w) \in Domains$ **s.t.** $w \in Worlds$ **and** $w \preceq w'$
            do $v'' := v \cap v'$
                % updates the domain of X in w if modified
                if $v'' \neq v$
                    then $Domains := Domains \setminus \{(v, w)\}$
                        $v = v''$
                        $Domains := Domains \cup \{(v, w)\}$
                        % requests associated DRF's if search is set for w
                        if $w \in SearchWorlds$
                            then send (v, w) on port Out
                        fi
                fi
            od
    fi

Note that updating domains of a world "smaller" than or "equal" to w' can be optimized by considering worlds in decreasing order: if a world is not modified, smaller worlds cannot be modified.

Splitting When the Split agent decides to split the variable X, it sends to X a set V of new indexed domains. X must then update the set of worlds it knows about, its set of indexed domains, and its set of splits.

split: V on input port $InpSplit$
      $Domains := Domains \cup V$
      $Worlds := Worlds \cup \{w' \mid (v', w') \in V\}$
      $Splits := Splits \cup \{w' \mid (v', w') \in V\}$

Since splitting and reductions are asynchronous, we keep in *Domains* the domain of X in the world that has just been split. If we don't keep this information, the following problem can arise: consider x the domain of X in $\top$, x' the domain of X in $\top$ after reduction by the drf d_1, and x'_1, x'_2 domains of X after a split on x'. Then, consider y the domain of Y in $\top$, and y_1 a domain of Y after a split of Y from $\top$. Then, a drf d_2 computing with x and y_1 can compute a domain x'' larger than x' for X in the world of y_1. If we don't keep x', we cannot intersect x'' with any domain, and thus we obtain the domain x'' for X in the world of y_1. If we consider that domain reduction functions are always contracting domains, this is not a real problem: x is larger than or equal to x'', some reductions may be lost, but they will be computed again from x'', and we will not loop. But if we don't require any special properties for domain reduction functions (and this is the case in our framework), then we cannot ensure termination anymore, because x'' can be larger than x.

Orienting the search The next guarded action collects a set of worlds W sent by the Search agent. W represents the worlds on which a variable will focus in its next steps:

search: W on input port *InpSearch*
    SearchWorlds := W

Jumping to another sub-space of the search When the solutions in the worlds defined by the Search agent are found, the Termination agent (see Section 4.5) raises the "solution_ack" event to inform all the variables. Then, the variable X sends its domains for the current worlds to the Master agent, updates its own structures (especially *Splits* that is used for termination detection), and requests the Search agent to change its set of worlds to concentrate on:

solution: solution_ack
    foreach $w \in SearchWorlds$
        do find (v,w) in *Domains*
            send (v,w) on output port *OutMaster*
            Domains := *Domains* \ $\{(v,w)\}$
            SearchWorlds := *SearchWorlds* \ $\{w\}$
            Worlds := *Worlds* \ $\{w\}$
            Splits := *Splits* \ $\{w\}$
    od
    % *asks for some new worlds to search in*
    send Worlds on output port *OutSearch*

Reporting state The Split agent observes the variables and their domains in order to decide which variable to split, and when. For this purpose, it needs to be informed of the state of the variables, i.e., their domains, and their *SearchWorlds*, in order to work in cooperation with the Search agent:

state_requested: domain? on input port *InSplit*

send *Domains* on output port *OutSplit*
send *Search Worlds* on output port *OutSplit*

4.2   Domain Reduction Functions

A DRF implements a domain reduction function given as input to the CDA algorithm. Thus, as many DRF's as drf's fed in the CDA algorithm are created by the Master agent.

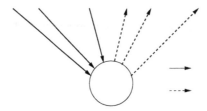

Fig. 2. a DRF agent

Assume a CSP over a set $\mathcal{X}$ of variables, and a drf f such that:

$$f : xi_1, ..., xi_m \longrightarrow xo_1, ..., xo_l$$

where $xi_1, ..., xi_m, xo_1, ..., xo_l$ are variables in $\mathcal{X}$. Then, the DRF F implementing the function f has the following structure (see Figure 2):

- m input ports $Inp\_Xi_1, ..., Inp\_Xi_m$ connected respectively to the m variable processes $Xi_1, ..., Xi_m$ implementing $xi_1, ..., xi_m$;
- l output ports $Out\_Xo_1, ..., Out\_Xo_l$ connected, respectively, to the l variable processes $Xo_1, ..., Xo_l$ implementing $xo_1, ..., xo_l$;
- m sets $Domains\_Xi_1, ..., Domains\_Xi_m$ of indexed variables for each input variable. These stores are initialized with the initial domains (i.e., in the $\top$ initial world) of input variables during the creation of F by the Master agent;
- m sets $Worlds\_Xi_1, ..., Worlds\_Xi_m$ of worlds known for the input variables;
- the code of the function f,

We now present the guarded actions a DRF can execute.

Reduction request When a DRF receives a reduction request from X_i, one of its input variables (i.e., it receives a new indexed domain (v, w) for this variable), it updates the domain of X_i: either the new indexed domain is added to the set $Domains_{X_i}$ (when the DRF does not know yet the world w for X_i), or the indexed domain is replaced in the set $Domains_{X_i}$. The DRF then selects the smallest w-compatible domains of each other input variables. Then, it reduces its output variables using the drf it represents. Finally, it sends their new indexed domains to each of its output variables. For the DRF F, mentioned above, we obtain the following guarded action for each of its input variables:

reduction_request: (v, w) on input port Inp_Xi_j
　　　% *Update of the indexed domains of* Xi_j
　　　if $w \in Worlds\_Xi_j$
　　　　　then **find** (v', w') in $Domains\_Xi_j$ **s.t.** $w' = w$
　　　　　　　　$Domains\_Xi_j := Domains\_Xi_j \setminus \{(v', w')\}$
　　　　　else $Worlds\_Xi_j := Worlds\_Xi_j \cup \{w\}$
　　　fi
　　　$Domains\_Xi_j := Domains\_Xi_j \cup \{(v, w)\}$
　　　% *Find the smallest compatible domains for each input variable*
　　　$I_j = v$
　　　foreach $k \in [1..m]$ **s.t.** $k \neq j$
　　　　　do $w'' = min_{\prec}\{w \in Worlds\_Xi_k \mid w \preceq w'\}$
　　　　　　　find (v'', w'') in $Domains\_Xi_k$
　　　　　　　$I_k = v''$
　　　od
　　　% *Compute new domains for output variables using drf*
　　　$(O_1, \ldots, O_l) = drf(I_1, \ldots, I_m)$
　　　% *send new indexed (by* w*) domains of output variables*
　　　foreach $k \in [1..l]$ sends (O_k, w) on output port Out_Xo_k

Note that we can optimize this guarded action by 1) directly updating the set $Domains\_X_i$ and reducing again new domains when the output variable X_i is also an input variable and the drf is not idempotent, and 2) sending new indexed domains only to variables that have effectively been modified.

Initializing the propagation process Each function must be applied at least once, i.e., in the CDA algorithm the set G of functions still to be applied is initialized with the set F of drf's. We consider the *start* event raised by the Master agent when the network is installed. We can start reduction with the initial domains (i.e., domains indexed by the initial world $\top$) of $Xi_1, \ldots, Xi_m$ given at creation time with the following guarded action:

starting: start
　　　　% *find initial domains of input variables*
　　　　foreach $j \in [1..m]$
　　　　　　do **find** $(v'', \top)$ in $Domains\_Xi_j$
　　　　　　　$I_j = v''$
　　　　od
　　　　% *compute and send new indexed domains to output variables*
　　　　$(O_1, \ldots, O_l) = drf(I_1, \ldots, I_m)$
　　　　foreach $j \in [1..l]$ sends $(O_j, \top)$ on output port Out_Xo_j

4.3　The Split Agent

This agents aims to dynamically (i.e., depending on the progress of constraint propagation) split the domain d of a variable into several (sub)domains such that their union is equal to d. In terms of constraint solving, this means that a CSP $\mathcal{P}$ is split into several sub-CSP's such that their union is equivalent to (i.e., correctness and completeness of the set of solutions) $\mathcal{P}$.

This agent observes all the variables (by periodically inquiring their states), analyzes the evolution of the propagation, and decides which variable must be split, and splits the variable. Thus, this agent needs a local memory in order to store pieces of global information involved in its decision making.

The Split agent is connected to each variable with two streams: one to receive the states of variables, the other, to request states, and to send the split domains. Moreover, this agent is linked to the Termination agent that detects its termination, and informs it when constraint propagation for some branch of the search-space is finished. Hence, the Split agent is able to establish one of its strategies: either wait for the end of propagation before splitting, or split as soon as domain reduction becomes tedious and slow.

We consider the Split agent as a coordinator, not as a simple worker. By this we mean that the termination of the network of agents depends on a correct and sensible agent, i.e., an agent able to take beneficial decisions, e.g., not to split numerous variables simultaneously, not to split again the same variable before noticing the effect of the previous split, etc.

We don't give the details of this agent because, depending on the desired splitting strategies (see Section 6), numerous algorithms are possible.

4.4   The Search Agent

The task of this agent is to dynamically determine how the search space must be explored. When variables encounter a new world, they ask the Search agent to decide which branches (worlds) must be exploited first. Since this agent collects information from variables, the Split agent, and the Termination agent, it can also lead the search without being queried by any variable.

The behavior of this agent depends not only on the evolution of the computation in the network of agents, but also on the needs of the end user: should only one solution be computed, several, all, or only some with specific given properties? Depending on these strategies and requirements, the Search agent then decides whether functions and variables must use all their domains in different worlds (this implements a breadth first search), one single domain at a time (this implements a depth first search), or several domains simultaneously (i.e., a mixed search).

In order to manage the search of solutions, and the exploration of the search space, the Search agent is connected to every variable to receive the set of worlds they know about, and to inform them which branches to explore. This coordinator is not linked to the Termination agent, since as soon as a branch is completely explored the Termination agent will be warned indirectly by the variables involved through a decision request. However, we can imagine connecting it to the termination agent in order to avoid some intermediary data exchange, and to the Split agent in order to work in tighter collaboration with it. But then, the decoupling of propagation, termination, splitting, and search becomes less obvious.

We assume that this agent takes correct and compatible decisions for each variable, i.e., its decisions are global and not only local. An agent that forces a variable to explore a world, and another variable to concentrate on another (non-compatible) world can lead to non-termination: some solutions can be computed, but we can never be sure to compute all solutions of the initial CSP.

4.5   The Termination Agent

This agent is responsible to detect four types of termination. Note that the framework we present is very generic and allows numerous strategies, explorations of the search space, and splitting techniques. Thus, detection of termination in such a case assumes that the Split agent and the Search agent are mutually correct, i.e., they do not loop, and they give compatible information (such as *SearchWorlds*) to every variable.

Termination of propagation Constraint propagation terminates when 1) no domain reduction function is busy anymore, 2) no variable is busy anymore with domains associated with worlds they must currently concentrate on (i.e., worlds of *SearchWorlds* as determined by the Search agent), and 3) no message is pending in a stream between a variable and a domain reduction function. When constraint propagation is finished, the Termination agent signals it to the Split agent, because the latter may need this information to fully realize its strategies.

Current branches totally explored This case happens when the solutions in one/several branches have been found. This means that propagation for these branches is finished, and the Split agent can no longer split their corresponding domains of variables. This termination is thus detected when both propagation and the Split agent terminate.

The whole search space has been explored In this case, all solutions of the initial CSP have been computed. The Termination agent detects this state when current branches are totally explored and the *Splits* set of every variable (worlds directly derived from a split of the variable itself) is empty.

Termination required by the Master agent When a user is not interested in all solutions, the Master agent can decide to stop resolution as soon as a/several satisfying solution(s) have been collected. In this case, the Master agent can request the Termination agent to stop all activity in the network of agents. Note that this feature can be used for optimization when computing a "good" solution (not necessarily the best) within a given time, or when the ratio of solution quality over elapsed time becomes sufficient.

We do not give here the details of the mechanism used by this agent. Informally, using features of **MANIFOLD**, we can easily implement a generic termination protocol scanning activities of agents, and the presence of messages pending in streams. We just require this agent to be connected to variables, drf's, the Split agent, and to be able to observe streams inbetween these agents.

4.6   The Master Agent

The task of this agent is rather static. The Master agent is mainly concerned with initialization and creation of the network of agents, and collecting solutions. Given a CSP, a set of "meta" domain reduction functions, a search algorithm, and a split algorithm, the Master agent derives the drf's needed for the resolution of the CSP, and establishes the network of agents with their connecting streams. Moreover, the Master agent is connected to each variable (to receive its values when necessary), and to the termination agent (to stop the resolution when sufficently many solutions or sufficiently good solutions have been computed).

5   An Example

We now illustrate our framework by solving an example of Boolean constraints. We assume three types of constraints: 1) $and(x, y, z)$ with the usual meaning $z = x \wedge z$, 2) $not(x, y)$ meaning $x = \bar{y}$, and 3) the standard equality "=". We now consider solving the CSP:

$$\langle \{and(x, y, z), not(x, z), y = t\}, \{x \in \{0, 1\}, y \in \{0, 1\}, z \in \{0, 1\}, t \in \{0, 1\}\} \rangle$$

The Master agent creates 4 generalized variables X, Y, Z, and T implementing x, y, z, and t, with initial domains $\{0, 1\}$. Assume that, using some meta domain reduction functions, the Master agent identifies 5 drf's f_1, f_2, f_3, f_4, and f_5 [1]:

$$f_1 : y \rightarrow z$$
$$f_1(y) := \{0\} \qquad \text{if y=\{0\}}$$
$$f_1(y) := \{0, 1\} \qquad \text{otherwise}$$

$$f_2 : z \rightarrow x$$
$$f_2(z) := \{1\} \qquad \text{if z=\{0\}}$$
$$f_2(z) := \{0\} \qquad \text{if z=\{1\}}$$
$$f_2(z) := \{0, 1\} \qquad \text{otherwise}$$

$$f_3 : t \rightarrow y$$
$$f_2(t) := t$$

$$f_4 : x, z \rightarrow y$$
$$f_4(x, z) := \{0\} \qquad \text{if x=\{1\} and z=\{0\}}$$
$$f_4(x, z) := \emptyset \qquad \text{if x=\{0\} and z=\{1\}}$$
$$f_4(x, z) := \{0, 1\} \quad \text{otherwise}$$

$$f_5 : x \rightarrow z$$
$$f_5(x) := \{1\} \qquad \text{if x=\{0\}}$$
$$f_5(x) := \{0\} \qquad \text{if x=\{1\}}$$
$$f_5(x) := \{0, 1\} \qquad \text{otherwise}$$

---

[1] To simplify the example, we consider here only 5 functions, a subset of the complete set of functions that can be automatically generated using algorithms such as in [4]. Constraint propagation based on these four functions, together with the Split agent, are sufficient for solving our example CSP.

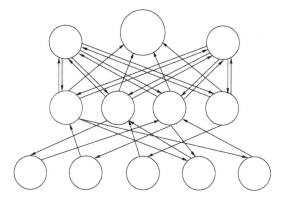

Fig. 3. A Boolean Example

Consider now that we want to perform a depth first search, and we want to perform a complete constraint propagation before splitting. We thus consider DFS as the Search agent that implements a depth first search, and PF as the Split agent that waits for the termination of propagation before splitting. We obtain the network illustrated in Figure 3. The agents F_1, F_2, F_3, F_4, and F_5 (respectively, X, Y, Z, and T) implement the functions f_1, f_2, f_3, f_4, and f_5 (respectively, the variables x, y, z, and t) as described in the previous section.

As soon as the start event is raised by the Master agent, the reduction process starts. Each function is applied only once, since none of them is able to modify the domains of the variables. Thus, propagation terminates without any change of domain.

Assume now that PF decides to split the variable T into $\{0\}$ in the world of T_1 and $\{1\}$ in the world of T_2. When requested by T, DFS has two possibilities: explore the world T_1 or the world T_2. Assume DFS first selects T_1. Then, T forwards $\{0\}$ to F_3, and the reduction starts again. When the propagation finishes, PF also terminates (no other variable can be split), and we obtain the first solution: $X = \{1\}$, $Y = \{0\}$, $Z = \{0\}$, and $T = \{0\}$. The Termination agent detects that current branches have been fully explored, and raises the solution_ack event. Variables catch this event, and thus forward (their respective parts of) this solution to the Master.

Next, the variables again query DFS, which can now decide to explore the world T_2. After propagation, the domains of T and Y are fixed to $\{1\}$. Another splitting is required for, say, X. We obtain two new worlds: the world of $T_2.X_1$ with the X value $\{0\}$, and $T_2.X_2$ with the X value $\{1\}$.

Suppose DFS selects $T_2.X_2$. Then, after the fixed point of propagation is reached, and no other split is possible, we obtain $X = \{1\}$, $Y = \emptyset$ (since F_4 deduces that $Y = \{0\}$, and then the Y agent intersects $\{0\}$ with $\{1\}$), $Z = \{0\}$, and $T = \{1\}$. This branch is totally explored, and the domains are forwarded to the Master, which deduces that this branch leads to an inconsistency (i.e., no valid solution since $Y = \emptyset$). DFS then selects $T_2.X_1$, which also leads to an inconsistency. At this point, the entire search space has been explored, and the computation stops.

6   Comments

We now discuss some important advantages of our framework with regards to its generality, its component-based aspect, and its dynamic behavior.

Interleaving of propagation and splitting In [13], a coordination-based chaotic iteration algorithm is presented. However, constraint propagation is generally not powerful enough to solve a CSP, i.e., reduction alone is not able to narrow domains of variables to singletons. Thus, such a framework cannot generally extract solutions. In this paper, we extend this framework and integrate splitting mechanisms and search techniques in a distributed environment, without requiring any synchronization, or any mutual exclusion among tasks. We thus obtain a single distributed and generic framework, in which propagation and splitting can be interleaved in order to realize complete distributed solvers. Furthermore, the decoupling of constraint propagation, splitting mechanism, and search technique is total. Thus, we can envisage designing in our framework most of the usual strategies realized for sequential computation at low cost: strategies are numerous, but they are all based on a mix of a small number of different splitting mechanisms and search techniques. We can also tackle new strategies, such as the ones based on the simultaneous exploration of several sub-spaces (worlds). Finally, we consider propagation and splitting at the same level, similarly to the sequential framework of [10].

Different types of splitting mechanisms Depending on the Split agent we plug in the network, we can realize several types of splitting strategies, such as:

- splitting a domain into two (or more) domains of the same size. This is a good strategy when we consider an even probability of solution containment in each zone of the domain, or when we want to favour propagation and avoid enumeration.
- splitting a domain into one value and the rest of the domain. This strategy is also known as "labeling" or enumeration. It is generally useful in search for one solution, when performing a depth-first search, or when one assignment can significantly ease reduction.
- shaving technique: a domain is split into three sub-domains, two narrow ones to include the bounds, and one for the rest. This is especially efficient when a domain reduction function is used that can push the left and the right bounds of the interval, until a local solution is reached. Then, one can hope that the global solutions are close to the bounds.

Different types of search By changing only one agent, we can perform different kinds of search, either a usual search such as depth-first or breadth-first, or unusual searches that our framework makes possible, such as simultaneously exploring several branches.

To perform a depth-first search, the Search agent selects a single world on which variables and domain reduction functions will focus. Breadth first search is realized by letting variables and function to simultaneously work on every world they know about. Searching in several branches is similar, but the Search agent selects a subset of all the worlds that are known at a given point in time.

In depth first (or when exploring several branches), we have the possibility of changing the branch, if desired. For instance, when exploring a branch takes too long (due to slow reduction), then the Search agent can decide to jump to another branch in order to extract a solution more quickly.

Splitting before termination of propagation It is generally accepted that splitting a CSP before reaching the termination of propagation can significantly improve the resolution speed (e.g., when reduction is converging slowly [11], it is generally better to split a variable first and then reduce each sub-CSP). Our framework is generic enough to allow this type of strategy. The Split agent gets enough information from variables to analyze the convergence, and it is free to act before the end of propagation. Thus, splitting of variables can be dynamically triggered if necessary before the fixed point of propagation is reached.

7   Conclusion and Future Works

In this paper we extend the framework of [13] in order to integrate a distributed splitting mechanism. This technique has three main advantages: 1) propagation and splitting can be interleaved in order to realize complete distributed solvers, 2) agents are decoupled, and thus by changing only one agent, we can perform different kinds of search and split, and 3) splitting of variables can be dynamically triggered before the fixed point of a propagation is reached.

We plan to establish the minimal properties jointly required of the Search and the Split agents (i.e., a kind of mutual agreement) in order to be able to ensure termination. This must ensure termination even for special cases such as when several branches are simultaneously explored, search sub-spaces to be explored are changed, variables not currently being explored split, an arbitrary number of search sub-spaces split, etc.

We also plan to tackle optimization problems by using the dynamic features of **MANIFOLD** and the properties of specific Search agents. When a solution is extracted, a new constraint (i.e., its reduction functions) can be added to state that the next solution must be better than the one just extracted.

Finally, we plan to extend this framework to constraint reduction, i.e., adding, changing, and removing constraints, and thus adding, changing and removing drf's. This is crucial when considering symbolic transformation of constraints (such as simplification of constraints, and addition of redundancies that can speed-up propagation) during propagation. This will open some other forms of splitting strategies such as partioning the search space with additional constraints (e.g., $X < Y$ or $X \geq Y$).

References

1. K. R. Apt. Component-based framework for constraint programming. Manuscript, 1999.
2. K. R. Apt. The Essence of Constraint Propagation. *Theoretical Computer Science*, 221(1–2):179–210, 1999.
3. K. R. Apt. The Rough Guide to Constraint Propagation". In J. Jaffar, editor, *Proc. of the 5th International Conference on Principles and Practi ce of Constraint Programming (CP'99)*, volume 1713 of *Lecture Notes in Computer Science*, pages 1–23. Springer-Verlag, 1999. Invited lecture.
4. K. R. Apt and E. Monfroy. Automatic Generation of Constraint Propagation Algorithms for Small Finite Domains. In J. Jaffar, editor, *Proceedings of Fifth International Conference on Principles and Practice of Constraint Programming, CP'99*, volume 1713 of *Lecture Notes in Computer Science*, pages 58–72, Alexandria, Virginia, USA, October 1999.
5. F. Arbab. Coordination of massively concurrent activities. Technical Report CS–R9565, CWI, Amsterdam, The Netherlands, November 1995. Available on-line `http://www.cwi.nl/ftp/CWIreports/IS/CS-R9565.ps.Z`.
6. F. Arbab. The IWIM model for coordination of concurrent activities. In Paolo Ciancarini and Chris Hankin, editors, *Coordination Languages and Models*, volume 1061 of *Lecture Notes in Computer Science*, pages 34–56. Springer-Verlag, 1996.
7. F. Arbab. *Manifold2.0 reference manual*. CWI, Amsterdam, The Netherlands, May 1997.
8. F. Benhamou and W. Older. Applying interval arithmetic to real, integer and Boolean constraints. *Journal of Logic Programming*, 32(1):1–24, March 1997.
9. P. Codognet and D. Diaz. A simple and efficient Boolean constraint solver for constraint logic programming. *Journal of Automated Reasoning*, 17(1):97–128, 1996.
10. L. Granvilliers. Résolution approchée de contraintes réelles par transformations symboliques et consistance de bloc. *Technique et Science Informatiques*, 18(2):209–232, 1999.
11. O. Lhomme, A. Gotlieb, and M. Rueher. Dynamic Optimization of Interval Narrowing Algorithms. *Journal of Logic Programming*, 37(1–2):165–183, 1998.
12. E. Monfroy. Using "Weaker" Functions for Constraint Propagation over Real Numb ers. In J. Carroll, H. Haddad, D. Oppenheim, B. Bryant, and G. Lamont, editors, *Proceedings of The 14th ACM Symposium on Applied Computing, ACM SAC'99, Scientific Computing Track*, pages 553–559, San Antonio, Texas, USA, March 1999.
13. E. Monfroy. A Coordination-based Chaotic Iteration Algorithm for Constraint Propagation. In J. Carroll, E. Damiani, H. Haddad, and D. Oppenheim, editors, *Proceedings of the 2000 ACM Symposium on Applied Computing (SAC'2000)*, pages 262–269, Villa Olmo, Como, Italy, March 2000. ACM Press.
14. E. Monfroy and F. Arbab. *Constraints Solving as the Coordination of Inference Engines*, chapter in "Coordination of Internet Agents: Models, Technologies, and Applications". Springer-Verlag, 2000. To appear.

Law-Governed Internet Communities

Xuhui Ao, Naftaly Minsky, Thu D. Nguyen, and Victoria Ungureanu

Rutgers University, New Brunswick, NJ 08903, USA,
{ao,minsky,tdnguyen,ungurean}@cs.rutgers.edu

Abstract. We consider the problem of coordination and control of large heterogeneous groups of agents distributed over the Internet in the context of Law-Governed Interaction (LGI) [2,5]. LGI is a mode of interaction that allows a group of distributed heterogeneous agents to interact with each other with confidence that an explicitly specified policy, called the *law* of the group, is complied with by everyone in the group.

The original LGI model [5] supported only *explicit* groups, whose membership is maintained and controlled by a central server. Such a central server is necessary for applications that require each member of the group to know about the membership of the entire group. However, in the case where members do not need to know the membership of the entire group, such a central server can become an unnecessary performance bottleneck, as group size increases, as well as a single point of failure.

In this paper, we present an extension to LGI allowing it to support *implicit groups*, also called *communities*, which require no central control of any kind, and whose membership does not have to be regulated, and might not be completely known to anybody.

1 Introduction

We consider the problem of coordination and control for large heterogeneous groups of agents distributed over the Internet in the context of Law-Governed Interaction (LGI) [2,5]. LGI is a mode of interaction that allows a group of distributed heterogeneous agents to interact with each other with confidence that an explicitly specified policy, called the *law* of the group, is complied with by everyone in the group. LGI has been designed specifically to satisfy the following principles, which we consider critical for coordination in large heterogeneous systems: (1) coordination policies need to be formulated explicitly rather than being implicit in the code of the agents involved, (2) coordination policies need to be enforced, and (3) the enforcement needs to be decentralized, for scalability. LGI has been implemented in a toolkit called Moses, which has been applied to a broad range of coordination and control applications, including: on-line reconfiguration of distributed systems [6], security [4], and electronic commerce [3].

A group of agents interacting via LGI under a given law $\mathcal{L}$ is called an $\mathcal{L}$-group. LGI distinguishes between two kinds of $\mathcal{L}$-groups, called *explicit* and *implicit* groups, that differ in the manner in which a group is deployed and in the management of its membership. Explicit groups have been discussed in detail in [5]. The purpose of this paper is to introduce implicit groups, also called

A. Porto and G.-C. Roman (Eds.): COORDINATION 2000, LNCS 1906, pp. 133–147, 2000.

communities, which are more general than explicit ones, and more suitable for very large groups of heterogeneous agents operating over the Internet.

Currently, an explicit $\mathcal{L}$-group $\mathcal{G}$ is established in Moses by creating a distinguished agent called the *secretary* of $\mathcal{G}$, denoted as $\mathcal{S}_\mathcal{G}$, and defining into it the law $\mathcal{L}$, and specifying the initial membership and structure of $\mathcal{G}$. Subsequent to its initialization, $\mathcal{S}_\mathcal{G}$ serves as a "gateway" to the group by admitting new members into it, subject to law $\mathcal{L}$. $\mathcal{S}_\mathcal{G}$ also functions as a name-server for the group, helping members to find each other's location, and to verify mutual memberships in the same group.

Such a secretary is necessary whenever the entire membership of the group needs to be known, and it is appropriate for relatively small groups. This is the case, for example, for a group operating under a token-ring protocol, where the structure of the group, i.e., the placement of its members along a ring and the existence of a single token among the members of the ring, are essential to protocol. This ring structure can be defined by the secretary of the group as its initial state, and, as demonstrated in [6], can be maintained as an invariant, even if the membership of the group is allowed to change dynamically.

But such group management is neither necessary nor appropriate where no knowledge of the entire group membership is required, or available, and where the size of the group is too large to be comfortably handled by a single secretary. An everyday example for such a situation is provided by the group of all car drivers in a given city. All these drivers must obey the traffic laws of the city, but generally there is nobody that knows the names of all these drivers, or their total membership. Such conditions are becoming increasingly common in modern distributed computing, as is illustrated by the following example.

Consider a distributed set of databases servers that provides access to an heterogeneous set of clients. Suppose that for a client to consult an item in a database or to update it, it needs to lock the item first. It is possible for a single agent to maintain locks for several items (at several databases) at a time. It is well known that this activity would be *serializable* if the following kind of two-phase locking (TPL) protocol is strictly observed by all clients [10]:

> New locks cannot be acquired after the first release of a lock (until the agent has released all locks that it currently holds). That is, each transaction (representing some set of changes) is divided into two phases: a *growing phase* of locking, and a *shrinking phase* of releasing locks. A locked resource can be used during both phases.

While this protocol can be enforced by a *central coordinator* that mediates the interaction between the distributed set of servers and their clients, such coordination would be quite unscalable. Under LGI, on the other hand, this protocol can be formulated as a law $\mathcal{TPL}$ that is enforced locally at each client, allowing for scalability, provided that the set of servers and their clients is not maintained as an *explicit* $\mathcal{TPL}$-group. Because the number of clients in this case might be very large, the requirement that each of them enters the group via a single secretary would create a bottleneck and a dangerous single point of failure. Moreover, the maintenance of an explicit group seems quite unnecessary here: none of the agents in this case needs to know the membership of the entire $\mathcal{TPL}$-group. In fact, the clients can be quite oblivious to the very existence of other clients.

Our concept of implicit groups, or communities, has been designed to deal with this kind of siltation. Broadly speaking, a community operating under law $\mathcal{L}$—or, an $\mathcal{L}$-community—is defined as the set of all agents that happen to be operating under law $\mathcal{L}$. Such a community is never formally established and there is no formal admission into it. Anybody can become a member of this community, simply by adopting the law $\mathcal{L}$ when using LGI.

While agents operating in an implicit group may not need to know the membership of the entire group, they still need to interact with one another—this, after all, is the purpose of a community. Thus, to support implicit groups, we need to provide the following capabilities (which for an explicit groups are provided by its secretary): (a) means for an agent operating under law $\mathcal{L}$ to ensure that its interlocutors are also operating under $\mathcal{L}$, i.e., that they indeed belong to the same community, (b) a convenient naming scheme that assigns a unique name to each member of an $\mathcal{L}$-community, and (c) means for supplying certain agents in an $\mathcal{L}$-community with *exclusive* privileges. The importance of these capabilities, and the manner in which we have extended LGI to provide for them, is described in this paper.

The remainder of the paper is organized as follows. In Section 2, we give a brief description of LGI and discuss how agents can join an $\mathcal{L}$-community and how they can name and locate each other. In Section 3, we describe how certificates can be used to supply certain agents in an $\mathcal{L}$-community with exclusive privileges. We conclude the paper in Section 4.

2   Law-Governed Community

2.1   Law Governed Interaction – An Overview

LGI is a mode of interaction that allows a group of distributed heterogeneous agents to interact with each other with confidence that an explicitly specified policy, called the *law* of the group, is complied with by everyone in the group. We call such a group of agents a community, or more specifically, an $\mathcal{L}$-community, where $\mathcal{L}$ is the law of the community. LGI does not assume any knowledge about the structure and behavior of the members of a given $\mathcal{L}$-community: LGI only deals with the interaction between these agents. However, LGI does maintain some state for each member of the community, which is called the *control-state*. Such per-agent states enable the law to differentiate between specific agents, and to be sensitive to changes in their states, which are, themselves, subject to the law. The control-state, whose semantics for a given community is defined by its law, could represent such things as the role of an agent, various kinds of privileges and tokens it carries, and dynamic identification of the state of computations in which the agent is involved.

The Concept of Law: The *law* $\mathcal{L}$ of a community is an *explicit and enforced* set of "rules of engagement" between members of this community, regulating the interaction between them via what we call $\mathcal{L}$-messages. More specifically, the law of a community $\mathcal{C}$ regulates certain types of events occurring at members of $\mathcal{C}$, mandating the effect that any such event should have; this mandate is called the *ruling* of the law for a given event. In LGI, events subjected to regulation include message *sends* and *receipts* of $\mathcal{L}$-messages, the *coming due of an obligation* previously imposed on a given object. One additional type of event regulated under LGI will be introduced in this paper.

The ruling of the law for a given event can involve the execution of *operations*, called *primitive operations*. LGI currently support primitive operations for testing the control-state of an agent and for its update, operations on messages, and some others – a sample of primitive operations (written in Prolog) is presented in Figure 1.

Operations on the control-state	
`t@CS`	returns true if term `t` is present in the control state, and fails otherwise
`+t`	adds term `t` to the control state;
`-t`	removes term `t` from the control state;
`t1←t2`	replaces term `t1` with term `t2`;
`incr(t(v),d)`	increments the value of the parameter `v` of term `t` with quantity `d`
`dcr(t(v),d)`	decrements the value of the parameter `v` of term `t` with quantity `d`

Operations on messages	
forward(x,m,y)	sends message `m` from `x` to `y`; triggers at `y` an `arrived` `(x,m,y)` event
deliver(x,m,y)	delivers the message `m` from `x` to agent `y`

Fig. 1. Some primitive operations in LGI

Generally speaking then, a law $\mathcal{L}$ regulates the exchange of $\mathcal{L}$-messages between members of an $\mathcal{L}$-community based on the control-states of the participants. Furthermore, it can mandate side effects for message-exchanges such as the modification of the control-states of the sender and/or receiver of a message, and the emission of extra messages (for monitoring purposes, say).

On The Local Enforceability of Laws: Although the law $\mathcal{L}$ of a community $\mathcal{C}$ is *global* in that it governs the interaction between all members of $\mathcal{C}$, it is enforceable *locally* at each member of $\mathcal{C}$ because:

- $\mathcal{L}$ only regulates local events at individual agents,
- the ruling of $\mathcal{L}$ for an event e at agent x depends only on e and the local control-state $\mathcal{CS}_x$ of x.
- The ruling of $\mathcal{L}$ at x can mandate only local operations to be carried out at x, such as an update of $\mathcal{CS}_x$, the forwarding of a message from x to some other agent, and the imposition of an obligation on x.

The fact that a law is enforced at all agents of a community gives LGI its necessary global scope, establishing a *common* set of ground rules for all members of C and providing them with the ability to trust each other, in spite of the heterogeneity of the community. The locality of law enforcement, however, critically enables LGI to scale with community size.

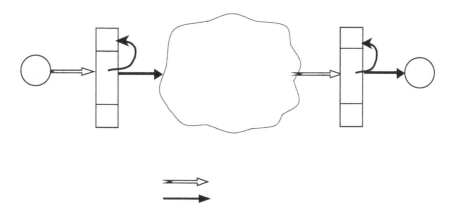

Fig. 2. Law enforcement in Moses.

On the Current Implementation of LGI, via Moses: We have implemented LGI via the *Moses* toolkit. In Moses, laws are written as Prolog programs and the law L of an L-community C is enforced by a set of trusted agents called *controllers*, which mediate the exchange of L-messages between members of C. Each member x of C must request some controller to maintain its control-state C_x and enforce L on its behalf. Figure 2 illustrates law enforcement in Moses, where controllers are logically placed between the members of C and the communication medium.

A controller is *generic* in that it can interpret and enforce any well formed law. In the current implementation, a controller operates as an independent process and may be placed on the same machine as its clients or on some remote machine. To help agents locate and contact controllers, we have implemented a *controller-naming* server, which maintains a set of available controllers. To be effective, for a widely distributed environment (such as the Internet), this set of controllers need to be well dispersed geographically, so that it would be possible to find a controller reasonably close to any prospective client.

2.2   Engaging in an L-Community

For an agent x to be able to exchange L-messages with other members of an L-community, it must: (a) find an LGI controller, and (b) notify this controller that it wants to use it, under law L. We will discuss these two steps below, and then explain how and why x can trust its interlocutors to observe the same law L.

Locating an LGI Controller: As already discussed, the Moses toolkit includes a controller-naming server, which can be used to maintain a set of active controllers. This server provides the address (host and port) of the available controllers to any agent that wishes to engage in LGI. One may have any number of such servers so that controllers can be distributed in different regions of the Internet. Efficiency-wise, x would do best by selecting a controller closest to it (to minimize the overhead of forwarding $\mathcal{L}$-messages through the controller). But functionally, one is free to choose a controller anywhere on the Internet, and several agents may share a single controller, without knowing of each other.

Adopting a law: Upon selecting a controller C, x would send C the message

    `adopt(law,name),`

where `law` is the law that it wants to adopt, and `name` is the name that it wants to be known by. The argument `law` can take the form of either the text of the law to be adopted or the name of such a law, given to it by a specified *law-repository* service, which is another tool provided by Moses—we will not discuss here the details of this service but rather assume that the text of the entire law is always passed to the controller.

When controller C receives the `adopt` message, it checks the supplied law for syntactic validity, and the chosen name for uniqueness among the names of all current agents handled by C. If these two conditions are satisfied, and if C is not already loaded to capacity, it will set up a starting control-state for agent x, as specified in the preamble of the law adopted by x, allowing x to start operating under this law[1].

The basis for trust between members of a community: The point of adopting a given law is to be able to interact with other agents operating under it. For this, one needs to be able to locate such agents—which will be discussed in the next section – and one needs to be able to trust its interlocutors to operate under the same law. More specifically, one needs the following assurances: (a) that the exchange of $\mathcal{L}$-messages is mediated by controllers interpreting the *same law* $\mathcal{L}$; and (b) that all these controllers are *correctly implemented*. If these two conditions are satisfied, then it follows that if y receives an $\mathcal{L}$-message from some x, this message must have been sent as an $\mathcal{L}$-message. In other words, $\mathcal{L}$-messages cannot be forged.

To ensure that a message forwarded by a controller C_x under law $\mathcal{L}$ would be handled by another controller C_y operating under the *same* law, C_x appends a hash H of law $\mathcal{L}$ to the message it forwards to C_y. (The hash of the law is obtained using one way functions that transform any string into a considerably smaller bits sequence with high probability that two strings will not collide [7,9].) C_y would accept this as a valid $\mathcal{L}$-message under $\mathcal{L}$ if and only if H is identical to the hash of its own law.

---

[1] If any one of these conditions is not satisfied, then x would receive an appropriate diagnostic, and will be able to try again.

With respect to the correctness of the controllers, if an agent is not concerned with malicious violations, then it can trust a controller provided by our controller-naming service, or a controller provided by the operating system—just like we often trust various standard services on the Internet, such as DNS and gateways. When malicious violations are a concern, however, the validity of controllers and of the host on which they operate needs to be certified. In this case, the controller-naming service needs to operate as a *certifying authority* for controllers. Furthermore, messages sent across the network must be digitally signed by the sending controller, and the signature must be verified by the receiving controller, allowing the two controllers to trust each other. Such secure inter-controller interaction has been implemented in Moses ([3]).

2.3   Naming within a Community

As already mentioned, when an agent joins a community, it must have a way of *naming* and *locating* other members of the community. After all, one joins a community only if one wishes to interact with some of its members. In the case of an explicit group, where there is a server, called secretary, that maintains group membership, then naming is easy. The secretary simply acts as a naming and locating service, negotiating with agents wishing to join the group in order for each agent to have a unique name within that group. In the case of a community, however, there is no such server. Thus, we need to develop a naming scheme to support communities.

In a distributed environment like the Internet, any naming scheme must meet the following requirements: (1) it must be possible to locally choose names that are globally unique, and (2) given a name, it must be possible (and easy) to locate the controller of the named agent

In addition, it would be convenient if names are human readable, selectable and well organized (so that we can easily understand names and not require translations from the machine representation to a human-parsable representation).

To satisfy the above requirements, we use a naming scheme that is very similar to current e-mail addressing. In our scheme,

```
memberName = localName@domainName
```

where **domainName** is the Internet host name of the controller of the agent and **localName** is the name negotiated between the agent and its controller when the agent first adopted the law of the community at its controller. Since **localName** is unique to the controller and the controller's host name is unique in the Internet, we can be sure that the whole name is globally unique.

Note that this simple naming scheme satisfies all of our requirements. Choosing a name is entirely a local operation between an agent and its controller. Yet, because we are leveraging the globally unique host names of controllers, a name that is chosen locally is guaranteed to be unique globally. Given an agent's name such as **bill@athos.rutgers.edu**, we simply leverage the already existing DNS service to locate the server `athos.rutgers.edu`. Finally, these names are certainly human readable—in fact, they are very familiar because current users already use this naming scheme every day for e-mail.

Since the member name of a community is globally unique, one can have a bunch of community name servers all over the Internet to publish the member names of the community. So one agent can easily locate other members in that community.

2.4   The $\mathcal{TPL}$ Law — An Example

To illustrate the nature of $\mathcal{L}$-communities , and the structure of their laws, we now show how the two phase locking (TPL) policy introduced informally in Section 1 can be formalized into a law, called $\mathcal{TPL}$ and specified in Figure 3. The rules of this law are followed by comments (in italic), which, together with the following discussion, should provide the reader with some understanding of the nature of LGI laws. Besides its rules, every law under LGI has a *preamble* that contains an `initialCS([...])` clause, specifying the initial control state of every agent that adopts this law. The preamble may also contain other types of clauses, one of which will be discussed in the following section.

Under this particular law, all new agents start with an empty control-state, and are, thus, indistinguishable from each other. But any agent can designate itself as a *server*, simply by sending a message `role(server)` to itself; which, by Rule $\mathcal{R}1$, would cause the term `server` to be added to its control-state. (In the following section, we will present constraints on such self appointments.) We also note here that under this law, a term `shrinking` is added to the control state of an agent x the first time it issues a request to unlock a resource, to record that it entered the second phase of a transaction (the *growing* phase is designated by the absence of the `shrinking` term in the control state). We will now discuss how resources can be locked under this law, how they can be used, and finally, how they are unlocked.

First, by Rule $\mathcal{R}2$, if a client x issues a request to `lock` a resource r, then this message is forwarded to the destination server s only if x has not yet entered in the shrinking phase. Also a term `lock(r,s,pending)` is added to the control state of x, to record that x has issued a `lock` request for r. Now, if the resource is available, the server s is expected to respond with a `locked(r)` message, which it can do by Rule $\mathcal{R}7$. When x receives such a message, then, by Rule $\mathcal{R}3$, the term `lock(r,s,pending)` is replaced by a term `lock(r,s,granted)`.

Once one has the term `lock(r,s,granted)` in its control-state, indicating a lock over resource r, one can, by Rule $\mathcal{R}4$, send service requests to s for this resource. Note that the response of the server to such a request is left unregulated by this law.

A client x may release any resource r that it previously locked, by sending an `unlock(r)` message to the server s managing r. Such messages are regulated by Rule $\mathcal{R}5$ which mandates that the corresponding `lock` term is to be removed from the control state of x. Also, if this is done during the growing phase, i.e., when the `shrinking` term is absent form the control-state of x, then the `shrinking` term is added, indicating the beginning of the shrinking phase. Finally, if r was the last resource hold by x then, the term shrinking is removed from the control state, thus allowing x to start a new transaction, in its growing phase.

Note that Rule $\mathcal{R}6$ allow servers to receive arbitrary messages. Although servers do not provide here any specific control, the very fact that they use $\mathcal{TPL}$-messages to communicate with their clients, forces agents that want to be their clients to use the same law, which is what ensures that policy TPL is satisfied.

Discussion: We end this description of law $\mathcal{TPL}$ with two additional comments. First, the capacity of LGI to provide control at the *client side* is essential for the implementation of this protocol. Pushing enforcement on the *server side*, like conventional mechanisms do, would make the support of this protocol very difficult, if at all possible in the case considered here, where servers are distributed and may belong to possible different administrative domains. Such an implementation would require each server to know what resources, if any, the agent locked from other servers in the past, and even what it is requesting from them concurrently.

Second, the correctness of two phase locking protocol rests on the assumption that at any given time only one client may hold a lock on a resource. $\mathcal{TPL}$ law does not attempt to regulate lock management, thus implicitly trusting the servers to respond correctly to lock messages. Since there are no restrictions on becoming a server, such assumption is appropriate, only when one trusts all agents to be non-malicious and bug-free. We will see in the next Section how this over-reliance on the correct behavior of agents can be removed.

3   Making Some Agents More Equal than Others

An important (but not always desirable) property of communities under LGI as described so far is that they are intrinsically *egalitarian*. That is, it is not possible to endow certain agents of a community with *exclusive privileges*.

The need for such exclusive privileges is evident from our locking example. Law $\mathcal{TPL}$ allows anybody to become a server, simply by sending the role(server) message to itself—which everybody is allowed to do by Rule $\mathcal{R}1$, and which causes a server term to be added to the control-state of the sender. But since servers must be trusted to actually lock resources upon a valid request, it would be useful to be able to allow only certain trusted agents to play this role.

For further illustration of the need to provide some agents with more power than others, consider the following elaboration of our example. Suppose that for the sake of load balancing or security or both, we would like to introduce *brokers* into our $\mathcal{TPL}$-community to mediate between the clients and the servers. Under the revised community, to be governed by law $\mathcal{TPL}'$ (introduced below), a client would need a broker's referral to a server in order to use it; and each broker is to be responsible for a subset of servers. Under law $\mathcal{TPL}'$, a broker is to be

---

$\mathcal{P}$*reamble:*
      initialCS([]).

   The initial control state of all members is empty.

$\mathcal{R}$1. `sent(X,role(server),_) :- do(+server).`

   Under this law an agent can act a server—i.e., have a term `server` *in its initial control state—simply by sending a message* `role(server)`.

$\mathcal{R}$2. `sent(C,lock(R),S) :- !shrinking@CS,`
            `do(forward),`
            `do(+lock(R,S,pending)).`

   A message to lock resource `R` *is forwarded to its destination, only if the sender* `C` *is not in the shrinking phase. Also a term* `lock(R,S,pending)`, *denoting the pending status of this request, is added to the control state of* `C`.

$\mathcal{R}$3. `arrived(S,locked(R),C)`
          `:- do(lock(R,S,pending) ←lock(R,S,granted)),`
             `do(deliver).`

   If lock for resource `R` *is granted to an agent* `C` *then a term* `lock(R,S, pending)` *is replaced by* `lock(R,S,granted)` *to record that the lock has been acquired for* `R`. *The message then is delivered to the agent itself, in order to keep it informed.*

$\mathcal{R}$4. `sent(C, request(R,Param),S) :- lock(R,S,granted)@CS,`
            `do(forward).`

   A request by client `C` *regarding resource* `R` *is forwarded to server* `S` *only if the lock for* `R` *has been granted by* `S` *to* `C` .

$\mathcal{R}$5. `sent(C, unlock(R),S) :- lock(R,S,granted)@CS,`
            `do(-lock(R,S,_)),`
            `(!shrinking@CS →do(+shrinking);true),`
            `(!lock(_,_,_)@CS →do(-shrinking);true),`
            `do(forward).`

   An unlock request is forwarded if the sender currently hold this lock; also, the correspondent `lock` *term is removed from the control state of the issuer. If this agent is not yet in its shrinking phase, it enters this phase by adding the term* `shrinking` *to its CS; and if* `R` *is the last locked resource held by* `C`, *the term* `shrinking` *is removed.*

$\mathcal{R}$6. `arrived(C,M,S) :- server@CS,`
            `do(deliver).`

   Any message that arrives at a server is delivered, without further ado.

$\mathcal{R}$7. `sent(S,locked(R),C) :- server@CS,`
            `do(forward).`

   `locked(R)` *messages sent by a server are forwarded without further ado.*

Fig. 3. Law $\mathcal{TPL}$ ensuring serializability of transactions

designated as such by the term **broker** in its control-state, and we will see later how such designation provides one with the power implied by it. What concerns us here, given the sensitive role played by brokers in this community, is how one can designate only selected agents as brokers, not allowing anybody else to play this role. The problem is that such exclusivity cannot be ensured for implicit groups under LGI, as described so far. The reason for this is given below.

Since all members of an implicit community C start with identical control-state, the only way for an agent x to gain an exclusive status under the law of its community is as follows: x must be the only agent capable of having a certain term, such as broker, to be added to its control-state during its lifetime. But the addition of a new term to the CS of x, is, by definition, the consequence of some sequence of interactions between the members of a subgroup G of C, which contains x. But if this is possible, then there can be nothing to prevent C to have another subgroup G', equivalent to G, which could add the term broker to the control-state of some agent x', violating exclusivity.

We now show how this equality-under-the-law of implicit communities under the present LGI can be broken by appealing to outside authorities via the well known concept of *certificates*.

3.1   The Role of Certificates in Distributed Systems

Computing over the Internet increasingly involves interaction between agents that are physically distant and have no knowledge of each others. As pointed out in [1], "such parties need to establish some trust in each other by receiving references from trusted intermediaries." Such intermediaries are often called *certifying authorities* (CAs), or simply *authorities*, and the references they produce are called *certificates*.

A certificate [8] is a four-tuple

$$\langle issuer, subject, attributes, signature \rangle$$

where, *issuer* is the public-key of the CA that issued and signed this certificate, *subject* is the public-key of the principal that is the subject of this certificate, *attributes* is what is being certified about the *subject*, and *signature* is the digital signature of this certificate by the *issuer*. Note that the *attributes* field is essentially a list of (attribute, value) pairs, represented here as a list of attribute(value) terms. For example, the attributes of a certificate might be the list [name(johnDoe), role(manager)], asserting that the name of the subject in question is JohnDoe and his role in this community is a manager.

3.2   Using Certificates to Get Exclusive Privileges Under LGI

We now describe how a member of an $\mathcal{L}$-community C can obtain exclusive privileges and status by presenting a certificate issued by some outside authority. The degree of control over a given community thus provided to an authority outside of it is determined by the law of this community. That is, (a) it is the law of a community that determines the authorities whose certificates are acceptable to the community, and (b) the law determines the effect that a given certificate may have.

Submitting Certificates. Consider an agent x that has a certificate c from an authority u. We have extended Moses with two Java methods that x can use for submitting a certificate to its controller C_x.

The first method is for submitting what we call a *self-certificate*: a self-certificate submitted by x is one where the *subject* field is a public-key whose private counterpart is held by x itself. Such a certificate states something about its holder, such as the role he should be playing in a community. To submit such a certificate, x would use the following method:

```
sendSelfCertificate(c, sig),
```

where c is the certificate to be sent, presumably signed by some authority u, and sig is a digital signature generated by x itself, using the private counterpart of the public-key provided in the subject-field of c. This signature is used by the controller to validate that the agent it serves is in fact the subject of the presented certificate.

The second method is for the case where the subject of certificate c is *not* x himself. Such a certificate can be submitted to the controller via the method

```
sendCertificate(c),
```

requiring no digital signature by the sender.

Specifying Acceptable Certifying Authorities. Of course, not every certifying authority would (nor should) be acceptable to a given community. Those that are acceptable, if any, can be specified in the law using clauses of the form:

```
authority(name, publicKey),
```

where name provides a convenient id for this authority within the law and publicKey provides a cryptographic identification for this authority to be used for verifying its signatures. Such clauses can be included in the *"preamble"* of the law, as in Figure 4. The set of all such clauses is called the *initial authority table* of the law. This is only an initial table, because LGI provides means for dynamically adding authorities to the authority table of an agent. (But space limitation prevents us from discussing these means and their use.)

Specifying the Effect of a Valid Certificate. The submission of a certificate c by an agent x operating under law $\mathcal{L}$ to a controller C_x triggers the following sequence of events. First, an attempt is made to confirm that c is a valid certificate, duly signed by an authority that is acceptable to law $\mathcal{L}$, i.e., an authority that is represented in the authority table of the agent. An exception event is triggered if the certificate cannot be confirmed.

Second, if the confirmed c is a self-certificate, then an attempt is made to confirm the signature of x on it. An exception event is triggered if this signature is not confirmed.

Third, if no exception has been triggered thus far during the processing of c, then the following event would be triggered:

```
certified(X, certificate(issuer(I), subject(Y), attributes(A))),
```

where X is the agent who presented the certificate, I is the the local name (in the authority table under this law) of the issuer of the certificate, and A is the list of attributes of the certificates. As to parameter Y of this event, we need to distinguish between two cases: if c is a self-certificate, then Y is equal to X; otherwise, Y should be the public-key of the subject of this certificate.

Finally, what happens once the **certified** event is triggered depends entirely on the law in question. For example, in the case of law $\mathcal{TPL}'$ (see Figure 4), if an agent x sends a self-certificate

$$\langle issuer, subject, [role(broker)], signature \rangle$$

to his controller and if this certificate is duly signed by the certifying authority called **authority** in this law, then event:

```
certified(x, certificate(issuer(authority),

        subject(x), attributes([role(broker)]))),
```

will be triggered. Given Rule $\mathcal{R}8$, this event will result in the insertion of the term **broker** into x's control-state. The effect of such certification on a community is illustrated by the following refinement of our $\mathcal{TPL}$ law.

$\mathcal{TPL}'$: A Revision of the $\mathcal{TPL}$. Law A revision of the $\mathcal{TPL}$ law which supports brokers is displayed in Figure 4. This revision consist of (a) two **authority**-clauses, that define the initial authority table of the law; (b) replacement of Rules $\mathcal{R}1$, $\mathcal{R}2$ of $\mathcal{TPL}$ with Rule $\mathcal{R}1'$, $\mathcal{R}2'$; and (c) three new rules.

To understand this law, first note that by Rule $\mathcal{R}2'$, a lock request will be forwarded only if the destination server is recorded in the **serverList** term in the control-state of the requesting client. Now, every member starts with an empty **serverList** in its control-state. And only an agent having a term **broker** can add names of servers to this list (see Rule $\mathcal{R}9$ and $\mathcal{R}10$). This is what gives agents with a term **broker** their privileged role. The issue to be considered next is how does one appoint a specific agent to this role.

By Rule $\mathcal{R}8$, an agent can become a broker by presenting a certificate signed by one of the two authorities recognized by this law, which assert the right of the presenter to be a broker. Thus, one needs an authorization by a recognized authority to become a broker under this law. Similarly, an agent can act as a server only when presenting an appropriate certificate attesting its role (Rule $\mathcal{R}1'$).

4 Conclusion

Distributed computing on the Internet increasingly involves coordinating large groups of heterogeneous agents. This coordination is only possible if such agents have a credible basis for trusting each other. Under LGI such trust is established

$\mathcal{P}$reamble:

    authority(serverAuthority, publicKey).

    authority(brokerAuthority, publicKey').

    initialCS(serverList([])).

    The authorities recognized by this law are: `serverAuthority` *and* `brokerAuthority`.

    The initial control state of a member contains an empty server list.

$\mathcal{R}1'$.

```
certified(X,certificate(issuer(serverAuthority),subject(X),
        attributes([role(server)]))) :-
        do(+server).
```

If an agent presents a certificate signed by `serverAuthority` *asserting that it has the role of server, then the term* `server` *is added to its control state.*

$\mathcal{R}2'$.

```
sent(C,lock(R),S) :-
        serverList(SL)@CS, member(S,SL),
        !shrinking@CS,
        do(forward), do(+lock(R,S,pending)).
```

A message to lock resource R *is forwarded to its destination, only if the sender* C *is not in the shrinking phase, and if the destination is in the* `serverList` *of the sender.*

$\mathcal{R}8$.
```
certified(X,certificate(issuer(brokerAuthority),subject(X),
        attributes([role(broker)]))) :-
        do(+broker).
```

If an agent presents a certificate signed by `brokerAuthority` *asserting that it has the role of broker, then the term* `broker` *is added to its control state.*

$\mathcal{R}9$.
```
sent(B,assignServer(S),C) :- broker@CS,
        do(forward).
```

Only a broker can assign a server to a client C.

$\mathcal{R}10$.

```
arrived(B,assignServer(S),C) :-
        do(serverList(SL) <- serverList([S|SL])),
        do(deliver).
```

The arrival of the message `assignServer(S)` *to a client* C *causes the* `serverList` *of* C *to be appended with* S.

Fig. 4. $\mathcal{TPL}'$: a revision of the $\mathcal{TPL}$ law of Two-Phase-Locking

by imposing a single law over all members of the group. In this paper we extend the LGI mechanism by introducing a concept of *implicit groups*, or *communities*, whose membership is left uncontrolled, and which require no central management of any kind. Specifically, we have discussed how an agent can join a community by adopting its law, how agents can name and locate each other, and how agents can use certificates and certifying authorities to acquire exclusive privileges.

References

1. A. Herzberg, Y. Mass, J. Mihaeli, D. Naor, and Y. Ravid. Access control meets public key infrastructure, or: Assigning roles to strangers. In *Proceedings of the 2000 IEEE Symposium on Security and Privacy*, 2000.

2. N.H. Minsky and V. Ungureanu. Regulated coordination in open distributed systems. In David Garlan and Daniel Le Metayer, editors, *Proc. of Coordination'97: Second International Conference on Coordination Models and Languages; LNCS 1282*, pages 81–98, September 1997.

3. N.H. Minsky and V. Ungureanu. A mechanism for establishing policies for electronic commerce. In *The 18th International Conference on Distributed Computing Systems (ICDCS)*, pages 322–331, May 1998.

4. N.H. Minsky and V. Ungureanu. Unified support for heterogeneous security policies in distributed systems. In *7th USENIX Security Symposium*, January 1998.

5. N.H. Minsky and V. Ungureanu. Law-governed interaction: a coordination and control mechanism for heterogeneous distributed systems. *TOSEM, ACM Transactions on Software Engineering and Methodology*, 2000. (to be published, and currently available through `http://www.cs.rutgers.edu/~minsky/`).

6. N.H. Minsky, V. Ungureanu, W. Wang, and J. Zhang. Building reconfiguration primitives into the law of a system. In *Proc. of the Third International Conference on Configurable Distributed Systems (ICCDS'96)*, March 1996. (available through `http://www.cs.rutgers.edu/~minsky/`).

7. R. Rivest. The MD5 message digest algorithm. Technical report, MIT, April 1992. RFC 1320.

8. R. Rivest and B. Lampson. SDSI-a simple distributed security infrastructure. Technical report, MIT, 1996. http://theory.lcs.mit.edu/~rivest/sdsi.ps.

9. B. Schneier. *Applied Cryptography*. John Wiley and Sons, 1996.

10. A. Tanenbaum. *Distributed Operating Systems*. Prentice Hall, 1995.

Reconfiguration of Software Architecture Styles with Name Mobility

Dan Hirsch[1] *, Paola Inverardi[2] **, and Ugo Montanari[3] ***

[1] Departamento de Computación, Universidad de Buenos Aires,
Ciudad Universitaria, Pab.I, 1428, Buenos Aires, Argentina
dhirsch@dc.uba.ar
[2] Dipartamento Di Matematica, Universitá dell'Aquila,
Via Vetoio, Localita' Coppito, L'Aquila, Italia
inverard@univaq.it
[3] Dipartimento di Informatica, Universitá di Pisa,
Corso Italia 40, I-56125, Pisa, Italia
ugo@di.unipi.it

Abstract. An important issue in the area of software architecture is the specification of reconfiguration and mobility of systems. This paper presents an approach for the specification of software architecture styles using hyperedge replacement systems and for their dynamic reconfiguration using constraint solving. A system architecture is represented as a graph where edges are components and nodes are ports of communication. Then, a style is represented as a graph grammar where the instances of the style are the graphs generated by the corresponding grammar. The construction and dynamic evolution of the style are represented as context-free productions and graph rewriting. To model reconfigurations we allow the declaration, creation and matching of new nodes (i.e. ports of communication) and use constraint solving over the productions of the style grammar for achieving synchronization. In this way complex evolutions can be specified in a more expressive and compact form than using π-calculus style languages for mobility.

1 Introduction

An important issue in the area of software architecture is the specification of reconfiguration and mobility of systems. In [5,6] we presented a first approach for the specification of software architecture styles using hyperedge replacement

---

* Partially supported by ARTES Project, PIC 11-00000-01856, ANPCyT, TW72, UBACyT.
** Partially supported by MURST project *Software Architectures and Languages to Coordinate Distributed Mobile Components.*
*** Partially supported by CNR Projects *Metodi per Sistemi Connessi mediante Reti* and GNIM *N*uovi Paradigmi di Calcolo: Linguaggi e Modelli; by MURST project *Theory of Concurrency* and *Higher Order and Types;* by TMR Network GET-GRATS; and by Esprit Working Groups *APPLIGRAPH* and *COORDINA.*

A. Porto and G.-C. Roman (Eds.): COORDINATION 2000, LNCS 1906, pp. 148–163, 2000.

systems and constraint solving to specify styles and their evolution. A system architecture is represented as a graph where hyperedges are components and nodes are ports of communication. Then, a style is represented as a hyperedge graph grammar where the instances of the style are the graphs generated by the corresponding grammar. The construction and dynamic evolution of the style are represented as *context-free* productions and graph rewriting.

To model evolution we used graph rewriting combined with constraint solving allowing to specify how components will evolve and communicate. Constraint productions are used to coordinate the dynamic evolution of the system. This is done by using constraints on ports to represent communications between components. This technique was first applied in [2,15,16] for distributed systems. In order to evolve, one component may need to synchronize with adjacent components on some port. If they agree, then all of them can evolve. This is modeled by a two phased approach where, context-free productions (a set for each component type) are equipped with synchronization conditions for each of the possible moves. After that, context-sensitive rewriting rules are obtained by combining some context-free productions in such a way that they agree on the shared ports (this is called *the rule-matching problem*) [1]. Applying one of these context-sensitive rules, allows for the evolution of a subpart of the system consisting of several components. Applying the rule means making all such processes (and not a proper subset of them) evolve, each with one of its context-free productions.

This method let us represent styles and their dynamic evolution, but with a limited ability to express the complex reconfigurations that real systems may experience. In this paper we investigate how to enhance the method to specify reconfigurations of a style. Here we allow the declaration, creation and matching of new nodes (i.e. ports of communication) and use constraint solving over the productions of the style grammar for synchronization. In this way complex evolutions can be specified in a more expressive and compact form than using π-calculus style languages for mobility. The formal definition of synchronized edge replacement in terms of logical sequents and inference rules is new. It allows for a compact and clear presentation of an otherwise cumbersome material.

As related work on using graph transformations for software architecture reconfiguration we can mention [9], where a dual approach is taken using a central coordinator for dynamic evolution (opposite to the self organising approach [12] we take). Also, the dynamic changes modeled in [9] must satisfy the original style, while we do not consider the problem here and approach it differently in [3,4]. Other works are [22] and [20] where reconfigurations are modeled by the categorical notion of pushout [18]. In [22] a program design language (COMMU-NITY) is used to represent program states and computations, and algebraic graph rewriting is employed for architecture reconfigurations. In [20] distributed graph transformation for dynamic change management is applied. These approaches also handle reconfiguration via transformation rules but they are based on general graph rewriting rules and thus assume a global, centralized control driving reconfigurations. Other related work on architectural reconfiguration and dynamics are [11], [13] and [17]. In [11] some features for dynamic architectures are analyzed based on the language Darwin used for specification of distributed system structure; [13] discusses the compositional specification and behavior analysis of dynamic changes of software architectures; and [17] investigates the role of connectors in supporting the runtime modification of software architectures.

Our proposed method is analogous to π-calculus [14], but with the advantage of the graphical, distributed approach which allows for multiple synchronizations in one step (instant reconfiguration). In our setting, name mobility means that the structure of the reconfigured system can be as tightly connected as needed.

The increased expressiveness is achieved while keeping the simplicity of context free descriptions for the behavior of each component and connector, and implementing the coordination policies through the synchronization and constraint mechanism at the production application level. This seems to be a nice way to express, synthetically but explicitly coordination specification at the architectural level.

2   Edge Replacement Systems and Syntactic Judgements

In this section we introduce the notions of graphs and synchronized edge replacement adding to it the capability of name creation and mobility. We formalize these notions as well formed syntactic judgements generated from a set of axioms and inference rules, allowing to model in a simple way the synchronization and reconfiguration of graphs. Also, using judgements to represent graphs and their rewriting will be useful for analyzing different synchronization policies and the expressive power of the approach. For an extensive presentation on the foundations of graph transformation we refer to [18].

2.1   Graphs

A *hyperedge*, or simply an edge, is an atomic item with a label (from a ranked alphabet $LE = \{LE_n\}_{n=0,1,...}$) and with as many (ordered) tentacles as the rank of its label. A set of *nodes* together with a set of such edges forms a *hypergraph* (or simply a *graph*) if each edge is connected, by its tentacles, to its *attachment* nodes. Graphs are considered in this paper up to isomorphism.

Here we represent graphs as *syntactic judgements* (or simply judgements) of the form

$$\Gamma \vdash G,$$

where G is a term containing the edges of the graph and $\Gamma \subseteq N$ is a set of names (out of an infinite set N of names) corresponding to the nodes of the graph. Term G can only use names on Γ. We use the notation Γ, x to denote the set obtained by adding x to Γ, assuming $x \notin \Gamma$. Similarly, we will write also Γ_1, Γ_2 to state that the resulting set of names is the disjoint union of Γ_1 and Γ_2. Given a signature $LE = \{LE_n\}_{n=0,1,...}$, judgments are built according to the following grammar

$$G ::= L(\boldsymbol{x}) \mid G|G \mid nil$$

where $\boldsymbol{x}$ is a vector of names. The *well-formed judgements* for constructing graphs over signature LE are those generated by applying the rules in Table 1.

Table 1. Well-formed judgments

Structural Axioms

$(AG1)$ $\quad \dfrac{\Gamma \vdash G \ = \ \rho\Gamma \vdash \rho G}{with \ \ \rho \ \ an \ \ injective \ \ substitution}$

$(AG2)$ $(G_1|G_2)|G_3 = G_1|(G_2|G_3)$

$(AG3)$ $G_1|G_2 = G_2|G_1$

$(AG4)$ $G|nil = G$

Syntactic Rules

$(RG1)$ $\dfrac{}{x_1, \ldots, x_n \vdash nil}$

$(RG2)$ $\dfrac{L \in LE_m \quad y_i \in \{x_j\}}{x_1, \ldots, x_n \vdash L(y_1, \ldots, y_m)}$

$(RG3)$ $\dfrac{\Gamma \vdash G_1 \quad \Gamma \vdash G_2}{\Gamma \vdash G_1|G_2}$

Rule *(RG1)* creates a graph with no edges and n nodes and rule *(RG2)* creates a graph with n nodes and one edge labelled by L and with m tentacles (note that there can be repetitions among nodes in $\boldsymbol{y}$, i.e. some tentacles can be attached to the same node). Equivalence of judgements up to α-conversion is obtained with *(AG1)*; substitution function ρ is injective so it cannot identify distinct nodes. *(AG2)*, *(AG3)* and *(AG4)* define the associativity, commutativity and identity over *nil* for operation $|$, respectively. Finally, rule *(RG3)* allows to put together (using $|$) two graphs that share the same set of nodes. We can state the following correspondence theorem.

Theorem 1 (Correspondence of Graphs and Judgements). *Well-formed syntactic judgements up to structural axioms are isomorphic to graphs up to isomorphism.*

Proof Sketch

A translation function $[\![-]\!]$ can be defined as follows:

1. *$[\![x_1, \ldots, x_n \vdash nil]\!]$ is a graph with no edges and n nodes.*
2. *$[\![x_1, \ldots, x_n \vdash L(y_1, \ldots, y_m)]\!]$ is a graph with n nodes and one edge.*
3. *$[\![\Gamma \vdash G_1|G_2]\!]$ is the graph obtained from $[\![\Gamma \vdash G_1]\!]$ and $[\![\Gamma \vdash G_2]\!]$ by identifying homonymous nodes.*

Conversely, rule (RG1) creates the graphs with no edges. All the other graphs can be created by starting with as many rules (RG2) as edges, and applying several times rule (RG3).

Ring Example We use graphs to represent system software architectures. In this context, edges are components and nodes are ports of communication. Edges sharing a node mean that there is a communication link among them. So, let us take the graph in figure 1*a* that represents a ring of four components. Edges representing components are drawn as boxes attached to their corresponding ports. The label of an edge is the name of the component and the arrow indicates the order of the attachment nodes. In this case we only have edges with two tentacles. Names in nodes are not needed but they are included to make easier the correspondence with terms. Figure 1*b* shows how the corresponding well-formed judgement is obtained. Note that *(RG3)* needs the same set of names Γ in both premises.

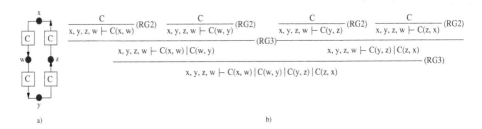

Fig. 1. The graph and the corresponding judgement for the ring example

2.2   Synchronized Edge Replacement

As we represent software architectures as graphs, we represent architectural styles as graph grammars. So a style is represented as a set of productions. More specifically, we use *context-free* grammars where for each component type, a set of productions is defined. The construction and dynamic evolution of the style are obtained as graph rewriting over the productions. In [6] we grouped productions in three sets, the static productions to construct the initial topology of systems, the communication pattern productions to model interactions among components types, and the dynamic productions to create and remove components during evolution. Now the dynamic productions will include productions for reconfiguration. To model evolution we used graph rewriting combined with constraint solving allowing to specify how components will evolve and communicate. Constraint productions are used to coordinate the dynamic evolution of the system. This is done by using constraints on ports to represent coordination among components.

The problem of finding the set of productions to use in a synchronized rewriting step is called *the rule-matching problem* [1]. The solution of the rule-matching problem is implemented considering it as a finite domain constraint problem [10]. Note that to specify styles, there is no need to worry about the possibly complex problem of finding such sets of productions, leaving the rule matching problem to the system. However, it may take a long time to solve such a problem. An analysis of some techniques to solve this problem in a distributed and efficient way can be found in [15]. In this paper we will not describe these techniques and the interested reader can refer to the references.

This method let us represent styles but with a limited ability to express the complex reconfigurations that real systems may experience. The following definitions present an extension to synchronized replacement systems where we allow the declaration and creation of new names on nodes and use synchronized rewriting for name mobility. In this way it is possible to specify reconfigurations over the graphs by changing the connections between edges. This means that, by creation and sharing of ports, more complex evolutions can be specified, reconfiguring components by identifying newly created ports.

A *context-free edge replacement production* rewrites a single edge into an arbitrary graph. Productions will be written as $L \to R$. A production $p = (L \to R)$ can be applied to a graph G yielding H ($G \Rightarrow_p H$) if there is an occurrence of an edge labeled by L in G. A result of applying p to G is a graph H which is obtained from G by removing an edge with label L, and embedding a fresh copy of R in G by coalescing the corresponding attachment nodes. This notion of edge replacement yields the basic steps in the derivation process of an edge replacement grammar.

To model coordinated rewriting, it is necessary to add some labels to the nodes in productions. Assuming to have an alphabet of actions $\mathcal{A}$, then we associate actions to some of the nodes. In this way, each rewrite of an edge must match actions with its adjacent edges and they have to move as well. For example, consider two edges which share one node, such that no other edge is attached to that node, and let us take one production for each of these edges. Each of these productions have an action on that node (a and b). If $a \neq b$, then the edges cannot be rewritten together (using these productions). If $a = b$, then they can move, via the context-sensitive rewriting rule obtained by merging the two context-free productions (*rule-matching problem*). The use of synchronized graph productions in a rewriting system implies the application of several productions where all edges to be rewritten and sharing a node must apply productions that satisfy the same actions.

A *synchronized edge replacement grammar*, or simply a grammar, consists of an initial graph and a set of productions. A derivation is obtained by starting with the initial graph and applying a sequence of rewriting rules, each obtained by synchronizing possibly several productions.

Now that we have coordinated rewriting, we need to add to productions the capability of sharing nodes. This is obtained by letting a production to declare new names for the nodes it creates, and by sharing these names with the rest of the graph using the synchronization process. This is done in a production by adding to the action in a node, a tuple of names that it wants to communicate. So now the synchronization of a rewriting rule has to match not only actions, but also the tuples of names. After the matching is obtained and the productions applied, the declared names that were matched are used to obtain the final graph of the rewriting by merging the corresponding nodes.

To formalize synchronized rewriting we use, as in section 2.1, judgements and define the notion of *transitions*, which are of the following form

$$\Gamma_1 \vdash G_1 \xrightarrow{\Lambda} \Gamma_1, \Gamma_\Lambda, \Gamma_2 \vdash G_2$$

$$\Lambda \subseteq \{axy \mid a \in \mathcal{A}, \ x \in \Gamma_1, \ |y| \cap \Gamma_1 = \emptyset\} \qquad \Gamma_\Lambda = \bigcup_{axy \in \Lambda} |y|$$

$$\Lambda \ is \ well \ formed \ \Leftrightarrow \begin{cases} axy, \ a'xy' \in \Lambda \Rightarrow a = a' \ and \ y = y' \\ \varepsilon xy \in \Lambda \Rightarrow |y| = \emptyset \end{cases}$$

A transition is represented as a logical sequent which says that G_1 is rewritten into G_2 satisfying a set of *requirements* Λ. Graph G_2 must include the nodes in G_1 and can include a set of new nodes (Γ_Λ) that are used in synchronization and a set of new internal nodes (Γ_2).

The set Λ contains requirements of the form axy where the names $|y|$ of vector y are not included in Γ_1, and has to be well formed. The first condition requires that Λ is functional on the second component of triples, which means that all edges in G_1 attached to node x, must agree on the same action and on the same shared names. Note that condition $|y| \cap \Gamma_1 = \emptyset$ implies that only new nodes can be shared. Since not all nodes need to be loci of synchronization, an identity action ε is defined which is required in a node by all the productions which do not synchronize on that node. The second well formedness condition states that if an identity action is imposed on a node then no name can be shared on that node.

A *production* is a special transition of the form

$$x_1, \ldots, x_n \vdash L(x_1, \ldots, x_n) \xrightarrow{\Lambda} x_1, \ldots, x_n, \Gamma_\Lambda, \Gamma_2 \vdash G$$

and in particular *id productions* are as follows

$$x_1, \ldots, x_n \vdash L(x_1, \ldots, x_n) \xrightarrow{\{\varepsilon x_1, \ldots, \varepsilon x_n\}} x_1, \ldots, x_n \vdash L(x_1, \ldots, x_n).$$

The context-free character of productions is here made clear by the fact that the graph to be rewritten consists of a single edge with distinct nodes. Productions are alpha convertible. To model edges which do not move in a transition we need productions with identity actions on their nodes, where an edge with label L is rewritten to itself. This is called the *id production id(L)*.

A *grammar* consists of an initial graph $\Gamma_0 \vdash G_0$ and a set of synchronized productions P over a ranked alphabet LE and an alphabet of actions $\mathcal{A}$. Set P must include productions $id(L)$ for all symbols L in LE. A *derivation* is a finite sequence of the form $\Gamma_0 \vdash G_0 \xrightarrow{\Lambda_1} \Gamma_1 \vdash G_1 \xrightarrow{\Lambda_2} \ldots \xrightarrow{\Lambda_n} \Gamma_n \vdash G_n$, where $\Gamma_{i-1} \vdash G_{i-1} \xrightarrow{\Lambda_i} \Gamma_i \vdash G_i$, $i = 1 \ldots n$ is a transition in the set $T(P)$ of transitions generated by P. Transitions $T(P)$ are generated by P applying the rules in Table 2.

Table 2. Transition Rules

$$(RT1)\quad \frac{x_1,\ldots,x_n \vdash L(x_1,\ldots,x_n) \xrightarrow{\Lambda} x_1,\ldots,x_n,\Gamma_\Lambda,\Gamma_2 \vdash G \in P \quad \rho \bigwedge wf}{\rho(x_1,\ldots,x_n),\Gamma_1 \vdash \rho(L(x_1,\ldots,x_n)) \xrightarrow{\rho\bigwedge} \rho(x_1,\ldots,x_n),\Gamma_1,\Gamma_{\rho\bigwedge},\Gamma_2 \vdash \rho G}$$

with $\rho : \{x_1,\ldots,x_n\} \to \{x_1,\ldots,x_n\}$

$$(RT2)\quad \frac{\Gamma_1 \vdash G_1 \xrightarrow{\Lambda} \Gamma_1,\Gamma_\Lambda,\Gamma_2 \vdash G_2 \quad \Gamma_1 \vdash G_1' \xrightarrow{\Lambda'} \Gamma_1,\Gamma_{\Lambda'},\Gamma_2' \vdash G_2' \quad \Lambda \cup \Lambda' \ wf}{\Gamma_1 \vdash G_1|G_1' \xrightarrow{\Lambda \cup \Lambda'} \Gamma_1,\Gamma_{\Lambda \cup \Lambda'},\Gamma_2,\Gamma_2' \vdash G_2|G_2'}$$

Rule *(RT1)* is necessary to allow to apply a production to a graph which consists of (possibly many nodes and of) a single edge that may have some tentacles attached to the same node (this is done by ρ that is a possibly non-injective substitution). Notice that for $\rho \bigwedge$ to be well formed, the requirements on nodes identified by ρ must coincide. Also, no requirement is imposed on isolated nodes (those in Γ_1). Rule *(RT2)* is the one that completes the synchronization process. The well-formed condition of $\Lambda \cup \Lambda'$ assures that the rule can only be applied when the synchronization requirements on the nodes are satisfied and the shared nodes are actually identified.

Ring-Star Example Let us consider again the ring architecture style. In this example an instance of this style starts with a ring configuration and at some point in its evolution is reconfigured to a star.

Figure 2a shows the grammar that includes the **initial graph** that starts with a ring of one component and the productions. Also the corresponding terms are included. Due to space limitations we only give the necessary productions to show how rings are constructed and reconfiguration is modeled. Productions for the communication pattern and other reconfigurations can be added.

The initial graph together with production **Brother** are used to construct rings. A component contains a name (i.e. C and S) and a state that changes during evolution. In this case the state is *idle* to specify that the reconfiguration can only occur when there are no communication interactions among the involved components [8].

Production **Star Reconfiguration** is used to reconfigure a ring into a star by creating and declaring a new node *(w)* and synchronizing with the rest of the components by coordinated rewriting using action r. Together with action r, the new node is distributed among components to identify it as the port for the center of the star. The coordination is communicated through the ring ports and after reconfiguration those ports are no longer used. Once the star is obtained the system can evolve using productions corresponding to the star substyle (not mentioned here). Figure 2b shows a derivation where a ring of four components is reconfigured after a coordinated rewriting (thick arrow).

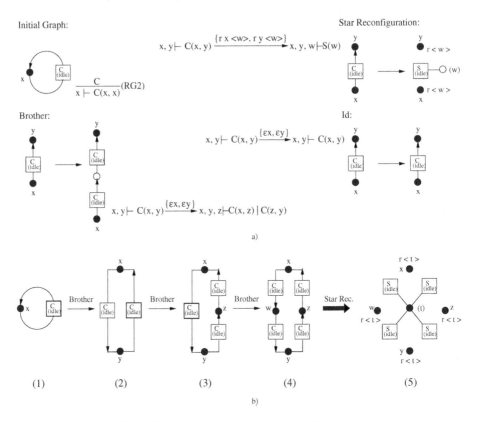

Fig. 2. Ring grammar with star reconfiguration

Figure 3 shows the proof from a ring of four components to a star that corresponds to the final step of the derivation in Figure 2*b*. As part of the proof, the construction of the four component ring is needed and corresponds to the proof of figure 1.

This simple example shows how the approach can be used to specify complex reconfigurations including the combination of different styles. Constraint productions allow a clear and explicit specification of style reconfigurations.

One important point to mention about using transitions and judgements for modelling the synchronized rewriting process, is that in this paper we use a general policy for synchronization, so all edges sharing a node have to agree on a requirement to be rewritten at the same time (we can call this a *broadcast* synchronization). The "implementation" of this policy is very easily identified, using the term representation, in inference rule *(RT2)* as the well-formed union of $\Lambda \cup \Lambda'$. If other policies are wanted the only thing that is needed is changing the union for a more elaborate operation.

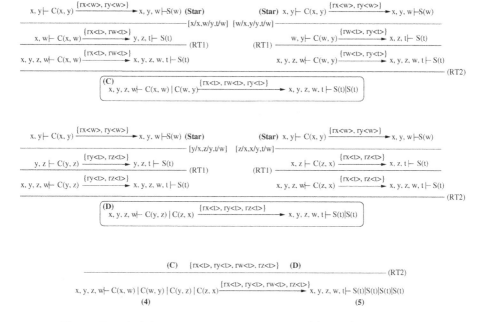

Fig. 3. Proof of the transition between graphs (4) and (5) in figure 2*b*

Another point to mention is the relation of this approach with π-calculus [14]. The approach we present only allows for the declaration and sharing of new nodes, which may seem restrictive, but this can be seen to correspond to πI-calculus [19]. It has been demonstrated that the πI-calculus can achieve essentially the same expressiveness as π-calculus.

The full power of π-calculus could be achieved by adding an inference rule coalescing a new and an old node in a transition. If repeated application of the rule is allowed, also several, old nodes could be coalesced, similarly to the fusion calculus [21]. However, with respect to both π-calculus and fusion calculus, our method has the advantage of the graphical distributed approach which allows for multiple synchronizations in one step.

Another comment is about the accumulation of isolated nodes, which can happen (as in figure 2*b* (5)) since nodes are never discarded. If isolated nodes are meaningless, they can be automatically erased by a structural axiom of the form

$$\Gamma, x \vdash G \ = \ \Gamma \vdash G, \ x \notin freevar(G).$$

3   Case Study

This section presents the application of our approach to a more realistic case study from the telemedicine area. This case study is motivated by a real system developed as part of a project carried out by University of L'Aquila and Parco

Scientifico e Tecnologico d'Abruzzo, a regional consortium of public and private research institutions and manufacturing industries. It is due to Paola Inverardi and Henry Muccini, with the help of Debra Richardson and additions by Stephen Fickas, and is proposed as a working case study for the Tenth International Workshop on Software Specification and Design (IWSSD-10) [7].

The current trend in healthcare is to transition patients from hospital care to home care as quickly as feasible. The *Teleservices and Remote Medical Care System (TRMCS)* is intended to provide and guarantee assistance services to at home or mobile users. This type of patient does not need continuous assistance but may need prioritized assistance when urgencies happen, in which case the patient would call a help center for assistance. The system must handle help request to a help center from patients with a medical emergency. Also, patients may have internet-based medical monitors that give continuous readouts. A help center may be contracted to read these monitors over the net and raise alerts when dangerous values are detected.

The case study can be examined from many perspectives like requirements, safety critical aspects, security, design and user interface. Some of the requirements of the system related to dynamic changes and reconfigurations are as follows.

1. Be open to new service installations.
2. Handle users that are geographically distributed and heterogeneously connected, offering homogeneous service costs.
3. Handle dynamic changes of users and their locations.
4. Support mobile users.

Others requirements not directly related with dynamics but which can affect the possible solutions include

1. Guarantee continuous service of the system.
2. Guarantee the delivery of help service in response to a help request in a specific critical time range.
3. Handle several help request in parallel that compete for service by overlapping in time and space.
4. Support conflict resolution according to resolution policies that minimize user damage.

We think that the method we propose in this paper (with respect to the software architecture level) can be useful to cope with many of the above requirements.

Taking advantage of the self organizing coordination policy of our approach and its flexibility to extend existing specifications (simply by adding new productions), we propose a general style that can be applied to the management of patients/users of the system with respect to the level of monitoring and criticality of the care they need. Also the proposed architecture is intended to consider the costs that this type of systems implies, making possible to use different technologies (for routers and communications) at different levels (i.e. more robust and reliable components and communication links at the higher levels than at the lower ones).

The proposed architecture style in figure 4a creates system instances that define a hierarchical architecture of *Routers* (i.e. a tree) hanging from a main *Server*. To each of the Routers a number of *Users* (patients) can be connected. Each level of routers in the tree defines the level of criticality of their users. That is, the closest the Routers level is to the root (i.e. the Server) the most critical patients are connected to those Routers. The idea for the style in figure 4 is based on the path compression techniques employed in search algorithms like *Find/Merge*.

For clarity, the operations of the different components have been simplified. The three types of units operate as follows.

- **User** sends either alarm (i.e. help requests) or check signals (i.e. control messages) on the user subsystem state or on the user health state, respectively.
- **Router** accepts signals (control or alarm) from the users. It forwards the alarm requests upwards to the Server and checks the behavior of the user subsystem through the control messages.
- **Server** dispatches the help requests.

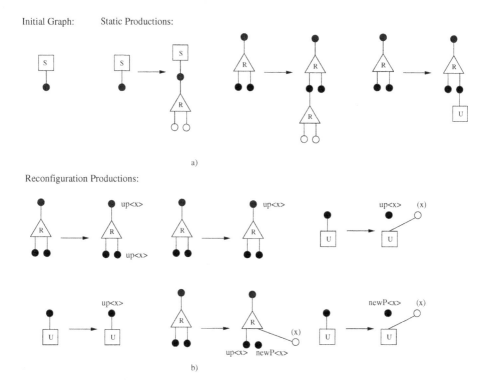

Fig. 4. TRMCS software architecture style

Due to space limitations productions in figure 4 are only part of the specification of the style. We include only the static productions to construct the trees and the reconfiguration productions to move users up one level. Some of the productions not included are the ones for moving Users down one level, move Users among Routers of the same level (maybe due to limitations of the Routers), communication productions, and dynamic productions for creating and removing of Users and Routers during evolution. For simplicity the state of the component is omitted assuming that all the productions shown can only occur in the *idle* state. The static productions are the ones that construct the trees starting from the server (the root). Routers (and the Server) create their sons (Routers on the left port and Users on the right port).

A general reconfiguration policy is defined to handle the following requirements

- Accept a variable number of users and other routers connected to each router.
- Based on the history of alarms sent by a user, move a user up or down in the tree.

Looking at the reconfiguration productions in figure 4b, it is worthwhile noticing that the six productions specify the global coordination policy that all the system components have to agree upon when moving a user one level up. Each production expresses what a single actor is supposed to do. The first production for example, refers to the Router whose User has to move one level up. The second production refers to the brothers of the Router that moves the User, agreeing on the reconfiguration (constraint $up < x >$). The third one refers to the User moving while the fourth one (as with the Routers) let all the moving User's brothers be aware of its move by agreeing on the same constraint ($up < x >$). The fifth production talks about the Router component one level up, which should be prepared to receive the new user on the new port x. The sixth production then let all the Users of that Router migrate on the new port (synchronizing on $newP < x >$). The configuration step will only be possible when all the productions can synchronously be applied, thus realizing an instant reconfiguration step. It is worth to notice that the application of these productions allows for many users to be reconfigured at the same time.

Figure 5 shows the application of the reconfiguration over a specific architecture. The User in bold box is the one to be moved. Figure 5a is the system before the reconfiguration and shows the ports where the participants have to synchronize. Figure 5b shows the result of the reconfiguration, where the User was moved up one level connecting the receiving Router, the moved User and its brothers to the new port.

4   Conclusions and Future Work

This paper presents a technique for the specification of software architecture style reconfigurations following a self organizing criterion. With respect to previous work, we maintain the use of context free productions - allowing for a

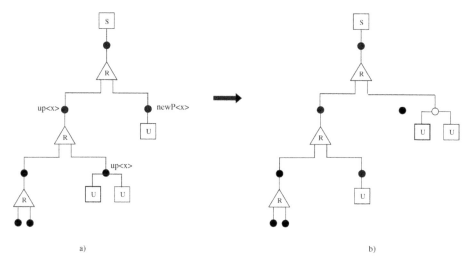

Fig. 5. Reconfiguration of a User one level up

clear separation of component descriptions - and the rule matching approach - based on constraint solving for finding the distributed solutions - which have been proposed in the simpler case with no name mobility. Our work goes in the direction of finding suitable ways of modeling SA without embodying in the description a specific coordination policy, rather the approach is to specify the minimal requirements on the coordination policy which can then be refined in the subsequent development steps into a specific one. To this respect we think the approach we present in this paper is a step in the right direction. Constraint matching and synchronized rule selection allows for an explicit, declarative but minimal specification of the coordination policies that can be legitimately adopted when implementing the system. Moreover the context free nature of the productions allows for a clean and simple specification of the reconfiguration step at the component level, in a completely distributed fashion.

It is our intention to apply this ongoing work to real case studies and finally to implement the simulation of software architecture derivations and reconfigurations.

References

1. Corradini, A., Degano, P., Montanari, U.: Specifying Highly Concurrent Data Structure Manipulation. In Bucci, G. and Valle, G., editors, COMPUTING 85:A Broad Perspective of Concurrent Developments. Elsevier Science,1985.
2. Degano, P., Montanari, U.: A Model of Distributed Systems Based on Graph Rewriting. Journal of the ACM Vol. 34, N2, April 1987, pp. 411-449.
3. Hirsch, D., Montanari, U.: Consistent Transformations for Software Architecture Styles of Distributed Systems. Proceedings of the Workshop on (formal methods applied to) Distributed Systems, Gheorghe Stefanescu, Ed., Iasi, Rumania, Septem-

ber 2-3. Electronic Notes in Theoretical Computer Science, Vol. 28, pp. 23-40, 1999. http://www.elsevier.nl/locate/entcs/volume28.html.

4. Hirsch, D., Montanari, U.: Higher-Order Hyperedge Replacement Systems and their Transformations: Specifying Software Architecture Reconfigurations. Proceedings of the Joint APPLIGRAPH/GETGRATS Workshop on Graph Transformation Systems (GRATRA 2000). Satellite Event of ETAPS 2000, H. Ehrig, G. Taentzer, Eds., Berlin, Germany, March 25-27. Technical Report of Computer Science Department/TU Berlin, No. 2000-02, pp. 215-223, 2000.

5. Hirsch, D., Inverardi, P., Montanari, U.: Graph Grammars and Constraint Solving for Software Architecture Styles. Proceedings of the Third International Software Architecture Workshop, Orlando, E.E.U.U., November 1-2, 1998.

6. Hirsch, D., Inverardi, P., Montanari, U.: Modeling Software Architectures and Styles with Graph Grammars and Constraint Solving. In Proceedings of the First Working IFIP Conference on Software Architecture, San Antonio, Texas, E.E.U.U., February 22-24, 1999.

7. Inverardi, P., Muccini, H.: The Teleservices and Remote Medical Care System (TRMCS). Workshop Case Study. 10th International Workshop on Software Specification and Design (IWSSD-10), San Diego, California, November 5-7, 2000. http://www.ics.uci.edu/IRUS/iwssd/cfp.html

8. Kramer, J., Magee, J.: The Evolving Philosophers Problem: Dynamic Change Management. IEEE Transactions on Software Engineering, SE-16 (11), pp.1293-1306, 1990.

9. Le M'etayer, D. : Describing Software Architecture Styles using Graph Grammars. IEEE Transactions on Software Engineering. Vol. 24, Nr 7, July 1998.

10. Mackworth, A.K.: Encyclopedia of IA, chapter Constraint Satisfaction. Springer Verlag, 1988.

11. Magee, J., Kramer, J.: Dynamic structure in software architectures. Proceedings of the Fourth ACM SIGSOFT Symposium on the Foundations of Software Engineering, ACM Software Engineering Notes, 1996.

12. Magee, J., Kramer, J.: Self organising software architectures. Proceedings of the Second International Software Architecture Workshop, 1996.

13. Magee, J., Kramer, J.: Analysing Dynamic Change in Software Architectures: A case study. Proceedings of the IEEE 4th International Conference on Configurable Distributed Systems (CDS 98), pp.91-100, Annapolis, May 1998.

14. Milner, R., Parrow, J., Walker, D.: A Calculus of Mobile Processes (parts I and II). Information and Computation, 100:1-77, 1992.

15. Montanari, U. and Rossi, F.: Graph Rewriting, Constraint Solving and Tiles for Coordinating Distributed Systems. Applied Categorical Structures, Vol.7, pp.333-370, 1999.

16. Montanari, U., Pistore, M. and Rossi, F.: Modeling Concurrent, Mobile and Coordinated Systems via Graph Transformations. In: H. Ehrig, H.-J. Kreowski, U. Montanari and G. Rozenberg, Eds., Handbook of Graph Grammars and Computing by Graph Transformation, Vol.3: Concurrency, Parallelism, and Distribution, World Scientific, 1999.

17. Oreizy, P., Medvidovic, N., Taylor, R.: Architectural-Based Runtime Software Evolution. Proceedings of the International Conference on Software Engineering (ICSE'98), Kyoto, Japan, 1998.

18. Rozenberg, G., editor: Handbook of Graph Grammars and Computing by Graph Transformation: Foundations, volume I. World Scientific, 1996.

19. Sangiorgi, D.: π-calculus, Internal Mobility and Agent-passing Calculi. Theoretical Computer Science 167(2), 1996.

20. Taentzer, G., Goedicke, M., Meyer, T.: Dynamic Change Management by Distributed Graph Transformation: Towards Configurable Distributed Systems. Proc. 6th Int. Workshop on Theory and Application of Graph Transformation, 1998.
21. Victor B.: The Fusion Calculus: Expressiveness and Symmetry in Mobile Processes. PhD Thesis, Uppsala University, Dept. of Computer Science, June 1998.
22. Wermelinger, M., Fiadeiro, J.: Algebraic Software Architecture Reconfiguration. Software Engineering-ESEC/FSE'99, LNCS Vol. 1687, Springer-Verlag, pp. 393-409, 1999.

An Agent Mediated Approach to Dynamic Change in Coordination Policies

Prasanta Bose[1] and Mark G. Matthews[2]

[1] Information and Software Engineering Department, George Mason University,
Fairfax, VA 22030
bose@mgfairfax.rr.com
[2] The MITRE Corporation, 1820 Dolley Madison Blvd.,
McLean, VA 22012
mmatthew@mitre.org

Abstract. Distributed information systems for decision-support, logistics, and e-commerce involve coordination of autonomous information resources and clients according to specific domain independent and domain dependent policies. A major challenge is handling dynamic changes in the priorities, preferences, and constraints of the clients and/or the resources. Addressing such a challenge requires solutions to two problems: a) Reasoning about the need for dynamic changes to coordination policies in response to changes in priorities, preferences, and constraints. b) Coordinating the run-time assembly of policy changes in a dependable manner. This paper introduces the NAVCo approach to address these problems. The approach involves exploiting negotiation-based coordination to address the first problem and model-based change coordination to address the second problem. These two key features of the approach are well suited for realization using an agent-based architecture. The paper describes the architecture with specific emphasis on the analysis and design of the agent specifications for negotiation and change coordination.

1   Introduction

Distributed information systems for decision-support applications, logistics, and e-commerce involve coordination of autonomous information resources and clients according to specific domain independent and domain dependent policies. A major challenge is handling dynamic changes in the preferences and constraints of the clients and/or the resources.

Consider the domain of distributed decision-support applications where autonomous information resources are coordinated to meet the information demands of client specific decision-support views. In such a domain, there is continuous change in Quality of Service (QoS) properties and constraints of the clients, information resources, and shared communications infrastructure. Current architectures for coordination of distributed information resources to support client specific views are static in nature; that is the coordination policies cannot be dynamically changed to meet changing demands. As an example, consider the following scenario from the supply-chain application domain:

A. Porto and G.-C. Roman (Eds.): COORDINATION 2000, LNCS 1906, pp. 164-181, 2000.
© Springer-Verlag Berlin Heidelberg 2000

A decision-support view for inventory management is maintained from multiple autonomous information resources within a supply-chain. Customer order information from customer sites, product assembly information from manufacturer sites, and parts inventories from parts supplier sites are configured to support an order-fulfillment view used by inventory managers of the suppliers and consumers. As orders, product assembly requirements, and parts inventories constantly change, changes in the view must be coordinated to achieve consistency and to support management decisions.

There are multiple view maintenance policies available to support the above inventory management task. Typical systems are based on static architectural decisions (on view maintenance policies) at design time by considering tradeoffs between consistency, communications costs, and processing costs. Suppose a high-cost complete consistency view maintenance policy was selected for implementation at design time. Further suppose that several inventory managers are simultaneously executing intensive on-line analytical processing (OLAP) queries against the order fulfillment view. The queries are competing with the view maintenance policy for system resources. Under these conditions, both the queries and the view maintenance task are likely to suffer from poor performance. Short of shutting down, reconfiguring, and restarting the system, current architectures have no way of prioritizing preferences and dynamically responding to changing preferences and constraints.

1.1 Self-Adaptive Software: Requirements

A key observation to be made from the above discussion is that automated and dynamic approaches to addressing the problem of changing preferences and constraints require architectures and adaptive mechanisms that achieve dynamic self-design in response to changing preferences and constraints. The four major capabilities of such self-adaptive software systems are: i) *Detecting a change in context or a change in needs.* The system should be able to monitor its behavior and detect deviations from its commitments or the presence of new opportunities. It should be able to accept new needs from external sources and evaluate for deviations with respect to current commitments. ii) *Knowing the space of adaptations.* It must have knowledge of the space of self-changes it can choose from to reduce deviations. iii) *Reasoning for adaptation decision.* It should be able to reason and make commitments on the self-changes and commitments on revised goals. iv) *Integrating the change.* It should be able to package the change if required and perform assembly/configuration coordination to insert the change into the existing system in a dependable manner with minimal disruption to existing behaviors.

1.2 NAVCo Approach: Key Ideas

The NAVCo approach described in this paper considers a family of adaptive systems for information view management. The key distinctive features of the approach are: a) Changes in committed preferences and context assumptions trigger the adaptation process. b) An adaptation space defined by a set of view maintenance policy objects that forms the basis of design for a set of middleware coordination agents.

c) Reasoning for change accomplished through a negotiation based process involving the clients and information resource agents. d) Use of verified assembly plans for change integration. The above features of the NAVCo approach are well suited for realization using agent-based concepts and an agent-based architecture.

The following sections of the paper describe the agent-based architecture. The paper focuses primarily on the negotiation-based coordination used to reach a change decision and the consequent coordination used to incorporate the change decision. In the context of NAVCo, a change decision equates to a decision to switch between view maintenance policies at run time.

2   Multi-resource View Maintenance Policies: Background

Multi-resource view maintenance falls within the domain of distributed decision-support database systems. A simplified model of this domain is illustrated in Figure 1. As illustrated in Figure 1, a view (V) is maintained from a set of autonomous data sources $(S_1, S_2,...,S_n)$. The view is a join of relations (r_1, r_2, r_n) within the data sources. The update/query processor and view maintenance policy components execute a distributed algorithm for incrementally maintaining the view. As data within a source changes, the associated update/query processor sends notification of the update to the view maintenance policy (VMP) component in Figure 1, which in turn queries the other sources to compute the incremental effect of the source update. After the incremental effect of the update has been computed, it is propagated to the client view. Client applications, such as on-line analytical processing (OLAP) and data mining, execute queries against the view. The data sources also support transactional environments, which result in updates to source relations that participate in the view.

The agent-based architecture presented in this paper focuses on providing mechanisms to allow run-time switching of view maintenance policies. Four VMPs are briefly discussed and compared in this section. A complete description of these policies can be found in [1, 21].

The Strobe algorithm is an incremental VMP that achieves strong consistency. The Strobe algorithm processes updates as they arrive, sending queries to the sources when necessary. However, the updates are not performed immediately on the materialized view (MV); instead, a list of actions (AL) to be performed on the view is generated. The MV is updated only when it is certain that applying all of the actions in AL (as a single transaction at the client) will bring the view to a consistent state. This occurs when there are no outstanding queries and all received updates have been processed.

The Complete-Strobe (C-Strobe) algorithm achieves complete consistency by updating the materialized view after each source update. The C-Strobe algorithm issues compensating queries for each update that arrives at the VMP between the time that a query is sent from the VMP and its corresponding answer is received from a source. The number of compensating queries can be quite large if there are continuous source updates.

The SWEEP algorithm achieves complete consistency of the view by ordering updates as they arrive at the VMP and ensuring that the state of the view at the client preserves the delivery of updates. The key concept behind SWEEP is on-line error correction in which compensation for concurrent updates is performed locally by using the information that is already available at the VMP. The SWEEP algorithm contains two loops that perform an iterative computation (or sweep) of the change in the view due to an update.

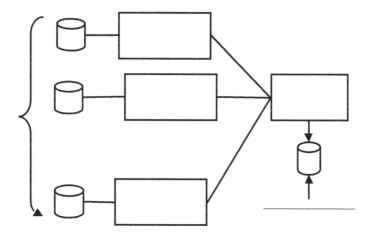

Fig. 1. Distributed Decision-Support Database System Domain

The Nested SWEEP algorithm is an extension of the SWEEP algorithm that allows the view maintenance for multiple updates to be carried out in a cumulative fashion. Nested SWEEP achieves strong consistency by recursively incorporating all concurrent updates encountered during the evaluation of an update. In this fashion, a composite view change is computed for multiple updates that occur concurrently.

2.1 Cost-Benefit Analysis

The performance of VMPs can be compared based on the communications and processing costs required to maintain a certain level of consistency. Communications costs can be measured with respect to the number and size of messages required per update. Processing costs can be measured with respect to the processing burden that the algorithm places on both the client and the data sources.

Table 1 compares the communications and query processing cost of four VMPs. The cost of the algorithms is dependent on the number of data sources, n. The costs of the C-Strobe and Nested SWEEP algorithms are highly dependent on a workload characterization factor, a where $0 \leq a \leq 1$, which reflects the rate of updates received. If updates arrive infrequently $a=0$ and if updates arrive continuously $a=1$. The client processing cost of a delete update in the Strobe and C-Strobe algorithms is highly dependent on the number of pending updates, p. The costs in Tables 1 and 2 depict the case in which the VMP components are co-located with the client.

Table 1. VMP Cost Comparison

Algorithm	Update Type	Comm. Cost	Client Cost	Server Cost
Strobe	Delete	1	1+p	0
	Insert	2n-1	(n-1)+1	1
C-Strobe	Delete	1	1+p	0
	Insert	2(n-1)+2a(n-1)!+1	(n-1)+a(n-1)!+1	1+a(n-2)!
SWEEP	delete/insert	2n-1	(n-1)+1	1
Nested SWEEP	delete/insert	2(1-a)(n-1)+1	(1-a)(n-1)+1	(1-a)

As illustrated in Table 1, the cost of the algorithms is highly sensitive to the volume and types of updates. To illustrate, consider the inventory management scenario introduced in Section 1. Further assume that there are four information resources, one client view, and the following dynamic workload:

- Period 1 -high volume, high insert (100 inserts, 0 deletes, X seconds)
- Period 2 - low volume, balanced (50 inserts, 50 deletes, 3X seconds)
- Period 3 - medium volume, high delete (0 inserts, 100 deletes, 2X seconds)

The cost of each algorithm over these periods can be calculated using the formulas in Table 1. The value of the parameter p is assumed to be 0 for low traffic, 10 for medium traffic, and 100 for high traffic. The value of the parameter, a, is assumed to be 0 for low traffic, 1/3 for medium traffic, and 1 for high traffic. The cost of the four algorithms over Periods 1-3 is illustrated in Table 2.

Table 2. Cost in Inventory Management Scenario

Algorithm	Comm Cost	Client Cost	Server Cost
Strobe	1200	1750	150
C-Strobe	2400	2350	350
SWEEP	2100	1200	300
Nested SWEEP	1250	775	158
Example 1	750	1525	75
Example 2	950	625	108

Currently a single algorithm is selected at design time and cannot be changed without shutting down and reconfiguring the system. Design-time tradeoffs must be made with respect to consistency versus client, server, and communications costs. The design-time decision can have a profound effect on the processing and communications requirements to support the view. If, however, the algorithm can be dynamically changed at run-time, these tradeoffs can be made continuously as preferences and constraints change. As illustrated in the two examples at the bottom of Table 2, the ability to dynamically switch algorithms can result in significant cost savings and improved performance in a constrained environment.

Example 1 shows that communications cost can be minimized by initially implementing the Nested SWEEP algorithm and then dynamically switching to the Strobe algorithm between periods 1 and 2. This results in a cost reduction of 450 messages over a static implementation of the Strobe algorithm. This frees up valuable shared communications resources for more critical applications.

Example 2 shows that client processing cost can be minimized by implementing the Nested SWEEP algorithm during periods 1 and 3, and the Strobe algorithm during period 2. This results in a cost reduction of over 1000 queries over a static implementation of the Strobe algorithm. This frees up valuable resources for processing-intensive analysis queries and results in a significant performance improvement for analysis users.

3 NAVCo Agent-Based Architecture

The NAVCo approach to adapting view maintenance policies in response to changes in the needs of the clients or changes in the constraints imposed by the resources is based on negotiation reasoning between the clients and resources followed by dynamic change coordination. The approach is based on a layered architecture with agent-based middleware in each layer. The layers in the architecture, shown in Figure 2 as a UML class diagram, separate the concern for policy change reasoning, policy change coordination and application specific information view maintenance based on a policy. The architectural components and connections are modeled as stereotypes of the UML class. For the sake of brevity, we limit our discussions in the rest of the paper to an example involving switching between the Strobe and C-Strobe policies described in the previous section. The architectural components in each layer, the connections between the components and the connections between the layers are briefly described below.

3.1 Negotiation Coordination Layer

The key component types of the negotiation coordination layer (bottom layer in Figure 2) are a negotiation facilitator agent (NFA), a client negotiation agent (CNA), and resource negotiation agents (RNAs) that communicate via a shared data space called the Negotiation space (NSpace). The CNA and RNAs provide an agent-oriented negotiation interface to the client and resources. The negotiation is based on a formalization of the WinWin model [2, 3]. The communication of a negotiated change decision from the negotiation layer to the change coordination layer is via the shared Nspace.

3.2 Change Coordination Layer

The change coordination layer (middle layer in Figure 2) performs the actions required to dynamically switch between view maintenance policies in response to a communicated switching decision from the negotiation coordination layer. The change coordination layer consists of a Strobe tracking agent (STA), a C-Strobe tracking agent (CTA), a change coordination agent (CCA), and a shared data space (CSpace). There is one tracking agent per scheduler agent in the application coordination layer. A tracking agent interacts with the monitoring interface of its associated scheduler agent via the change coordination event channel (CChan). Each time a scheduling agent experiences a qualitative change in one of its state variables, the change is propagated to the associated tracking agent which abstractly tracks the execution state of the scheduling agent. The CCA accepts the communicated switching decision from the NFA via the NSpace and, based on the current tracking information maintained by the tracking agents, executes the set of configuration and control actions required to bring about the dynamic switching between VMP scheduling agents within the application coordination layer. The CCA interacts with the control interface of the scheduling agents via the CChan. The CSpace is used to communicate the tracking knowledge from the tracking agents to the CCA.

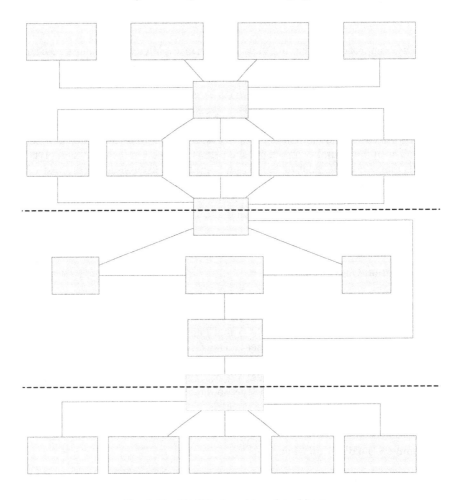

Fig. 2. The NAVCo Agent-based Architecture

3.3 Application Coordination Layer

The application coordination layer (top layer in Figure 2) consists of agent representatives of the application specific service components that act to perform view maintenance. The application component interfaces necessary to support distributed view maintenance are achieved by the resource and client manager agents (RMA and CMA respectively) as depicted in Figure 2. The RMAs provide the functionality of the update/query processor depicted in Figure 1. To allow flexible switching of view maintenance policies, the activities of a view maintenance policy are decomposed and realized by a set of modular agents (scheduler, queue, and query processor) that allow reuse and flexible switching by localizing the change element to the scheduler agent. The scheduler agents (SSA for Strobe and CSA for C-Strobe) dynamically schedule updates and queries according to a specific VMP. The query processor agent (QPA) executes a query processing schedule. The input buffer (IB) component queues update tasks to be scheduled by the scheduling agent. An application coordinator agent (ACA) delegates view maintenenace tasks (in terms of updates) to the active scheduler agent. The agents interact via the application coordination event-channel (AChan). The SSA, CSA, IB, and QPA each contain a control interface and associated methods to allow the change coordination and control agent to perform configuration and control actions. The SSA and CSA also include a monitoring interface and associated methods to allow tracking agents to track policy execution states.

4   Design and Analysis of Negotiation Coordination Layer

The model for negotiation coordination used in our approach is based on the WinWin [2, 3] model used in multi-agent (representing stakeholders) requirements negotiation. In such a model, the participating agents collaboratively and asynchronously explore the WinWin decision space that is represented by four main conceptual artifacts: i) WinCondition - capturing the preferences and constraints of a participant. ii) Issue - capturing the conflict between WinConditions or their associated risks and uncertainties. iii) Option - capturing a decision choice for resolving an issue. iv) Agreement - capturing the agreed upon set of conditions which satisfy stakeholder WinConditions and/or capturing the agreed options for resolving issues. The artifacts specify the message objects passed between the agents. The object model for the WinCondition object developed for negotiating VMPs is shown in Figure 3. The object explicates attributes relevant to expressing preferences and constraints for the distributed view maintenance problem.

NAVCo incorporates three types of negotiation reasoning schemes that extend the WinWin model to consider a reactive model of negotiation. The first method, used during the initial establishment of the task and for negotiation of the initial policy, takes a task-driven approach and is triggered when a new client WinCondition is submitted. As illustrated in Table 3, the client initiates the task through submission of a WinCondition containing the task parameters and any preferences and constraints. The second method, depicted in Table 4 and used for run-time dynamic renegotiation of policies, is conflict driven and is triggered by changes in preferences and constraints. In this scheme any team participant may submit a revised WinCondition based on changing component preferences and constraints.

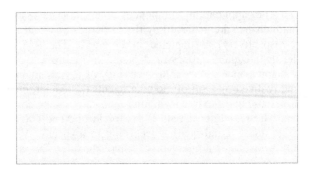

Fig. 3. The WinCondition Object Model

Table 3. Task Driven Negotiation Protocol

1. CNA submits a WinCondition to NFA. The WinCondition identifies the task preferences and constraints of the Client
2. The NFA analyzes the posted WinCondition and identifies Issue(s)
3. The NFA generates potential Options that Resolve the Issue(s): Options are policy decisions that are either derived from a) the resource (RNA) preferences or b) global policy knowledge
4. NAs (both CNA and RNAs) evaluate the Option(s)
5. If an option is accepted by all NAs
Then {Agreement = Accepted Option, Agreement propagated to CCA for implementation}
Else {one or more NAs post revised WinConditions
Go To Step 2 }   End If

Table 4. Conflict Driven Negotiation Protocol

1. CNA or RNA submits revised WinCondition to the NFA.
2. NFA analyzes revised WinCondition against existing related WinConditions to generate Issue(s) resulting from conflicting interaction
3. NFA generates potential Options that Resolve the Issue(s)
4. If there is no change in existing Options (i.e., Option has already been Agreed upon)
Then {NFA marks the issue as Resolved}
Else { CNA and RNAs evaluate the Option(s)
.   If an option is accepted by all NAs
Then {Agreement = Accepted Option, Agreement propagated to CCA}
Else {CNA and/or RNAs post revised WinConditions, Go To Step 2 }
End If
End If

The third method is priority driven and is used when an acceptable policy cannot be negotiated among all team participants in a predetermined amount of time. In this scheme, team participants are assigned a priority based on inputs from the task owner. The option with the highest overall utility, based on global and team member priorities, is selected.

The above negotiation reasoning methods exploit the context and view maintenance problem domain to generate the issues and options and to evaluate the options as follows: 1) Given one or more WinConditions, *issue generation* involves formulating a query to identify VMP specification objects that satisfy the WinConditions. Here the issue is formalized as a query object (global goal generation). 2) Given the formulation of the issue, *option generation* involves evaluation of the query to retrieve plausible VMP specification objects and their refinements based on action-theory knowledge of the NFA. 3) Given the options, *option evaluation* involves checking for consistency of an option against the committed WinConditions representing active beliefs of the RNAs.

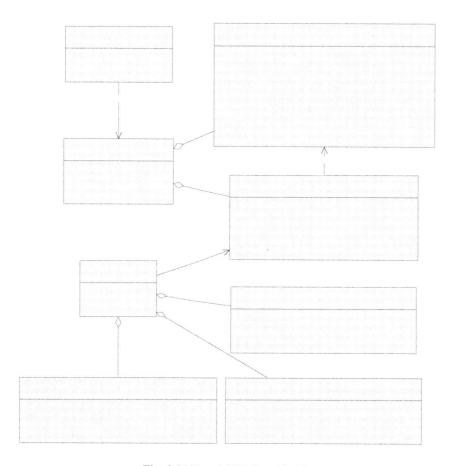

Fig. 4. RNA and CNA Data Model

4.1 Models to Support Negotiated Selection of VMP

In order to support the agent negotiation coordination protocols outlined above, NAVCo defines the client and resource negotiating agents to have a) declarative models of preferences and constraints represented as a database of facts, and b) action-theory for issue generation, option generation and evaluation that are represented as a set of rules. We briefly describe below the data models and some examples of the rules that have been formulated and prototyped in our initial experiments.

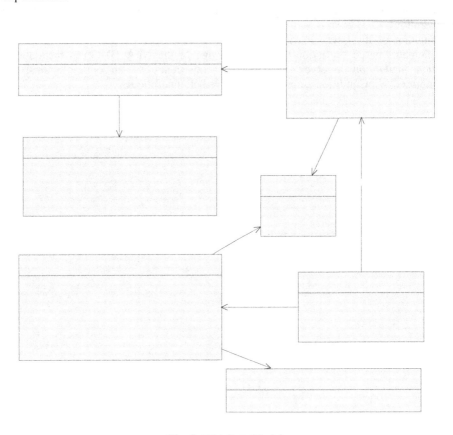

Fig. 5. NFA Data Model

The class diagram shown in Figure 4 captures the data model underlying the information maintained by the CNA of the clients and the RNA of the resources. The model in essence articulates the WinCondition as consisting of two parts: a) Task part of type provides or requires depending on the component type (resource or client). The task part explicates the role to be played, prioritization of tasks, task preferences, and update volume and distribution submitted to the team in support of the task. b) QoS constraint part articulating the constraints imposed on the task. The QoS schema specifies the component workload to support the task and the component QoS constraints based on the status of component resources captured as QoS metrics. The data model also specifies global integrity constraints in terms of the capacity of the clients and resources.

The data model specifying the content of the information in the NFA is given in Figure 5. The data-model captures specifications of the VMPs and their associated costs. The data model also contains models of the WinConditions, Issues, and Options that get posted to or generated by the NFA. Some of the important data elements are a) identification, characteristics, and costs of available coordination policies, b) task-specific meta-data, and c) overall team-level workload characterization, preferences, and constraints.

The rules for issue and option generation are modeled as database trigger rules that analyze an update and create issues, options and option evaluations. The trigger rule in Table 5 creates an Issue, whose semantics is that of a query assertion to select a Policy, in the Issues tables when there is an update in the WinCondition table. It accesses relevant constraints imposed by a task specific WinCondition that must be met by a VMP.

Table 5. An Example of an Issue Generation Rule modeled as a Trigger Rule

TRIGGER <Issue generation> on INSERT into WinConditions
(INSERT into Issues (…)
WHERE Issue.Assertion =
(SELECT Policy
FROM PolicyCost |x| Policy
WHERE UpdateVolume = WinCondition.UpdateVolume
AND UpdateDistribution =WinCondition.UpdateDistribution
AND ConsistencyLevel = WinCondition.ConsistencyLevel
AND UpdateMode=WinCondition.UpdateMode
AND RelativeClientCost < =WinCondition.ComponentCostTolerance))

5 Design and Analysis of Change Coordination Layer

A major requirement on the agent-based mechanisms for run-time change coordination of view maintenance policies is ensuring *application state independence.* This involves ensuring that the sequence of change actions, imposed by the change agents, leads to a connection state that is consistent with the application level processing state without the policy change. The key idea underlying the NAVCo approach to addressing the above requirement is based on the understanding that ensuring such a property involves a) use of knowledge of the processing state of the current view maintenance policy components, b) exploiting knowledge of the behavior of the new policy component to identify the starting state of the new policy such that continued processing from that state would be a consistent progress of the processing state of the current policy, and c) a sequence of actions that brings about the change in activities of the policies and their respective states.

The above understanding is translated into agent design constraints by having 1) tracking agents that use abstract specifications of the view maintenance policies to track their processing states, and 2) a change agent to coordinate the actions required to bring about the change.

The design of the change agents is based on decision rules for control and configuration of the policy-based application layer coordination agents. The rules are obtained by systematic pairwise analysis of switching from one policy to another and identifying changes that do not introduce any inconsistencies in the application specific processing states (such as inconsistent workloads). The questions then are: 1) What are the right abstract behavioral specifications of the view maintenance policy agents that need to be tracked? 2) What is the method for obtaining the specifications of the change agents? 3) Given the error-prone manual generation of the decision rules that get used to program the change agents, how do we analyze and debug the correctness of the decision rules used by the change agents? The following two subsections describe the NAVCo approach to specifying the agent-behaviors for tracking and generation of the rule-based specifications of the change agents.

5.1   Tracking Agent: Behavior Specification

The answer to the first question, raised above, is based on domain analysis of the algorithms for view maintenance. In particular, we identify the state variables underlying the scheduling agent, the query processing agent and the input buffer that represent the application specific processing state and are manipulated by the algorithms to provide view maintenance. Based on such analysis, we have identified the following set of explicit state variables represented by the different components: a) the scheduler's current workload defining the incoming updates from the application specific information resources, b) the query processor's pending tasks (called here the unanswered query set), c) the tasks that have been completed but yet to be scheduled for propagation into the client view, and d) the concurrent update tasks that arrive at the buffer during the processing of an update (necessary to identify and execute compensating queries to eliminate the inconsistency of the current answer due to interacting concurrent updates).

For a given view maintenance policy, the abstract behavior specification is based on qualitative abstractions of the state variables. The abstractions aid in characterizing the overall workload of the different components in the design for a specific policy, that must be gracefully preserved during transitions between view maintenance policies in order to satisfy the application state independence criteria.

5.2   Change Agent: Behavior Specification

The behavior specification of the Change Agent is modeled as a decision tree captured by a finite state machine model (activity diagram in UML) where the decision conditions are captured by the transitions and the actions are captured by the activity states. The decision tree is obtained by a two-step process.

Step 1 - Identify intermediate states. In this step, different workload scenarios are considered and the policies are manually executed to generate event traces for each policy against each workload scenario.

Figure 6 shows a scenario consisting of a single insert operation with no concurrent updates. The scenario modeled as a sequence diagram shows a partial interaction between the application components and the view maintenance agents, where: 1) An insert is submitted by the RMA of an information resource and received by the active scheduling agent (SA). 2) The SA generates a query based on the received insert and schedules it for execution by the query processing agent (QPA). 3) The QPA decomposes the query and sends sub-queries to other resources as required to generate an incremental view update. 4) The QPA sends the query answer to the SA. 5) The SA processes the update and propagates it to the CMA of the client view.

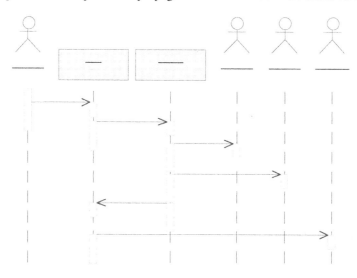

Fig. 6. An example workload scenario

Table 6 shows the event trace table generated by C-Strobe based on the workload scenario in Figure 6. The table shows the sequence of the distinct abstract state vectors (corresponding to the qualitative abstractions of the state variables identified in the previous sections and tracked by the tracking agents in the architecture) that result from the execution of the view maintenance objects. Similarly, Table 7 shows the event trace table for the Strobe policy objects.

Step 2 - Obtain change plans. The second step involves analyzing for pairwise switching of policies to identify workload constraints of the active policy in a given state (specified by the abstract state vector) in the trace and the matching workload constraints of the new policy to be activated in a specific state. The configuration action for activating the new policy is then setting up the workload state variables according to the valid transitions obtained from the above analysis.

This step consists of two sub-steps: 1) identifying the entry in the second trace such that continued processing from that point in the trace would be a consistent progress of the processing state of the first trace, and 2) determining the sequence of actions required to map the state variable values of the first trace to appropriate state variable values of the second trace.

Table 6. Partial event trace generated by C-Strobe

Table 7. Partial event trace generated by Strobe

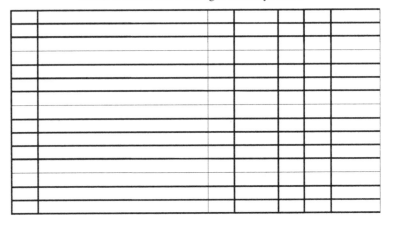

6 Prototype

The adaptive view coordination architecture has been modeled using Rationale Rose 98 Enterprise Edition. Use cases, class diagrams, object collaboration diagrams, and sequence diagrams have been developed. Initial prototypes have been developed for both the negotiation and application views (layers). Prototypes for resource manager, resource negotiation, change coordinator, and negotiation facilitator agents have been developed. Each prototype agent consists of a Java application and a Microsoft Access database.

All agent-to-agent coordination is accomplished through the use of the Nspace, which is implemented using JavaSpaces technology. WinConditions, options, dynamic switching plans and other objects are written as entries into the Nspace. The Nspace notify and read methods are utilized to route the entries to the appropriate agents. The prototype agents currently utilize input and output text files to simulate interactions with clients and resources. Initial results show that the NAVCo reactive reasoning methods can exploit the JavaSpaces based design environment to make negotiated decisions on the policy objects.

7 Related Work

There has been a significant amount of work conducted in the area of view maintenance resulting in a spectrum of solutions ranging from a fully virtual approach where no data is materialized at one extreme to a fully replicated approach where full base relations are copied at the other extreme. The Strobe [21] and SWEEP algorithms [1] are a hybrid of these two extremes and are designed to provide incremental view maintenance over multiple, distributed resources.

The NAVCo work builds on the negotiation research performed by the community in requirements negotiation as well as automated negotiation. Negotiation is a complex and difficult area of active research pursued by researchers in different fields of study. Research progress has been made in different approaches to negotiation: a) Human Factors approach - here the major focus is understanding methods and techniques employed by humans to negotiate so as to manage the human factors of pride, ego, and culture [8, 15, 16]. The work on understanding people factors in requirements negotiation falls in this category. b) Economics, Game Theory and Bargaining approach - here research progress has been made on theoretical models of outcome driven negotiation and self-stabilizing agreement to achieve some equilibrium [11] and process driven negotiation [14]. Research on negotiation focuses on the group decision context where the power to decide is distributed across more than one stakeholder/agent as opposed to group decision making where a single decision maker relies on a set of analysts [12]. Two key aspects of the negotiated decision studied in most of the research are conflict and interdependence of decisions. Conflict has been used constructively in cooperative domains to explore negotiation options [3]. c) Artificial Agents approach - here the focus has been on developing computational agents that negotiate to resolve conflict [6], to distribute tasks [17, 19], to share resources [22], to change goals so as to optimize multi-attribute utility functions [18]. In general, the models for agent cooperation and negotiation consider negotiation between multiple agents driven by global utility functions or driven by independent local utility functions. The WinWin [2, 3] model used in NAVCo considers both types of drivers typical of negotiating teams having local preferences as well as global constraints.

The NAVCo approach is also similar in spirit to the work on architecture-based run-time evolution [13]. Our approach and reasoning tools differ from [13] in terms of the nature of automation. The work in [13] focused on providing a support environment where the necessary analysis for dynamic change and consequent operationalization can be performed. The NAVCo approach and prototype discussed in the paper is motivated by automated switching via automated negotiation reasoning and change coordination realized by the middleware agents in the negotiation layer and the change coordination layer.

8 Summary and Future Work

This paper develops a Negotiation-based Adaptive View Coordination (NAVCo) approach for a class of distributed information management systems that allows view maintenance policies to be dynamically adapted to meet changes in QoS preferences and constraints in a run-time environment. The key ideas in the NAVCo approach involve negotiation-based coordination and model-based tracking and policy change coordination. The ideas are well suited for realization using agent-based concepts and architecture. The paper describes the layered agent-based architecture with specific emphasis on the agent-oriented middleware at each layer that supports a) cooperative change reasoning via multi-agent negotiation coordination and negotiated artifacts representations, and b) change coordination via model-based tracking and change agents. With respect to the change-coordination layer, the paper details systematic approaches to specifying the tracking agents and synthesizing the rule-based specifications of the change agents. Current work is targeted towards developing monitoring agents that monitor the application layer middleware agents and can be used to trigger the policy switching process based on reifying the run-time performance concern as a change in committed WinConditions. Also such monitors would be useful to validate the adaptation in terms of performance benefits gained as a result of switching. Future work will focus on debugging the agent specifications using model checking approaches as well as further extensions to the capability of the negotiating agents for issue generation, option generation and evaluation rules.

9 References

1. D. Agrawal, A. El Abbadi, A Singh, and T. Yurek, Efficient View Maintenance at Data Warehouses. In Proceedings of the ACM SIGMOD '97, pp. 417-427, 1997.
2. B. Boehm, P. Bose, E Horowitz and M. J. Lee, "Software Requirements Negotiation and Renegotiation Aids: A Theory-W Based Spiral Approach," In IEEE Proceedings of the 17th ICSE Conference, 1995.
3. P. Bose and Z. Xiaoqing, "WinWin Decision Model Based Coordination," International Joint Conference on Work Activities Coordination and Collaboration, 1999.
4. P. Bose and M. G. Matthews, "An Architecture for Achieving Dynamic Change in Coordination Policies," Proceedings of the 4th International Software Architecture Workshop (ISAW4), June 2000.
5. W. R. Collins et. al., "How Good is Good Enough?" Communications of the ACM, pp. 81-91, January 1994.
6. E. H. Durfee, V. R. Lesser, and D. D. Corkill, "Cooperation Through Communication in a Distributed Problem Solving Network," In M. N. Huhns ed., Distributed Artificial Intelligence, Chapter 2, 29-58.
7. J. Farley, "Java Distributed Computing," O' Reilly Press, 1998.
8. R. Fisher and W. Ury, "Getting to Yes," Houghton-Mifflin, 1981. Also Penguin Books, 1983.
9. R. Hull and G. Zhou, A Framework for Supporting Data Integration Using the Materialized and Virtual Approaches. In Proceedings of the ACM SIGMOD International Conference on Management of Data, pp. 481-492, June 1996.
10. T. W. Malone and K. Crowston, "The Interdisciplinary Study of Coordination," ACM Computing Surveys, Vol. 26, No. 1, pp. 87-119, Mar. 1994.
11. J. F. Nash, "The Bargaining Problem," Econometrica 28, pp. 155-162, 1950.

12. J. F. Nunamaker, A. R. Dennis, J. S. Valacich and D. R. Vogel, "Information Technology for Negotiating Groups: Generating Options for Mutual Gain," Management Science, October 1991.
13. P. Oreizy, N. Medvidovic, and R. N. Taylor, "Architecture-based Runtime Evolution," In Proceedings of ICSE 1998.
14. M. J. Osborne and A. Rubinstein, "A Course in Game Theory," MIT Press, MA, 1994.
15. M. Porter, "Competitive Strategy: Techniques for Analyzing Industries and Competitors," Free Press, NY, 1980.
16. H. Raiffa, "The Art and Science of Negotiation,, Harvard University Press, Cambridge, MA, 1982
17. R. G. Smith, "The Contract Net Protocol: High-level Communication and Control in a Distributed Problem Solver," IEEE Trans. On Computer, 29, pp. 1104-1113, 1980.
18. K. P. Sycara, "Resolving Goal Conflicts Via Negotiation," In Proceedings of AAAI, pp. 245-250, 1988.
19. M. P. Wellman, "A General Equilibrium Approach to Distributed Transportation Planning," In Proceedings of AAAI-92, San Jose, CA 1992.
20. T. Winograd, "Bringing Design to Software," Addison Wesley Publishers, 1996.
21. Y. Zhuge, H. Garcia-Molina, and J. Wiener, "The Strobe Algorithms for Multi-Source Warehouse Consistency," In Proceedings of the International Conference on Parallel and Distributed Information Systems, December 1996.
22. G. Zlotkin, and J. S. Rosenschein, "Mechanism Design for Automated Negotiation and Its Application to Task Oriented Domains," Artificial Intelligence, Vol. 86, pp. 195-244, 1996.

Coordination Models
for Dynamic Resource Allocation

Stefan Johansson, Paul Davidsson, and Bengt Carlsson

Department of Software Engineering and Computer Science,
University of Karlskrona/Ronneby,
Soft Center, 372 25 Ronneby, Sweden
{sja, pdv, bca}@ipd.hk-r.se,

Abstract. A number of different coordination models for dynamic resource allocation are proposed. The models are based on an asynchronous
and distributed approach which makes use of mobile agents to distribute
the resources of the providers between the consumers. Each provider has
a broker, i.e., the mobile agent, that continually visits all or a subset
of the consumers, offering the resources currently available at the corresponding provider. The models are increasingly complex, starting with a
rather simple static mechanism, and ending with a sophisticated solution
that balance the allocations both from the consumer and the provider
perspective. Finally, an evaluation of the models in a realistic Intelligent
Network domain is presented.

1   Introduction

Dynamic resource allocation is a problem that arises in various areas such as:

- *Telecommunication networks*, where resources sometimes need to be reallo-
  cated in order to avoid overload situations in a distributed switching system,
  such as a SS7 network. One proposed solution make use of traditional prob-
  abilistic heuristics e.g. Call Gapping and Percentage Blocking [2].
- *Utility distribution* in which the goal is to, as efficiently as possible, make
  sure that utility is delivered to the customers. Here the preferences of the
  customers may vary over time, e.g. it may be important for one customer
  to have enough warm water for a shower in the morning, while it is less
  important to have it during the day when nobody is home. The allocation can
  efficiently be achieved through the use of distributed, hierarchical auctions
  [13].
- *CPU load balancing*, where the mean job flow time in a network of processors may be minimized through dynamically allocating different processes
  to different CPUs. Agent technology and a market based approach based on
  centralized auctions is one way to cope with this coordination problem [5].

It is doubtless an important problem to be able to handle, in order to meet
the ever increasing expectations of the customers of systems such as the ones
described above.

A. Porto and G.-C. Roman (Eds.): COORDINATION 2000, LNCS 1906, pp. 182–197, 2000.
© Springer-Verlag Berlin Heidelberg 2000

From a general point of view, dynamic resource allocation deals with the problem of allocating resources produced by a set of *providers* to a set of *customers*. The amount of available resources, as well as the rate of consumption (and thus the need for the resources) may vary over time, and the resources cannot be saved for later usage. The problem is to dynamically update the allocation in a way that the following goals are achieved:

1. If the total capacity of the providers exceeds the total demand of the customers, all customers should get as much resources as they need.
2. In all situations, the deviation between the relative amount of resources given to the consumers should be kept as small as possible. By "relative amount of resources", we mean the amount of resources a customer gets divided by the amount of resources it demands. This is one possible way to describe consumer fairness in a dynamic resource allocation problem.
3. In all situations, the deviation between the utilizations of the providers should be kept as small as possible, i.e. the utilization of the resources should be balanced between the providers. Just as in the previous goal, this is a measure of fairness, but from the provider side, – each provider should be utilized equally much.
4. The utilization of a provider should not exceed its target capacity, i.e. the limit telling how much of the available resources of the provider that should be used maximally. For instance the target capacity may be lower than the actual capacity when the provider have to save some of its resources for higher prioritized tasks, such as alarm calls, electricity for essential equipment such as water pumps, and CPU power for operating system calls.

In other words, we would like to allocate the resources in a fair way (both from the perspective of the provider and the consumer) without wasting any resources or violating any target capacities.

1.1   Outline of the Paper

Firstly, in section 2 we describe four different distributed approaches to the problem of dynamic resource allocation. Some properties are common for all the proposals, such as the overall architecture and the abilities to communicate, and some are different, i.e. the calculation of demands and allocations. This section also includes a table at page 185 of the notations and abbreviations used in the paper. We then in section 3 describe a typical instance of a dynamic resource allocation, namely the one that is performed in Intelligent Networks in the area of telecommunication. This application domain has been simulated and a description of the simulations and their results is found in sections 4 and 5. We then discuss the results and draw some conclusions in the last sections (6 and 7).

2   Mobile Broker Coordination in Dynamic Resource Allocation

We present four different distributed approaches to dynamic resource allocation: the Naive Broker (NB) model, the Greedy Customer (GC) model, the Broker Balanced (BB) coordination model, and the Dually Balanced (DB) coordination model. Common for all of the presented coordination models are the following:

- Each provider has a broker that acts on its behalf by visiting the consumers.
- Each broker follows a route specifying the order in which the consumers are visited.
- In the case of two brokers visiting a consumer during the same time period, the one that gets there first will be the first to negotiate with the consumer.
- When a broker arrives to a consumer, the consumer starts by telling the broker how much capacity it would like to have. The broker responds with the amount it will allocate for that consumer. No further iterations of the negotiation is performed.
- The brokers are assumed to have full knowledge of the target capacity of its corresponding provider.[1]
- There is no *other* coordination between consumers, providers and brokers, than the ones described above.
- The brokers and the consumers may cooperate (within the given model of coordination above) in order to find the best global (allocation) solution.
- The predicted demand of the consumer is the same as the actual demand during the last second, i.e. it is assumed that the consumers are not able to predict any changes in demand.

Since no information at all is used to coordinate the demands and allocations neither in the NB model nor in the GC model, we will regard them as *statically coordinated*, whereas BB and DB are the *dynamically coordinated* models.meet new demands of the environment (as is the case with the BB and the DB).

2.1   The Naive Broker Model

In the NB model, the broker has a very simple relation to its consumers. It gives every consumer exactly the amount of resources it asks for until the target capacity of its provider is reached. Thus, if a broker has given away all of its resources, the next consumer in the route will not be able to increase its share of the resources. The consumer only asks for the amount of resources that it predicts it will need.

2.2   The Greedy Consumer Model

An improvement of the NB is the GC. Here we let the consumers ask for more than they think they need, i.e. a bid that exceeds their predicted demand and the

---

[1] Note that this is *not* the same as being fully updated on the current available capacity of the provider.

broker still gives the consumer the exact amount of resources it asks for. This is a greedy behavior that protects against each individual consumer's risk of running out of resources, however asking for more than it need may cause a lack of resources even though the provider run below target capacity. The GC range from the pure NB model to a strictly selfish behavior, in which the consumers always ask for all the available capacity that the broker has. This means that only the first consumer along the route of the broker gets any resources. This *degree of greediness* can be seen as a mixed strategy in a cooperative game as has been discussed e.g. in previous work by Johansson [8].

Table 1. The symbols and abbreviations used in the paper

Notation	Explanation
BB	The Broker Balanced model of coordination
DB	The Dually Balanced model of coordination
GC	The Greedy Consumer model of coordination
NB	The Naive Broker model of coordination
IN	Intelligent Network
OL	Optimal Load
SSP	Service Switching Point, – a consumer node in the SS7 network
SCP	Service Control Point, – a provider node in the SS7 network
d_i^j	The demand of consumer i given to broker j
D^j	The total demand of all consumers of the route of broker j
ϕ_i^j	The balancing factor calculated by consumer in order to modify the demand given to broker j
g	The function describing the difference between the actual and the wanted demand
m_i^j	The modified demand of consumer i given to broker j
r_i^j	The relative load of broker j according to consumer i
T^j	The target capacity the provider of broker j
u_i^j	The upper limit of resources given to consumer i by broker j

2.3   The Broker Balanced Coordination Model

In the BB coordination model, each broker j keeps track of two values for each consumer i in its route: the *demand*, d_i^j, i.e., how much capacity the consumer asked for, and the *upper limit*, u_i^j, which is capacity actually given to the consumer. The broker then calculates the upper limit for that consumer using the following formula:

$$u_i^j = \frac{(d_i^j \cdot T_j)}{D^j}, \tag{1}$$

where D^j is the total demand, $\sum_i d_i^j$, and T_j is the target capacity. Note that in case of a sudden increase in demand, as soon as D^j becomes greater than T_j, the broker will give the allocator less than it requested. On the other hand, the sum of the upper limits, $\sum_i u_i^j$, may momentarily exceed T_j, which in the worst case will lead to a transient overload situation. The mechanism is self-stabilizing, and will find an equilibrium within one route (given that the demands, d_i^j, stabilize on new levels).

2.4   The Dually Balanced Coordination Model

In addition to having brokers balance the load among its consumers, each consumer may help the brokers by demanding in a way that the total resource utilization is spread out evenly between the providers, whose brokers visit the consumer. This coordination model, denoted DB, take both supply and demand into account when allocating the resources.

Since a consumer i knows its own previous demand given to a broker j, and also the amount of resources that it is given as an upper limit, it may calculate the relative load r_i^j of that broker, i.e. its total amount of demand from the consumers in its route, $\sum_i d_i^j$, divided by its target capacity T_j.[2] Similar to the broker, it may now calculate its demands in a way that it balances the load, but in this case it balances the load between the different visiting brokers, rather than, as the broker, balancing the allocation relative to the needs of the consumers.

We implement this by letting the consumer calculate the average of the relative loads of its providers $S_i = \sum_j r_i^j/k$, (where k is the number of visiting brokers) and $\sum_{j\neq b} r_i^j/(k-1)$, (where b is the broker visiting i at the moment). The modified demand m_i^j sent to b's provider is then a product of the actual demand of the consumer d_i^j and a balancing factor ϕ made out of the relative loads:

$$m_i^j = d_i^j \cdot \phi_i^j \qquad (2)$$

where ϕ_i^j is (approximately):

$$\phi_i^j = \frac{\sum_{j\neq b} r_i^j/k - 1}{\sum_j r_i^j/k} = \frac{k \cdot d_i^j \cdot \sum_{j\neq b} r_i^j}{(k-1) \cdot \sum_j r_i^j} \qquad (3)$$

To use the quotient of the relative loads directly as a regulator may cause oscillations in the demand, but using a PID-regulator to stabilize ϕ_i^j, results in less fluctuating values. The idea behind such a regulator is to damp the oscillations in demand that appear when the consumers are trying to balance their demands between their providers. This can be done by looking at the function g that describes the difference between the actual value and the wanted value. By numerically calculating the integration and the derivative of g and by feeding these values back to the balancing factor ϕ, such an effect may be achieved if the weights of the feedback are appropriate. More about PID-regulators can be found in text books about control theory, e.g. in [7].

---

[2] In a fully cooperative system this information may be provided directly by the broker at the time of arrival, instead of being derived from previous visits.

3   Intelligent Network Resource Allocation

The Intelligent Network (IN) concept was developed in order to enable operators of telecommunication networks to create and maintain services quickly [11]. Two important entities of an IN are the Service Switching Points (SSPs) and the Service Control Points (SCPs). The SSPs continuously receive requests of services which they cannot serve without the help of the SCPs where all service software resides. Thus, the SCPs are provide rs and the SSPs are consumers. The SSPs and SCPs communicate via a signaling network which we here will represent as a *cloud* rather than a specific topology of signaling links and nodes. This is because we assume the computational power at the SCPs to be the bottleneck, i.e. the ability to handle the requests, rather than the signalling network itself. It is assumed that a small part of the available bandwidth of this network is reserved for the load control mechanism, in our case agent communication and transportation. If n is the number of SCPs and m is the number of SSPs, where typically $n < m$,

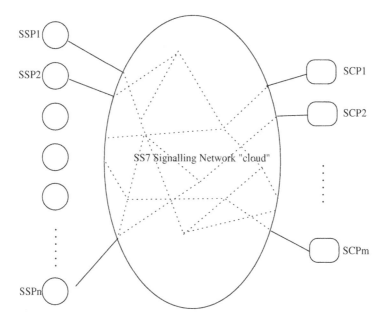

Fig. 1. An Intelligent Network (IN) with m SCPs and n SSPs

we have the simplified IN configuration shown in Fig. 1 (taken from Arvidsson et al. [1]). It is assumed that all SCPs support the same set of service classes and that all service requests can be directed by a SSP to any SCP.

As been observed by Arvidsson et al. [1], IN load control can be seen as a distributed resource allocation problem:

"On one hand, there is the desire to serve all service requests that are often unpredictable and bursty with regard to time, rate and volume.

On the other hand, all the resources in the network have finite capacity and must be managed for optimal allocation amongst different usage requests. Resource allocation in IN involves three tasks:

1. monitoring utilization levels of resources (in particular SCP processors),
2. control of the allocation of these resources and
3. granting/denial of permission to individual service requests to use the resources."

More specifically, there are a number of goals that an ideal solution to this load control problem would meet. For instance, SCP load levels should be as close to the target load (e.g., 0.9 Erlangs, corresponding to 90% of its capacity) as possible but not exceed it.[3] If an overload situation is approaching, the SSPs should throttle new requests. The system should also be able to quickly react to sudden increases in offered loads and increase the carried load correspondingly. Finally, it should balance the load equally between the SCPs.

4   Simulation Model of a Distributed Resource Allocation Problem

We have compared four mobile broker coordination models in a IN resource allocation problem described in section 3 above in a simulation study. A comparison between the BB and other non-distributed coordination models can be found in [4].

We use the same simulation model as Arvidsson et al. [1]. The IN configuration has 8 SCPs and 32 SSPs, which are assumed to be statistically identical respectively. The processors at the SCPs are engineered to operate at a nominal load of 35% and with a maximum permissible load of 90%. All messages passing through the network experience a constant delay of 5 ms, and it is assumed that no messages are lost and network resources do not overload. The network supports two service classes which are modified services of the two services defined by Karagiannis et al. [9]. The call holding times of both services are negative exponentially distributed with a mean of $100s$. Each call consists of a connection phase, which corresponds to a processing load of $4.1ms$ for service 1 and $6.4ms$ for service 2, and a disconnection phase, which corresponds to a processing load of $1.4ms$ and $0.16ms$ respectively. Service requests arrive according to independent Poisson processes. In the simulations below, the arrival rate is stated in terms of offered load corresponding to aggregated SCP load (between 0 and 2 Erlangs, i.e., between no traffic and severe overload).

For all broker-based approaches, we assume that the time needed for a broker to negotiate and move from one SSP to another is $200ms$. A smaller delay would imply even better reactions to changes in offered load, but would also demand more network bandwidth. Moreover in the simulations below, each broker's route

---

[3] This is due to the requirement of having certain capacity dedicated to e.g. the resource allocation itself, maintenance, urgent services etc.

initially consists of eight SSP as defined in Table 2. Thus, each SSP belongs to the route of exactly two brokers. Another condition that is fulfilled with the routes is that each route shares at least one SSP with every other route.[4]

Table 2. The visiting order of the consumers in the broker routes of our simulations

Place in Route	b_1	b_2	b_3	b_4	b_5	b_6	b_7	b_8
1	8	28	21	4	16	24	10	26
2	7	27	3	20	15	14	11	32
3	6	2	26	19	23	13	31	8
4	5	1	25	22	17	18	9	10
5	4	32	24	21	29	30	7	12
6	3	31	27	28	14	11	15	16
7	2	30	23	18	13	6	19	20
8	1	29	22	17	5	12	25	9

We then simulate the following scenario:

- Initially, all consumers are offered a load corresponding to an expected SCP load of 0.35 Erlang.
- At time 200, eight consumers get a peak in demand reaching up to 2.0 Erlang. All of these eight are in the route of broker 1 (SSPs 1, 2, 3, 4, 5, 6, 7 and 8).
- At time 500, the overloaded SSPs get back to a normal demand of 0.35 Erlang.

The scenario is a worst case scenario for a distributed coordination model without any centralized possibility to communicate capacities and demands between the providers and the consumers. This is because the SSPs getting a peak in their demand all belong to the route of the same broker, thus making the demands in the system very unbalanced. Our goal is to find out if our coordination model proposals are able of handling such displacements in demands.

5   Results of the Simulation

We describe the results of the simulations from the four different perspectives discussed in the general problem description in Section 1, the ability to deliver the amount of resources asked for without waste, the ability to allocate the resources in a fair way according to changes in demands, the ability to spread out the loads evenly between the providers of capacity, and the ability to stay below target capacity for all providers.

---

[4] To find out what SSP should belong to which route is not hard; however, to find a set of routes that is optimal with respect to the visiting order as a whole is NP-complete.

5.1   The Ability to Deliver Requested Resources

We use the average ability to deliver the resource in the given scenario as a measure of the capability of the coordination models in this matter. Since the total demand of the system is below the total target capacity, an optimal allocation should manage to reach a full acceptance rate at 100%. In Fig. 2 and Table 3 we see that the NB is well below the others and that DB is slightly better on allocating, than the other two top coordination models.

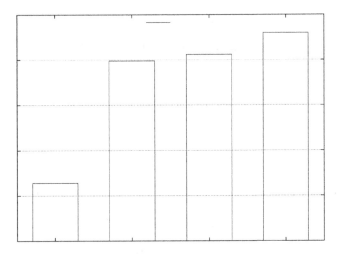

Fig. 2. The averaged rate of acceptance over all SCPs in 10 simulations for the different coordination models.

Table 3. The average acceptance rates of the different coordination models (graphically shown in Figs. 2 and 3)

	NB	GC	BB	DB
SSP 1–8	0.740	0.910	0.923	0.981
SSP 9–36	0.897	0.993	0.993	0.978
All SSPs	0.814	0.949	0.956	0.980

5.2   The Deviation in the Fulfillment of Demands

Since the relative allocation should be kept as fair as possible, i.e. the rates of acceptance of each SSP should be kept as close to the average acceptance rate as possible, we compare the SSPs that have a constant expected rate of requests (that is SSP 9–32) with the ones that get a peak in demand (SSP 1–8). In Fig. 3 we see that the DB manage to balance the allocation rates, while the others have more or less problems in doing so (even though both GC and BB manage to give the unpeaked SSPs a higher rate of acceptance, they fail to fulfill the needs of the overloaded SSPs).

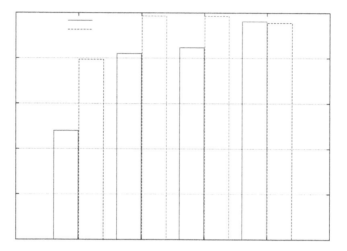

Fig. 3. The averaged rate of acceptance for the different coordination models in the 10 simulations. The left bars show the rate of SSP 1–8, whereas the right bars show the rate of SSP 9–32.

5.3   The Deviation in Loads of the Providers

In Figs. 4 – 7 we see how the load is spread between the SCPs. For reasons of clarity, three (out of eight) characteristics of loads are shown:

- The load of SCP 1, which is the provider whose customers all get a peak in their demand.
- The load of SCP 2, which shares two customers with SCP 1, and whose customers' *other* brokers visit a customer with a peak in its demand right before it visits the customer shared with SCP 2 (see Table 2).
- The load of SCP 5, which is a typical representative of all other providers in the system (i.e. SCP 3 – 8).[5]

---

[5] All of SCPs 3–8 have almost identical characteristics, justifying the approximation of all of them through just plotting one of them.

Figure 4 show the load for the naive broker approach. We clearly see how SCP 1 has a higher load than the *optimal load* (OL).[6] SCP 2 has a slightly lower load, and the rest of the brokers have a significantly lower load, staying at approximately. 0.5 Erlang. This is because they only visit one consumer with the a peak demand and no mechanism is implemented that coordinate the allocation in a way that the load is spread out between the SCPs.

In Fig. 5, which shows the carried load for the greedy consumer model, we see an improvement in that both SCP 1 and 2 is closer to the OL, and the rest of the providers are much closer to the OL than in the NB.

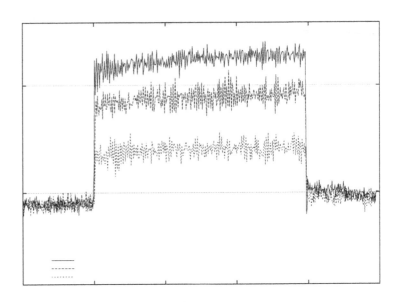

Fig. 4. The average load of SCP 1, 2 and 5 in the NB over time based on 10 simulations.

We see in Fig. 6 that yet some improvement is made when using the BB model of coordination. This is because the SCP 5 – type of providers are getting closer to the OL and that SCP 1 and 2 manage to increase their total load. Note that the BB gives rise to a sudden peak in load for SCP 1 as the demand peaks. This is due to the brokers ability to momentarily allocate more capacity than its target capacity, and the consumer's ability to use all of the capacity it has got allocated.

---

[6] The optimal load is calculated through dividing the expected total demand of all consumers with the number of providers. We assume that all providers have the same capacity. The OLs are shown as thin lines in the diagrams on the levels of 0.35 Erlang and 0.7625 Erlang.

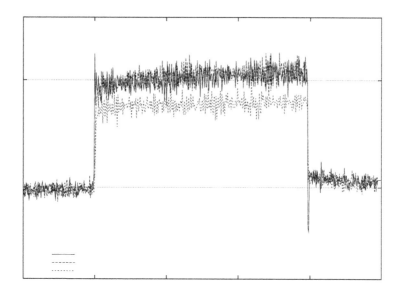

Fig. 5. The average load of scp 1, 2 and 5 in the gc over time based on 10 simulations.

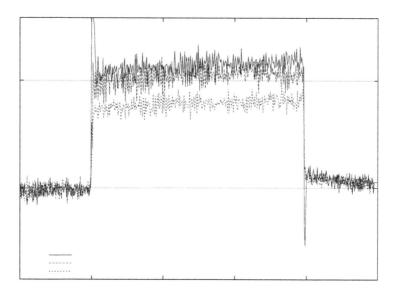

Fig. 6. The average load of scp 1, 2 and 5 in the bb over time based on 10 simulations.

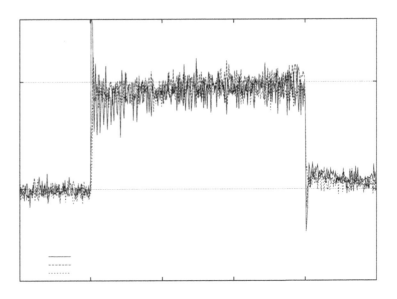

Fig. 7. The average load of SCP 1, 2 and 5 in the DB over time based on 10 simulations.

The last of our simulations concerned the DB. We used a simple numeric integration and derivation to stabilize the balancing factor that is used by the allocator to decide how to split its demands between its providers. In Fig. 7, we see that the system reallocates the resources in a way that all SCPs get about the same load near the OL.

5.4   On Not Exceeding the Target Capacity

The two coordination models that best achieve the *other* goals of this simulation, i.e. the BB and the DB, are the ones that are violating the restriction of not exceeding the target capacity (as can be seen in Figs. 6 and 7). This is because the brokers in both coordination models use the balancing mechanism described in Section 2.3, which momentarily may allocate more capacity to their customers than their corresponding providers may provide, but since that mechanism stabilizes in one iteration of the broker route, such violations only occur when a sudden peak in demand strikes at several SSPs in a broker route at the same time. Also, since they to a higher degree manage to utilize the capacity of the providers, they run a higher risk of reaching the target (and above).

6   Discussion

What the fairness in allocation and load is concerned, nothing beats a centralized solution, since it has access to all data when it makes the allocation, e.g. in market-based control mechanisms using centralized auctions [6], but as pointed out by Carlsson et al., there are several advantages with a distributed coordination model such as increased robustness and the ability to model owner preferences [4]. These advantages may be implemented through mobile brokers, and the results in Section 5 show that near-optimal *distributed* coordination models are possible through the use of the DB approach.

There is always a tradeoff between the degree of decentralization on the one hand, where a fully decentralized system have advantages such as the ones described above, and the degree of availability of global information on the other hand, where a pure centralized solution have this information, but inherently lack the advantages of decentralized approaches.

In comparison to related work, we present an evaluation of four mobile agent-based coordination mechanisms in the domain of resource allocation in telecommunication networks. We have previously shown that a decentralized mechanisms (in that case the BB coordination mechanism) is a feasible alternative to the centralized auction–based ones [4], and the results here show further improvements along this line.

Several projects are dealing with solutions to different dynamic resource allocation problems, most of them by using traditional centralized non-agent mechanisms (e.g. [3,2,10]), some use agents to negotiate in central markets, for instance centralized auctions [1,12] and some use local distributed markets, e.g. hierarchical markets [13]. Our solution differs in that we introduce local markets based on the routes of the mobile agents and that the consumers are buyers on more than one market, which facilitate global equilibria through local interactions without any other explicit coordination than the exchange of demands and delivered resources.

7   Conclusions and Future Work

Dynamic resource allocation is not a new problem. However, as far as we know, the idea of using *mobile broker agents* in order to balance *both* resources and demands between providers and consumers in a truly distributed way (i.e. the DB approach) is novel.

We have studied a dynamic resource allocation problem by means of using mobile brokers to allocate the resources between the consumers and providers. Four different coordination models for dynamic resource allocation in a IN domain were used and we may, by the result of the simulations draw the following conclusions:

- All of the proposed models allocate the resources without use of any global knowledge, i.e. the architectures of the approaches are truly distributed.
- Apart from the NB, the proposed models manage to balance the resources in a IN scenario fairly well.
- By using the DB, it is possible to coordinate allocations in dynamic resource allocation in a way that fulfills the goals 1–3 stated in Section 1.

- Goal 4 is not perfectly fulfilled by any model, however, all models reach the goal to an acceptable degree.

We believe that the exchange of ideas between the traditional application areas such as telecommunication networks, and utility distribution on the one hand, and new emergent technologies such as agent technology on the other, is fruitful. We will for sure see an increase in use of decentralized coordination mechanisms for traditional dynamic resource allocation problems.

In the future we will study how the coordination models presented here may be extended to other domains than the IN scenario in Section 4. We will also try to develop the ideas on route generation, possibly by letting the system adapt the routes to the current load situation dynamically. Last but not least, we will extend our evaluation of multi-agent solutions to include other coordination mechanisms such as distributed auctions and leaky buckets.

Acknowledgements

The authors would like to acknowledge the EC ACTS-project AC-333 MARINER for partial funding and inspiration. We would of course also like to thank the anonymous reviewers and the following colleagues for helping us with various details: Rune Gustavsson, Åke Arvidsson, Michael Mattsson, Christoffer Jerrebo, Magnus Svensson, Mårten Folkler, Richard Krejstrup, Per Liden, and Mikael Svanberg.

References

1. Å. Arvidsson, B. Jennings, L. Angelin, and M. Svensson. On the use of agent technology for IN load control. In *16th International Teletraffic Congress*. Elsevier Science, 1999.
2. A.W. Berger. Comparison of call gapping and percent blocking for overload control in distributed switching systems and telecommunication networks. *IEEE Trans. Commun.*, 39:574–580, 1991.
3. A.W. Berger. Performance analysis of a rate-control throttle where tokens and jobs queue. *IEEE J. Select. Areas Commun.*, 9:165–170, 1991.
4. B. Carlsson, P. Davidsson, S.J. Johansson, and M. Ohlin. Using mobile agents for IN load control. In *Proc. of Intelligent Networks '2000*. IEEE, 2000.
5. A. Chavez, A. Moukas, and P. Maes. *Challenger*: a multi-agent system for distributed resource allocation. In *Proceedings of Autonomous Agents '97*. ACM, 1997.
6. S.H. Clearwater, editor. *Market-Based Control: Some early lessons*. World Scientific, 1996.
7. P. Harriott. *Process Control*. McGraw–Hill, New York, 1964.
8. S.J. Johansson. Game theory and agents. licentiate thesis, November 1999. Dept. of Software Engineering and Computer Science, University of Karlskrona/Ronneby.
9. G. Karagiannis, V.F Nicola, and I.G.M.M. Niemegeers. Quantitative evaluation of scalability in broadband intelligent networks. In Körner and Nilsson, editors, *Performance of Information and Communication Systems*, pages 65–82. Chapman & Hall, 1998.

10. T. Kimura and T. Asaka. Leaky-bucket-with-gate algorithm for connection setup congestion control in multi-media networks. *IEICE Trans. Commun.*, E80-B(3):448–455, March 1997.
11. T. Magedanz and R. Popescu-Zeletin. *Intelligent Networks*. International Thomson Computer Press, 1996.
12. M.P. Wellman. Market-based control: A paradigm for distributed resource allocation. In S. Clearwater, editor, *Market-Oriented Programming: Some early lessons*, chapter 4. World Scientific, 1996.
13. F. Ygge. *Market-Oriented Programming and its Application to Power Load Management*. PhD thesis, Lund University, Sweden, 1998.

MobileML : A Programming Language for Mobile Computation

Masatomo Hashimoto and Akinori Yonezawa

Department of Information Science, Faculty of Science, University of Tokyo,
7-3-1 Hongo, Bunkyo-ku, Tokyo 113-0033, Japan
{masatomo,yonezawa}@is.s.u-tokyo.ac.jp

Abstract. This paper describes a language which facilitates programming for *mobile computation* i.e., computation in which code migrates and continues to run across network nodes. Such languages allow us to develop novel distributed applications (such as workflow systems, flexible software distribution, and intelligent search systems) more easily and efficiently. However, many of existing programming language systems are often insufficient because they lack the support for concise description of migration and formal models for reasoning about program's properties including type safety and security. Our goal is to construct a programming language system which adequately supports mobile computation on a solid theoretical basis. As an attempt to achieve that, we have designed a programming language based on ML which has well-founded theoretical bases. The features of this language include: transparent migration, dynamic linking with distributed resources by means of *contexts*, and semantics consistent with the original ML. Especially, our notion of contexts allows us to succinctly describe the interaction between mobile code and environments at destination nodes. We briefly explain a simple semantic model based on Plotkin's λ_v-calculus and *tuple spaces*. Though our model currently guarantees only type soundness, we believe that theoretical results such as prevention of security violation (of Heintze and Rieckes' SLam Calculus) can be incorporated into our system rather easily. We have also implemented an experimental interpreter system as a first step of the full-fledged language system.

1 Introduction

With explosive growth of global computer networks, programming languages are expected to have some sophisticated mechanisms for networkwide programming. Java [12] popularized the notion of *mobile code* which can travel on a heterogeneous network and automatically runs upon arrival at the destination. Some of modern distributed languages [4,13,28,20,25] facilitate a novel form of distributed computation, called *mobile computation* [28,13,5] i.e., computation in which code migrates and continues to run across network nodes. Mobile computation is expected to be a promising framework for construction of distributed systems. The main advantages of constructing a distributed system in the style of mobile computation are efficiency and flexibility. For example, suppose that

A. Porto and G.-C. Roman (Eds.): COORDINATION 2000, LNCS 1906, pp. 198–215, 2000.

we are trying to search the Internet for routes of a tour and to reserve tickets from a mobile terminal. Connection between mobile terminals and the Internet is usualy very poor in speed and too expensive in cost. Therefore, we would like to avoid connecting to the Internet for a long period. In the framework of mobile computation, search and reservation programs migrate from mobile terminals to servers of travel agencies on the Internet [15,28].

It is desirable for programming languages for mobile computation to have at least the following features:

Transparent migration. Mobile code is a program which migrates from one node to another in a network. It can suspend its execution at arbitrary program points, move to another node, and resume execution with exactly the same execution state at the destination node. We call such a form of migration *strong* or *transparent* [13]. Transparent migration is desirable because it allows succinct description of migration and offers clear semantics of migration [13]. This feature reduces programmer's burden considerably.

Abstraction of local environments. When a piece of code moves to a network node, its execution environment also changes. In the style of mobile computation, pieces of mobile code naturally make use of local environments including processors, displays, hard disks, and local data such as strings, images and sounds. Therefore, appropriate abstractions for local environments are necessary in order to simplify programming.

Formal models. In mobile systems, external code may be executed at a user's machine and user's private code may be executed elsewhere in the network. Therefore security and safety are important issues. Solid formal models are the key to formal reasoning about such properties of programs.

However, none of the existing programming languages satisfy all the above. Obliq [4] is a distributed object-oriented language based on static scoping rules. In Obliq, we can transmit closures to other network nodes, and construct mobile applications [3]. However, transparent migration and abstractions for local environments are not supported. Telescript [28] is a pioneer of mobile language. It can describe migration by only writing "**go** *destination*" at almost an arbitrary program point. Although Telescript supports transparent migration, it does not have the notion of local environment and any formal model. D'Agents [14], once called AgentTcl [13], is based on a scripting language Tcl and supports transparent migration. However, no formal model exists. JavaGo [25] realizes transparent migration by source to source transformation in Java with Remote Method Invocation. Its transformation mechanism is based on a formal framework [26]. However, Java language itself is far from rigorously specified. Distributed Join-Calculus [10] is a distributed concurrent language based on a solid formal model. This language can represent *locations* which contain running processes, and may fail. However, it cannot directly describe utilization of local environments.

Our goal is to construct a programming language system which adequately supports mobile computation on a rigorous theoretical basis. As an approach to that goal, we have designed a language called *MobileML* based on ML [6], and implemented an experimental interpreter system. The main features of this language include: transparent migration, dynamic linking with distributed resources by means of *contexts*, and semantics consistent with the original ML. Above all, our notion of contexts allows us to succinctly describe various forms of interactions between mobile code and environments at the destination nodes. (Examples include a description of runtime update of libraries used in an application.) Of course, we can utilize theoretical results and implementation techniques developed for the family of ML languages such as OCaml and SML/NJ. We have also developed a simple semantic model for MobileML based on Plotkin's λ_v-calculus and *tuple spaces* [11].

The rest of this paper is organized as follows. Section 2 introduces the key notions in our system. Then MobileML system is described in Sect. 3. Section 4 outlines a semantic model for MobileML. After coding examples are given in Sect. 5, Sect. 6 mentions a related work, and finally Sect. 7 concludes this paper. A summary of a formal model for MobileML is presented in the Appendix.

2   Key Notions

2.1   Transparent Migration

When a computation transparently migrates, it suspends its execution, moves to another machine, and resumes its execution at the destination machine preserving all of the execution states. Suppose that we are evaluating the following expression, assuming the standard call-by-value semantics.

$$\textbf{let } f = \lambda x.x + 1 \textbf{ in } (\text{ print\_int } (f\ 3)\ )$$

The evaluation can be divided into two phases:

(1) evaluation of $\lambda x.x + 1$ (and binding f to the result), and
(2) evaluation of (print_int $(f\ 3)$).

If we want the second phase to be executed somewhere else, say at a destination l, all we have to do is to put a **go** expression as follows:

$$\textbf{let } f = \lambda x.x + 1 \textbf{ in } (\textbf{ go } l;\ \text{print\_int } (f\ 3)\ )$$

Evaluating the above expression makes the code of "print_int $(f\ 3)$" be sent to and executed at the destination designated by l. Note that the binding for f is kept throughout the migration, and then $(\lambda x.x + 1)\ 3$ is executed at the destination. The state of the execution stack is also preserved. Consider the expression below.

$$\textbf{let } f = \lambda x.(\textbf{go } l;\ x + 1) \textbf{ in}$$
$$\textbf{let } g = \lambda x.\text{print\_int } (x * 2) \textbf{ in } (\ g\ (f\ 3)\ )$$

If this expression is evaluated, the code of "$((\lambda x.\text{print\_int}\ (x * 2))\ (3 + 1))$" will be executed at l.

2.2   Contexts

A context [17] is a program expression with holes in it. The basic operation for a context is to fill its hole with an expression. For example, consider the following context.

$$\boxed{\textbf{let } x = 3 \textbf{ in } 1 + \boxed{\text{Hole}}}$$

If its hole is filled with $(x * 2)$, we obtain expression **let** $x = 3$ **in** $1 + (x * 2)$. In this expression, x in $(x * 2)$ is bound by the **let**-construct. That is, the hole-filling operation is essentially different from *capture-avoiding* substitution in the lambda calculus [2]. Our hole-filling operation *captures* free variables. Moreover, each hole may provide a different set of bindings. The following context:

$$\boxed{\textbf{let } a = 1 \textbf{ in let } \_ = \boxed{A} \textbf{ in let } b = \text{true} \textbf{ in let } \_ = \boxed{B} \textbf{ in } ()}$$

will bind a and b occurring in an expression filled in "B" to 1 and true, respectively. A piece of code filled in "A" can get only the binding for a.

2.3   Assimilation

In our system, mobile code travels on a network, interacting with (being filled in the holes of) contexts local to nodes. A destination is designated by the name of a context and its hole. As seen in the previous subsection, contexts act as dynamic binders. Mobile code can utilize functions and data through the variables which the destination context binds. When a variable in a piece of mobile code is dynamically bound with some value by a context, we say the value is *assimilated* through the variable by the mobile code. We call such a variable an *assimilation variable* denoted by `x. Assimilation is our term for dynamic binding. For example, evaluating an expression

$$\textbf{let } f = \lambda x.x + 1 \textbf{ in } (\textbf{ go } l;\ (f\ `a)\ )$$

causes the code of "$(f\ `a)$" to migrate to the context designated by l. If the context l is

$$\boxed{\textbf{let } a = 3 \textbf{ in } \boxed{\text{Hole}}}$$

(the name of hole is omitted since the above context has a single hole) then,

$$\textbf{let } a = 3 \textbf{ in } ((\lambda x.x + 1)\ a)$$

will be evaluated, and the value 3 will be assimilated through a into $(f\ `a)$. The variable f is bound to $\lambda x.x + 1$ since the execution state is preserved by transparency of the migration.

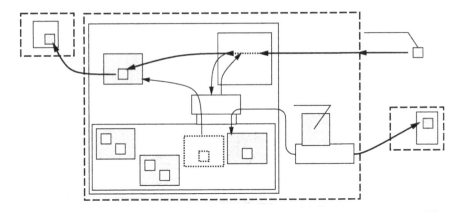

Fig. 1. MobileML system

Note that assimilation through an assimilation variable is done at the time of each migration. For example,

go l_1; **while** true **do go** $`l$ **done**

causes ever lasting migration as long as destination contexts exist and as long as assimilation through $`l$ succeeds.

3   MobileML System

This section outlines the system of MobileML, and briefly introduces the syntax of MobileML.

3.1   The System

Figure 1 depicts the overview of our MobileML system. The MobileML (MML for short) system consists of two parts: MML interpreter which executes user programs, and MML server which maintains contexts. The interpreter can interpret and execute programs in MML. Users can implement various mobile applications by writing programs which specify migration to contexts and registration of contexts with MML servers. Note that migration (transmission) of mobile code in MML is one-way and asynchronous like message sending in Actors [1].

The server consists of three parts: typechecker, repository, and repository manager. The typechecker checks if the type of incoming mobile code (the type information sent with the code) matches with the type of the destination context. Contexts are stored in the repository, which contains a pre-defined context named "guest" implicitly. The repository manager searches the repository for the destination context and its type, or registers and stores new contexts, in response to the users' requests. In case the name of context is omitted in a search

$d ::= \cdots$ original ML declarations
$\quad | \; \textbf{context } k \textbf{ with } X_1 \cdots X_n = e$ definition of a context

$e ::= \cdots$ original ML expressions
$\quad | \; (\!| X \textbf{ hides } x_1, \ldots, x_n |\!)$ a hole
$\quad | \; \textbf{register } e_1 \textbf{ as } e_2 \textbf{ with } e_3$ registration of a context
$\quad | \; \textbf{go } e$ trigger of migration
$\quad | \; \langle\!| \textbf{assim } \{x_1, \ldots, x_n\} \textbf{ in } e |\!\rangle$ delimiter for migrant
$\quad | \; \grave{x}$ assimilation variable

Fig. 2. MobileML syntax

request, context "guest" is returned as the result of search. (An MML sever also includes an interpreting engine not shown in Fig. 1, in order to execute mobile code filled in a hole of a context.)

Figure 1 also shows a system snapshot where a piece of mobile code migrates to a context. In the figure, A, B, C, and D denote contexts named "A", "B", "C", and "D", respectively. Mobile code M is migrating to the destination indicated by the string "//mml.harp/C" where "//mml.harp" indicates an MML server running at the host machine "harp". Note that the name of hole is omitted in the destination name since C has a single hole. (In the case of multiple holes, we will write "//mml.harp/A:hole1" for instance.) Code M first arrives at the MML server, and its typechecker checks whether the type of the destination context (C in this case) and the type required by M are unifiable. For that purpose, the typechecker requests the repository manager to search the repository for the type of the context named "C". If the typechecker returns OK, the code obtained by filling C's hole with the mobile code M is executed in the server.

3.2   MobileML Syntax

The syntax of MML is obtained by extending the original ML declarations and expressions with the constructs shown in Fig. 2. Contexts are defined by declaration **context** k **with** $X_1 \cdots X_n = e$. This declaration defines a context which has body e with holes $X_1, \ldots, X_n$, and names the context k. $(\!| X \textbf{ hides } x_1, \ldots, x_n |\!)$ denotes a hole whose name is X and the bindings for variables $x_1, \ldots, x_n$ are *invisible* from the code to be filled in the hole X. For example, the following declaration:

$$\textbf{context } k \textbf{ with } X =$$
$$\textbf{let } a = 1 \textbf{ in let } b = \textbf{true in } (\!| X \textbf{ hides } a |\!)$$

defines a context k which never binds a. When a piece of code which requires a binding for a migrates to X, a type error will occur. $(\!| X \textbf{ hides} |\!)$ is abbreviated as $(\!| X |\!)$. In order to register contexts with an MML server's repository, we write

register e_1 **as** e_2 **with** e_3. Evaluating this expression registers a context e_1 as a name e_2 with the repository of the server e_3.

When **go** e is evaluated, the rest of the computation runs at the destination denoted by e. Then the migrating part in the expression, which we call *migrant*, is specified by the innermost ⟨**assim** {_} **in** _⟩ which surrounds the **go** expression. We write ⟨|e|⟩ as an abbreviation for ⟨**assim** {} **in** e⟩. For example, when we evaluate

$$⟨ ⟨\textbf{go } l;\ \text{print\_string "Hello!"}⟩;\ \text{print\_string "Where is here?"} ⟩,$$

"Hello!" is printed at l, and "Where is here?" is printed locally. The migrant in this case is (print_string "Hello!"). An assimilation variable `x appearing in a migrant gets bound at the destination. In case `x is not bound anywhere, an exception will be raised. A delimiter ⟨**assim** $\{x_1, \ldots, x_n\}$ **in** e⟩ determines an *assimilating migrant* for assimilation variables `$x_1, \ldots,$ `x_n occurring in e. That is, it specifies a migrant which is responsible for assimilation of the variables. For example, consider the following expression:

$$⟨\textbf{assim } \{\} \textbf{ in go } l;\ ⟨\textbf{assim } \{a\} \textbf{ in go } l';\ \underline{\text{print\_string `a}}⟩⟩$$

The assimilating migrant for `a is the underlined part of the above expression, and assimilation through `a occurs at the destination l' of the migrant. If we slightly modify the above expression as

$$⟨\textbf{assim } \{a\} \textbf{ in go } l;\ \underline{⟨\textbf{assim } \{\} \textbf{ in go } l';\ \text{print\_string `a}⟩}⟩,$$

the assimilating migrant for `a becomes the underlined part above. In this case, assimilation through `a occurs at l. Delimiter ⟨**assim** $\{x_1, \ldots, x_n\}$ **in** e⟩ is the only binder for the assimilation variables. It binds the free occurrences of `$x_1, \ldots,$ `x_n in e. Scoping for **assim**-binders obeys the scoping rule similar to the lambda abstraction in the lambda calculus.

By using assimilation variables, **go**, and ⟨**assim** {_} **in** _⟩, we can describe a bit more complex migration like

```
let go_or_not = λx.if test then go l' else ()
in
⟨assim {a, b} in
  go l;
  print_string `a;
  ⟨assim {} in go_or_not (); print_string `b⟩
⟩
```

where "test" is a value of type bool. In the above code, assimilation through a and b is done at l. As the head part of the inner **assim**-construct does not declare b, `b in the construct is assimilated (bound) at $l$. So, whether "test" is "true" or "false", assimilation through $b$ is done at $l$, although "print_string `b" is executed at l' when "test" is "true".

3.3   Types

In addition to the types in the original ML, the set τ of MML types contains context types specified by the following form:

$$\mathsf{cnt}(X_1 : [\Gamma_1 \rhd \tau_1], \dots, X_n : [\Gamma_n \rhd \tau_n])^\tau$$

and Γ is written as $\{x_1 : \tau_1, \dots, x_n : \tau_n\}$ where each x_i denotes a variable and τ_i is its type. A context of this type has holes $X_1, \dots, X_n$. We can fill X_i with an expression e_i of type τ_i, and then the variables occurring in e_i which appear in Γ_i become bound. When all of the holes are filled, the context yield an expression of type τ, which we call *result type*. The type deduction system and the type reconstruction algorithm are essentially the same as the ML type system extended with first-class contexts [16]. For example, a type of the context defined by the following declaration:

> **context** k **with** $X =$
> **let** $a = 1$ **in let** $b =$ true **in** $\langle\!\langle X \rangle\!\rangle$;

is automatically inferred as $\mathsf{cnt}(X : [\{a : \text{int}, b : \text{bool}\} \rhd \alpha])^\alpha$.

As mentioned in Sect. 3.1, the typechecker in an MML server dynamically checks if the type required by mobile code and the type of the destination context match. Suppose that a piece of mobile code is migrating to a context of type $\mathsf{cnt}(X : [\Gamma \rhd \alpha])^\beta$ with expectation of assimilating values through variables $x_1 : \tau_1, \dots, x_n : \tau_n$. (The information of these variables and their types are added to the code by the system.) Then the typechecker in the MML server checks whether $\{x_1 : \tau_1, \dots, x_n : \tau_n\} \subseteq \Gamma$ is satisfied. Since this check cannot be statically made, MML is not a strongly typed language. That is, well-typed programs in MML may cause runtime type errors. For example, the type of the following expression:

$$\langle\!\langle \text{assim } \{a\} \text{ in go } l; \text{print\_string } `a \rangle\!\rangle$$

is inferred as unit; however, a type error will occur at l if destination context l does not provide a value of type string for a. This is to some extent inevitable in the setting of distributed computation. However, we can cope with such kind of type error by exception-handling mechanisms.

4   Outline of a Semantic Model

This section outlines a semantic model for MML. As mentioned in Sect. 2, the key notions in MML are transparent migration, contexts, and assimilation. They can be described by a simple formal model, which we call λ_{mv}-calculus, although it is not a general model for distributed computation. Our intention here is to concentrate on the essence of MML. The issue of constructing more general models by extending λ_{mv}-calculus is discussed in the technical report [18].

This calculus is based on a simply typed version of Plotkin's λ_v-calculus [22]. The main extensions are as follows:

- representation for expressions to be evaluated concurrently by *processes* (as in CML [23]),
- the notion of first-class contexts [17], and
- representation for transparent migration.

In order to model transparent migration, we use the notion of partial continuations [9,7]. Then, execution states of programs are abstracted as partial continuations [26,27].

In λ_{mv}-calculus, a network state is represented as a set of *hosts* each of which is a pair of a host name and a set of processes. Contexts are registered with hosts (we identify MML servers with hosts in this calculus) and wait for mobile code to be filled in their holes. A piece of mobile code is transmitted from a host to a registered context by means of *tuple space* [11]. In our calculus, a tuple space acts as a virtual global buffer for mobile code transmission. That is, when a piece of mobile code is shipped off, it is first stored in the tuple space as a tuple of the destination name, the code, and the type information of what bindings the code requires. (This phase always succeeds.) Then, a context picks up the tuple whose destination and type information matches the name of the context and its type, respectively, and then fill its hole with the code in the tuple. In this way, asynchronous features of mobile code transmission in MML is modeled in our calculus.

The type system of λ_{mv}-calculus is based on the type system of Hashimoto and Ohoris' Context Calculus [17]. In our type system, a hole is assigned the set $\{x_1, \ldots, x_n\}$ of variables whose binders λx_i surround the hole. The set is extended in the typing rule for lambda abstraction. A summary of the definition of λ_{mv}-calculus and its dynamic and static semantics are given in the Appendix. This calculus enjoys subject reduction lemma and type soundness theorem at the cost of runtime typecheck.

For more precise modeling of MML, we must extend the simple type system of λ_{mv}-calculus to a polymorphic one. We can utilize techniques elaborated for ML with first-class contexts [16] and ML with **shift/reset** [7].

5   Program Examples

This section gives two small examples of programming with MML. The first one is a simple example of distributed information retrieval. Applications of such a kind are often referred to as a typical example of mobile computation. The second one indicates a novel use of mobile computation: runtime update of program fragments of an application without restarting its execution.

5.1   News Collector

A news collector is a program which travels around a network and collects news texts. We assume that a number of contexts which provide news are already registered with MML servers running on the network. The following program registers a news server (which is a context) named "NewsS" with an MML server running on the host "harp."

```
val top_news = ref "MobileML has been released!";
```

```
context news with READER WRITTER =
  let fun get_news () = !top_news;
      val _ = [<READER>];
      fun write_news s = top_news:= s;
      val _ = [<WRITTER>]
  in () end;
```

```
register news as "NewsS" with "//mml.harp/";
```

This context has two holes READER and WRITTER. It binds a variable get_news occurring in a piece of code to be filled in READER, and variables get_news and write_news occurring in one to be filled in WRITTER. We can write a news collector as follows:

```
fun collector () =
  let val result = ref "";
      val locs = [ "//mml.harp/NewsS:READER",
                   "//mml.lute/NewsS:READER",
                             ...
                   "//mml.banjo/NewsS:READER" ]
  in
    <|assim {get_news} in
      iter
      (fn loc =>
        go loc; result:= !result ^ ('get_news()) ^ "\n"
      ) locs;
      go "//mml.halle/MyHome";
      print_string !result
    |>
  end;
```

where iter is the usual iteration function of type $(\alpha \to \text{unit}) \to \alpha \text{ list} \to \text{unit}$. A migrant is created by evaluating "collector ()", and travels around the destinations given in the list locs in order to collect the news. A reference cell result is used to accumulate the items. The result will be displayed at "//mml.halle/MyHome". Note that reference cells are always copied and do not create a remote reference in MML.

5.2   Runtime Library Update

Usually, an application software is constructed so that necessary libraries are linked only at starting time. If we want to try a new version of a library, we must reboot the application. Rebooting an application would be very irritating if it needs much time. In our scheme of "runtime library update", an application (or its main program) is represented by a piece of mobile code which uses a library and the library is considered as a context. The following programs illustrate our scheme.

```
val lib_name = ref "";
context lib1 with APPL =
  let val new_lib = lib_name;
      val f1 = ...;
      val f2 = ...;

          ...

      val fn = ...
  in [<APPL>] end;
```

```
register lib1 as "lib-v1" with "//mml.harp/";
```

The above code defines and registers a context representing a library. A piece of code migrating to hole APPL can use functions f1, ..., fn in the library. In this setting, an application starts its execution by migrating to such a context. An application is defined as follows:

```
fun run () =
  <|assim {new_lib} in
     go "//mml.harp/lib-v1";
     while true do
        if {!'}new_lib <> "" then go {!'}new_lib else do_jobs();
     done
  |>;
```

By evaluating "run ()", a migrant migrates to the library lib1, and repeats the execution of "do_jobs ()" while the content of new_lib is "".

Meanwhile, a developer of the library completes a new version lib2 of the library. He distributes the new version using a function named updator given below.

```
val lib_name = ref "";
context lib2 with APPL =
  let val new_lib = lib_name;
      val f1 = ...;
      val f2 = ...;

          ...

      val fn = ...
  in [<APPL>] end;

fun updator () =
  <|go "//mml.harp/";
     register lib2 as "lib-v2" with "//mml.harp/";
     <|assim {new_lib} in
        go "//mml.harp/lib-v1"; 'new_lib:= "//mml.harp/lib-v2"
     |>
  |>;
```

By applying () to **updator**, a migrant (1) migrates to the server at "harp", (2) registers the new version with the server, (3) migrates to the old library, (4) lets the application know the name of the new version, by updating the content of shared variable **new_lib** to the (full) name of the new version. Finally, the application becomes aware of the name of the new version in the **while**-loop, and migrates to the new version of the library. Due to transparency of migration, the application can continue to run with the new library without being rebooted.

6   Related Work

Facile [20] supports a mechanism similar to that of our "assimilation". It is a concurrent distributed language based on a higher-order strongly typed language. This language supports closure transmission similar to that of Obliq [4]. The feature of this language that we should pay attention to is a mechanism for dynamic binding with remote resources. However, that is slightly different from our mechanism. Facile uses *proxy structures* in order to specify the variables which become bound at a remote site. A proxy structure is generated from a *remote signature* which specifies names and types of the values provided at the remote site. We can treat proxy structures as if they were local structures. That is, by means of proxy structures, a closure can refer the remote structures which match the remote signature at the compilation time. When a closure arrives at the destination, the closure is linked with the structures specified by remote signatures, assuming that such structures always exist. Therefore, in case specifications of remote structures are modified, it is necessary to get the new remote signatures and to recompile programs which refer the structures. Our MML does not need such recompilation since such consistency is dynamically checked.

7   Concluding Remarks

Mobile computation has the advantages of high efficiency and productivity in developing novel distributed applications such as workflow systems, flexible software distribution, and intelligent search systems. In our current work, we have designed a language which facilitates programming for mobile computation. The innovative features of our language include the notion of contexts which allows us to succinctly describe the interaction between mobile code and environments at destination nodes. Since our language is based on ML, we can expect that theoretical developments and implementation techniques elaborated for ML are readily applicable to our system. We have also developed a semantic model for our language based on CML-style semantics and tuple spaces. In our model, tuple spaces act as virtual global buffers for mobile code transmission. This model enjoys type soundness theorem assuming that we can always determine at runtime if the type of a migrant matches the type of the destination context.

There are several interesting issues that merit further investigation. We briefly mention some of them.

Communication between migrants. In the current MML system, migrants running at the same context can communicate by using reference cells visible in the context. However, special mechanisms for communication between migrants are not provided. If we extend MML with a communication mechanism using channels as found in CML [23] or *transiently shared tuple spaces* of LIME [21], the convenience will increase especially in case of inter-migrant communication in the same context or host machine.

Security. In the present system, visibility of resources from mobile code can naturally be controlled by means of **hide** and multiple different holes. However, security issues such as authentication and verification of mobile code are not addressed yet. For example, we would like to incorporate into our system theoretical results such as prevention of security violation by SLam Calculus [19], and type-based specification mechanisms of access control policies of KLAIM [8] or Dπ [24].

Efficient implementation. We have implemented an experimental interpreter system on OCaml. However, there is plenty of room for improvements to make our system be suitable for the practical use. We are planning to construct a bytecode based compiler system. Techniques for closure transmission developed in Facile [20] will be applicable to our code transmission.

Acknowledgments

The authors would like to acknowledge fruitful discussions with the members of the AMO Project.

References

1. Gul Agha. *ACTORS : A Model of Concurrent Computations in Distributed Systems.* The MIT Press, Cambridge, Mass., 1986.
2. H.P. Barendregt. *The Lambda Calculus*, volume 103 of *Studies in Logic and the Foundations of Mathematics.* North-Holland, 1984. revised edition.
3. Krishna A. Bharat and Luca Cardelli. Migratory Applications. In *Proceedings of the 8th Annual ACM Symposium on User Interface Software and Technology*, Pittsburgh, Pa., November 1995. Also available as Digital Systems Research Center Research Report 138.
4. Luca Cardelli. A language with distributed scope. *Computing Systems*, 8(1):27–59, 1995. Also available as Digital Systems Research Center Research Report 122.
5. Luca Cardelli. Mobile Computation. In J. Vitek and C. Tschudin, editors, *Mobile Object Systems - Towards the Programmable Internet*, number 1222 in Lecture Notes in Computer Science, pages 3–6. Springer-Verlag, April 1997.
6. L. Damas and R. Milner. Principal type-schemes for functional programs. In *Proc. ACM Symposium on Principles of Programming Languages*, pages 207–212, 1982.
7. Olivier Danvy and Andrzej Filinski. A Functional Abstraction of Typed Contexts. Technical report, Institute of Datalogy, University of Copenhagen, 1989. DIKU 89/12.

8. R. De Nicola, G. Ferrari, and R. Pugliese. Types as Specifications of Access Policies. In J. Vitek and C. Jensen, editors, *Secure Internet Programming: Security Issues for Distributed and Mobile Objects*, volume 1603 of *LNCS*, pages 117–146. Springer-Verlag, 1999.

9. M. Felleisen, M. Wand, , D. P. Friedman, and B. F. Duba. Abstract Continuations: A Mathematical Semantics for Handling Full Functional Jumps. In *ACM Conference on Lisp and Functional Programming*, pages 52–62, 1988.

10. Cédric Fournet, Georges Gonthier, Jean-Jacques Lévy, Luc Maranget, and Didier Rémy. A Calculus of Mobile Agents. In Ugo Montanari and Vladimiro Sassone, editors, *CONCUR '96: Concurrency Theory (7th International Conference, Pisa, Italy, August 1996, Proceedings)*, volume 1119 of *LNCS*, pages 406–421. Springer-Verlag, 1996.

11. David Gelernter. Generative Communication in Linda. *ACM Transactions on Programming Languages and Systems*, 7(1):80–112, January 1985.

12. J. Gosling and H. McGilton. The Java Language Environment. White paper, Sun Microsystems, 1995.

13. Robert S. Gray. Agent Tcl: A transportable agent system. In *Proceedings of the CIKM Workshop on Intelligent Information Agents*, Baltimore, Md., December 1995.

14. Robert S. Gray, George Cybenko, David Kotz, and Daniela Rus. D'Agents: Security in a multiple-language, mobile-agent system. In Giovanni Vigna, editor, *Mobile Agent Security*, Lecture Notes in Computer Science, pages 154–187. Springer-Verlag: Heidelberg, Germany, 1998.

15. Colin G. Harrison, David M. Chess, and Aaron Kershenbaum. Mobile Agents: Are they a good idea? Research report, IBM T. J. Watson Research Center, March 1995.

16. Masatomo Hashimoto. First-Class Contexts in ML. In *Proc. 4th Asian Computing Science Conference*, volume 1538 of *Lecture Notes in Computer Science*, pages 206–223. Springer, 1998.

17. Masatomo Hashimoto and Atsushi Ohori. A Typed Context Calculus. Preprint 1098, Research Institute for Mathematical Sciences, Kyoto, Japan, 1996. Revised version to appear in TCS.

18. Masatomo Hashimoto and Akinori Yonezawa. A Typed Language for Mobile Computation. Technical report, Univ. Tokyo, 2000. In preparation.

19. Nevin Heintze and Jon G. Riecke. The SLam Calculus: Programming with Secrecy and Integrity. In *Conference Record of POPL 98: The 25TH ACM SIGPLAN-SIGACT Symposium on Principles of Programming Languages, San Diego, California*, pages 365–377, New York, NY, January 1998. ACM.

20. Frederick C. Knabe. An overview of mobile agent programming. In *Proceedings of the 5th LOMAPS Workshop on Analysis and Verification of Multiple-Agent Languages*, Stockholm, Sweden, June 1996.

21. Gian Pietro Picco, Amy L. Murphy, and Gruia-Catalin Roman. LIME: Linda Meets Mobility. In *Proceedings of the 21st International Conference on Software Engineering*, pages 368–377. ACM Press, May 1999.

22. G. Plotkin. Call-by-name, call-by-value, and the λ-calculus. *Theoretical Computer Science*, 1:125–159, 1975.

23. J. H. Reppy. CML: A higher-order Concurrent Language. In *Proceedings of ACM SIGPLAN'91 Conference on Programming Language Design and Implementation*, pages 293–305, 1991.

24. James Riely and Matthew Hennessy. A Typed Language for Distributed Mobile Processes. In *Proc. ACM Symposium on Principles of Programming Languages*, pages 378–390. ACM Press, January 1998.
25. Tatsurou Sekiguchi, Hidehiko Masuhara, and Akinori Yonezawa. A Simple Extension of Java Language for Controllable Transparent Migration and its Portable Implementation. In *Proceedings of the Third International Conference on Coordination Models and Languages*, 1999.
26. Tatsurou Sekiguchi and Akinori Yonezawa. A Calculus with Code Mobility. In H. Bowman and J. Derrick, editors, *Proceedings of Second IFIP International Conference on Formal Methods for Open Object-based Distributed Systems*, pages 21–36. Chapman&Hall, 1997.
27. Takuo Watanabe. Mobile Code Description using Partial Continuations: Definition and Operational Semantics. In *SWoPP '97*, pages 61–66. IPSJ, August 1997.
28. James E. White. Mobile Agents. In Jeffrey Bradshaw, editor, *Software Agents*. The MIT Press, 1996.

A   Summary of λ_{mv}-Calculus

In this appendix, we briefly introduce λ_{mv}-calculus – a simply typed lambda calculus with the features of mobile computation in MML. This calculus is based on a simply typed version of Plotkin's λ_v-calculus [22]. A dynamic semantics of this calculus is obtained by defining a transition system between *configurations* which represent network states. A configuration is a pair of a *tuple space* [11] and a set of *hosts*. The tuple space acts as a virtual global buffer for code transmission. A host is a pair of host name and a set of processes (i.e., named programs which are evaluated locally and concurrently).

We use the following notation for sets. Let A and B be sets. Then $A \cup B$ is their union, $A \uplus B$ is their disjoint union, and $A \setminus B$ is their difference. We sometimes omit braces for singletons, for instance, we use $\{a, b\} \uplus c$ for $\{a, b\} \uplus \{c\}$. Let M and N be multisets. Then $M \oplus N$ denotes their union.

A.1   Types and Expressions

The set of types (ranged over by τ) of λ_{mv} is given by the following syntax:

$$\tau ::= b \mid \tau \to \tau \mid \mathsf{cnt}_\rho$$

where b stands for a given set of base types, cnt_ρ for *context types*, and ρ for *assimilation variable sets* $\{a_1^{\tau_1}, \dots, a_n^{\tau_n}\}$ of *assimilation variables* a_i annotated with their types τ_i. We assume that each context has a single hole of type unit, and its result type is unit. Thus, cnt_ρ suffices for context type.

Let $x^{a:\tau}$ range over a countably infinite collection of variables labeled with their types and assimilation variables where a on the shoulder of x denotes the external name of x. And let X range over a countably infinite collection of holes. The sets of values ranged over by v and expressions ranged over by e are given by the following syntax:

$$v ::= c^\tau \mid a^\tau \mid x^{a:\tau} \mid \lambda x^{a:\tau}.e \mid X \mid \delta X : \rho.e$$

$$e ::= v \mid e\, e \mid \langle\!| e |\!\rangle_\rho \mid \mathbf{go}(e, e) \mid \mathbf{reg}(e, e)$$

where $\delta X : \rho.e$ stands for contexts, and c^τ for a given set of constants labeled with their types. The set of constants contains host names h^{hstn} and process names p^{procn}. We write $\langle\!\langle e\rangle\!\rangle$ as an abbreviation for $\langle\!\langle e\rangle\!\rangle_{\{\}}$. The set $\mathrm{FV}(e)$ of free variables in e is defined in the usual way, according to the structure of e. The following clauses are examples.

$$\mathrm{FV}(x^{a:\tau}) = \{x^{a:\tau}\} \qquad \mathrm{FV}(\lambda x^{a:\tau}.e) = \mathrm{FV}(e) \setminus \{x^{a:\tau}\}$$
$$\mathrm{FV}(\delta X : \rho.e) = \mathrm{FV}(e) \qquad \mathrm{FV}(\langle\!\langle e\rangle\!\rangle_{\{a_1^{\tau_1},\dots,a_n^{\tau_n}\}}) = \mathrm{FV}(e)$$

The set $\mathrm{FAV}(e)$ of free assimilation variables in e is defined similarly. The following clauses are also examples.

$$\mathrm{FAV}(a^\tau) = \{a^\tau\} \qquad \mathrm{FAV}(\lambda x^{a:\tau}.e) = \mathrm{FAV}(e)$$
$$\mathrm{FAV}(\delta X : \rho.e) = \mathrm{FAV}(e) \qquad \mathrm{FAV}(\langle\!\langle e\rangle\!\rangle_\rho) = \mathrm{FAV}(e) \setminus \rho$$

We denote the set of free holes in e by $\mathrm{FH}(e)$. We can safely assume α-renaming of bound holes just as bound variables in the lambda calculus. By $e\{x^{a:\tau} \mapsto e'\}$ and $e\{a^\tau \mapsto e'\}$, we denote the expressions obtained by substituting e' for any free occurrence of $x^{a:\tau}$ in e and a^τ in e, respectively. The notion of α-congruence in λ_{mv} is defined as:

$$\lambda x^{a:\tau}.e \equiv_\alpha \lambda y^{a:\tau}.e\{x^{a:\tau} \mapsto y^{a:\tau}\} \quad (\text{if } y \notin \mathrm{FV}(e))$$

A.2   Type System

A *hole type assignment*, ranged over by Δ, is $\emptyset$ or a singleton of a pair of a hole and its assimilation variable set. The type system of λ_{mv} is defined as a proof system to derive a *typing judgment* of the form:

$$\Delta \vdash e : \tau$$

where expression e has type τ under hole type assignment Δ. The set of typing rules is given in Fig. 3. In type inference, we do not apply the inference rules which add redundant elements to the hole type assignments.

A.3   Local Evaluation

We first define an evaluation relation "$\longrightarrow$" local to processes, following the line of λ_v. An evaluation context is an expression containing a single "[ ]" which marks the next redex. Evaluation contexts are standard evaluation contexts for call-by-value evaluation, and are defined by the following syntax:

$$E ::= [\,] \mid E\ e \mid v\ E \mid \langle\!\langle E\rangle\!\rangle_\rho$$

The local evaluation relation "$\longrightarrow$" is the smallest relation satisfying the following rule:

$$\begin{aligned}
(prim) && E[c^\tau\ v] &\longrightarrow E[\mathrm{Prim}(c^\tau, v)] \\
(\beta) && E[(\lambda x^{a:\tau}.e)\ v] &\longrightarrow E[e\{x \mapsto v\}] && (\mathrm{FH}(e) = \mathrm{FH}(v) = \emptyset) \\
(migr) && E[\langle\!\langle v\rangle\!\rangle_\rho] &\longrightarrow v
\end{aligned}$$

Cst $\emptyset \vdash c^\tau : \tau$ Asv $\emptyset \vdash a^\tau : \tau$ Var $\emptyset \vdash x^{a:\tau} : \tau$

Fun $\dfrac{\{X : \rho\} \vdash e : \tau'}{\{X : \rho \uplus \{a : \tau\}\} \vdash \lambda x^{a:\tau}.e : \tau \to \tau'}$ App $\dfrac{\Delta_1 \vdash e_1 : \tau_1 \to \tau_2 \quad \Delta_2 \vdash e_2 : \tau_1}{\Delta_1 \uplus \Delta_2 \vdash e_1\,e_2 : \tau_2}$

Hol $\{X : \{\}\} \vdash X : \mathsf{unit}$ Cnt $\dfrac{\{X : \rho\} \vdash e : \mathsf{unit}}{\emptyset \vdash \delta X : \rho.e : \mathsf{cnt}_\rho}$

Go $\dfrac{\Delta_1 \vdash e_1 : \mathsf{hstn} \quad \Delta_2 \vdash e_2 : \mathsf{procn}}{\Delta_1 \uplus \Delta_2 \vdash \mathbf{go}(e_1, e_2) : \mathsf{unit}}$ Mig $\dfrac{\Delta \vdash e : \mathsf{unit}}{\Delta \vdash \langle\!| e |\!\rangle_{\{a_1^{\tau_1}, \ldots, a_n^{\tau_n}\}} : \mathsf{unit}}$

Reg $\dfrac{\Delta_1 \vdash e_1 : \mathsf{cnt}_\rho \quad \Delta_2 \vdash e_2 : \mathsf{procn}}{\Delta_1 \uplus \Delta_2 \vdash \mathbf{reg}(e_1, e_2) : \mathsf{unit}}$

Fig. 3. Typing rules

where "Prim" denotes a partial function which gives meanings to the function constants. We assume that if $\emptyset \vdash v : \tau$, then $\mathrm{Prim}(c^{\tau \to \tau'}, v)$ is defined and $\emptyset \vdash \mathrm{Prim}(c^{\tau \to \tau'}, v) : \tau'$.

A.4   Global Evaluation

Global evaluation is defined by a transition system of configurations. This is similar to the style of CML [23]. The global evaluation relation "$\Longrightarrow$" extends "$\longrightarrow$" to configurations, and adds additional rules for context registration and migration. We denote by $\lfloor e \rfloor^p$ a process which is named p and executes e. A host containing its name h and a set $\mathcal{P}$ of processes is denoted by $\langle h, \mathcal{P} \rangle$. We denote a set of hosts by $\mathcal{H}$. A migrant is denoted by $\lceil h, p, e, \rho \rceil$, and a migrant set is a multiset (tuple space) of migrants ranged over by $\mathcal{M}$. We denote a configuration by $\mathcal{M}, \mathcal{H}$.

A process set $\mathcal{P}$ is well-formed if for all $\lfloor e \rfloor^p \in \mathcal{P}$, the following hold: $\mathrm{FV}(e) = \mathrm{FAV}(e) = \emptyset$ and there is no $e' \neq e$ such that $\lfloor e' \rfloor^p \in \mathcal{P}$. A host set $\mathcal{H}$ is well-formed if for all $\langle h, \mathcal{P} \rangle \in \mathcal{H}$, the following hold: $\mathcal{P}$ is well-formed, and there is no $\mathcal{P}' \neq \mathcal{P}$ such that $\langle h, \mathcal{P}' \rangle \in \mathcal{H}$. A migrant set $\mathcal{M}$ is well-formed if for all $\lceil h, p, e, \rho \rceil \in \mathcal{M}$, $\mathrm{FV}(e) = \emptyset$. A configuration $\mathcal{M}, \mathcal{H}$ is well-formed if both $\mathcal{M}$ and $\mathcal{H}$ are well-formed.

A *process typing* PT is a finite map from long process names (each of which is a pair of a host name and a process name) to types. A well-formed configuration $\mathcal{M}, \mathcal{H}$ has type PT, denoted by $\vdash \mathcal{M}, \mathcal{H} : \mathrm{PT}$, if the following hold: $\{(h, p) | h \in \mathrm{dom}(\mathcal{H})$ and $p \in \mathrm{dom}(\mathcal{H}(h))\} \subseteq \mathrm{dom}(\mathrm{PT})$, for all e such that $\lfloor e \rfloor^p \in \mathcal{P}$ and $\langle h, \mathcal{P} \rangle \in \mathcal{H}$, $\emptyset \vdash e : \mathrm{PT}(h, p)$, and for all $\lceil h, p, e, \rho \rceil \in \mathcal{M}$, $\emptyset \vdash e : \mathsf{unit}$ and $\mathrm{FAV}(e) \subseteq \rho$.

The global evaluation relation is defined by four inference rules each of which defines a single step evaluation. The first rule simply extends the local evaluation relation to configurations:

Exp $\dfrac{e \longrightarrow e'}{\mathcal{M}, \mathcal{H} \uplus \langle h, \mathcal{P} \uplus \lfloor e \rfloor^p \rangle \implies \mathcal{M}, \mathcal{H} \uplus \langle h, \mathcal{P} \uplus \lfloor e' \rfloor^p \rangle}$

In the following rule, context $\delta X : \rho.e'_1$ is registered as p with h.

Reg $\dfrac{e_1 \longrightarrow \delta X : \rho.e'_1 \qquad e_2 \longrightarrow p}{\mathcal{M}, \mathcal{H} \uplus \langle h, \mathcal{P} \uplus \lfloor E[\mathbf{reg}(e_1, e_2)] \rfloor \rangle \implies \mathcal{M}, \mathcal{H} \uplus \langle h, \mathcal{P} \uplus \lfloor E[()] \rfloor \uplus \lfloor \delta X : \rho.e'_1 \rfloor^p \rangle}$

In the following, $R[\_]$ denotes an evaluation context which does not contain any $\langle\!\lfloor\_\rfloor\!\rangle$. The expression $R[()]$ is packed in a tuple, which is added (**out**-ed) to $\mathcal{M}$.

Go $\dfrac{e_1 \longrightarrow h \qquad e_2 \longrightarrow p}{\mathcal{M}, \mathcal{H} \uplus \langle h', \mathcal{P} \uplus \lfloor E[\langle\!\lfloor R[\mathbf{go}(e_1, e_2)] \rfloor\!\rangle_\rho] \rfloor \rangle \implies \mathcal{M} \oplus \lceil h, p, R[()], \rho \rceil, \mathcal{H} \uplus \langle h', \mathcal{P} \uplus \lfloor E[()] \rfloor \rangle}$

We denote by $e\{e'/X\}$ an expression obtained from e by filling its hole X with e'. Let X occur in the scopes of $\lambda x_1^{a_1 : \tau_1}, \dots, \lambda x_n^{a_n : \tau_n}$ in e. Then we define *renamer* $\theta_e^{X : \{a_1^{\tau_1}, \dots, a_n^{\tau_n}\}}$ as substitution $\{a_1^{\tau_1} \mapsto x_1^{a_1 : \tau_1}, \dots, a_n^{\tau_n} \mapsto x_n^{a_n : \tau_n}\}$. A migrant can access local resources provided by a context through assimilation variables, by applying the migrant to the renamer before hole-filling. The rule below shows that a migrant matching with a context can arrive at the context.

Fill $\dfrac{\rho' \subseteq \rho \qquad p' \text{ is fresh}}{\mathcal{M} \oplus \lceil h, p, e', \rho' \rceil, \mathcal{H} \uplus \langle h, \lfloor \delta X : \rho.e \rfloor^p \uplus \mathcal{P} \rangle \implies \mathcal{M}, \mathcal{H} \uplus \langle h, \lfloor e\{\langle\!\lfloor \theta_e^{X : \rho}(e') \rfloor\!\rangle / X\} \rfloor^{p'} \uplus \lfloor \delta X : \rho.e \rfloor^p \uplus \mathcal{P} \rangle}$

A process $\lfloor e \rfloor^p$ is *stuck* if e is not a value and there do not exist well-formed configurations $\mathcal{M}, \mathcal{H} \uplus \langle h, \mathcal{P} \uplus \lfloor e \rfloor^p \rangle$ and $\mathcal{M}', \mathcal{H}'$ such that $\mathcal{M}, \mathcal{H} \uplus \langle h, \mathcal{P} \uplus \lfloor e \rfloor^p \rangle \implies \mathcal{M}', \mathcal{H}'$, with p a selected process of this transition. A well-formed configuration is *stuck* if one or more of its processes are stuck.

We have the following lemma and theorem. The proof is given in the technical report [18].

Lemma 1 (Subject Reduction). *If a configuration $\mathcal{M}, \mathcal{H}$ is well-formed, $\mathcal{M}, \mathcal{H} \implies \mathcal{M}', \mathcal{H}'$, and $\vdash \mathcal{M}, \mathcal{H} : \mathsf{PT}$, then there exists a process typing PT' such that $\mathsf{PT} \subseteq \mathsf{PT}'$, $\vdash \mathcal{M}', \mathcal{H}' : \mathsf{PT}'$, and $\vdash \mathcal{M}, \mathcal{H} : \mathsf{PT}$.*

Theorem 1 (Type Soundness). *Well-formed configurations do not get stuck.*

Hybrid Models for Mobile Computing

Mika Katara

Software Systems Laboratory
Tampere University of Technology
P.O. Box 553, FIN-33101 Tampere, Finland
Tel. +358 3 365 3822, Fax +358 3 365 2913
mika.katara@cs.tut.fi

Abstract. Hybrid specifications, i.e. ones containing both discrete and continuous changes, are used mainly in modelling systems that control some physical phenomena. In this paper, we propose hybrid modelling of novel wireless mobile systems, which generally fall under the term mobile computing. The particular systems consist of agents capable of moving in a physical reality and communicating wirelessly when in each other's proximity. In this paper we concentrate on agents not capable of controlling their own movement, e.g. the ones designed to be carried around. Their environment comprises of a user and the physical reality whose nature is continuous rather than discrete. An approach to modelling of such systems is presented. The approach, which is based on the DisCo method, takes into account the continuous nature of the environment. Joint actions and closed system modelling are used to coordinate multi-agent interactions at a high level of abstraction. An example is presented where the approach is illustrated by a specification modelling file transfer operation between two agents.

1 Introduction

Hybrid specifications, i.e. ones containing both discrete and continuous changes, are used mainly in modelling systems that control some physical phenomena. In this paper, we propose hybrid modelling of novel wireless mobile systems, which generally fall under the term mobile computing.

The systems of interest are those consisting of agents capable of moving in a physical reality and communicating wirelessly when in each other's proximity. Consider for instance PDAs (Personal Digital Assistants) communicating with each other through short range radios. In this paper we concentrate on agents not capable of controlling their own movement, e.g. the ones designed to be carried around. Their environment comprises of a user and the physical reality whose nature is continuous rather than discrete.

There is interaction between an agent and its continuous environment. Applications available to the user of the agent may depend on the physical characteristics of the agent's environment. For example, communication between other agents depends on mutual distance which changes continuously. Capturing this

A. Porto and G.-C. Roman (Eds.): COORDINATION 2000, LNCS 1906, pp. 216–231, 2000.

interaction in the specifications calls for hybrid models. In this paper an approach to hybrid modelling of mobile systems is presented.

The approach is based on the DisCo[1] method [8,1], a formal specification method for distributed *reactive systems*, i.e., systems that are in constant interaction with their environments. The basis of DisCo is the *joint action* theory [4,5], which enables the specification of *collective behavior* at a high level of abstraction. Specifications describe *closed systems*, i.e. systems together with their environments. Joint actions and closed system modelling are used to coordinate multi-agent interactions at high levels of abstraction. Specifications are refined towards implementation using a form of *superposition* [7], which preserves all *safety* properties ("something bad will never happen") by construction, while *liveness* properties ("something good will eventually happen") lead to proof obligations.

The rest of the paper is structured as follows. In Section 2, an introduction to the DisCo method is given. The hybrid approach to modelling of mobile systems is presented in Section 3. In Section 4, an example is presented. Conclusions are stated in Section 5.

2 Introduction to DisCo

2.1 Classes and Actions

The DisCo method [8,1] is based on the joint action theory [4,5] which has been found suitable for specifying and reasoning about reactive and concurrent systems. In DisCo, the focus is set on collective behaviour at high levels of abstraction, where objects communicate by *participating* in atomic actions. The formal basis of the DisCo language is in the *Temporal Logic of Actions, TLA* [13]. TLA is a linear time logic where attention is on infinite sequences of states called *behaviours* and their properties. An infinite number of *state variables* is assumed and in each state of a behaviour every variable has a unique value.

A DisCo specification has an operational interpretation. All variables are encapsulated in objects. DisCo also has *classes* and (multiple) *inheritance*, familiar from other object-oriented languages. Methods are replaced by multi-object actions, having neither callers nor callees. Objects can be associated with each other using *relations* and *references*. The life cycle of objects begins at *creation*, where the initial state of the specification is given, they cannot be created or destroyed at run time.

In an action each participant is assigned a *role*. Objects are capable of participating in actions in certain roles. No object can participate in more than one role at a time. Actions may also have *parameters* which refer to immutable values rather than mutable objects. Parameters, which have nondeterministic values, can be used to introduce nondeterminism.

In an action definition the roles and the classes of participating objects are given. A Boolean expression, called the *guard*, and the *body* of the action are also

---

[1] Acronym for *Dist*ributed *Co*-operation.

given. In the body, unprimed and primed variable names are used to distinguish values of variables before and after executing the action, respectively. Functions can be used to abbreviate complex expressions.

Actions in DisCo are atomic, i.e., their executions are bound to be finished without outside interference. Concurrency is modelled by *interleaving* the executions of actions. An action is said to be *enabled* if there exist potential participants and values for parameters so that the guard evaluates to true. If more than one action is enabled the one to be executed is selected nondeterministically.

If a role name is given in braces, the role is said to be *quantified*. It means that a nondeterministic (possibly empty) set of objects that satisfy the guard can participate in the role. The guard and the body are evaluated for each object participating in a quantified role.

As an example, consider a simple specification given below, which models sending and delivering messages holding integer values. It includes classes Message and Receiver and actions Sending and Delivery. The parameter *data* of action Sending, the value of which is copied to the message participating as m, models the data to be sent. In action Delivery the value within participant m is delivered to all receivers participating in the quantified role r. The sequence *received* models the sequence of received values in each Receiver:

$$\textbf{class } Message = \{data : integer\}$$

$$\textbf{class } Receiver = \{received : \textbf{sequence } integer\}$$

$$Sending(m : Message; data : integer) :$$
$$m.data = 0$$
$$\wedge\ data \neq 0$$
$$\rightarrow m.data' = data$$

$$Delivery(m : Message; \{r\} : Receiver) :$$
$$m.data \neq 0$$
$$\rightarrow r.received' = r.received +\ < m.data >$$
$$\wedge\ m.data' = 0$$

Messages that are currently in use are distinguished from others by non-zero value of variable *data*. These variables should be initialized as zero, which can be required by an initial condition:

$$\textbf{initially } \forall m \in Message : m.data = 0$$

The execution model does not guarantee that all enabled actions are finally executed. Fairness requirements have to be given to ensure liveness. Prefixing the name of a (possibly quantified) role with an asterisk indicates that if an action is infinitely often enabled so that the same object can participate in the same prefixed role, then the action has to be executed infinitely often with this object in the prefixed role. If fairness is required for more than one participant, the above is required for each combination of such participants. Explicit fairness requirements are the biggest difference between the execution models of DisCo and UNITY [6].

2.2   Timed Specifications

Real time is a continuous quantity that can be incorporated in the above scheme as follows (for more detailed discussion, see e.g. [10]). Each action is assumed to be executed instantaneously. A clock variable $\Omega \in \mathbb{R}^{0+}$, belonging to the set of nonnegative reals and initialized as 0, is introduced to record time from the beginning of a behaviour. An implicit parameter τ representing the time when an action is executed is added to each action. Also, all guards are implicitly strengthened by the conjunct

$$\Omega \leq \tau \leq min(\Delta) \ ,$$

where Δ denotes a multiset of *deadlines*. Moreover, conjunct $\Omega' = \tau$ is added to the bodies of all actions.

Minimal separation requirement between actions A and B can be enforced by strengthening the guard of action B by conjunct $\tau \geq \tau_A + d$, where τ_A denotes the most recent execution moment of A. For bounded response requirements, deadlines are used. When a deadline $\tau + d$ is needed for some future action, a conjunct of the form $x' = \Delta_{on}(d)$ is given in the action body to add this deadline to Δ and to store it in a variable x. An implicit conjunct $\tau \leq min(\Delta)$ in all guards then prevents advancing Ω beyond this deadline, until some action has removed the deadline with $\Delta_{off}(x)$. In the initial state, Δ can hold initial deadlines. Furthermore, a type time, a synonym type of real, can be used in timed specifications.

It should be noted that fairness still remains the only execution force. Actions are not executed because time passes, but the passing of time is noticed as a result of executing an action. This may lead to *Zeno behaviours*, where time is not allowed to grow beyond any bound. However, as discussed in [3], Zeno behaviours are harmful only if there are no other alternatives where time may grow unboundedly.

2.3   Superposition and Layers

In DisCo, the specification process is started at a high level of abstraction. Specifications are *stepwise refined* towards implementation applying the *superposition* principle. In superposition, classes can be extended with new variables, and totally new classes can be added. New actions can be given, and new participants and parameters can be added to the old actions. Guards can be strengthened and action bodies extended. Different refined versions for one action can be given.

However, actions are not allowed to modify old variables. This restriction is necessary to ensure the preservation of safety properties. Superposition relation is trivial to check mechanically.

A DisCo specification consists of a set of superposition steps called *layers*. One specification can be refined in several parallel layers yielding several branches of the specification. These branches correspond to different aspects of the system. Different specifications and different branches of the same specification can be *composed* together. In composition, actions can be *synchronized* to be executed in parallel.

To illustrate the use of superposition, a simple refinement of the previous specification is presented. In superposition, actions can be *specialized*. Specializing means introducing a new action that is specialized for a subclass, i.e., it is enabled only for objects of the subclass. The guards of the other versions of the action are implicitly strengthened so that they are no longer enabled for the subclass.

A subclass FirstClassMessage of Message is introduced and both Sending and Delivery are specialized for it. Moreover, every sent FirstClassMessages *fcm* must be read by some number of Receivers within certain time interval from sending. The minimum number of Receivers and the interval are given by variables *read_by* and *d* of class FirstClassMessage, respectively. The above is satisfied by a simple real-time requirement and a conjunct in the guard of action FirstClassDelivery. The conjunct requires that the number of objects participating in role r is greater than or equal to the value of $fcm.read\_by^2$:

$$\textbf{class } FirstClassMessage = Message +$$
$$\{d : time;$$
$$t : time;$$
$$read\_by : integer\}$$

$$FirstClassSending(fcm : FirstClassMessage; data : integer) :$$
$$\textbf{refines } Sending(fcm, data)$$
$$\rightarrow fcm.t' = \Delta_{on}(fcm.d)$$

$$FirstClassDelivery(*fcm : FirstClassMessage; \{r\} : Receiver) :$$
$$\textbf{refines } Delivery(fcm, r^{\{\}})$$
$$\wedge |r^{\{\}}| \geq fcm.read\_by$$
$$\rightarrow \Delta_{off}(fcm.t)$$

After this superposition step there are two versions of Sending and Delivery, the ones for Messages which are not FirstClassMessages, and the others, named

---

[2] The notation $r^{\{\}}$ refers to the set formed by all objects participating in role r.

FirstClassSending and FirstClassDelivery, for FirstClassMessages. As discussed earlier, a fairness requirement is needed for a participant in action FirstClass-Delivery to force the action into execution.

3   Hybrid Modelling of Mobility

3.1   Capturing Hybrid Interaction

In *closed system* modelling the system under development is specified together with its assumed environment. The greatest advantage of closed specifications over *open specifications* is that the specification process can be started without first fixing the interfaces between different components of the system.

In DisCo, joint actions allow specification of *interaction* between agents at a high level of abstraction. Specifications are always closed allowing to capture the essential collective behaviour before partitioning the specification into components with fixed interfaces [11,12].

The behaviour of a system consisting of mobile agents depends on the physical localities of the agents. Locations of the agents change as they move. The movement of agents may affect the enabledness of actions. Consider for example a situation where the locations of agents A and C stay the same and agent B moves from the proximity of A to the proximity of C. An action modelling communication between two agents which are in each other's proximity, may first be enabled for A and B, later disabled for all agents and again later enabled for B and C. Alternatively, the action may at some point be enabled for both A and B, and B and C.

A fundamental question is whether an agent can *control* or only *observe* its motion. The former approach relates to mobile robotics and controller design. The latter relates to systems designed to be carried around in a pocket or, for instance, moved in a car or train. In this case the system can only give suggestions to the user on where to move next, but the decision to do so lies beyond its capabilities. In the sequel we will concentrate on the latter scenario.

An environment of such an agent consists of a user, other agents, and the physical reality in which it exists. The user uses the applications provided by the agent and decides to move in a physical reality to a certain direction with a certain speed. Depending on the location, the agent may be able to communicate with other agents. The applications that are available to the user may depend on the proximity of other agents. The physical reality serves as a medium for wireless communication between agents.

The behaviour of an agent can be described as a sequence of states. A state consists of values of variables. Actions are used to describe how states in a behaviour relate to each other. The values of variables can change only in actions. The nature of phenomenas in the physical reality is continuous, i.e. changes do not occur only in discrete steps but also between them.

There is interaction between an agent and its continuous environment. Consider for example an agent transmitting data to another agent. On one hand the transmission causes changes in the environment, which make it possible for the other agent to receive the transmission. On the other hand the changes in the signal to noise ratio caused by movement of the agent, for instance, can affect the data transfer rate between the agents.

Capturing this interaction in the specifications of mobile agents calls for hybrid models, i.e. models capable of describing not only discrete changes but also continuous ones. In the DisCo approach, joint actions and closed system modelling are used to capture hybrid interaction.

3.2   Superposing Localities

A group of mobile agents communicates in joint actions. Mobile agents are modelled as objects with localities. Their behaviours and willingness to communicate depends on their locations relative to other objects.

We will assume that the movement of an agent is continuous, but the agent has no control over it. However, the agent is always capable of measuring its location. The measuring takes place in actions. The current location of a participating agent can be modelled as a parameter and assigning a parameter value to a state variable corresponds to a measurement.

Based on the measurements, an agent can estimate its future motion or even guide movement of the user. This approach, where ordinary state variables and time are used to estimate continuous quantities was applied in [9] to general hybrid systems.

Actions are used to coordinate both individual and joint behaviour of agents. Aspects related to physical location, the corresponding state variables and coordination can be given in one or more superposition steps.

For simplicity and without loss of generality, we will concentrate on agents moving in a two-dimensional Euclidean space. Type Physical_Location describes the actual physical location of an instance of class Object in a two-dimensional space. The variables x and y are the values of the coordinates, and ref is a reference to the associated instance:

$$\textbf{type } Physical\_Location = \{x, y : real$$
$$ref : \textbf{reference } Object\}$$

Whenever an action that has parameters of type Physical_Location is executed, the values of the parameters correspond to the actual physical locations of the referenced objects at the moment the action is executed. Additionally, function Distance is defined. It gets two physical locations as parameters and returns their mutual distance:

$$\textbf{function } Distance(pl1, pl2 : Physical\_Location) : real \textbf{ is}$$
$$\sqrt{(pl1.x - pl2.x)^2 + (pl1.y - pl2.y)^2}$$

3.3   Hybrid Deadlines

Typical inputs to a hybrid system come from sensors monitoring a physical phenomena. Values from sensors are typically obtained at discrete moments, thus actions and non-deterministic parameters can be used to capture the correct behavior. However, modelling an action that has to be executed at a moment when a continuous quantity reaches some limit poses a problem. The problem is determining the right moment of time when the action should happen. Obviously, the moment the quantity reaches the limit is not known beforehand, so we cannot give a time deadline for the action.

One solution is to introduce priorities to actions and require that actions should be chosen for execution based on them. However, we consider priorities as an implementation level mechanism and feel that fairness is a much more convenient execution force at high levels of abstraction.

For other continuous quantities than time we will use *hybrid deadlines* which are analogous to time deadlines. In this paper, they are applied to mutual distances between objects which change continuously as the objects move.

For this purpose, for each pair $o1, o2 \in Object$, a multiset $\Delta^{Distance(o1,o2)}$ is introduced to hold hybrid deadlines concerning the mutual distance between the objects. Furthermore, it is assumed that between executions of actions, the mutual distance between any pair of objects changes *monotonically*.

We can use hybrid deadlines in conjunction with fairness to force some actions into execution before certain distance grows beyond some deadline. Similarly to time deadlines, hybrid deadlines can be added and removed using Δ_{on} and Δ_{off}, respectively. However, the parameter of Δ_{on} is treated as an absolute value, not as an offset from the current value of distance. Every new deadline less than the current value is treated as the current value.

In each action there is an implicit parameter PL which is a set of type Physical_Location and it holds that

$$\forall o \in Object \; \exists pl \in PL : pl.ref = o$$

and

$$\forall pl1, pl2 \in PL : pl1.ref = pl2.ref \Rightarrow pl1.x = pl2.x \land pl1.y = pl2.y \; .$$

Furthermore, in all guards there is an implicit conjunct

$$\forall pl1, pl2 \in PL : Distance(pl1, pl2) \leq min(\Delta^{Distance(pl1.ref,pl2.ref)}) \; ,$$

which prevents the mutual distance between any pair of objects to grow beyond any hybrid deadline set for the distance until some action removes the limiting hybrid deadline with $\Delta_{off}^{Distance(pl1.ref,pl2.ref)}$.

The requirement of monotonicity means that, between executions of actions, for every pair of objects their mutual distance is either nonincreasing or nondecreasing. Nonincreasing means that the distance cannot increase and nondecreasing that the distance cannot decrease. If actions are executed with sufficient frequency, this is not a vital restriction.

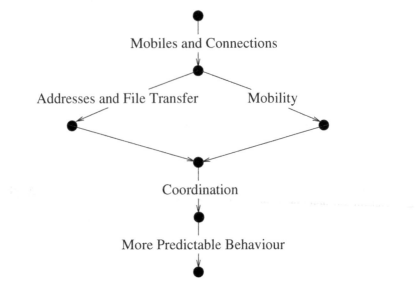

Fig. 1. The layered structure of the specification

If a distance for which there is a hybrid deadline, reaches this deadline and then starts to decrease, the action that removes the deadline may or may not be executed. The deadline mechanism ensures only that deadlines are not passed.

4   Example

To illustrate the use of hybrid modelling in conjunction with mobility, a simple example is presented. The specification describes agents capable of moving and transferring files when in each other's proximity. The specification consists of five layers (see Fig. 1).

4.1   Mobiles and Connections

In the highest level layer named Mobiles and Connections, the agents are modelled as instances of class Mobile, a subclass of Object. At this level there are no attributes in the class. Relation Connection can hold between two instances of class Mobile:

$$\textbf{class } Mobile = \; Object + \{\}$$

$$\textbf{relation } (0..1) \cdot Connection \cdot (0..1) : Mobile \times Mobile$$

Action Connect sets a relation between two participating Mobiles. It can be executed if neither one is already in relation with some other Mobile:

$Connect(m1, m2 : Mobile) :$
$$\forall m \in Mobile : \neg(m1 \cdot Connection \cdot m \vee m \cdot Connection \cdot m1$$
$$\vee m2 \cdot Connection \cdot m \vee m \cdot Connection \cdot m2)$$
$$\rightarrow m1 \cdot Connection' \cdot m2$$

Action Disconnect resets a relation between two Mobiles:

$$Disconnect(m1, m2 : Mobile) :$$
$$m1 \cdot Connection \cdot m2$$
$$\rightarrow \neg m1 \cdot Connection' \cdot m2$$

At a high level of abstraction the system comprises only of entities called Mobiles. They can be connected to at most one other Mobile at a time. This safety property will be preserved by all later refinements, because superposition preserves all safety properties by construction.

4.2 Addresses and File Transfer

In layer Addresses and File Transfer a file transfer operation between two Mobiles is specified. A Mobile can push a file to another Mobile.

The layer introduces types Address and File:

type $Address, File$

Moreover, the class Mobile is extended with four variables. Variable *address* is a unique physical network address hard coded into each device and *others* is a set of addresses of other instances of class Mobile known by this instance. Variable *files* is a set of Files and *pushing* is a variable where a file to be pushed to another Mobile is stored. There is also an initial condition requiring that the address fields have unique values:

class $Mobile = Mobile +$
$\{address : $**constant** $Address;$
$others : $**set** $Address;$
$files : $**set** $File;$
$pushing : File\}$

initially $\forall m, n \in Mobile : m.address = n.address \Rightarrow m = n$

If a Mobile is not connected, it can broadcast its address to other Mobiles. This is modelled as action Broadcast_Address. In the action, the address of the participant $m1$ is made known to Mobiles participating in the quantified role $m2$:

$$Broadcast\_Address(m1, \{m2\} : Mobile) :$$
$$\forall m \in Mobile : \neg(m1 \cdot Connection \cdot m \vee m \cdot Connection \cdot m1)$$
$$\rightarrow m2.others' = m2.others + \{m1.address\}$$

Action Connect is refined and renamed to Start_File_Push. A file to be pushed and its recipient are chosen nondeterministically from sets $files$ and $others$, respectively. The body of the action assigns the file to variable pushing:

$$Start\_File\_Push(m1, m2 : Mobile; f : File) :$$
$$\textbf{refines } Connect(m1, m2)$$
$$\wedge f \in m1.files$$
$$\wedge m2.address \in m1.others$$
$$\rightarrow m1.pushing' = f$$

Nondeterministic choice is a natural way to model that the user chooses the file and its recipient from the lists displayed in the graphical user interface of an agent. However, the Mobiles whose addresses are in the set may have connected to other Mobiles after broadcasting their addresses. Nevertheless, the guard of Connect ensures that only those Mobiles that are not connected can be connected to.

Action Stop_File_Push is a refinement of action Disconnect. It completes the file transfer by adding the file that was pushed to the set $files$ of the recipient:

$$Stop\_File\_Push(m1, m2 : Mobile) :$$
$$\textbf{refines } Disconnect(m1, m2)$$
$$\rightarrow m2.files' = m2.files + \{m1.pushing\}$$

There is also another refinement of action Disconnect, modelling the end of an unsuccessful file transfer operation. It is named Abort_File_Push and it is similar to the original action:

$$Abort\_File\_Push(m1, m2 : Mobile) :$$
$$\textbf{refines } Disconnect(m1, m2)$$

Moreover, there is an action modelling removal of obsolete addresses from the set $others$ of a participating Mobile:

$$Remove\_Addresses(m1 : Mobile; obsolete : \textbf{set } Address) :$$
$$obsolete \subseteq m1.others$$
$$\rightarrow m1.others' = m1.others - obsolete$$

4.3   Mobility

In layer Mobility the variables needed to store the measured location information are added. Type Location is used to store values of physical locations and also the speed of the Mobile relative to both x and y axes:

$$\textbf{type } Location = \{x, y \; : real;$$
$$x\_speed, y\_speed : real\}$$

Variables x and y should be initialized to reflect the initial physical location of the Mobile.

Class Mobile is extended to include variable l of type Location. Variable *period* indicates the time period between successive updates of the location information and variable *deadline* holds the next moment of time when the update is to be done:

$$\textbf{class } Mobile = Mobile +$$
$$\{l : Location;$$
$$period : time;$$
$$deadline : time\}$$

The update is modelled by action Update which is executed periodically. It has a parameter of type Physical_Location, which is the physical location of the participant $m1$. There is also the implicit parameter PL containing the physical locations of all Objects. The action computes the speed relative to both axes based on the current place and the previous place. The speed is stored with current place in l. The guard of the action ensures that it is not executed too early and the deadline mechanism that it is not executed too late. The fairness requirement ensures that it will be executed. When executed, the deadline is removed and a new one is set to $\tau + period$:

$$Update(^{*}m1 : Mobile; pl1 : Physical\_Location) :$$
$$\tau \geq m1.deadline$$
$$\wedge \; pl1.ref = m1$$
$$\rightarrow m1.l.x\_speed' = (pl1.x - m1.l.x)/m1.period$$
$$\wedge \; m1.l.y\_speed' = (pl1.y - m1.l.y)/m1.period$$
$$\wedge \; m1.l.x' = pl1.x$$
$$\wedge \; m1.l.y' = pl1.y$$
$$\wedge \; \Delta_{off}(m1.deadline)$$
$$\wedge \; m1.deadline' = \Delta_{on}(m1.period)$$

This layer leaves actions Connect and Disconnect unchanged.

4.4   Coordination

Layer Coordination refines the composition of specification branches corresponding to layers Addresses and File Transfer, and Mobility (see Fig. 1).

A real-valued constant Max_Distance defines a maximum distance between two Mobiles capable of communicating with each other:

$$\textbf{constant } Max\_Distance : real$$

Action Broadcast_Address is refined by strengthening its guard by two conjuncts. The first one requires that all participants in the quantified role $m2$ must be within Max_Distance from $m1$. The second one requires that all Mobiles within Max_Distance from m1 are participating in the role:

$Broadcast\_Address(*m1, \{m2\} : Mobile) :$

$\qquad \textbf{refines } Broadcast\_Address(m1, m2^{\{\}})$

$\qquad \wedge \exists pl1, pl2 \in PL : (pl1.ref = m1 \wedge pl2.ref = m2$

$\qquad\qquad \wedge Distance(pl1, pl2) \leq Max\_Distance)$

$\qquad \wedge \neg \exists pl1, pl2 \in PL : (pl1.ref = m1 \wedge pl2.ref \in Mobile \wedge pl2.ref \neq m1$

$\qquad\qquad \wedge Distance(pl1, pl2) \leq Max\_Distance$

$\qquad\qquad \wedge \neg pl2.ref \in m2^{\{\}})$

The guard of action Start_File_Push is strengthened so that the distance between the two participants must be less than or equal to Max_Distance. When executed, it adds a hybrid deadline regarding the distance between the participants to Max_Distance:

$Start\_File\_Push(m1, m2 : Mobile; f : File; pl1, pl2 : Physical\_Location) :$

$\qquad \textbf{refines } Start\_File\_Push(m1, m2, f)$

$\qquad \wedge pl1.ref = m1$

$\qquad \wedge pl2.ref = m2$

$\qquad \wedge Distance(pl1, pl2) \leq Max\_Distance$

$\qquad \rightarrow \Delta_{on}^{Distance(m1,m2)}(Max\_Distance)$

The guard of action Stop_File_Push is strengthened similarly. It removes the hybrid deadline added in action Start_File_Push:

$Stop\_File\_Push(*m1, m2 : Mobile; pl1, pl2 : Physical\_Location) :$

$\qquad \textbf{refines } Stop\_File\_Push(m1, m2)$

$\qquad \wedge pl1.ref = m1$

$\qquad \wedge pl2.ref = m2$

$\qquad \wedge Distance(pl1, pl2) \leq Max\_Distance$

$\qquad \rightarrow \Delta_{off}^{Distance(m1,m2)}(Max\_Distance)$

Action Lose_Connection is a refinement of action Abort_File_Push. It is assumed to be executed by the environment. It models the losing of the connection in the case when the distance between connected Mobiles grows too large. When this happens, the guard, the hybrid deadline and the fairness requirement ensure that the action is executed exactly when the distance equals Max_Distance. When executed, it removes the hybrid deadline:

$$Lose\_Connection(^{*}m1, m2 : Mobile; pl1, pl2 : Physical\_Location) :$$
$$\textbf{refines } Abort\_File\_Push(m1, m2)$$
$$\wedge \; pl1.ref = m1$$
$$\wedge \; pl2.ref = m2$$
$$\wedge \; Distance(pl1, pl2) \geq Max\_Distance$$
$$\rightarrow \; \Delta_{off}^{Distance(m1,m2)}(Max\_Distance)$$

Fairness is required for a participant in all actions except Start_Object_Push, which is considered to be executed by the user. This layer leaves action Update unchanged.

4.5 More Predictable Behaviour

In the final superposition step, state variables and time are used to estimate the future values of distance between two Mobiles. The objective is to make the file transfer operation more predictable.

An integer-valued constant Bandwidth describes the data transfer rate between any two Mobiles:

$$\textbf{constant } Bandwidth : integer$$

The type File is extended with attribute indicating the size of the file:

$$\textbf{type } File = File +$$
$$\{size : integer\}$$

Function Within_Range_Till_End computes a Boolean return value estimating whether or not the two Mobiles are still within each other's range after some time t assuming the latest coordinates and speed:

$$\textbf{function } Within\_Range\_Till\_End(m1, m2 : Mobile;$$
$$pl1, pl2 : Physical\_Location; t : time) : boolean \textbf{ is}$$
$$\sqrt{((pl1.x + m1.l.x\_speed \times t) - (pl2.x + m2.l.x\_speed \times t))^2 +}$$
$$\overline{((pl1.y + m1.l.y\_speed \times t) - (pl2.y + m2.l.y\_speed \times t))^2} \leq Max\_Distance$$

The only action that is refined in this layer is Start_File_Push. To make the file transfer more predictable its guard is strengthened by a conjunct that ensures that either the transfer is likely to succeed or the user confirms the transfer:

$$Start\_File\_Push(m1, m2 : Mobile; f : File; pl1, pl2 : Physical\_Location;$$
$$confirmation : boolean) :$$
$$\textbf{refines } Start\_File\_Push(m1, m2, f, pl1, pl2)$$
$$\wedge \; (Within\_Range\_Till\_End(m1, m2, pl1, pl2, f.size/Bandwidth)$$
$$\vee \; confirmation)$$

From the point of view of the user, the effects of the refinement can been seen as follows. After the user has chosen a file and a recipient, an estimation is made on whether the file can be transferred successfully or not. In the former case the transfer begins immediately, but in the latter case a dialogue box is displayed to the user asking whether to begin transfer or not. If the user chooses to continue, the transfer is started, otherwise it is cancelled.

5   Conclusions

We have proposed the use of hybrid modelling in specification of novel wireless mobile systems. We believe that their development would benefit from modelling also aspects related to the continuous nature of the environment in which they operate. Furthermore, an approach to hybrid modelling of mobile systems was presented, where the locations of mobile agents change continuously. Moreover, it was demonstrated how discretely changing state variables and time can be used to estimate continuously changing distance between two agents. The approach can be generalized to other kinds of continuous quantities as well.

The way mobility was modelled in this paper was inspired by previous work done in related state-based formalisms, especially action systems [15] and Mobile UNITY [16]. Real time has been modelled previously in mobile specifications, e.g. in [14] where integer valued clock variables were used. However, the author is unaware of any previous work on modelling other continuous quantities in high level specifications of mobile systems.

To support the DisCo method a new toolset is under construction [2]. However, supporting all the issues raised in this paper remains as future work. Other interesting directions for future work include modelling variable bandwidth and other characteristics related to quality of service (QoS).

Acknowledgements

The author would like to thank all members of the DisCo project for their creative ideas and constructive comments. Tampere Graduate School in Information Science and Engineering (TISE) and Academy of Finland (project 57473) have funded the research presented in this paper. Moreover, the anonymous reviewers provided helpful comments.

References

1. The DisCo project WWW page. At URL http://disco.cs.tut.fi, 1999.
2. T. Aaltonen, M. Katara, and R. Pitkänen. Disco toolset – the new generation. FM-TOOLS 2000: The 4th Workshop on Tools for System Design and Verification, July 2000.
3. M. Abadi and L. Lamport. An old-fashioned recipe for real time. *ACM Transactions on Programming Languages and Systems*, 16(5):1543–1571, Sept. 1994.
4. R. J. R. Back and R. Kurki-Suonio. Distributed cooperation with action systems. *ACM Transactions on Programming Languages and Systems*, 10(4):513–554, Oct. 1988.
5. R. J. R. Back and R. Kurki-Suonio. Decentralization of process nets with centralized control. *Distributed Computing*, 3:73–87, 1989.
6. K. M. Chandy and J. Misra. *Parallel Program Design, A Foundation*. Addison-Wesley, 1988.
7. E. W. Dijkstra and C. S. Scholten. Termination detection for diffusing computations. *Information Processing Letters*, 11(1):1–4, Aug. 1980.
8. H.-M. Järvinen, R. Kurki-Suonio, M. Sakkinen, and K. Systä. Object-oriented specification of reactive systems. In *Proceedings of the 12th International Conference on Software Engineering*, pages 63–71. IEEE Computer Society Press, 1990.
9. R. Kurki-Suonio. Hybrid models with fairness and distributed clocks. In *Hybrid Systems*, number 736 in Lecture Notes in Computer Science, pages 103–120. Springer–Verlag, 1993.
10. R. Kurki-Suonio and M. Katara. Logical layers in specifications with distributed objects and real time. *Computer Systems Science & Engineering*, 14(4):217–226, July 1999.
11. R. Kurki-Suonio and T. Mikkonen. Liberating object-oriented modeling from programming-level abstractions. In J. Bosch and S. Mitchell, editors, *Object-Oriented Technology, ECOOP'97 Workshop Reader*, number 1357 in Lecture Notes in Computer Science, pages 195–199. Springer–Verlag, 1998.
12. R. Kurki-Suonio and T. Mikkonen. Harnessing the power of interaction. In H. Jaakkola, H. Kangassalo, and E. Kawaguchi, editors, *Information Modelling and Knowledge Bases X*, pages 1–11. IOS Press, 1999.
13. L. Lamport. The temporal logic of actions. *ACM Transactions on Programming Languages and Systems*, 16(3):872–923, May 1994.
14. P. J. McCann and G.-C. Roman. Modeling mobile IP in mobile UNITY. *ACM Transactions on Software Engineering and Methodology*, 8(2):115–146, Apr. 1999.
15. L. Petre and K. Sere. Coordination Among Mobile Objects. In P. Ciancarini and A. Wolf, editors, *Coordination Languages and Models, Third International Conference, COORDINATION'99*, number 1594 in Lecture Notes in Computer Science, pages 227–242, Amsterdam, The Netherlands, Apr. 1999. Springer-Verlag.
16. G.-C. Roman, P. J. McCann, and J. Y. Plun. Mobile UNITY: Reasoning and specification in mobile computing. *ACM Transactions on Software Engineering and Methodology*, 6(3):250–282, July 1997.

Mobile Agents Coordination in Mob$_{adtl}$

Gianluigi Ferrari, Carlo Montangero, Laura Semini, and Simone Semprini

Dipartimento di Informatica, Università di Pisa.
{giangi,monta,semini,semprini}@di.unipi.it

Abstract. We present and formalize Mob$_{adtl}$, a model for network–aware applications, extending the Oikos–*adtl* temporal–logic based approach to the specification and verification of distributed systems. The model supports strong subjective mobility of *agents* under the control of stationary *guardians*. Communications are based on asynchronous message passing. The approach exploits the notions of coordination and refinement to deal separately with the specification of functional issues in the agents, and with the specification of coordination policies, e.g. security, routing, etc., in the guardians. The goal is to specify mobile agents as independently as possible of the requirements related to the other facets of distribution. The specification of an application is obtained by instantiating the general model, refining it along different dimensions corresponding to the different aspects of interest, and finally composing the refinements. The main advantage, besides the increased flexibility of the specification process, is that it is possible to specify rich coordination policies incrementally, while the functional units remain relatively simple. We use Mob$_{adtl}$ to specify a simple electronic commerce application, paying particular attention to the incremental specification of the policies. We show how refined policies lead to stronger system properties.

1 Introduction

Present–day network computing technologies exploit mobile entities (either *logical*, like program codes and agents, or *physical*, like hand–held devices) that execute certain computational activities while moving around the network. A basic concern in such a context is the complexity of the development of these *network–aware* applications. Network–awareness means that behaviours strongly depend on the network environment of the host in which the application is running. Moreover, the programming focus is on structural or architectural rather than algorithmic issues. The emerging network–aware programming mechanisms and languages [15,10] provide effective infrastructures to support forms of mobility and control of dynamically loaded software components and physical devices.

A certain amount of success has been achieved in the development of network–aware applications over the WEB; however these experiences have shown the difficulties of using traditional software technologies in the context of network–aware computing. Therefore, from a Software Engineering perspective there is a new challenging issue: the definition of structural and computational models to provide designers with conceptual and programming abstractions to master

A. Porto and G.-C. Roman (Eds.): COORDINATION 2000, LNCS 1906, pp. 232–248, 2000.

the overall architecture and the structure of the components of network–aware applications.

In this paper we present Mob$_{adtl}$, a temporal logic based model to specify and develop network–aware applications. We introduce the model and its axiomatic presentation in Oikos–*adtl* [22], a linear–time temporal logic specifically designed to deal with distributed systems with asynchronous communications. Our approach is based on the notions of *coordination* [7,1] and *refinement calculus* [4]. Coordination provides a powerful conceptual tool to specify and develop systems in a compositional way. The refinement calculus simplifies the design of a system by using incremental development techniques. In Mob$_{adtl}$, we can specify network–aware applications by separating functionality from structural design: coordination provides primitives to glue together independent computational units, like those realizing the functionalities and those realizing security and routing policies. Hence, coordinators are the basic conceptual and programming abstractions to make applications adapt and react to the dynamic changes of their network environments. However, functional specifications cannot abstract completely from the policies: a policy that does not allow a component to enter into a site may have a visible functional effect. Mob$_{adtl}$ provides the necessary hooks to provide a very abstract description of the consequences of the policies, allowing at the same time to postpone to the appropriate points in the refinement process the specific decisions about the policies themselves. Indeed, Mob$_{adtl}$ does not provide directly any specific policy: effective policies must be explicitly specified through suitable refinement steps.

To illustrate how Mob$_{adtl}$ supports system specification we consider electronic commerce. Electronic commerce has many aspects including security, distribution and recovery. It involves strong interaction patterns among the actors (e.g. clients and vendors). These are typical features of network–aware applications having a set of controlled activities with strong interactions over a distributed environment. In the example, we first define the behaviour of a pair of components: a customer, and an agent sent to order a pizza, and derive the overall properties of the application assuming that the involved sites behave as the generic sites of our model. We then refine the application by fixing some policies for these sites, and show which new properties of the application can be derived.

The remainder of this paper is organized as follows. In Section 2, we present our abstract model for network–aware computing. Section 3 reviews Oikos–*adtl*. The axiomatization of the model is subsequently defined in Section 4. In Section 5 we apply the framework to the specification of a simple electronic commerce application. We conclude the paper with some remarks about related works and future research directions.

2   A Model for Network–Aware Computing

This section presents our abstract model for network–aware computing. First, we classify the models for network–aware computing presented in the literature along the following axis.

The nature of mobile units: They can be any combination of code, data and control [15,10]. Models where only pieces of code can be moved are said to support a *weak* form of mobility, while models where the units of mobility are *processes* (code + control) or *agents* (code + control + data) support *strong* mobility.

There are programming languages designed only to provide the ability of downloading code for execution (e.g. Java [3]). More sophisticated languages support migration of entire computations (e.g. Telescript [29]). A number of *Distributed process calculi* have been proposed as formal models for network–aware programming. We mention the *Distributed Join-Calculus* [14], the *Distributed π-Calculus* [18], the *Ambient Calculus* [6], and the *Seal Calculus* [28]. All these calculi advocate programming models which support strong mobility. Coordination-based models of behaviours have been adopted in the design of the Klaim experimental programming language [11], the $\sigma\pi$ calculus [2] and Mobile Unity [21]. Klaim extends the Linda [16,8] model with multiple distributed tuple spaces and provide programming abstractions to support process mobility. $\sigma\pi$ permits the specification of dynamic networks of components (i.e. networks which reconfigure their communication linkages): a component name is the unit of mobility. In Mobile Unity the unit of mobility is a component. Program states are equipped with a distinguished variable, the *location variable*, and a change of the value of the location variable corresponds to a component migration.

Mobility extent: If not all the components can move, it is useful to distinguish between mobile and *stationary* components. In the Aglets API [19], the *aglet context* provides a bounded environment where mobile components live. Aglet contexts are considered as not transferable. Similarly, Telescript's *places* are stationary components.

The dichotomy between stationary and mobile components also emerges in the foundational calculi. For instance, Klaim's nodes and Distributed π calculus allocated threads are stationary components. In the Ambient calculus, instead, ambients are the units of movement and they can be always moved as a whole including subambients. However, it is difficult to prove behavioural properties of ambients as the control of movements is distributed over all ambients (any of them can exercise the movement capabilities). A type system that constraints mobility of ambients has been proposed in [5]. Using type information one can express whether an ambient is mobile or stationary. To constrain explicitly ambient movements, an extension of the basic calculus has been proposed in [20]: the movement interactions become synchronous operations, and any movement can take place only if the two participant ambients agree.

Location awareness: The units can be either *location aware* or not. Location awareness results in the ability of choosing between a set of possible next actions depending on the current location. Locations reflect the idea of administrative domains and computations at a certain location are under the control of a specific authority.

Basically, in all models the units are location aware. The notions of ambients in the Ambient calculus, of seals in the Seal calculus, and localities in the Distributed Join calculus and Distributed π calculus correspond to variants of the general notion of locations. Finally, in Mobile Unity, location awareness is modelled by the value hold by the location variable.

Location control: The mobile units can control their location (*proactive* or *subjective* mobility), or can be moved by other entities (*reactive* or *objective* mobility). For instance, in Mobile Unity and Klaim only a proactive form of mobility is allowed, while the *seals* are moved by their parent in the Seal calculus. The Ambient calculus is an hybrid: ambients can decide to move, but they carry their sub–ambients with them, which are thus moved in an objective way.

Communication model: Examples are the transient shared memory of Mobile Unity; the name passing over a named channel in the Distributed Join calculus; the anonymous asynchronous message passing via explicit addressing of Klaim. In general, remote interactions are handled through explicit naming: a component which interacts over a non-local channel has to know the place where the channel is located. An exception to this schema is the Ambient calculus: the knowledge of an ambient name is not enough to access its services; it is necessary to know the route to the ambient. Finally, interposition mechanisms (*wrappers*), which encapsulate components to control and monitor communications have been exploited in [27]. Wrappers support the enforcement of security properties by constraining communications between trusted and untrusted components: wrappers explicitly specify which are the allowed communications among components.

In our model, a system is based on an immutable net of elaboration nodes: the *neighborhoods*. The neighborhood is a bounded environment where several components (both stationary and mobile) live. Components have a unique name, e.g. determined by the initial neighborhood and a suffix to distinguish siblings.

The notion of neighborhood basically corresponds to that of location. Each neighborhood is associated with a stationary component, the *guardian*. The knowledge of their own guardian makes components (both stationary and mobile) location aware. A guardian acts as an interposition interface among components and neighborhoods: it specifies and implements communication and movement policies. In other words, guardians monitor the components and limit the resources they can use. More precisely, communications between components occur via the guardians. Communications are based on *asynchronous message passing*. Guardians provide also routing facilities to forward messages and to handle migrating components.

The model supports strong mobility and mobility is *subjective*, but component migration requests can be refused by guardians, for instance because of security reasons. Indeed, guardians intercept messages and components and can decide which messages and components can enter or leave the neighborhood they control. The following figure provides a pictorial representation of our model.

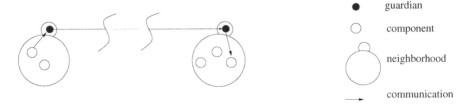

Fig. 1. Communication among components in different neighborhoods: messages and migrating components are routed via the guardians at both ends. Which other guardian may be involved is fixed by the routing and security policies at lower refinement steps.

The notion of neighborhood permits to model several crucial issues of network–aware programming. For instance a neighborhood can be used to represent an administrative domain where components are under the control of a single authority (the guardian), a naming domain where components adopt a given naming policy, and also an address space. The current notion of neighborhood is not complete. For instance, important requirements are not covered: the ability to define new neighborhoods and merge existing neighborhoods is missing.

Asynchronous communication permits to keep the model abstract from any specific communication protocol. The model itself does not embody any routing or security policy for the communications between guardians. Effective routing and security policies must be explicitly specified through suitable refinement steps. The development approach deals separately with functional, security, and mobility issues. For instance, we can fully specify the functionality of a component by giving only very abstract description of the security requirements. A complete system specification is therefore obtained by plugging together different refinements corresponding to different aspects of the system.

3   Background: Oikos–*adtl*

Oikos–*adtl* is a specification language for distributed systems based on asynchronous communications. It is based on an asynchronous, distributed, temporal logic, which extends Unity [9] to deal with components and events.

The language, its semantics, and a number of theorems have been introduced in [22,26]. We recall here the most important concepts.

The Computational Model. A system is characterized by a list of component names, and a set of state transitions, each associated to a component. A computation is a graph of states like the one in the figure below (dotted arrows denote multiple transition steps, plain arrows single transitions or message emission). Any state of component M is either the result of the application of a local transition, (as the one establishing q in the figure below), or the result of a send operation originated in a distinguished component (as message r).

$$M: p \xrightarrow[\text{establish q}]{\text{locally}} p, q \cdots\!\!\succ p \xrightarrow[\text{r in } N]{\text{establish}} p \cdots\!\!\succ$$

$$N: \quad\cdots\cdots\cdots\cdots\cdots\cdots\cdots\cdots\cdots\cdots\cdots\cdots\!\!\succ o \longrightarrow o, r \cdots\!\!\succ$$

Syntax and Semantics. A specification consists of a set of component names, and a set of formulae. Formulae are built over *state formulae*, which express properties of single computation states. They shape $M:p$, where M is a component name and p a 1st order logic formula. Formulae describe computations relating state formulae by the temporal operators CAUSES_C, CAUSES, NEEDS, BECAUSE_C, BECAUSE, WHEN, and those of Unity. Formulae are interpreted on computations. Transitions and communications define the *next state* relation: its reflexive and transitive closure define the *future state* relation. Formulae shape like:

$$M:p \text{ WHEN } c \text{ CAUSES } (S:q \wedge M:r) \tag{1}$$

$$S:q \text{ WHEN } c \text{ BECAUSE } (S:r \wedge M:p) \tag{2}$$

$$M:q \text{ CAUSES } N:r \tag{3}$$

$$S:q \text{ NEEDS } S:c \tag{4}$$

An event *occurs* when a given property is established, i.e. it *becomes* true. State formulae preceding the temporal operators are to be read as events. The con–(dis–)junction of state properties following the temporal operators are called *conditions*: for instance, in (3) operator CAUSES relates an event and a condition, and specifies that the establishment of q in M is sufficient to let r hold in the future in N. BECAUSE also relates an event and a condition, and specifies that the condition is necessary for the event to occur: it must hold before the event occurs. NEEDS requires a condition to hold when an event occurs. Finally, WHEN is used to express more sophisticated properties, by *subjecting* the effects of an event to additional conditions. For instance, (1) states that any state of M in which c holds and p is established is followed by states of S and M satisfying, respectively, q and r, as in the computations to the left, below. Formula (2) states that q can be established in S when c holds only if previously r and p have hold in S and M, respectively, like in the computation to the right. The same computation satisfies also (4): when q is established in S, c must hold.

$$M: \cdots\!\!\succ c, \neg p \longrightarrow c, p \cdots\!\!\succ \cdots\!\!\succ r \cdots\!\!\succ \qquad M: \cdots\!\!\succ p \cdots\!\!\succ \cdots\!\!\succ$$

$$S: \cdots\cdots\cdots\cdots\cdots\!\!\succ \cdots\!\!\succ q \cdots\!\!\succ \qquad S: \cdots\!\!\succ r \cdots\!\!\succ c, \neg q \longrightarrow c, q \cdots\!\!\succ$$

Suffix c stands for *closely*: CAUSES_C requires the condition to occur in the same state in which the event occurs, or in the next one; BECAUSE_C requires that the condition enabling the event happened in the *close past*, i.e. in the same (like NEEDS) or in the previous state.

Addressing readability in specifications, we avoid explicit quantifications [26]: variables in the premises of a formula (before the temporal operator) are universally quantified, while those appearing free in the conclusions are existentially quantified. Finally, a large set of theorems is available to be used to reason on Oikos–*adtl* specifications. Two interesting examples are a weak form of transitivity for CAUSES (5), and WHEN elimination (6):

$$\frac{M:A \text{ CAUSES } O:C \qquad O:C \text{ CAUSES } N:B \qquad O:C \text{ BECAUSE } M:A}{M:A \text{ CAUSES } N:B} \tag{5}$$

$$\frac{M:A \text{ WHEN } B \text{ CAUSES } N:C_1 \qquad M:A \text{ WHEN } \neg B \text{ CAUSES } O:C_2}{M:A \text{ CAUSES } N:C_1 \vee O:C_2} \tag{6}$$

4   Axiomatization

The goal of the axiomatization is to capture the most general model which satisfies the properties of Sect. 2 and to provide the necessary hooks to specify applications as refinements of the axioms. In particular we want to deal separately with the specification of functional issues in the agents, and the specification of coordination policies in the guardians. Thus, the axioms fix an "interface" for agents and guardians. This permits to specify applications by instantiating the axioms and then adding sets of formulae which state the application specific functionalities and the communication and security policies in use. These sets can be defined independently of each other.

In the axioms, location awareness is encoded in the component state via predicate *guardedby(G)*, which identifies the current guardian, i.e. the current location. Stationary components are characterised by the invariance of this predicate. Dually, each guardian holds a representation of the neighborhood it controls via two mutually exclusive predicates, *guarding(A)* and *moving(A, T)*: one of these predicates always holds in the guardian for each mobile component (*agent*, for short) which ever entered the neighborhood.

To move to another neighborhood, an agent A issues a mobility request to its guardian. If no veto is raised (events *veto(_)*), the successful movement of an agent A to location T is represented by a suitable coordination of the events *guardedby(T)* in the agent and *guarding(A)* in the guardian T. Predicate *moving(A, T)* identifies those agents that asked to leave the neighborhood and are not back yet. To guarantee the correct behavior, the mobility requests of agents that already asked to move, are intercepted and the originator is notified by *double_req*. Similarly, to send a message, a component sends a communication request to the guardian of the neighborhood it currently belongs to. If no veto is raised and the message is delivered, delivery occurs via the receiver's guardian.

The general model (hence the axioms in this section) does not describe how messages or agents reach their target, or why and where a veto is raised: the axioms only make clear that any of the guardians involved in a communication or a movement, can veto it. Also, the guardians at both ends are necessarily involved. Which other guardians may be involved, is fixed by the routing and security policies at lower refinement levels. The formulae introduced there detail the guardians, and take care of what happens in between the sender and target guardians, who raises vetoes, and why.

In particular, the general axioms do not describe how to deliver a message to a moving target. However, they imply that any refinement either guarantees the *control stabilization property* (i.e. that any message actually reaches its target, if not vetoed) or has ways to stop tracing a target which is moving too fast, and eventually notify a veto (e.g. after a given number of hops between guardians). Another issue which is left unspecified in the general model is how vetoes are routed: the model only requires that vetoes are delivered. A first realistic refinement could impose that also vetoes are delivered via the destination guardian. Finally, the general model is insecure, and malicious agents could fake vetoes or communication and mobility requests wrapping them in messages. Again, the specification of suitable safety properties to avoid these misbehaviours is left to further refinements.

4.1 Communications

When a component S needs to send a message M to component R, the event communication request *msg(M, S, R)* is raised in G, the guardian of the neighborhood S currently belongs to. The request can either succeed, i.e. the message is delivered to the receiver, or fail, in which case a veto is notified to the sender. If the request is successful, delivery occurs via the receiver's guardian.

The top of Table 1 displays the communication liveness axioms. CL1: event *out(M,R)* in S represents the agent's need to communicate and causes a request *msg(M, S, R)* to the agent's guardian G, to handle the communication. CL2: there are two possible consequences of an event in G which carries the request to handle a message for an agent G is not currently guarding. Either there is a guardian G' that in a future state will be guarding the receiver and serve the request, or a veto is raised. The first case calls for control stabilization, as mentioned above. The second case takes care of the model assumption that any guardian involved in a communication can stop it, raising a veto. Vetoes can originate similarly in other axioms, and are no longer discussed. CL3: when a

Table 1. Axioms for communications

CL1: S: out(M, R) WHEN guardedby(G) CAUSES G: msg(M, S , R)

CL2: G: msg(M, S, R) WHEN ¬ guarding(R) CAUSES
      G': (msg(M, S, R) ∧ guarding(R)) ∨ S: veto(msg(M, S, R))

CL3: G: msg(M, S, R) WHEN guarding(R) CAUSES_C
      R: in(M, S) ∨ S: veto(msg(M, S, R))

CS1: R: in(M, S) BECAUSE_C G: (msg(M, S, R) ∧ guarding(R))

CS2: S: veto(msg(M, S, R)) BECAUSE G: msg(M, S, R)

CS3: G: msg(M, S, R) BECAUSE
      S: (out(M, R) ∧ guardedby(G)) ∨ G': (msg(M, S, R) ∧ G ≠ G')

---

guardian receives and accepts a message for a component it is guarding, it delivers the message $(in(M, S))$. CAUSES_C is needed to force the guardian to deliver the message before reacting to a possible movement request by the receiver R.

The last axioms in Table 1 express communication safety properties. CS1: components receive messages only if their guardian received a message delivery request. CS2: communication requests are vetoed only if some guardian received a message delivery request. CS3: guardians receive communication requests only if a component in its neighborhood attempted to send a message or another guardian forwarded the request.

The following property holds: G: $msg(M, S, R)$ BECAUSE S: $out(M, R)$. The proof exploits the second disjoint in CS3 and BECAUSE transitivity, to connect G and the guardian of the sender, where the first disjoint of CS3 applies. The proof is an interesting example of well–founded recursion: the chain of intermediate guardians must be finite, since time is limited in the past. By BECAUSE transitivity, it follows from CS1 and the property above that there are no spurious messages: R: $in(M, S)$ BECAUSE S: $out(M, R)$.

4.2   Mobility

When agent A decides to move to a target neighborhood T, it notifies a mobility request $to(A, T)$ to its guardian O, which can either veto or accept the request. If the origin guardian O allows the agent to attempt to leave the neighborhood it controls, the mobility request may reach the destination neighborhood, or be vetoed along the route. If it reaches the destination, the target guardian can still reject the request instead of taking the agent under its own control.

Table 2 lists the mobility liveness axioms. ML1: event $moveTo(T)$ in A represents its commitment to move to T. The reaction to this event is a mobility request $(to(A, T))$ to the current guardian O. ML2: guardians immediately record (CAUSES_C) mobility requests from the agents they are guarding $(O: moving(A, T))$. This "freezes" the requesting agents, and prevents their guardians from considering other mobility requests from the same agent, before the current request

Table 2. Axioms for mobility: liveness

ML1: A: moveTo(T) WHEN guardedby(O) CAUSES O: to(A, T)

ML2: O: to(A, T) WHEN guarding(A) CAUSES_C O: moving(A, T)

ML3: O: to(A, _) WHEN moving(A, _) CAUSES A:double_req

ML4: O: moving(A, T)) CAUSES
            T: from(A, O) ∨ (O: guarding(A) ∧ A: veto(mob(A, O, T)))

ML5: T: from(A, O) CAUSES (T: guarding(A) ∧ A: guardedby(T)) ∨
            (O: guarding(A) ∧ A: veto(mob(A, O, T)))

ML6: C: guardedby(G′) WHEN guardedby(G) ∧ G≠G′ CAUSES_C
            C: ¬ guardedby(G)

Table 3. Axioms for mobility: safety

MS1: A: veto(mob(A, O, T)) BECAUSE O: to(A, T)
MS2: O: to(A, T) BECAUSE A: moveTo(T) ∧ guardedby(O)
MS3: O: moving(A, T) BECAUSE_C O: to(A, T)
MS4: T: from(A, O) BECAUSE O: moving(A, T)
MS5: T: guarding(A) BECAUSE T: from(A, _)
MS6: A: guardedby(G) UNLESS guardedby(G')
MS7: A: guardedby(G) BECAUSE G: guarding(A)
MS8: A: double_req BECAUSE O: moving(A, _)
MS9: G: INV ¬ (guarding(A) ∧ moving(A, _))
MS10: G: STABLE (guarding(A) ∨ moving(A, _))
MS11: G: INV ¬ guardedby(_)
MS12: *for all g and c, c initially in g's neighborhood*
          g: INIT guarding(c) ∧ from(c, _) *and*
          c: INIT guardedby(g) ∧ moveTo(g)

---

is handled. Indeed, ML3 states that a request from a frozen agent causes a veto of the kind *double_req*: safety axioms guarantee that only a frozen agent can cause a request to leave O, when O is not guarding A, i.e. only a frozen agent can cause the event in ML3. ML4: a mobility request may be forwarded, or may result in a veto, as usual. If the request is vetoed, the agent is unfrozen, and returns under the control of the origin guardian. ML5: if a request to enter neighborhood T is accepted, the guardian starts controlling the requesting agent (*T: guarding(A)*), which enters the neighborhood (*A: guardedby(T)*). ML6: when an agent changes neighborhood, the data recording its old location are immediately removed.

The general form $veto(mob(A, O, T))$ permits to accommodate vetoes generated in the refinements by intermediate guardians.

Mobility safety conditions are in Table 3. MS1: agents receive mobility vetoes only if a guardian handled their request to move. MS2: guardians receive mobility requests from an agent they are guarding, only if the agent actually requested to move. MS3: guardians handle mobility requests only if they received them. MS4: guardians receive mobility requests by agents they are not guarding only if the origin guardian accepted the request. MS5: guardians control only agents that previously asked to move in. MS6: agents are always aware of their location, i.e. of the guardian that guards them. MS7: agents can enter a neighborhood only if accepted by the guardian. MS8: mobility requests are considered double only if one is actually pending. MS9 and MS10: once an agent entered a neighborhood, the guardian always either guards it or serve a mobility request of its, but not both at the same time; also, guardians keep track of the agents that left. The interplay of guarding, moving and guardedby is such that the model does not constrains implementation choices with respect to mobility. E.g. there is no need to stop the execution of a frozen agent immediately after a request to move: the implementation can wait to do so until permission to leave is granted by the local guardian. The model has nothing to say on the local computations in the meantime. It only entails that communication and mobility requests of a frozen agent are dealt with differently: communications are regularly served, while mobility attempts are captured as double requests. MS11: guardians are not guarded, i.e. they are not location aware. MS12: in the initial state, every guardian knows the agents it is controlling, and every agent knows the name of its guardian. The other terms are needed to fulfill the other safety conditions in the initial state.

The next section gives an example of independent specification of functionality and policy, and of their composition.

5   A Simple Example

This section shows how Mob$_{adtl}$ supports the specification of network–aware applications. We specify a simple electronic commerce application where some activities strongly interact in a distributed environment. We focus on the coordination, communication and mobility concerns which guide the design phases.

To demonstrate how Mob$_{adtl}$ supports the composition of specifications addressing different concerns, we specify independently the functionality of the system (i.e. the components) and the coordination policies, i.e. the constraints on the guardians. We show that the coordination policies lead to stronger properties of the system, namely that some vetoes which are possible in the general model, no longer arise when the policies are in place. Finally, since the example is very simple (only two neighborhoods), there is no need to specify routing policies: should the system be expanded, routing policies could also be added.

5.1   Functional Description

In our scenario, a hungry customer sends an agent to buy a pizza: if allowed to enter the shop, the agent will buy the pizza and, once back home, inform the customer of the delivery time. Otherwise, the customer will be informed of the failure. The involved components are the customer c, a stationary component belonging to the Home neighborhood; the agent a, initially in the Home neighborhood; the guardian of the Home neighborhood h; the guardian of the Shop neighborhood s, which plays the role of the shopkeeper.

We omit to instantiate the general axioms to this particular system and just give the formulae to describe the functionalities of the components. Formulae c1 and c2 in Table 4 define the customer's behavior. When the *hungry* event occurs, a message is sent to the buyer agent (*out(buy_pizza, a)*). The second formula states that c is stationary.

The remaining formulae describe the behavior of the agent. a1: a reacts to a request from the customer (*in(buy(i), c)*) committing to move to the Shop neighborhood. a2 and a3: once in the Shop, the agent records the result of its request (*delivery_at(T)*) and goes back Home; once at Home, it communicates the delivery time to the customer. a4: the agent will inform the customer if not allowed

Table 4. Specification of the customer c and the agent a

---

c1 c: hungry CAUSES c: out(buy_pizza, a)
c2 c: INV guardedby(h)
a1 a: in(buy_pizza, c) CAUSES a: moveTo(s)
a2 a: guardedby(s) CAUSES a: (delivery_at(T) ∧ moveTo(h))
a3 a: guardedby(h) WHEN delivery_at(T) CAUSES a: out(pizza_at(T), c)
a4 a: veto(mob(a, _, _)) CAUSES a: out(failure, c)
a5 a: delivery_at(T) NEEDS guardedby(s)
a6 a: delivery_at(T) UNLESS out(pizza_at(T), c)
a7 a: out(failure, c) BECAUSE a: veto(mob(a, _, _))

---

to accomplish this task (*out(failure, c)*). a5 and a6 express safety conditions: the former states that the event *delivery_at(T)* can occur only if the agent is at the shop, and prevents the agent from not actually going there. The last formula guarantees that data about the delivery will be kept till the agent communicates them to the customer, i.e. the agent has a good memory.

The following properties hold:

P1: c: hungry CAUSES
c:(in(pizza_at(T), a) ∨ in(failure, a) ∨ veto(msg(buy_pizza, c, a))) ∨
a:(double_req ∨ veto(msg(pizza_at(T), a, c)) ∨ veto(msg(failure, a, c)))

P2: c: in(failure, a) BECAUSE a:veto(mob(a, h, s)) ∨ veto(mob(a, s, h))

P1 is a liveness property, i.e. it describes a particular behaviour of the system: the hungry customer will receive the pizza, provided that no vetoes are raised, i.e. the agent is allowed to move to the shop and come back home and the guardians do not refuse to serve communications requests by the customer and the agent. It is useful to understand why vetoes are originated, to define policies to avoid undesired behaviours. The first veto is a communication denial raised by one of the guardians involved in a communication from c to a. Similarly, the last two vetoes may be caused by the generic refusal by a guardian to let a communicate with c. *double_req* is raised if a attempts to leave a neighborhood twice. Mobility vetoes due to refusals by either h or s to let a move in or out are subsumed by the expression *c: in(failure, a)* (cfr. a4, Table 4). The safety property P2 states that the causes of failure notifications to the customer are mobility vetoes. Proofs are available at www.di.unipi.it/~semprini.

The next section introduces policies to allow free communications between the components when they are in the same neighborhood, and to let a move freely to and from the shop.

Table 5. Specification of the guardians h and s

---

h1 h: to(A, T) CAUSES T : from(A, h)
h2 h: from(a, _) CAUSES h: guarding(a)
h3 h: msg(M, S, R) WHEN guarding(R) CAUSES_C R: in(M, S)
h4 h: msg(M, S, R) WHEN ¬guarding(R) CAUSES S: veto(msg(M, S, R))
s1 s: from(A, _) WHEN open CAUSES s: guarding(a)
s2 s: from(A, O) WHEN ¬open CAUSES a: veto(mob(a, O, s)) ∧ O: guarding(a)
s3 s: moving(a, T) CAUSES T: from(a, s, T)

5.2   Coordination Policies

The policies for h are specified in Table 5 (first four axioms). h1: h allows any agent to leave its neighborhood. h2: h always allows a to come in. h3: h delivers any message for a component it is guarding, hence messages to the customer are always delivered since c is stationary. h4: h vetoes any attempt to communicate with the outside world, thus forbidding any attempt of the customer to reach the agent when it is busy buying a pizza.

The last formulae in Table 5 specify the shopkeeper: if the shop is open, the shopkeeper lets everyone in; if the shop is closed, enter requests are rejected and vetoes notified. s3: the agent can always leave the shop. Having fixed the policies adopted by the guardians, stronger properties hold:

P1′: c: hungry CAUSES a: double_req ∨
          c:(in(pizza_at(T), a) ∨ in(failure, a) ∨ veto(msg(buy_pizza, c, a)))

P2′: c: in(failure, a) BECAUSE s: ¬ open ∧ from(a, h)

P1′ and P2′ show that the specified policies reduce the number of vetoes and their causes. Since h lets the agent communicate freely with the customer, and a actually only sends messages to c when at home, vetoes to this communications are not raised. Similarly, since s and h let the agent move in and out freely, mobility vetoes can only represent the fact that the agent found the shop closed and are subsumed by the expression *c: in(failure, a)* (cfr. a4, Table4). However possible causes of vetoes still persist. As a matter of fact, h4 prevents c from communicating with a when a is at the shop, and nothing prevents c from attempting to do so, hence the possibility of a veto to a communication request by c. Similarly, nothing prevents a from attempting to leave twice, hence the possibility of a *double_req* kind of veto.

The safety property P2 states that the only cause of failure notifications to the customer is that the agent found the shop closed when trying to enter.

6   Discussion

Several works have addressed the problem of providing effective models for network aware applications. A temporal logic approach has been proposed by Roman and McCann [21]. Mobile Unity is based on the *transient* shared memory model: a variable shared by a pair of processes can be updated in an independent and non–coherent way when the processes are in distinguished localities. Specifications include a *coordination* section, which defines how coherence is achieved among the values of a shared variable when the processes move to the same or to *close* locations. The different communication model heavily influences the specification and verification style, and makes Mobile Unity and Mob$_{adtl}$ complementary approaches.

An important class of models is based on the Ambient Calculus [6]. Mobile Ambients support both subjective and objective mobility. However this generality can be seen as a source of *interferences* and wrong behaviours: imagine, for instance, the situation of an ambient wanting to move to a location and somebody else wanting to move it elsewhere.

Mobile Safe Ambients [20] has been defined to remove the most serious interferences. It introduces *coactions*, imposing both parties involved in a movement action to agree on it, and *single threaded* ambients, permitting only one process, the *pilot* process, to have the capability for making a move in each ambient, at any time. Abstractly, the model constrains subjective and objective moves (coactions impose synchronization and agreement) and introduces a form of control centralization with the notion of single thread.

The resulting model shows some similarities with Mob$_{adtl}$. The first is the notion of authority (pilot processes and guardians); the second is based on the fact that the action–coaction mechanism is similar to the interaction protocol between an agent (making a request to move) and its guardian (permitting the move). From this point of view, mobility in Safe Ambients is subjective and controlled.

An important aspect of our framework is that provides each authority (each guardian) with the ability to define its own coordination policy. For instance, different authorities may have different security requirements, and, therefore, there is a need to have considerable flexibility by allowing authorities to express different security policies. The approach has several advantages. First, it supports interoperability: different computing environments may need different security requirements. Moreover, the security policies of the guardians can be enforced and implemented by different mechanisms. On the contrary, most models for secure mobile systems base their policy on a specific mechanism. These can be:

- *Secure type programming languages.* Capability based type systems have been recently introduced to specify and enforce access control policies of mobile agents [5,20,18,27,12].

  The specification of the security policy can be transformed into a secure typed interface and implemented in a secure type language: the soundness of the type system ensures that program does not violate the security requirements implied by the type interface.

- *Cryptography.* The security policy has the role of establishing *trust* among guardians. Standard implementations exploit cryptography to enforce authority and identity of components. Cryptographic mechanisms are included in modern programming languages, e.g. the Java APIs [17].
- *Proof-Carrying Code.* Necula [23] has introduced an approach to ensure correctness of mobile code with respect to a fixed safety policy: code producers provide the code with a proof of correctness that code consumers check before allowing the code to execute.

  The security policy can be transformed into a safety policy and a Proof-Carrying Code mechanism is used to determine whether the component supplied by a different guardian satisfies the safety policy.

Notice also that our model works even if the guardians do not trust each other. The support for multiple authorities and multiple coordination policies makes the framework ideal to specify network aware applications with many different security policies. In [13] we have explored the usability of our formal framework in the specification of applications based on two distinct security policies.

To conclude this discussion, we observe how refinements or instantiations of our model can result in more elaborated or flexible models. For instance, we can encode hierarchical models, including nested neighborhoods, by defining appropriate routing policies to be applied to communications and migrations. Similarly, one of the proposed implementations for the Safe Ambients calculus is based on a flattening of the ambients hierarchy and on the explicitation of the hierarchical structure with routing rules [25].

We can also add flexibility allowing agents to change their course in an intermediate step towards their final destination, following an autonomous decision or an external request. This can be obtained defining the routing policies and the agents, in such a way that guardians wake up agents at each intermediate step, to permit them to assess the situation and take decisions.

7   Conclusions

We introduced Mob$_{adtl}$, a temporal-logic-based model to specify and develop network aware applications. The goal of this paper is to show how Mob$_{adtl}$ facilitates the specification and verification of network–aware applications by separating functionality from coordination policies. Mob$_{adtl}$ supports a development methodology where coordination policies are considered since early specification stages. This has the main advantage that coordination of mobile components, security and routing policies are taken into account in the design stages and not considered later on top of existing infrastructures. Furthermore, the impact of specific coordination policies on the overall architecture of the system can be evaluated in a natural manner.

We are currently exploring the use of the theorem prover Isabelle [24] to automatize reasoning on Mob$_{adtl}$ properties and policies. As a first step, we are representing in terms of Isabelle theories the axioms of Mob$_{adtl}$.

Acknowledgements

This work was partly supported by the ESPRIT W.G. 24512 COORDINA, and by the Italian M.U.R.S.T. national projects SALADIN and TOSCA.

References

1. J.-M. Andreoli, C. Hankin, and D. L. Métayer, editors. *Coordination Programming: Mechanisms, Models and Semantics.* Imperial College Press, 1996.
2. F. Arbab, M. Bonsangue, and F. de Boer. A coordination language for mobile components. In *Proc. of the 2000 ACM Symposium on Applied Computing (SAC 2000).* ACM Press, 2000.
3. K. Arnold and J. Gosling. *The Java Programming Language.* The Java Series. Addison-Wesley, Reading, MA, second edition, 1998.
4. R. Back and J. von Wright. *Refinement Calculus. A Systematic Introduction.* Graduate texts in computer science. Springer-Verlag, 1998.
5. L. Cardelli, G. Ghelli, and A. Gordon. Mobility Types for Mobile Ambients. In J. Wiederman, P. van Emde Boas, and M. Nielsen, editors, *26th Colloquium on Automata, Languages and Programming (ICALP) (Prague, Czech Republic)*, volume 1644 of *Lecture Notes in Computer Science*, pages 230–239. Springer-Verlag, July 1999.
6. L. Cardelli and A. Gordon. Mobile ambients. In M. Nivat, editor, *Foundations of Software Science and Computational Structures*, volume 1378 of *Lecture Notes in Computer Science*, pages 140–155. Springer Verlag, 1998.
7. N. Carriero and D. Gelernter. Coordination Languages and their Significance. *Communications of the ACM*, 5(2):97–107, 1989.
8. N. Carriero and D. Gelernter. Linda in Context. *Communications of the ACM*, 32(4):444–459, 1989.
9. K. Chandy and J. Misra. *Parallel Program Design: A Foundation.* Addison-Wesley, Reading Mass., 1988.
10. G. Cugola, C. Ghezzi, G. Picco, and G. Vigna. Analyzing Mobile Code Languages. In *Mobile Object Systems: Towards the Programmable Internet*, volume 1222 of *Lecture Notes in Computer Science*, pages 93–110. Springer-Verlag, Apr 1997.
11. R. De Nicola, G. Ferrari, and R. Pugliese. A Kernel Language for Agents Interaction and Mobility. *IEEE Transactions on Software Engineering*, 24(5):315–330, 1998.
12. R. De Nicola, G. Ferrari, R. Pugliese, and B. Venneri. Types for Access Control. *Theoretical Computer Science*, to appear, 2000. Available at http://rap.dsi.unifi.it/papers.html.
13. G. Ferrari, C. Montangero, L. Semini, and S. Semprini. Multiple Security Policies in Mob$_{adtl}$. In *Proc. Workshop on Issues in the Theory of Security (WITS'00)*, Geneva, 7,8 July 2000.
14. C. Fournet, G. Gonthier, J.-J. Lévy, L. Maranget, and D. Rémy. A Calculus of Mobile Agents. In U. Montanari and V. Sassone, editors, *Proc. CONCUR '96: Concurrency Theory, 7th International Conference*, volume 1119 of *Lecture Notes in Computer Science*, pages 406–421, Pisa, Aug. 1996. Springer-Verlag.

15. A. Fuggetta, G. Picco, and G. Vigna. Understanding Code Mobility. *IEEE Transactions on Software Engineering*, 24(5):342–361, 1998.

16. D. Gelernter. Generative Communication in Linda. *ACM Transactions on Programming Languages and Systems*, 7(1):80–112, 1989.

17. L. Gong. *Inside Java 2 Platform Security*. Addison-WESLEY, 1999.

18. M. Hennessy and J. Riely. Resource Access Control in Systems of Mobile Agents. In U. Nestmann and B. Pierce, editors, *Proc. HLCL '98: High-Level Concurrent Languages*, volume 16.3 of *Electronic Notes on Theoretical Computer Science*, pages 3–17, Nice, France, Sep. 1998. Elsevier Science Publishers.

19. D. B. Lange and M. Oshima. *Programming and Deploying Java Mobile Agents with Aglets*. Addison–Wesley, 1998.

20. F. Levi and D. Sangiorgi. Controlling Interference in Ambients. In *Proc. 27th Annual ACM Symp. on Principles of Programming Languages*, pages 352–264, Boston, Jan 00. ACM Press.

21. P. McCann and G.-C.Roman. Compositional programming abstractions for mobile computing. *IEEE Transactions on Software Engineering*, 24(2):97–110, Feb. 1998.

22. C. Montangero and L. Semini. Composing Specifications for Coordination. In P. Ciancarini and A. Wolf, editors, *Proc. 3nd Int. Conf. on Coordination Models and Languages*, volume 1594 of *Lecture Notes in Computer Science*, pages 118–133, Amsterdam, Apr. 1999. Springer-Verlag.

23. G. Necula. Proof–carrying code. In *Proc. of the ACM Symposium on Principles of Programming Languages*. ACM, 1997.

24. L. Paulson and T. Nipkow. Isabelle. www.cl.cam.ac.uk/Research/HVG/Isabelle/.

25. D. Sangiorgi. Personal Communication.

26. L. Semini and C. Montangero. A Refinement Calculus for Tuple Spaces. *Science of Computer Programming*, 34:79–140, 1999.

27. P. Sewell and J. Vitek. Secure Composition of Insecure Components. In *Proc. Computer Security Foundations Workshop 12, CSFW-12*. IEEE, 1999.

28. J. Vitek and G. Castagna. Towards a Calculus of Secure Mobile Computations. In *Proc. Workshop on Internet Programming Languages*, volume 1686 of *Lecture Notes in Computer Science*, Chicago, Illinois, May 1998. Springer-Verlag.

29. J. E. White. Mobile Agents. In J. Bradshaw, editor, *Software Agents*. AAAI Press and MIT Press, 1996.

A Logical Interface Description Language for Components

F. Arbab[1], F.S. de Boer[2], and M.M. Bonsangue[1]

[1] CWI, Amsterdam, The Netherlands
{farhad,marcello}@cwi.nl
[2] Utrecht University, The Netherlands
frankb@cs.uu.nl

Abstract. Motivated by our earlier work on the IWIM model and the Manifold language, in this paper, we attend to some of the basic issues in component-based software. We present a formal model for such systems, a formal-logic-based component interface description language that conveys the observable semantics of components, a formal system for deriving the semantics of a composite system out of the semantics of its constituent components, and the conditions under which this derivation system is sound and complete. Our main results in this paper are the theorems that formulate the notion of compositionality and the completeness of the derivation system that supports this property in a component-based system.

1 Introduction

Building applications out of software components is currently a major challenge for Software Engineering. The urgency and importance of this challenge are intensified by the continuous rapid growth of the supply and demand for software (components) on the internet, and the prospect of mobile computing. There are close ties between many of the issues investigated in the coordination research community in the past decade or so, on the one hand, and some of the basic problems in Component Based Software Engineering, on the other.

Motivated by our earlier work on the IWIM model and the Manifold language, in this paper we introduce a formal logic-based interface description language for components in component-based systems. We consider components as black box computational entities that communicate asynchronously via unbounded FIFO buffers. Each such FIFO buffer is called a channel and has a system-wide unique identity. The identity of a channel can also be communicated as a value through channels. This allows dynamic reconfiguration of channel connections among the components of a system.

The interface of a component describes its observable behavior abstracting away its implementation in a particular programming language. The interface of a component contains five elements: a name, a channel signature, and three predicates, namely a blocking invariant, a precondition, and a postcondition. The name of a component uniquely identifies the component within a system.

A. Porto and G.-C. Roman (Eds.): COORDINATION 2000, LNCS 1906, pp. 249–266, 2000.

The channel signature of a component is a list of channels representing its initial connections. The blocking invariant is a predicate that specifies the possible deadlock behavior of the component. The precondition is a predicate that specifies the contents of the buffers of the initial external channels (i.e., the ones in the channel signature) of the component. The postcondition is a predicate that specifies the contents of the buffers of the external channels that exist upon termination.

In order to simplify our presentation in this paper, we restrict ourselves to component-based systems that consist of a static number of components and channels, although the connections in the system can change dynamically and in an arbitrary manner. Semantically, we describe the behavior of a component by a transition system, abstracting away from its internal details and the language of its implementation. We define the observable behavior of a component in terms of sequences of values, one for each channel-end that the component has been connected to. Thus, we abstract away the ordering among the communications on different channels. The observable behavior of a component-based system is given by the set of final global states of successfully terminating computations, provided that the system is deadlock-free. The existence of a deadlocking computation is considered a fatal error. A global state records for each channel the contents of its buffer.

The main contribution of this paper is to show that it is possible to reason about the correctness of an entire system compositionally in terms of the interface specifications of its components, abstracting away their internal implementation details. Our notion of correctness of a component-based system is based on the above-mentioned concept of observable behavior. This extends the usual notion of partial correctness by excluding deadlocks.

Compositionality is a highly desirable, but elusive, property for formal models of component-based systems. For compositionality to hold, the formal system that relates the semantics of the whole system to that of its individual components must constitute a proof method that is both sound and complete. We show that our proof method is generally sound. On the other hand, it is not generally possible to derive the formal semantics of a whole system as a composition of the local semantics of its components only. Consequently, completeness of our proof method does not generally hold. However, we show that it is possible to obtain completeness for component-based systems that satisfy certain restrictions. Indeed, we show that these restrictions are both necessary and sufficient conditions for completeness.

To achieve completeness, we impose two restrictions on component-based systems. First, we restrict to channels that are one-to-one and uni-directional. This means that every channel is an exclusively point-to-point communication medium between a single producer and a single consumer. The producer or the consumer of a channel loses its exclusive control of its channel-end by writing its identifier end to another channel. Subsequently, a component may dynamically (re)gain the exclusive control of a specific end of a channel, simply by reading its identifier as a value from another channel. This allows dynamic reconfiguration of channel connections among the components in a system.

The second restriction imposes certain constraints on the forms of global non-determinism allowed in a system. We elaborate on this in Section 5.1.

We proceed as follows. In the next section we define a semantic model for components and define its observable behavior. In Section 3, we define the semantics of a component-based system. In Section 4, we introduce a formal language to describe interfaces of components, and formally define its semantics. Finally, in Section 5, we introduce a sound compositional proof system that allows to derive a system-wide correctness specification from the interface specifications of its components. We end this section by showing the completeness of the proof system for a certain class of component-based systems.

1.1   Comparison with Related Work

Over the past few years several component infrastructure technologies, such as Corba [16], ActiveX [14], and JavaBeans [12], have been developed, each of which embodies a different notion of "software components". Indeed, none of these technologies offers a formal definition of a component, and none of the twenty-or-so informal definitions for "component" commonly found in the literature on component-based systems is exact enough to be formalizable. Following [4], we strongly advocate a formal framework for componentware, to reflect the essential concepts in existing component-based approaches.

Our model for component-based systems is inspired by works in (1) architectural description languages, like UniCon [18], and (2) coordination languages, like Manifold [3]. Our model supports heterogeneity and reusability of components and provides modularity of description. Components communicate asynchronously and anonymously via identifiable channels. Thus, our model differs from models of asynchronously communicating process like CSP [13], parallel object-oriented languages [6], and actor languages [1], where communication between the processes, objects, or actors, is established via their identities.

Our notion of the interface of a component includes a description of its observable behavior. This is in contrast to most current interface description languages [16] which specify only some syntactic characteristics of a component, and thus reduce the analysis of a component-based system to mere syntactic consistency checks.

To the best of our knowledge, only [5] takes a similar semantical approach to the definition of a component interface. However, their model does not allow for dynamic reconfiguration of the connections, and gives no formal language for the description of the semantical information in a component interface. They, as well as many other systems, allow multiple interfaces for a single component. While our model has no specific features to support multi-interface components, it does not preclude them either: our model simply deals with component interfaces and is oblivious to the possible associations of (one or more) component interfaces with actual components.

Our semantic approach is based on the one taken in [7] for a language, introduced in [2], for describing confluent dynamically reconfigurable data-flow networks. In this paper we abstract away the syntactic representation of components, show the necessity of confluence to obtain a compositional semantics, and present a proof method for reasoning about the correctness of a component-based system. Generalization of data-flow networks for describing dynamically reconfigurable or mobile networks has also been studied in [9] and [11] for a different notion of observables using the model of stream functions.

Our computational model provides a framework for the study of the semantic basis of assertional proof methods for communicating and mobile processes. As such, our approach is different than the various process algebras for mobility, like the π-calculus [15] or the ambient calculus [10].

2   The Observable Behavior of Components

Components are the basic entities of a system. They interact by means of exchanging values via channels. A channel is an unbounded FIFO buffer. It represents a reliable and directed flow of information from its source to its sink. A component may send a value to a channel only if it is connected to its source. Similarly, it may receive a value from a channel only if it is connected to its sink. The identity of the source or the sink of a channel itself can also be communicated via a channel. As such, the connection topology in a system can dynamically change. Initially, we assume that each component is connected to a given set of sources and/or sinks of some channels. This defines the initial connection topology of a system.

In this section we introduce a formal model of the observable behavior of a component in terms of a transition system that abstracts away its internal behavior [8]. The internal behavior itself may be implemented in different programming languages.

For the rest of this paper, let $Chan$ be a set of channel identities with typical elements $c, c', \ldots$, and let $\overline{Chan}$ be the set $\{\overline{c} \mid c \in Chan\}$. For a channel $c \in Chan$, we denote by $\overline{c}$ its source-end and associate the channel identity c with its sink-end. The source-end $\overline{c}$ and the sink-end c of a channel c are also called its channel-ends. Furthermore, let Val be a set of values, with typical elements $u, v, \ldots$, that includes both c and $\overline{c}$ for every $c \in Chan$. We denote by Act the set of communication actions of the forms $\overline{c}!v$ and $c?v$ for each $c \in Chan$ and $v \in Val$, which respectively denote the sending and the receiving of a value v through a channel c. We assume the read action $c?v$ is destructive: as a result of this action, a value v is irrevocably removed from the FIFO buffer of c.

Definition 1. *A component C is specified by a transition system $\langle L, i, r, \longrightarrow \rangle$, where L is a set of (control) locations, with typical element l; $i \in L$ is an initial location; r is a set of channel-ends to which the component is initially connected; and $\longrightarrow \subseteq L \times Act \times L$ is a transition relation that describes the communication behavior of the component. As usual, we use $s \xrightarrow{a} s'$ to indicate that $(s, a, s') \in \longrightarrow$.*

Intuitively, a component may send a value v to the source-end of a channel c by performing a $\overline{c}!v$ action, and may receive a value v from the sink-end of a channel c by performing a $c?v$ action. If in some location, a component is willing to receive a value from the sink of a channel c, then it should be willing to accept any value from that sink. We call this property 'input reactiveness' formally expressed as the following condition that must be satisfied by the transition relation of every component $\langle L, i, r, \longrightarrow \rangle$:

$$\forall l \xrightarrow{c?v} l' . \forall u \in Val . \exists l'' \in L . l \xrightarrow{c?u} l'' .$$

In other words, we restrict to component-based systems that cannot put selection constraints on the values they receive. This restriction is introduced for technical convenience only (specifically, it allows a slightly simpler deadlock analysis).

A component can communicate only via channel-ends to which it is actually connected. Initially, a component $C \hat{=} \langle L, i, r, \longrightarrow \rangle$ is connected only to the channel-ends in its r. Other channel-ends can be used only after the component receives their identities through other channels. Formally, we require that, for every computation $i \xrightarrow{a_1} l_1 \xrightarrow{a_2} \ldots \xrightarrow{a_n} l_n$ of C:

1. if $a_n = c?v$ then $c \in r$ or there exists a preceding input $a_j = d?c$, $1 \le j < n$ and $d \ne c$; and
2. if $a_n = \overline{c}!v$ then $\overline{c} \in r$ or there exists a preceding input $a_j = d?\overline{c}$, $1 \le j < n$.

Note that the source end of a channel may be received through the sink end of the same channel, whereas its sink end, of course, cannot be received through the channel itself.

Next, we define the observable behavior of a component by mapping each computation to the sequence of values the component sends or receives through each channel-end. Information about the deadlock behavior of a component will be given in terms of a so-called ready set [17] consisting of those channel-ends on which the component is waiting for input. Note that as such, we do not have any information about the ordering among the communications of a component through different channel-ends. In practice, this abstraction simplifies reasoning about the correctness of the entire systems, as the value sent or received by a component at a particular point in time will be independent of the time other values are sent or received through other channels. However, we will record some information about when channels are exported.

To record when a channel (end) is exported by a component, we extend the set of values with a special element $\gamma \notin Val$. Let $Val_\gamma = Val \cup \{\gamma\}$. We define a component state to be a function s that maps the sink of each channel $c \in Chan$ to a sequence $s(c) \in Val_\gamma^*$ of values received from the channel c, and the source of each channel $c \in Chan$ to a sequence $s(\overline{c}) \in Val_\gamma^*$ of values sent to the channel c. The occurrence of the symbol γ in a sequence $w_1 \cdot \gamma \cdot w_2 \cdot \gamma \cdots$ indicates that the channel-end c (or $\overline{c}$) was exported in between the sequences of read (or sent) values $w_1, w_2, \ldots$.

For each component $C \hat{=} \langle L, i, r, \longrightarrow \rangle$ we formally model its observable behavior by means of a transition relation $\longrightarrow$ on configurations of the form $\langle l, s \rangle$, where s denotes a component state as defined above. This relation is defined as the least relation which satisfies the following rules:

$$\frac{l \xrightarrow{c?v} l'}{\langle l, s \rangle \longrightarrow \langle l', s[s(c) \cdot v/c] \rangle}$$

$$\frac{l \xrightarrow{\overline{c}!v} l' \text{ and } v \notin Chan \cup \overline{Chan}}{\langle l, s \rangle \longrightarrow \langle l', s[s(\overline{c}) \cdot v/\overline{c}] \rangle}$$

$$\frac{l \xrightarrow{\overline{c}!v} l' \text{ and } v \in Chan \cup \overline{Chan}}{\langle l, s \rangle \longrightarrow \langle l', s[s(\overline{c}) \cdot v/\overline{c}][s(v) \cdot \gamma/v] \rangle}$$

Here $s[a/x]$ denotes the function that maps x to a and otherwise acts as s. The effect of an input communication on a state s is that the received value is appended to the sequence $s(c)$ of values received so far from the channel c. Similarly, the effect of an output on a state s is that the sent value is appended to the sequence $s(\overline{c})$ of values sent so far along the channel c. Moreover, if the sent value is a channel-end, γ is appended to the sequence associated with that channel-end.

We now formally define the observable behavior of a component.

Definition 2. *Let $C \hat{=} \langle L, i, r, \longrightarrow \rangle$ be a component and s be a component state. We denote by $\longrightarrow^*$ the reflexive transitive closure of the transition relation $\longrightarrow$. Moreover, $\langle l, s \rangle \not\longrightarrow$ indicates that no further transition is possible from $\langle l, s \rangle$, i.e., l is a final location. Finally, let D be the set of locations l from which only input transitions $l \xrightarrow{c?v} l'$ are possible. The observable behavior $\mathcal{O}(C)(s)$ of component C in an initial state s is defined as a pair $\langle T, R \rangle$ where:*

$$T = \{s' \mid \langle i, s \rangle \longrightarrow^* \langle l, s' \rangle \not\longrightarrow\}$$
$$R = \{(s', \{c \mid l \xrightarrow{c?v} l'\}) \mid \langle i, s \rangle \longrightarrow^* \langle l, s' \rangle, \ l \in D\}.$$

Thus, the semantics of a component in isolation consists of the set T of all final states of successfully terminating computations, plus the set R of all those reachable states that may give rise to a deadlock, together with a corresponding ready-set. Given a reachable state which may give rise to a deadlock, its corresponding *ready-set* contains all channels on which the component is ready to perform an input action.

3   Component-Based Systems

A component-based system π consists of a finite collection of components $C_1 \parallel \cdots \parallel C_n$. In order to specify the dynamics of a system, we introduce the set Σ of system states, with typical element σ. A system state σ is a function that maps each channel sink c and channel source $\overline{c}$ to a sequence of indexed values (k, v), where $k \in \{1, \ldots, n\}$ and $v \in Val_\gamma$. The index k indicates that it was the component C_k that sent or received the value v through the given channel end.

We restrict ourselves to those system states σ that are *prefix invariant*, i.e., for every channel the sequence of values received from its source is a prefix of the sequence of values delivered through its sink:

$$\forall c \in Chan : Val(\sigma(\overline{c})) \sqsubseteq Val(\sigma(c)) .$$

Here, $\sqsubseteq$ is the prefix relation among sequences, and, for a sequence w of indexed values $(k_1, v_1), (k_2, v_2), \cdots (k_n, v_n)$, $Val(w)$ denotes the sequence of values $v_1, v_2, \cdots v_n$ obtained from w by removing the indices and the occurrences of the control symbol γ, if any.

Observe that, given a system state σ and a channel c, the sequence that is the difference between $Val(\sigma(c))$ and $Val(\sigma(\overline{c}))$ is the contents of the buffer of c in σ, denoted as $buf(\sigma, c)$.

Let $C_k \widehat{=} \langle L_k, i_k, r_k, \longrightarrow_k \rangle$, $k = 1, \ldots, n$, and $\sigma \in \Sigma$. The observable behavior of a component-based system $\pi = C_1 \parallel \cdots \parallel C_n$ is defined in terms of a global transition relation $\longrightarrow$ on global configurations of the form $\langle l, \sigma \rangle$, where $l \in L_1 \times \cdots \times L_n$ and σ denotes a system state as defined above. We define $\longrightarrow$ as the least transition relation satisfying the following three rules:

$$\frac{l_k \xrightarrow{c?v}_k l'_k \text{ and } buf(\sigma, c) = w \cdot v}{\langle (l_1, \ldots, l_k, \ldots, l_n), \sigma \rangle \longrightarrow \langle (l_1, \ldots, l'_k, \ldots, l_n), \sigma[\sigma(c) \cdot (k, v)/c]] \rangle}$$

$$\frac{l_k \xrightarrow{\overline{c}!v}_k l'_k \text{ and } v \notin Chan \cup \overline{Chan}}{\langle (l_1, \ldots, l_k, \ldots, l_n), \sigma \rangle \longrightarrow \langle (l_1, \ldots, l'_k, \ldots, l_n), \sigma[\sigma(\overline{c}) \cdot (k, v)/\overline{c}] \rangle}$$

$$\frac{l_k \xrightarrow{\overline{c}!v}_k l'_k \text{ and } v \in Chan \cup \overline{Chan}}{\langle (l_1, \ldots, l_k, \ldots, l_n), \sigma \rangle \longrightarrow \langle (l_1, \ldots, l'_k, \ldots, l_n), \sigma[\sigma(\overline{c}) \cdot (k, v)/\overline{c}][\sigma(v) \cdot (k, \gamma)/v] \rangle}$$

A component receives a value v from a channel-end c only if v is the first element of the buffer of channel c (which is thus non-empty). Otherwise it blocks. On the other hand, a component can always append a value to the buffer of a channel c by sending it through the channel-end $\overline{c}$.

Let $\overline{i}$ denotes the tuple $(i_1, \ldots, i_n)$ of initial locations. By $\overline{l}$ we denote a tuple $(l_1, \ldots, l_n)$ of locations l_i, $i = 1, \ldots, n$. Furthermore, we use the symbol $\delta \notin \Sigma$ in $\langle \overline{i}, \sigma \rangle \Rightarrow \delta$ to denote the existence of a *deadlocking computation* starting from state σ. This means that $\langle \overline{i}, \sigma \rangle \longrightarrow^* \langle \overline{l}, \sigma' \rangle$ and from the configuration $\langle \overline{l}, \sigma' \rangle$ no further transition is possible, although for some location l_k of $\overline{l}$ there exists a transition $l_k \xrightarrow{a}_k l'_k$, for some communication action a and location l'_k. Furthermore, $\langle \overline{i}, \sigma \rangle \Rightarrow \sigma'$ indicates a computation that starts from σ and *successfully terminates* in a system state σ'. This means that $\langle \overline{i}, \sigma \rangle \longrightarrow^* \langle \overline{l}, \sigma' \rangle$ and for all locations l_k of $\overline{l}$, communication action a, and location l'_k, there is no transition $l_k \xrightarrow{a}_k l'_k$.

We now define the observable semantics of a component-based system.

Definition 3. *Let* $\pi = C_1 \parallel \cdots \parallel C_n$, *with* $C_k \widehat{=} \langle L_k, i_k, r_k, \longrightarrow_k \rangle$, $k = 1, \ldots, n$ *and let* $\overline{i}$ *denote the tuple* $(i_1, \ldots, i_n)$ *of initial locations. We define*

$$\mathcal{O}(\pi)(\sigma) = \begin{cases} \delta & \text{if } \langle \overline{i}, \sigma \rangle \Rightarrow \delta, \\ \{\sigma' \mid \langle \overline{i}, \sigma \rangle \Rightarrow \sigma'\} & \text{otherwise.} \end{cases}$$

Thus, $\mathcal{O}(\pi)(\sigma)$ collects all the final states of the system that correspond to its successfully terminating computations, if it involves no deadlocks. Deadlock itself is considered a fatal error.

4   A Logical Interface Description Language

We introduce a formal assertion language for specifying the observable behavior of a component $C \hat{=} \langle L, i, r, \longrightarrow \rangle$ via an interface. The interface of a component consists of the following:

- the name of the component;
- an initial set of external connections (the sinks and/or sources of some channels);
- a blocking invariant;
- a precondition;
- a postcondition.

The blocking invariant specifies the possible deadlock behavior of a component. The precondition specifies the contents of the buffers of the initial external channels, and the postcondition specifies the sequences of values received from and delivered to the external channels that exist upon termination.

The above specification of a component involves a multi-sorted assertion language which includes the sort $Chan$ of channel-sinks and the sort $\overline{Chan}$ of channel-sources. In fact, c and $\overline{c}$ are introduced as constants in the assertion language for every $c \in Chan$. Apart from the sort of values that can be transmitted along channels (which thus includes the set $Chan \cup \overline{Chan}$) our specification language includes the sort of (finite) sequences of values. Finally, we assume that the sort set of $Chan$ and $\overline{Chan}$ is given.

We denote by Var, with typical elements $x, y, z, \ldots$, the set of all variables. For each sort we assume that a set of variables of that sort is given, and that these sets of variables are disjoint for different sorts. We denote by $\mathcal{S}$ the underlying signature of many-sorted operators f and predicates p. It includes, for example, the usual sequence operations like append, prefix, etc., and the usual set operations of union, intersection, etc. An example of a useful operator is $\overline{\cdot}$, that can be applied to a channel-end resulting into the other channel-end. Thus applying this operator to the sink-end of a channel c returns its corresponding source-end $\overline{c}$, and, likewise, $\overline{\overline{c}} = c$.

Given the above multi-sorted signature $\mathcal{S}$, we introduce the following set of expressions of the assertion language (we omitt sort restrictions).

Definition 4. *An expression* e *of the assertion language is defined as follows (we omit the type information).*

$$e ::= c \mid \overline{c} \mid x \mid e\downarrow \; \mid e\downarrow_k \; \mid f(e_1, \ldots, e_n),$$

where $k \in \{1, \ldots, n\}$, $f \in \mathcal{S}$ *denotes an operator,* $c \in Chan$, *and* $x \in Var$.

The *local* semantics of an expression e is formally given by $\mathcal{E}(e)(\omega)(s)$, where ω is a function that assigns to each variable a corresponding value (of the correct type), and s is component state. We have that

- $\mathcal{E}(c)(\omega)(s) = c$;
- $\mathcal{E}(\overline{c})(\omega)(s) = \overline{c}$;
- $\mathcal{E}(x)(\omega)(s) = \omega(x)$;
- $\mathcal{E}(e\downarrow)(\omega)(s) = s(\mathcal{E}(e)(\omega)(s))$
- $\mathcal{E}(e\downarrow_k)(\omega)(s) = s(\mathcal{E}(e)(\omega)(s))$
- $\mathcal{E}(f(e_1,\ldots,e_n)(\omega)(s) = f(\mathcal{E}(e_1)(\omega)(s),\ldots,\mathcal{E}(e_n)(\omega)(s))$, associating an operator f with its interpretation.

The constants c and $\overline{c}$, thus, denote the sink and the source of the channel c, respectively. The value of a variable is given by ω. Given an expression e denoting a channel-end, the expressions $e\downarrow$ and $e\downarrow_k$ both denote the sequence of values associated with that channel-end in the component state s. We will see later that these two expressions will receive a different interpretation at a global level. The definition of the semantics of a complex expression is standard.

Next, we introduce the syntax of assertions.

Definition 5. *An assertion ϕ of the assertion language is defined as follows.*

$$\phi ::= p(e_1,\ldots,e_n) \mid \neg\phi \mid \phi \wedge \phi \mid \exists x(\phi)$$

Here $p \in \mathcal{S}$ denotes a many-sorted predicate, and $x \in Var$ is a variable.

By $s,\omega \models \phi$ we denote that the assertion ϕ is true with respect to a variable-assignment ω and a component state s. This definition is standard. For example,

$$s,\omega \models p(e_1,\ldots,e_n) \text{ if and only if } p(\mathcal{E}(e_1)(\omega)(s),\ldots,\mathcal{E}(e_n)(\omega)(s)),$$

associates a predicate p with its interpretation. Thus, given the prefix relation $\sqsubseteq \in \mathcal{S}$ on sequences, the assertion

$$c\downarrow \sqsubseteq \overline{d}\downarrow$$

expresses that the sequence of values received through the channel c is sent along the channel d.

As another example, we show how to express in our assertion language that a channel x has been known to a given component initially connected to channels in a set r. In order to do so, we assume the presence of an operator *setchan* in our signature $\mathcal{S}$ whose interpretation is to return the set of sinks and sources of all channels occurring in a given sequence of values. Moreover, we use $\mu y(\phi)$ as a shorthand for a set-quantifier that gives the smallest set y for which ϕ holds (it is not hard to see that such a quantifier can be expressed in our assertion language). That a channel x has been known to a component can now be expressed as

$$x \in \mu y\,(r \subseteq y \wedge \forall z(z \in y \to setchan(z\downarrow) \subseteq y)).$$

In other words, the set of channels that have been known to a component is the smallest set containing the channels to which the component is initially connected, plus, for every channel, those channels stored in its associated sequence of values.

It is worthwhile to observe that we have the following algebraic characterization of the operator *setchan*:

$$
\begin{aligned}
setchan(\varepsilon) &= \emptyset \\
setchan(c \cdot w) &= \{c\} \cup setchan(w) \\
setchan(\overline{c} \cdot w) &= \{\overline{c}\} \cup setchan(w) \\
setchan(v \cdot w) &= setchan(w) \quad v \notin Chan \cup \overline{Chan}.
\end{aligned}
$$

Here ε denotes the empty sequence. Generally, reasoning about the properties of channels as expressed by our assertion language involves algebraic axiomatizations of the data types of sets and sequences.

The following definition introduces the notion of the interface of a component.

Definition 6. *The observable interface of a component is a labeled tuple of the form*

$$\langle Id\text{: } C,\, Chan\text{: } r,\, Inv\text{: } I(z),\, Pre\text{: } \phi(r),\, Post\text{: } \psi(r)\rangle$$

Here z is a variable that ranges over sets of channel sinks only, and $\phi(r)$ and $\psi(r)$ denote assertions with occurrences of r.

The blocking invariant $I(z)$, which denotes an assertion with free occurrences only of the variable z, specifies the possible deadlock behavior of C. It holds in all those component states where the component C is committed to get a value from channels in z, possibly blocking it. The assertions $\phi(r)$ and $\psi(r)$ denote the usual pre- and postconditions, where r denotes the set of channel-ends to which C is initially connected. For notational convenience only, we assume that initially the buffers of all the channels in r are empty (so we do not need a precondition). We then abbreviate a component interface by a triple $I(z)$: $C\{\psi(r)\}$. As a simple example, the interface

$$z = \{c\} \vee z = \{d\}\text{: } C\{c\!\downarrow = \overline{d}\!\downarrow\}$$

denotes a component named C, initially connected to the sinks of two channels, namely c and d and to the source of d. The component receives values from either c or d, and upon termination every values it has read from c it has been output to d in the same order.

Formally, we have the following semantics for component interfaces:

Definition 7. *Let $C \hat{=} \langle L, i, r, \longrightarrow \rangle$ be a component, and let $\mathcal{O}(C) = \langle T, R \rangle$ be its observable semantics. We define*

$$\models I(z)\text{: } C\{\psi(r)\}$$

if for all variable assignment ω, component state $s \in T$ and ready pair $(s', r') \in R$, we have $s, \omega \models \psi(r)$ and $s', \omega \models I(r')$. Here $I(r')$ denotes the result of replacing every occurrence of z in I by r'.

Basically, we have the same assertion language for the specification of correctness properties at the level of a system of components.

Definition 8. *Let* $\pi = C_1 \parallel \cdots \parallel C_n$ *be a component-based system, with* $r_1, \ldots, r_n$ *sets of initial connections for each component in the system. A system correctness specification for* π *is of the form* $\{\phi(r)\}\pi\{\psi(r)\}$, *where* $r = r_1 \cup \cdots \cup r_n$, *and* $\phi(r)$ *and* $\psi(r)$ *denote assertions with occurrences of* r.

The assertions $\phi(r)$ and $\psi(r)$ denote the usual pre- and postconditions. For technical convenience only, we assume that the buffers of all channels in r are empty. Consequently, we do not need to consider the precondition. Thus, we abbreviate a system specification as $\pi\{\psi(r)\}$.

In order to define the semantics of a system-wide correctness specification for a system $\pi = C_1 \parallel \cdots \parallel C_n$, we introduce a different *system-wide* interpretation for the assertion language. The semantics of an expression e is now given by $\mathcal{G}(e)(\omega)(\sigma)$, where σ is a system state of π. The main difference between the system-wide and the component-level interpretations is that we define for expression e of sort channel-source or channel-sink,

- $\mathcal{G}(e\downarrow)(\omega)(\sigma) = \sigma(\mathcal{G}(e)(\omega)(\sigma))$
- $\mathcal{G}(e\downarrow_k)(\omega)(\sigma) = \sigma(\mathcal{G}(e)(\omega)(\sigma))\downarrow_k,$

where $\downarrow_k$ projects a sequences of indexed values into the sequence of values (including the control symbol γ) indexed by k. Algebraically,

$$\begin{aligned}
\varepsilon\downarrow_k &= \varepsilon \\
((k, v) \cdot w)\downarrow_k &= v \cdot (w\downarrow_k), \quad v \in Val_\gamma \\
((j, v) \cdot w)\downarrow_k &= w\downarrow_k, \quad j \neq k.
\end{aligned}$$

At the level of the global assertion language, the expressions $c\downarrow$ and $\overline{c}\downarrow$, thus, denote sequences of *indexed* values (k, v), where $k \in \{1, \ldots, n\}$ is the index for the actor component C_k involved in the reading or the writing of v.

Analogous to the component-level interpretation, we denote by $\sigma, \omega \models \phi$ that ϕ is true with respect to the variable assignment ω and system state σ. An assertion ϕ is valid, indicated by $\models \phi$, if $\sigma, \omega \models \phi$, for every σ and ω.

As an example, we have for every channel c, the global validity of the assertion axiomatizing the FIFO nature of c:

$$Val(c\downarrow) \sqsubseteq Val(\overline{c}\downarrow),$$

where Val is algebraically characterized by

$$\begin{aligned}
Val(\varepsilon) &= \varepsilon \\
Val((k, \gamma) \cdot w) &= Val(w) \\
Val((k, v) \cdot w) &= v \cdot Val(w), \quad v \in Val.
\end{aligned}$$

The global validity of the above assertion follows from the fact that all system states are prefix invariant.

As another example, given two sequences w_1 and w_2 and that $w_1 - w_2$ yields the suffix of the sequence w_1 determined by its prefix w_2, the global interpretation of the expression

$$Val(\overline{c}\downarrow) - Val(c\downarrow)$$

denotes the contents of the buffer of a channel c. In the sequel, we abbreviate this expression as $buf(c)$. Note that, generally, we cannot denote the buffer of a channel by an expression interpreted in the state of a component.

We formally define the semantics of a system-wide correctness specification in terms of the above system-wide interpretation of the assertion language.

Definition 9. *Let $C_1, \ldots, C_n$ be some components with (disjoint) initial connection sets $r_1, \ldots r_n$, respectively. Let $\pi = C_1 \| \cdots \| C_n$ be a component-based system, and $r = r_1 \cup \cdots \cup r_n$. We define $\models \pi\{\psi(r)\}$ if $\mathcal{O}(\pi)(\sigma_0) \neq \delta$ and for all $\sigma \in \mathcal{O}(\pi)(\sigma_0)$ we have that $\sigma, \omega \models \psi(r)$, for every variable assignment ω. Here (for simplicity) σ_0 is the system state mapping each channel in r to the empty sequence ε.*

A global specification $\pi\{\psi(r)\}$, thus, is valid if π does not have a deadlocking computation and every successfully terminating computation in π results in a system state that satisfies $\psi(r)$.

4.1   Expressing Absence of Deadlocks

As a major example, we show how to express the absence of deadlocks in a system $\pi = C_1 \| \cdots \| C_n$ in our assertion language. First we need to introduce the assertion $\phi\downarrow_k$ that we derive from ϕ by replacing every occurrence of the operator $\downarrow$ by $\downarrow_k$. As discussed previously, this latter operator selects from a labeled sequence of values the sequence of only those values labeled by the index k.

Assume the interface specifications $I_1(z_1):C_1\{\psi_1\}, \ldots, I_n(z_n):C_n\{\psi_n\}$ are given for the components of π. Let $\overline{I}$ and $\overline{\psi}$ denote the sequences of assertions $I_1, \ldots, I_n$ and $\psi_1, \ldots, \psi_n$, respectively. Under our system-wide interpretation, the following assertion then defines $\delta(\overline{I}, \overline{\psi})$ to holds on all possible deadlock states in the system π.

$$\delta(\overline{I}, \overline{\psi}) \hat{=} \bigwedge_i (I_i' \vee \psi_i') \wedge \bigvee_i I_i' \wedge \bigwedge_i (I_i' \rightarrow \forall x \in z_i(buf(x) = \epsilon)).$$

Here, I_i' denotes the assertion $I_i\downarrow_i$ and, similarly, ψ_i' denotes the assertion $\psi_i\downarrow_i$. Note that the logical structure of this assertion reflects the semantic definition of a global deadlock situation given that I_i' represents the state of the component C_i as it tries to input from a channel in the set z_i, and ψ_i' represents its state of the component C_i upon termination: the first conjunct expresses that each component C_i of the system is either terminating in a state satisfying ψ_i' or it tries to input from a channel in the set z_i in a state satisfying I_i'. The second conjunct guarantees that there esists at least one component that tries to input from a channel, and the third conjunct expresses that all those components are actually blocked beacause the channels on which they are inputting are empty.

We explain the above assertion using a simple system $\pi = C_1 \| C_2$. In π, the component C_1 repeatedly writes a value to the channel d and subsequently reads a value from the channel c. The component C_2, on the other hand, repeatedly reads a value from d and subsequently writes that value to c. Let $r_1 = \{c, \overline{d}\}$ and $r_2 = \{\overline{c}, d\}$ be the sets of initial connections of C_1 and C_2, respectively. Also, let $I_1(z_1)$ and $I_2(z_2)$ denote the assertions

$$|c\downarrow| < |\overline{d}\downarrow| \wedge z_1 = \{c\} \wedge \forall z \notin r_1(z\downarrow= \epsilon)$$

and

$$|d\downarrow| = |\overline{c}\downarrow| \wedge z_2 = \{d\} \wedge \forall z \notin r_2(z\downarrow= \epsilon),$$

respectively, where the operation $|w|$ gives the length of the sequence w. Intuitively, the assertion $I_1(z_1)$ states that the number of values read from the channel c by the component C_1 is strictly smaller than the number of values written to the channel d by C_1 as it is about to read from c. Furthermore, it states that the component C_1 reads only from the channel c and writes only to the channel d. On the other hand, the assertion $I_2(z_2)$ states that the number of values read from d by the component C_2 is exactly equal to the number of values read from c by C_2, as it is about to read from d. Furthermore, it states that the component C_2 reads only from the channel d and writes only to the channel c.

We assume that C_1 and C_2 do not terminate, so that we can take *false* as the postcondition for both components. The assertion $\delta(\overline{I}, \overline{\psi})$ for $\overline{I} = I_1(z_1), I_2(z_2)$ and $\overline{\psi} = false, false$, thus, logically reduces to the assertion

$$I_1\downarrow_1 \wedge I_2\downarrow_2 \wedge buf(c) = \epsilon \wedge buf(d) = \epsilon, \tag{1}$$

which holds if the system can deadlock. Next, we prove that this assertion leads to a contradiction. We have

$$|c\downarrow_1| < |\overline{d}\downarrow_1| \wedge |d\downarrow_2| = |\overline{c}\downarrow_2|. \tag{2}$$

Moreover, from $buf(c) = \epsilon \wedge buf(d) = \epsilon$ it follows that

$$|c\downarrow| = |\overline{c}\downarrow| \wedge |d\downarrow| = |\overline{d}\downarrow|. \tag{3}$$

Since C_1 and C_2 are the only components and

$$\forall z \notin r_1(z\downarrow_1= \epsilon) \text{ and } \forall z \notin r_2(z\downarrow_2= \epsilon)$$

we derive from (3) the assertion

$$|c\downarrow_1| = |\overline{c}\downarrow_2| \wedge |d\downarrow_2| = |\overline{d}\downarrow_1|, \tag{4}$$

that is in contradiction with assertion (2). Since the assertion (1), above, describes all possible deadlock situations, we conclude that the system π cannot deadlock.

5   Composing Component Interfaces

In this section, we introduce a compositional proof system that allows us to derive a system-wide correctness specification from the interface specifications of the constituent components of a system.

In order to formulate this proof system, we observe that the following property holds for this projection operator.

Lemma 1. *For every assertion ϕ, variable assignment ω, and system state σ we have that*

$$\sigma, \omega \models \phi \downarrow_k \text{ if and only if } \sigma \downarrow_k, \omega \models \phi,$$

where $\sigma \downarrow_k$ denotes the component state resulting from applying $\downarrow_k$ to every sequence of labeled values $\sigma(c)$ and $\sigma(\bar{c})$ for all $c \in Chan$, i.e., $\sigma \downarrow_k (c) = \sigma(c) \downarrow_k$.

In other words, the above lemma states that the system-wide interpretation of $\phi \downarrow_k$ is the same as the component-level interpretation of ϕ.

We now formulate our proof system for deriving system-wide correctness formulas.

Definition 10. *Let $\pi = C_1 \parallel \cdots \parallel C_n$ be a component based system and let $I_1(z_1){:}C_1\{\psi_1\}$, ..., $I_n(z_n){:}C_n\{\psi_n\}$ be the interfaces of its components. We denote by $\vdash \pi\{\psi\}$ that the system correctness formula $\pi\{\psi\}$ is derivable from the following proof system:*

$$\frac{I_i(z_i){:} \ C_i\{\psi_i\} \text{ and } \models \neg\delta(\overline{I};\overline{\psi})}{\pi\{\bigwedge_i(\psi_i \downarrow_i)\}} \qquad \frac{\pi\{\psi\} \text{ and } \models \psi \to \psi'}{\pi\{\psi'\}}$$

where $\overline{I} = I_1(z_1), \ldots, I_n(z_n)$ and $\overline{\psi} = \psi_1, \ldots, \psi_n$.

In order to prove the soundness of the first and main rule of our proof system, we first need to show that the validity of the assertion $\neg\delta(\overline{I}, \overline{\psi})$ guarantees the absence of deadlocks. Indeed, the validity of the component-level correctness specifications $I_i(z_i){:} \ C_i\{\psi_i\}$, for each $i \in \{1, \ldots, n\}$, implies that every deadlocked system state σ of π satisfies the assertion $\delta(\overline{I}, \overline{\psi})$. More specifically, let $\mathcal{O}(C_i)(s_0) = \langle T_i, R_i \rangle$, where s_0 assigns to every channel-end the empty sequence (for notational convenience only, we assume that all channels are initially empty). Then either $\sigma \downarrow_i \in T_i$ or $(\sigma \downarrow_i, r_i) \in R_i$, for some set of input channels r_i on which the component C_i is blocked in the system state σ. By the validity of $I_i(z_i){:} \ C_i\{\psi_i\}$, we thus derive that either $\sigma \downarrow_i, \omega \models \psi_i$ or $\sigma \downarrow_i, \omega \models I_i(r_i)$. Moreover, since σ is a deadlock state, we have that $\sigma \downarrow_i, \omega \models I_i(r_i)$ implies that $\sigma, \omega \models \forall x \in r_i(buf(x) = \epsilon)$. Summarizing the above, and using Lemma 1, we conclude $\sigma, \omega \models \delta(\overline{I}, \overline{\psi})$. Similarly, it follows that every successfully terminating computation in π results in a final state σ such that $\sigma, \omega \models \bigwedge_i(\psi_i \downarrow_i)$.

Theorem 1. *For every component based system $\pi = C_1 \parallel \cdots \parallel C_n$ we have that $\vdash \pi\{\psi\}$ implies $\models \pi\{\psi\}$.*

5.1 Completeness and Compositionality

The main rule of our proof system for deriving system-wide specifications allows compositional reasoning in terms of the interface specifications of the constituent components of a system. Therefore, completeness of the proof system semantically boils down to showing that the observable behavior of a system can be obtained in a compositional manner from the observable behavior of its components. Generally, although compositionality is a highly desirable property, it is not readily present in the formal models of component-based systems. In fact, our abstract semantics for components decouples the inherent ordering of the transmission and reception of values through different channels, and is not compositional in the general case. The following example illustrate this.

Consider the following three transition systems describing three different components (we omit all transitions derivable by the input reactiveness property).

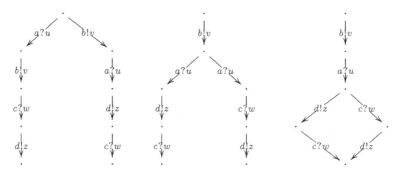

It is not hard to see that all three components have the same observable behavior. However, consider a system consisting of one of these components together with the following one:

$$\cdot \; -b?v \!\!\!\twoheadrightarrow \cdot \; -a!u \!\!\!\twoheadrightarrow \cdot \; -d?z \!\!\!\twoheadrightarrow \cdot \; -c!w \!\!\!\twoheadrightarrow \cdot$$

If the system includes the component in the middle then it may deadlock, whereas deadlock is not possible if it includes the rightmost or leftmost component.

The above example shows two situations where compositionality breaks down, leading to violation of the completeness of our proof system. The crux of these counter-examples is that the environment is allowed to influence the nondeterministic behavior of a component. In order to prevent this, we need to identify the forms of external nondeterminism that must be forbidden, to obtain a compositional characterization of the observable behavior of a system in terms of the observable behavior of its components.

There are three reasons why a component may exhibit a nondeterministic behavior that can be resolved by the influence of the environment: (1) a nondeterministic choice involving input actions; (2) receiving a value from a channelend shared with other components; and (3) sending a value to a channel-end shared with other components.

We rule out the first kind of external non-determinism by requiring a component to be *input confluent*. Formally, a component $C \hat{=} \langle L, i, r, \longrightarrow \rangle$ is said to be input confluent if, for all $l \in L$,

1. if $l \xrightarrow{c?v} l_1$ and $l \xrightarrow{c'!v'} l_2$ then there exists $l' \in L$ such that $l_1 \xrightarrow{c'!v'} l'$ and $l_2 \xrightarrow{c?v} l'$;

2. if $l \xrightarrow{c?v} l_1$ and $l \xrightarrow{c?v} l_2$ then $l_1 = l_2$; and

3. if $l \xrightarrow{c?v} l_1$ and $l \xrightarrow{c'?v'} l_2$ with $c \neq c'$ then there exists $l' \in L$ such that $l_1 \xrightarrow{c'?v'} l'$ and $l_2 \xrightarrow{c?v} l'$.

In other words, a nondeterministic choice involving an input communication (on different channels) may delay that communication but cannot discharge it. Note that this is the case when different input actions are executed by parallel processes within a component. Returning to our counter-example, the left component violates the first condition and the middle component violates the second one.

To avoid the interference caused by the sharing of channel-ends among several components, we restrict to channels that are uni-directional and one-to-one. This means that every channel is an exclusive point-to-point communication medium between a single producer and a single consumer. The producer or the consumer of a channel must then lose its exclusive ownership of its end of a channel when it writes the name of that channel-end to a channel. Subsequently, a component may dynamically regain the exclusive ownership of a specific end of a channel, by reading its identity as a value from another channel. This way, the components in a system can dynamically reconfigure their channel connections.

A formal characterization of uni-directional and one-to-one channels is expressed in the two conditions below. We require that every component in a system is input confluent and that every computation $i \xrightarrow{a_1} l_1 \xrightarrow{a_2} \ldots \xrightarrow{a_n} l_n$ in every component $C \hat{=} \langle L, i, r, \longrightarrow \rangle$ satisfies the following two conditions:

1. if $a_n = c?v$ then either $c \in r$ and $a_k \neq \bar{e}!c$, for all $1 \leq k < n$ and $e \in Chan$; or there exists $1 \leq i < j$ such that $a_i = d?c$, $d \neq c$, and $a_k \neq \bar{e}!c$ for all $j \leq k < n$ and $e \in Chan$.
2. if $a_n = \bar{c}!v$ then either $\bar{c} \in r$ and $a_k \neq \bar{e}!c$, for all $1 \leq k < n$ and $e \in Chan$; or there exists $1 \leq i < j$ such that $a_i = d?\bar{c}$ and $a_k \neq \bar{e}!c$, for all $j \leq k < n$ and $e \in Chan$.

Thus, a component can communicate via a channel-end only if (1) it has once been connected to the channel-end (either because the channel-end is included in the set of the initial connections of the component, or because the component has received the identity of the channel-end through a read action on another channel); and (2) the component has not subsequently relinquished its ownership of the channel-end by writing the identity of the channel-end to a channel.

We now show that the observable behavior of a system consisting of input confluent components (with exclusively point-to-point channels) can be described as a composition of the observable behavior of its components. Let

$\pi = C_1 \parallel \cdots \parallel C_n$ be a component-based system with $\mathcal{O}(C_k)(s_k) = \langle T_k, R_k \rangle$, $k \in \{0, \ldots, n\}$, as the semantics of its components. We define the set $\bigsqcup_k T_k$ of system states σ such that for every k there exists a component state $s'_k \in T_k$ with $\sigma(c) \downarrow_k = s'_k(c)$ and $\sigma(\overline{c}) \downarrow_k = s'_k(\overline{c})$, for every channel c. Recall that $\downarrow_k$ denotes the projection operation that, for a given sequence w of indexed values, yields the sequence of values indexed by k.

Similarly, we define the set $\bigsqcup_i \langle T_i, R_i \rangle$ of system states σ such that there is at least one k for which there exists a ready-set $(s'_k, r) \in R_k$ such that $\sigma(c) = \epsilon$ for every $c \in r$ and $\sigma(c) \downarrow_k = s'_k(c)$, and for every k for which this does not hold, there exists a component state $s'_k \in T_k$ with $\sigma(c) \downarrow_k = s'_k(c)$.

The following theorem states that for a system $\pi = C_1 \parallel \cdots \parallel C_n$ composed of input-confluent components connected only by point-to-point, uni-directional channels, we can describe the semantics of π, $\mathcal{O}(\pi)$, as a composition of the semantics of its components, $\mathcal{O}(C_k)$, $k = 1, \ldots, n$.

Theorem 2. *Let* $\pi = C_1 \parallel \cdots \parallel C_n$ *be as described above. Let* σ *be a system state and* $s_k = \sigma \downarrow_k$, $k = 1, \ldots, n$. *Given* $\mathcal{O}(C_k)(s_k) = \langle T_k, R_k \rangle$, *for* $k \in \{1, \ldots, n\}$, *we have*

$$\mathcal{O}(\pi)(\sigma) = \begin{cases} \bigsqcup_i T_i & \text{if } \bigsqcup_i \langle T_i, R_i \rangle = \emptyset \\ \delta & \text{otherwise.} \end{cases}$$

Assuming that we can express in the assertion language the observable behavior $\mathcal{O}(C)$ of a component C, we derive as a consequence of the above compositionality theorem the following (relative) completeness theorem.

Theorem 3. *For every component-based system* $\pi = C_1 \parallel \cdots \parallel C_n$ *where the behavior of every component* $C_k \hat{=} \langle L_k, i_k, r_k, \longrightarrow_k \rangle$ *is input confluent, and components are connected only by point-to-point, uni-directional channels, we have that* $\models \pi\{\psi\}$ *if and only if* $\vdash \pi\{\psi\}$.

6   Conclusion and Future Work

The work reported in this paper is a further development of [2] and [7]. In [2] a language for dynamic networks of components is introduced, and in [7] a compositional semantics for its asynchronous subset is given. In this paper we abstract from the syntactical representation of a component and present a sound and complete description of a system in terms of the interfaces of its components.

For simplicity, in this paper we restricted the class of component-based systems by disallowing dynamic creation of components and channels. Our semantic framework, however, can easily be extended to relax these restrictions, as shown in [7]. Currently, we are investigating other forms of communication among components in systems that retain a compositional semantics with respect to our notion of observables.

We also intend to extend our proposed assertional language with features we borrow from temporal logic, in order to reason about the reactive behavior of a component.

Acknowledgements. We like to thank the Amsterdam Coordination Group, especially Jaco de Bakker, Falk Bartels and Jerry den Hartog for discussions and suggestions about the contents of this paper. Thank also to Erika A'braham-Mumm for her helpful comments.

References

1. G. Agha, I. Mason, S. Smith, and C. Talcott. A foundation for actor computation *Journal of Functional Programming*, 1(1):1-69, 1993.
2. F. Arbab, M.M. Bonsangue, and F.S. de Boer. A coordination language for mobile components. In *Proc. of SAC 2000*, pages 166–173, ACM press, 2000.
3. F. Arbab, I. Herman, and P. Spilling. An overview of Manifold and its implementation. *Concurrency: Practice and Experience*, 5(1):23–70, 1993.
4. K. Bergner, A. Rausch, M. Sihling, A. Vilbig An integrated view on componentware: concepts, description techniques, and development process. In R. Lee, editor, *Proc. of IASTED Conference on Software Engineering*, pages 77–82, ACTA Press, 1998.
5. K. Bergner, A. Rausch, M. Sihling, A. Vilbig, and M. Broy. A formal model for componentware. In M. Sitaraman and G. Leavens, editors, *Foundation of Component-Based Systems*, Cambridge University Press, 2000.
6. F.S. de Boer. Reasoning about asynchronous communication in dynamically evolving object structures. In *Theoretical Computer Science*, 2000.
7. F.S. de Boer and M.M. Bonsangue. A compositional model for confluent dynamical data-flow networks. In B. Rovan ed., *Proc. 25th MFCS*, LNCS, 2000.
8. M.M. Bonsangue, F. Arbab, J.W. de Bakker, J.J.M.M. Rutten, A. Scutellá, and G. Zavattaro. A transition system semantics for the control-driven coordination language MANIFOLD. *Theoretical Computer Science*, 240(1), July 2000.
9. M. Broy. Equations for describing dynamic nets of communicating systems. In *Proc. 5th COMPASS workshop*, volume 906 of LNCS, pages 170–187, 1995.
10. L. Cardelli and A.D. Gordon. Mobile ambients. In *Proc. of Foundation of Software Science and Computational Structures*, volume 1378 of LNCS, pages 140-155, 1998.
11. R. Grosu and K. Stølen. A model for mobile point-to-point data-flow networks without channel sharing. In *Proc. AMAST'96*, LNCS, 1996.
12. JavaSoft. The JavaBeans component architecture, 1999. Available on line at the URL: http://java.sun.com/beans.
13. He Jifeng, M.B. Josephs, and C.A.R. Hoare. A theory of synchrony and asynchrony. In *Proc. of IFIP Working Conference on Programming Concepts and Methods*, pages 459-478, 1990.
14. Microsoft Corporation. ActiveX Controls, 1999 Available on line at the URL: http://www.microsoft.com/com/tech/activex.asp.
15. R. Milner, J. Parrow, and D. Walker. A calculus of mobile processes, parts I and II. *Information and Computation* 100:1, 1992, pp. 1–77.
16. Object Management Group. CORBA 2.1 specifications, 1997. Available on line at the URL:http://www.omg.org.
17. E.-R. Olderog and C.A.R. Hoare. Specification-oriented semantics for communicating processes. *Acta Informatica* 23:9–66, 1986.
18. M. Shaw, R. De Line, D. Klein, T. Ross, D. Young and G. Zelesnik. Abstraction for software architectures and tools to support them. *IEEE Transactions on Software Engineering* 21(4):356–372, 1995.

A Formalization of the IWIM Model

P. Katis, N. Sabadini, and R.F.C. Walters

Dipartimento di Scienze CC. FF. MM., Università degli Studi dell'Insubria, Como,
Italy

Abstract. The authors introduce case-place automata as an abstract
formal framework for the 'idealized workers and idealized managers'
(IWIM) model on which the language MANIFOLD is based. Case-place
automata are equipped with left/right interfaces and in/out conditions,
that are used to compose automata according to three main operations,
namely restricted product, free product, and restricted sum. These operations find natural interpretations in terms of parallel composition of
communicating workers and reconfigurations of modules. Taking the 'distributed sort' algorithm of [4] as a case study, it is shown that the manager process can be expressed as a recursive equation in the algebra of
automata.

1 Introduction

Arbab introduced in [1] a model of coordination he called 'idealized workers and
idealized managers' (IWIM) on which the language MANIFOLD is based. In
this model workers are rather like circuit components which process their input
and produce output without knowledge as to which other components they are
connected. In normal activity a group of workers is rather like a circuit. The
manager of a group of workers on the other hand knows nothing of the detailed
activities of its workers but is able to reconfigure them in response to certain
events.

The aim of this paper is to introduce a new kind of automaton, and operations on these automata, to formalize the IWIM model. In previous articles [8],
[9], the authors have introduced automata suitable for describing the normal
communicating-parallel activity of workers. The novelty of this paper is an extension which permits the description of the manager's activity in changing the
configuration of the workers.

The automata we introduce, which we call *case place automata* (CP automata), are in the first place graphs - the vertices represent states and the arcs
transitions. Each CP automata has in addition *interfaces* which allow parallel
communication. The interfaces are distinguished into *left* interfaces (often *input)*
and *right* interfaces (often *output*). An interface is represented mathematically
by a labelling of the transitions of the automaton in an alphabet. The idea is
that when a transition occurs in the automaton the corresponding label occurs
on the interface. Having such interfaces allows us to describe communicating
parallel composition (*restricted product* denoted $\cdot$, and *free product* denoted $\times$)

A. Porto and G.-C. Roman (Eds.): COORDINATION 2000, LNCS 1906, pp. 267–283, 2000.

of automata; in such a composite a state is a pair of states, and a transition is a pair of transitions, one of each automaton, which agree or synchronize on the common interface. An expression of automata using these compositions is a circuit.

The new aspect of CP automata is that they have in addition to interfaces also *conditions*. Very often the state space of an automaton decomposes naturally into a disjoint sum of *cases*. For example, in representing a system consisting of a producer, a buffer and a consumer, the actions of the producer and the consumer are determined by three relevant cases of the buffer *empty*, *full*, and *partly full*. We are concerned here with cases relevant to activating (creating) or disactivating (destroying) automata (including channels between automata), what we call *in-conditions* or *out-conditions* respectively. A condition is a subset of the set of states and it represents states in which the configuration may change in a particular way. However it is *crucial* not to think of conditions just as initial and terminal states. In purely sequential programming it is reasonable to think in this way, but when there are several active processes one of the active processes may die in a particular terminal state while the others are in general activity - that is, the global state of the system in which a change of configuration occurs is a terminal state in only one component. To permit a change of configuration in only one component of a system it is crucial to allow the whole state space among the in- and out-conditions. Formally, we gather the various in-conditions into a single *function* (usually not the inclusion of a subset) which lands in the set of states of the automaton. Similarly the out-conditions consist of a function into the state space of the automaton.

With the structure of in- and out-conditions we define the *restricted sum* (denoted $+$) of CP automata which expresses the deactivation of the first automaton in one of its out-conditions followed be the activation of the second in one of its in-conditions.

As a case study of the use of CP automata, we give a detailed description the distributed sort/numerical optimization of [4], showing that the manager process in these algorithms is the recursive equation

$$\mathcal{S} = \mathcal{A} + \mathcal{D} \cdot (\mathcal{A} \times \mathcal{S}) \cdot \mathcal{M},$$

which when instantiated to yield the sort algorithm, for example, yields

$$Sort = Atomsort + Divert \cdot (Atomsort \times Sort) \cdot Merge.$$

We prove distributive laws between the parallel and restricted sum operations which allow us to solve this recursive equation.

As an example of the use of CP automata in expressing mobility we describe another example, a variant of the Dining Philosopher problem in which diners may move, and which requires two further operations on CP automata *case feedback*, and *place feedback*.

In the remainder of the introduction we describe in more detail the IWIM model and introduce the notation we use for sets and functions and their operations. In section 2 we give the formal definition of CP automaton. In section 3 we introduce the operations of parallel composition and restricted sum. Section 4 is devoted to the description of the manager process of the distributed bucket sort. In section 5 we show how mobility of processes may be modelled using CP automata, introducing at the same time two extra feedback operations on CP automata. We finish with a section of conclusions.

1.1 The IWIM Coordination Model

Arbab in a series of papers [1], [2], [5], has described a conceptual model of coordination, idealized workers and idealized managers (IWIM), on which his language MANIFOLD is based. The essential features of IWIM are as follows:

- The elements of the model are processes; each process may partake of two roles - a worker role and a manager role. There is only one type of process however, a fact which leads to the possibility of describing hierarchical systems, in which the role of a process may be managerial at one level while that of a worker at the next.
- In the role of worker a process has no knowledge of the processes with which it may be communicating. In this sense it is like a component in an electrical circuit. Its role is simply to process what arrives at its ports and dispatch results to its ports. It can also broadcast events which allow the manager to make decisions about rearrangement of its workers.
  Its communications are anonymous, a feature that characterizes exogenous models.
- In the role of a manager a process has no knowledge of the precise activities of its workers. It knows simply their configuration and certain events, as a result of which it is able to decide on a change of topology of the workers.
- The manager may be useful for a variety of different jobs, in which workers of one type are substituted by workers of another type. This leads to reusability of management structures.

1.2 Notation

By a *graph* **G** we mean a set G_0 of vertices and a set G_1 of (directed) arcs, together with two functions $d_0, d_1 : G_1 \to G_0$ which specify the source and target, respectively, of each arc. A *morphism* from **G** to **H** consists of a function from vertices to vertices, and a function from arcs to arcs which respects the source and target functions; an isomorphism is a morphism for which both functions are bijections.

We shall frequently use the following simple algebra of sets and functions in our constructions below. Given two sets X and Y the cartesian product of X and Y will be denoted $X \times Y$, and the sum (disjoint union) of X and Y will be denoted $X + Y$. Associated with the cartesian product and sum constructions there are a variety of special functions: the projections $pr_X : X \times Y \to X, pr_Y : X \times Y \to Y$, the diagonal $\Delta_X : X \to X \times X$, the product twist $X \times Y \to Y \times X$; the injections of the sum $in_X : X \to X + Y, in_Y : Y \to X + Y$, the codiagonal $\nabla_X : X + X \to X$, and the sum twist $X + Y \to Y + X$. We denote the composition of function $\varphi : X \to Y$ with $\psi : Y \to Z$ by $\psi \circ \varphi : X \to Z$. Given two functions $\varphi : X \to Y$, $\psi : Z \to W$, there are functions $\varphi + \psi : X + Z \to Y + W$ and $\varphi \times \psi : X \times Z \to Y \times W$. Given two functions $\varphi : X \to Z$, $\psi : Y \to Z$, an abbreviation for the composite function $\nabla_Z \circ (\varphi + \psi) : X + Y \to Z$ is $(\varphi | \psi)$. Given sets X, Y, Z, there is the distributive law bijection $\delta_{X,Y,Z} : X \times Y + X \times Z \to X \times (Y + Z)$. If T is a one point set then for any X, there are isomorphisms $T \times X \cong X \cong X \times T$. Finally there is a unique function from the empty set $\emptyset$ to any other set X, and further $\emptyset \times X \cong \emptyset$. For further details of this algebra see [12].

1.3   Acknowledgements

The authors gratefully acknowledge stimulating conversations with Fahrad Arbab. In fact, the research of this paper was carried out in response to a remark of Arbab in [5], where he says: "An alternative approach to a mathematical foundation for the semantics of MANIFOLD can be sought in other category-theoretical models. The essence of the semantics of a coordinator process in MANIFOLD can be described as transitions between states, each of which defines a different topology of information–carrying streams among various sets of processes. What is defined in each such state is reminiscent of an (asynchronous) electronic circuit. Category theoretical models have been used to describe simple circuit diagrams [8]. Extensions of such models to account for the dynamic topological reconfiguration of MANIFOLD is a non–trivial challenge which, nevertheless, points to an interesting model of computation". We thank also Adriano Scutellà for interesting conversations. The research has been financially supported by the Dipartimento di Scienze Chimiche, Fisiche e Matematiche of the University of Insubria, Como, Italy, and by the Italian Progetto Cofinanziato MURST *Tipi di Ordine Superiore e Concorrenza* (TOSCA).

2   CP Automata

The algebra we use to formalize the IWIM model has as elements certain automata, which we call *case-place automata* (or CP automata).

Definition 1. *A CP automaton $\mathcal{G}$ consists of a graph* $\mathbf{G}$*, four sets* X, Y, A, B *and four functions*

$$\partial_0 : G_1 \to X, \ \partial_1 : G_1 \to Y,$$
$$\gamma_0 : A \to G_0, \ \gamma_1 : B \to G_0.$$

A behaviour *of $\mathcal{G}$ is a path in the graph* $\mathbf{G}$*.*

The graph $\mathbf{G}$ is called the *centre* of the automaton. We remark that ∂_0, ∂_1 may be thought of as *labellings* of the arcs of $\mathbf{G}$ in the alphabets X, Y, respectively. These labellings will be used in the restricted product of two CP automata, the operation which expresses communicating parallel processes. Alternatively, one may think of the vertices and arcs of $\mathbf{G}$ as the *states* and *transitions* of the system, whereas the elements of X, Y are the transitions of the interfaces. We call X the *left interface* of the automaton, and Y the *right interface* - automata communicate through these interfaces. Often the interface sets will be products of sets; for example the left interface of $\mathbf{G}$ may be $X = U \times V$, and the right interface may be $Y = Z \times W$, and we then speak of U and V as the left interfaces, and Z and W as the right interfaces. If we ignore the functions γ_0, γ_1 a CP automaton is a (particular type of) *span of graphs* as defined in [9], where the reader may find more details and examples.

The set A represents a *condition* on the states in which the automaton may come into existence, and the set B a condition in which it may cease to exist. We call A the *in-condition* of the automaton, and B the *out-condition*. The functions γ_0, γ_1 of a CP automaton will be used in the restricted sum of CP automata - an operation which expresses change of configuration of processes. The meaning of the in- and out-conditions will become clearer in the section on the restricted sum of automata, and in the example of the distributed sort. Often the condition sets will be sums of sets; for example the in-condition may be $A = D + E$, and we then speak of D and E as in-conditions.

There is a useful graphical representation of CP automata (ignoring the conditions this is described in [9]). For example, we will represent a CP automaton with left interface $U \times V$, right interface $Z \times W$, in-condition $D + E$, and out-condition B, by a diagram of the following sort:

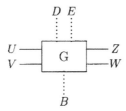

For simplicity we use the same names $\partial_0, \partial_1, \gamma_0, \gamma_1$ for the four functions of any CP automaton where there is no risk of confusion, introducing further suffixes when clarification is needed. We use symbols $X, Y, Z, U, V, W...$ for the (left and right) interfaces, and symbols $A, B, C, D, E, F, I, ...$ for the (in- and out-) conditions.

Example 1. An example of a CP automaton is provided by a Mealy automaton with input set X, output set Y, internal states G_0, initial states A and final states B. The arrows of the graph $\mathbf{G}$ are provided by the transitions of the automaton. The functions γ_0, γ_1 are inclusions. The reader is warned that this example gives a false impression of the strength of the model we are describing. It is essential, for example, in expressing the changing geometry of a system that the functions γ_0, γ_1 not be restricted solely to inclusions. The sets A and B are not to be thought of as initial and final states, but rather as conditions under which a change of geometry might occur. Another difference with Mealy automata is that the sets X and Y need not be input and output but rather interfaces on which synchronization occurs with connected components.

Remark 1. We want to describe a program for a manager that will co-ordinate a family of workers in order to produce a distributed bucket sort algorithm. There are three types of workers: an atomic sort, a divert and a merge. In terms of the model presented here, the manager will be a recursive equation built out of the operations of CP automata. There will be three variables in the expression, one variable $\mathcal{A}$ is to play the role of the atomic sort and will require the following structure: it has a single input line and a single output line; the in-condition has the form $A_0 + I + F$, where I is a one element set that represents the initial state of the atomic sort, F represents states in which the atomic sort is full, and A_0 denotes the set of all states of the atomic sort; the out-condition of $\mathcal{A}$ is $A_0 + F$. The second variable $\mathcal{D}$ is to play the role of the divert (input to second output line) which has the following structure: it has one input line and two output line; the in-condition is $I + D_0$, and out-condition D_0, where I is a one element set that represents the initial state and D_0 denotes the set of all states of the divert. The third variable $\mathcal{M}$ is to play the role of the merge (of two sorted lists) which has the following structure: it has two input lines and one output line; the in-condition is $I + M_0$, and out-condition M_0, where I is a one element set that represents the initial state and M_0 denotes the set of all states of the merge. In order to obtain from the manager program an actual sort it is necessary to instantiate the variables as CP automata with appropriate functionality. In this paper we will not describe such CP automata, but rather give some illustrative finite state abstractions. The same manager program can be used with different instantiation of the variables to produce other algorithms. This fact is in keeping with the spirit of the IWIM model; in particular, the separation of coordination from computation. The manager is not concerned with inner workings of its workers; the manager's only concern is the coordination of its workers. The manager's decision to create or destroy its workers, or to reconfigure its network of workers, is based on events it receives from the workers. In our framework, these events are represented by conditions.

Example 2. Consider the set $X = \{x, \_\}$ (the underscore symbol is intended to represent the null action). The following diagram specifies the centre **A** of a CP automaton $\mathcal{A}$, and its left and right interfaces, both being the set X. Note that we have indicated the functions ∂_0, ∂_1 by labelling the arcs of the graph.

To complete the definition of $\mathcal{A}$ we must also describe the in-conditions and out-conditions. The vertex set A_0 of the centre $\mathbf{A}$ of $\mathcal{A}$ will be one of the in- and also one of the out-conditions. Consider two further sets $I = \{i\}$ and $F = \{f\}$ (subsets of A_0); denote the inclusion of I in A_0 by inc_I, and the inclusion of F in A_0 by inc_F. Then the in-condition set of $\mathcal{A}$ is $A_0 + I + F$ and $\gamma_0 = (1_{A_0} \,|\, inc_I \,|\, inc_F)$. The out-condition set of $\mathcal{A}$ is $A_0 + F$ and $\gamma_1 = (1_{A_0} \,|\, inc_F)$.

Example 3. A behaviour of $\mathcal{A}$ (a path in the centre of $\mathcal{A}$) commencing in state i consists in repeatedly accepting symbols x in state i until perhaps a change either to state e or to state f when it can output symbols x. In any state it can idle by accepting and outputting null symbols. This CP automaton is quite abstract and has many possible meanings. One particular concrete realization is a bounded sorting program - what we will call an atomic sort. Symbol x is an abstraction of the symbols to be sorted. State i is an abstraction of those states in which the sorter is receiving symbols. State e is the abstraction of those states in which the sorter has received an end of list symbol. State f is an abstraction of those states in which the sorter has reached its capacity (full states). In either e or f the sorter may output symbols in sorted order.

Two more examples useful for the analysis of the distributed sort algorithm:

Example 4. Let $X = \{x, \_\}$. Consider the graph $\mathbf{D}$ with vertex set $D_0 = \{0\}$ and three labelled edges $x/\_, \_ : 0 \to 0$, $\_/\_, \_ : 0 \to 0$, $\_/\_, x : 0 \to 0$. This forms the centre of a CP automaton $\mathcal{D}$ with left interface X and right interface $X \times X$. Take the in-condition to be $I + D_0$, where I is a one element set, and out-condition D_0. Since the CP automaton has only one state the functions γ_0, γ_1 are uniquely defined.

Again $\mathcal{D}$ is an abstract automaton. One of its concrete realizations is a program which diverts input to the second line of its output only.

Example 5. Let $X = \{x, \_\}$. Consider the graph $\mathbf{M}$ with vertex set $M_0 = \{0\}$ and four labelled edges $x, \_/\_ : 0 \to 0$, $\_, \_/\_ : 0 \to 0$, $\_, x/\_ : 0 \to 0$, $\_, \_/x$. This forms the centre of a CP automaton $\mathcal{M}$ with left interface $X \times X$ and right interface X. Take the in-condition to be $I + M_0$, where I is a one element set, and out-condition M_0. Since the CP automaton has only one state the functions γ_0, γ_1 are uniquely defined.

One of the concrete realizations of $\mathcal{M}$ is the merge of two queues, which produces a sorted output if the two lists are sorted.

We will need in section 4.1 the notion of *isomorphism* of CP automata.

Definition 2. *Given two CP automata* $\mathcal{G} = (\mathbf{G}, X, Y, A, B, \partial_{0,\mathcal{G}}, \partial_{1,\mathcal{G}}, \gamma_{0,\mathcal{G}}, \gamma_{1,\mathcal{G}})$ *and* $\mathcal{H} = (\mathbf{H}, X, Y, A, B, \partial_{0,\mathcal{H}}, \partial_{1,\mathcal{H}}, \gamma_{0,\mathcal{H}}, \gamma_{1,\mathcal{H}})$ *an isomorphism from* $\mathcal{G}$ *to* $\mathcal{H}$ *is a graph isomorphism* $\varphi : \mathbf{G} \to \mathbf{H}$ *such that* $\partial_{0,\mathcal{H}} \circ \varphi = \partial_{0,\mathcal{G}}$, $\partial_{1,\mathcal{H}} \circ \varphi = \partial_{1,\mathcal{G}}$, $\varphi \circ \gamma_{0,\mathcal{G}} = \gamma_{0,\mathcal{H}}$, $\varphi \circ \gamma_{1,\mathcal{G}} = \gamma_{1,\mathcal{H}}$.

3 Operations

3.1 Parallel Composition

Definition 3. *Given two CP automata*

$$\mathcal{G} = (\mathbf{G}, X, Y, A, B, \partial_0, \partial_1, \gamma_0, \gamma_1),$$
$$\mathcal{H} = (\mathbf{H}, Y, Z, C, D, \partial_0, \partial_1, \gamma_0, \gamma_1)$$

the restricted product (communicating parallel composition) of $\mathcal{G}$ and $\mathcal{H}$, denoted $\mathcal{G} \cdot \mathcal{H}$ is the CP automaton whose set of vertices is $G_0 \times H_0$ and whose set of arcs is that subset of $G_1 \times H_1$ consisting of pairs of arcs (g, h) such that $\partial_1(g) = \partial_0(h)$. The interfaces and conditions of $\mathcal{G} \cdot \mathcal{H}$ are $X, Z, A \times C, B \times D$, and the four functions are

$$\partial_{0,\mathcal{G}\cdot\mathcal{H}}(g, h) = \partial_{0,\mathcal{G}}(g), \ \ \partial_{1,\mathcal{G}\cdot\mathcal{H}}(g, h) = \partial_{1,\mathcal{H}}(h),$$
$$\gamma_{0,\mathcal{G}\cdot\mathcal{H}} = \gamma_{0,\mathcal{G}} \times \gamma_{0,\mathcal{H}} \ , \ \ \gamma_{1,\mathcal{G}\cdot\mathcal{H}} = \gamma_{1,\mathcal{G}} \times \gamma_{1,\mathcal{H}} \ .$$

Diagrammatically we represent the restricted product as follows:

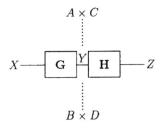

Closely related to the restricted product is the free product of CP automata.

Definition 4. *Given two CP automata*

$$\mathcal{G} = (\mathbf{G}, X, Y, A, B, \partial_0, \partial_1, \gamma_0, \gamma_1),$$
$$\mathcal{H} = (\mathbf{H}, Z, W, C, D, \partial_0, \partial_1, \gamma_0, \gamma_1)$$

the free product (parallel composition with no communication) of $\mathcal{G}$ and $\mathcal{H}$, denoted $\mathcal{G} \times \mathcal{H}$ is the CP automaton whose set of vertices is $G_0 \times H_0$ and whose set of arcs is $G_1 \times H_1$. The interfaces and conditions of $\mathcal{G} \times \mathcal{H}$ are $X \times Z, Y \times W, A \times C, B \times D$, and the four functions are

$$\partial_{0,\mathcal{G}\times\mathcal{H}} = \partial_{0,\mathcal{G}} \times \partial_{0,\mathcal{H}}, \ \ \partial_{1,\mathcal{G}\times\mathcal{H}} = \partial_{1,\mathcal{G}} \times \partial_{1,\mathcal{H}},$$
$$\gamma_{0,\mathcal{G}\times\mathcal{H}} = \gamma_{0,\mathcal{G}} \times \gamma_{0,\mathcal{H}} \ , \ \ \gamma_{1,\mathcal{G}\times\mathcal{H}} = \gamma_{1,\mathcal{G}} \times \gamma_{1,\mathcal{H}} \ .$$

Diagrammatically we represent the free product as follows:

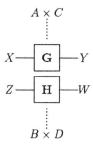

$$A \times C$$

$$B \times D$$

Example 6. Consider the following expression in three types of components described in Remark 1:

$$\mathcal{D} \cdot (\mathcal{A} \times \mathcal{A}) \cdot \mathcal{M}.$$

The diagrammatic representation of this is

$$(I + D_0) \times (A_0 + I + F) \times (A_0 + I + F) \times (I + M_0)$$

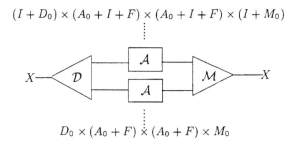

$$D_0 \times (A_0 + F) \times (A_0 + F) \times M_0$$

When the variables are instantiated with the particular automata described in examples 2, 3, and 4, a behaviour of the resulting CP automaton is (an abstracted version of) the following: the symbols received by $\mathcal{D}$ are passed to the second sorter $\mathcal{A}$, while both the first and second sorters continue to work in parallel eventually outputting their results to the merge $\mathcal{M}$. If the second sorter becomes full it can accept no further symbols.

If we ignore the functions γ_0, γ_1 of the CP automata the restricted product of CP automata is the *span composition* of [9] and the free product is the *tensor product* of the corresponding spans of graphs. For some examples of how these operations may be used to model concurrent systems see that paper. We will see further examples in the section on the distributed sort below. From a circuit theory point of view these operations correspond, respectively, to the series and parallel operations of circuit components. In the context of this paper the two operations correspond to the *communicating parallel composition of workers in their normal activity*. The communication of the parts of a product is anonymous - each automaton has a precisely defined interface, and has no knowledge of the automata with which it is communicating.

Remark 2. There are a variety of automata models of concurrent systems based on products of automata, the most prominent being asynchronous automata [13], and the synchronous product of automata of Arnold and Nivat [6]. These theories however are endogenous in the sense of Arbab; that is, the communication between automata is *not* anonymous - the automata use information about the state of neighbouring automata in deciding their actions. A further crucial limitation to these models is exactly the one we are addressing in (the next section of) this paper, namely that they have a fixed geometry. The fact that asynchronous automata have a fixed dependence relation has been regarded in the concurrency community as a serious drawback. Lastly these theories lack compositionality; to achieve compositionality is precisely the purpose of developing an algebra.

3.2   Restricted Sum

Definition 5. *Given two CP automata*

$$\mathcal{G} = (\mathbf{G}, X, Y, A, B, \partial_0, \partial_1, \gamma_0, \gamma_1),$$
$$\mathcal{H} = (\mathbf{H}, X, Y, B, C, \partial_0, \partial_1, \gamma_0, \gamma_1)$$

the restricted sum *(change of configuration) of $\mathcal{G}$ and $\mathcal{H}$, denoted $\mathcal{G} + \mathcal{H}$ is the CP automaton whose set of arcs is $G_1 + H_1$ and whose set of vertices is $(G_0 + H_0)/\sim$; that is $(G_0 + H_0)$ quotiented by the relation $\gamma_{1,\mathcal{G}}(b) \sim \gamma_{0,\mathcal{H}}(b)$ (for all $b \in B$). The interfaces and conditions of $\mathcal{G} + \mathcal{H}$ are X, Y, A and C, and the four functions are*

$$\partial_{0,\mathcal{G}+\mathcal{H}} = (\partial_{0,\mathcal{G}} \mid \partial_{0,\mathcal{H}}), \quad \partial_{1,\mathcal{G}+\mathcal{H}} = (\partial_{1,\mathcal{G}} \mid \partial_{1,\mathcal{H}}),$$
$$\gamma_{0,\mathcal{G}+\mathcal{H}} = in_{G_0} \circ \gamma_{0,\mathcal{G}}, \quad \gamma_{1,\mathcal{G}+\mathcal{H}} = in_{H_0} \circ \gamma_{1,\mathcal{H}} .$$

A behaviour of $\mathcal{G} + \mathcal{H}$ is initially a behaviour of $\mathcal{G}$, and then, if a state in the image of B is reached, the behaviour may change to a behaviour of $\mathcal{H}$. The intended interpretation is that initially only the process $\mathcal{G}$ exists; when a state in B is reached the process $\mathcal{G}$ may die and the process $\mathcal{H}$ be created. We will see in the next section that this is the correct interpretation in a dynamic algorithm like the distributed sort.

The diagrammatic representation of the restricted sum is as follows:

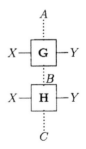

3.3   Adjusting the Conditions

Given two CP automata we wish to compose, it may happen that the conditions are not appropriate to allow the composition, but that a modification is necessary. To this end we allow adjustment of conditions by composition with any of the special functions described in section 1.2. For example, the atomic sort $\mathcal{A}$ is defined with in-condition $A_0 + I + F$ and out condition $A_0 + F$. Composing $\gamma_0 : A_0 + I + F \rightarrow A_0$ with $in_I : I \rightarrow A_0 + I + F$, and composing $\gamma_1 : A_0 + F \rightarrow A_0$ with $in_F : F \rightarrow A_0 + F$ we obtain a new CP automaton with the same centre and interfaces but new in-condition I and new out-condition F. This new automaton we denote $\mathcal{A}_F^I$. In general an adjustment of in-condition we denote by adding a superscript, and adjusting an out-condition by adding a subscript. This notation is very efficient, though there is clearly in some cases the possibility of ambiguity.

Remark 3. Notice that the restricted sum seems very close to sequential composition. However this is deceptive; consider the parallel composite $\mathcal{G} \times \mathcal{H}$ of two processes, where $\mathcal{G}$ has out-condition T (a one element terminal state), and $\mathcal{H}$ has in- and out-condition H_0. Notice that $\mathcal{G} \times \mathcal{H}$ has out-condition $T \times H_0$ which may be adjusted by composing with the isomorphism $T \times H_0 \cong H_0$. The interpretation of the restricted sum $(\mathcal{G} \times \mathcal{H})_{H_0} + \mathcal{H}$ is that the process $\mathcal{G}$ dies upon reaching its terminal state leaving the process $\mathcal{H}$ still running.

4   Distributed Sort

We will now describe the distributed sort algorithm using the components and operations described above. The idea is that the sort $\mathcal{S}$ begins with an atomic sort $\mathcal{A}$ which completes its activity *if* it receives an end of list before becoming full. If however the atomic sort becomes full a diversion $\mathcal{D}$, a new atomic sort $\mathcal{A}$, and a merge $\mathcal{M}$ are created and configured as $\mathcal{D} \cdot (\mathcal{A} \times \mathcal{A}) \cdot \mathcal{M}$ (see the diagram in section 3.1). The sort process is recursive; that is, if the second sort becomes full new diversions, atomic sorts, and merges are created, and so on.

First we describe how the transition from the atomic sort $\mathcal{A}$ to two parallel sorters $\mathcal{D} \cdot (\mathcal{A} \times \mathcal{A}) \cdot \mathcal{M}$ can be described using the restricted sum. Recall that $\mathcal{D} \cdot (\mathcal{A} \times \mathcal{A}) \cdot \mathcal{M}$ has in-condition

$$(I + D_0) \times (A_0 + I + F) \times (A_0 + I + F) \times (I + M_0).$$

We compose the in-condition function of $\mathcal{D} \cdot (\mathcal{A} \times \mathcal{A}) \cdot \mathcal{M}$ with the composite of $F \cong I \times F \times I \times I$ and $in_I \times in_F \times in_I \times in_I$ to obtain a new in-condition for $\mathcal{D} \cdot (\mathcal{A} \times \mathcal{A}) \cdot \mathcal{M}$, namely F. Similarly we can adjust the out-condition of $\mathcal{D} \cdot (\mathcal{A} \times \mathcal{A}) \cdot \mathcal{M}$ to be $D_0 \times A_0 \times F \times M_0$. We can obviously adjust the out-condition of $\mathcal{A}$ to be F, so now the restricted sum

$$\mathcal{A}_F^I + (\mathcal{D} \cdot (\mathcal{A} \times \mathcal{A}) \cdot \mathcal{M})_{D_0 \times A_0 \times F \times M_0}^F$$

may be formed. In the specific instantiation we have previously considered, the effect is to equate the full state f of single atomic sorter $\mathcal{A}$ to the quadruple of states, the initial state of $\mathcal{D}$, the state f of the first atomic sorter, the state i of the second atomic sorter of $\mathcal{D} \cdot (\mathcal{A} \times \mathcal{A}) \cdot \mathcal{M}$, and the initial state of the $\mathcal{M}$. That is, the first atomic sorter is just the continuation of the single sorter, whereas the second atomic sorter is newly created in its initial state. A diagram of the result is:

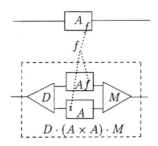

In a similar way the expression $\mathcal{A} + \mathcal{D} \cdot (\mathcal{A} \times \mathcal{S}) \cdot \mathcal{M}$ may be formed for any process $\mathcal{S}$ with appropriate in-condition of an initial state. The manager process of the recursive sort is then the *unevaluated equation*

$$\mathcal{S} = \mathcal{A} + \mathcal{D} \cdot (\mathcal{A} \times \mathcal{S}) \cdot \mathcal{M}.$$

For $\mathcal{A}, \mathcal{D}, \mathcal{M}$ as given above the solution of the evaluated expression is a distributed sort, but in [4] the authors show how the same protocol may be used to perform parallel/distributed numerical optimization of a complex function by supplying a different $\mathcal{A}$, an evaluator, each instance of which takes in an input unit describing a subdomain of a function, and produces its best estimate of the optimum value of the function in that subdomain; and a different $\mathcal{M}$, a selector, each instance of which produces as its output the best optimum value it receives as its input.

We will now do some *rough calculations* with this equation ignoring for the moment the important aspect of in- and out-conditions. The calculation will be made more precise and justified in the next section.

The equation $\mathcal{S} = \mathcal{A} + \mathcal{D} \cdot (\mathcal{A} \times \mathcal{S}) \cdot \mathcal{M}$ may be formally expanded using the distributive laws (section 4.1) which exist between the products and the restricted sum.

$$\begin{aligned}
\mathcal{S} &= \mathcal{A} + \mathcal{D} \cdot (\mathcal{A} \times \mathcal{S}) \cdot \mathcal{M} \\
&= \mathcal{A} + \mathcal{D} \cdot (\mathcal{A} \times (\mathcal{A} + \mathcal{D} \cdot (\mathcal{A} \times \mathcal{S}) \cdot \mathcal{M})) \cdot \mathcal{M} \\
&= \mathcal{A} + \mathcal{D} \cdot (\mathcal{A} \times \mathcal{A}) \cdot \mathcal{M} + \mathcal{D} \cdot (\mathcal{A} \times (\mathcal{D} \cdot (\mathcal{A} \times \mathcal{S}) \cdot \mathcal{M})) \cdot \mathcal{M} \\
&= \dots \\
&= \mathcal{A} + \mathcal{D} \cdot (\mathcal{A} \times \mathcal{A}) \cdot \mathcal{M} + \mathcal{D} \cdot (\mathcal{A} \times (\mathcal{D} \cdot (\mathcal{A} \times \mathcal{A}) \cdot \mathcal{M})) \cdot \mathcal{M} + \dots.
\end{aligned}$$

The terms in the final (infinite) expansion correspond precisely to the sequence of geometries possible for the distributed sort:

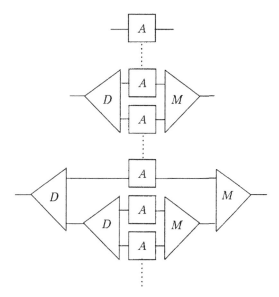

4.1   Distributive Laws

We would now like to make more precise the distributive laws we have used in expanding the expression for the distributed sort. Consider CP automata $\mathcal{G}$, $\mathcal{H}$, $\mathcal{K}$.

Proposition 1. *The following distributive laws hold provided the in- and out-conditions indicated are among those of the associated CP automaton, and the interfaces of the automata are appropriate for the operations:*

$$\mathcal{G}_B^A \cdot (\mathcal{H}_D^C + \mathcal{K}_E^D) \cong \mathcal{G}_{G_0}^A \cdot \mathcal{H}_D^C + \mathcal{G}_B^{G_0} \cdot \mathcal{K}_E^D, \tag{1}$$

$$(\mathcal{H}_D^C + \mathcal{K}_E^D) \cdot \mathcal{G}_B^A \cong \mathcal{H}_D^C \cdot \mathcal{G}_{G_0}^A + \mathcal{K}_E^D \cdot \mathcal{G}_B^{G_0}, \tag{2}$$

$$\mathcal{G}_B^A \times (\mathcal{H}_D^C + \mathcal{K}_E^D) \cong \mathcal{G}_{G_0}^A \times \mathcal{H}_D^C + \mathcal{G}_B^{G_0} \times \mathcal{K}_E^D, \tag{3}$$

$$(\mathcal{H}_D^C + \mathcal{K}_E^D) \times \mathcal{G}_B^A \cong \mathcal{H}_D^C \times \mathcal{G}_{G_0}^A + \mathcal{K}_E^D \times \mathcal{G}_B^{G_0}. \tag{4}$$

Proof. We give the proof of the first only. The arcs in the left-hand side are either pairs (g, h) $(g \in G_1, h \in H_1)$ such that $\partial_1(g) = \partial_0(h)$ or pairs (g, h) $(g \in G_1, h \in K_1)$ such that $\partial_1(g) = \partial_0(k)$. But this is precisely what arcs in the right-hand side are. The vertices on the left-hand side are pairs of the form $(g, [l])$ $(g \in G_0, l \in H_0 + K_0)$ where $[l]$ denotes the equivalence class of l with respect to the equivalence generated by $\gamma_1(d) \sim \gamma_0(d)$ $(d \in D)$. The vertices on the right-hand side are equivalence classes of pairs $[(g, l)]$ $(l \in H_0 + K_0)$ with respect to the equivalence relation generated by $\gamma_1(g, d) \sim \gamma_0(g, d)$, that is, $(g, \gamma_1(d)) \sim (g, \gamma_0(d))$ $(g \in G_0, d \in D)$. There is a clear bijection between the vertices of the left hand and right hand sides. This defines an isomorphism of graphs which clearly respects the interfaces and conditions.

In making a precise expansion of the equation

$$S = A + D \cdot (A \times S) \cdot M$$

we will see that there are some distinctions that are worth making which we have neglected until now. First the equation is not really an equation but an isomorphism. Second we must specify in- and out conditions for S - we take the in-condition to be a one point set I (the initial state) and the out-condition to be $\emptyset$ (the empty set). The equation now takes the precise form

$$S_\emptyset^I \cong A_F^I + D_{D_0}^I \cdot (A_{A_0}^F \times S_\emptyset^I) \cdot M_{M_0}^I.$$

Let us now expand this isomorphism using the distributive laws. Substituting for $S_\emptyset^I$ in the right hand side we get

$$
\begin{aligned}
S_\emptyset^I \cong{} & A_F^I + D_{D_0}^I \cdot (A_{A_0}^F \times (A_F^I + D_{D_0}^I \cdot (A_{A_0}^F \times S_\emptyset^I) \cdot M_{M_0}^I)) \cdot M_{M_0}^I \\
\cong{} & A_F^I + D_{D_0}^I \cdot (A_{A_0}^F \times A_F^I + A_{A_0}^{A_0} \times (D_{D_0}^I \cdot (A_{A_0}^F \times S_\emptyset^I) \cdot M_{M_0}^I)) \cdot M_{M_0}^I \\
\cong{} & A_F^I + D_{D_0}^I \cdot (A_{A_0}^F \times A_F^I) \cdot M_{M_0}^I + {} \\
& D_{D_0}^{D_0} \cdot (A_{A_0}^{A_0} \times (D_{D_0}^I \cdot (A_{A_0}^F \times S_\emptyset^I) \cdot M_{M_0}^I)) \cdot M_{M_0}^{M_0}.
\end{aligned}
$$

Careful examination of this expansion reveals that the in- and out-conditions of the various parts are exactly the appropriate ones.

5   Sofia's Birthday Party

We illustrate the use of CP automata in describing mobility of processes, introducing also two further operations, *case* and *place feedback*.

Definition 6. *Given a CP automaton*

$$\mathcal{G} = (\mathbf{G}, X \times Y, Z \times Y, A, B, \partial_0, \partial_1, \gamma_0, \gamma_1),$$

the place feedback of $\mathcal{G}$ with respect to Y, denoted $\mathsf{Pfb}_Y(\mathcal{G})$ is the CP automaton whose set of vertices is G_0 and whose set of arcs is that subset of G_1 consisting of arcs g such that $(pr_Y \circ \partial_1)(g) = (pr_Y \circ \partial_0)(g)$. The interfaces and conditions of $\mathsf{Pfb}_Y(\mathcal{G})$ are X, Z, A, B, with the four functions defined as follows:

$$\partial_{0,\mathsf{Pfb}_Y(\mathcal{G})} = pr_X \circ \partial_{0,\mathcal{G}}, \quad \partial_{1,\mathsf{Pfb}_Y(\mathcal{G})} = pr_Z \circ \partial_{1,\mathcal{G}},$$
$$\gamma_{0,\mathsf{Pfb}_Y(\mathcal{G})} = \gamma_{0,\mathcal{G}}, \quad \gamma_{1,\mathsf{Pfb}_Y(\mathcal{G})} = \gamma_{1,\mathcal{G}}.$$

The diagrammatic representation of $\mathsf{Pfb}_Y(\mathcal{G})$ involves joining the right interface Y to the left interface Y.

Definition 7. *Given a CP automaton*

$$\mathcal{G} = (\mathbf{G}, X, Y, A + B, C + B, \partial_0, \partial_1, \gamma_0, \gamma_1),$$

the case feedback *of $\mathcal{G}$ with respect to B, denoted $\mathsf{Cfb}_B(\mathcal{G})$ is the CP automaton whose set of arcs is G_1 and whose set of vertices is $G_0/\sim$; that is G_0 quotiented by the relation $(\gamma_1 \circ in_B)(b) \sim (\gamma_0 \circ in_B)(b)$ (for all $b \in B$). The interfaces and conditions of $\mathsf{Cfb}_B(\mathcal{G})$ are X, Y, A and C, and the four functions are defined as follows:*

$$\partial_{0,\mathsf{Cfb}_B(\mathcal{G})} = \partial_{0,\mathcal{G}}, \ \ \partial_{1,\mathsf{Cfb}_B(\mathcal{G})} = \partial_{1,\mathcal{G}},$$
$$\gamma_{0,\mathsf{Cfb}_B(\mathcal{G})} = \gamma_{0,\mathcal{G}} \circ in_A, \ \ \gamma_{1,\mathsf{Cfb}_B(\mathcal{G})} = \gamma_{1,\mathcal{G}} \circ in_C.$$

The diagrammatic representation of $\mathsf{Cfb}_B(\mathcal{G})$ involves joining the out-condition B to the in-condition B.

The example we would like to describe is a variant of the Dining Philosopher Problem which we call Sofia's Birthday Party. Instead of a circle of philosophers around a table with as many forks, we consider a circle of seats around a table separated by forks on the table. Then there are a number of children (not greater than the number of seats). The protocol of each child is the same as that of a philosopher. However in addition, if a child is not holding a fork, and the seat to the right is empty, the child may change seats - the food may be better there. To describe this we need six CP automata – a child $\mathcal{C}$, an empty seat $\mathcal{E}$, a fork $\mathcal{F}$, two transition elements $\mathcal{L}$ and $\mathcal{R}$, and an identity 1_X of X (a wire). The interface sets involved are $X = \{x, \_\}$ and $Y = \{\_, u, l\}$.

The transition elements have left and right interfaces $X \times Y$. The graph $\mathbf{L}$ of the transition element $\mathcal{L}$ has two vertices p and q and three labelled edges $\_, \_/\_, \_ : q \to q$; $x, \_/\_, \_ : q \to p$; $\_, \_/\_, \_ : p \to p$. Its in-condition is $Q = \{q\}$, and its out-condition is $P = \{p\}$. The graph $\mathbf{R}$ of the of the transition element $\mathcal{R}$ also has two vertices p and q, and has three labelled edges $\_, \_/\_, \_ : q \to q$; $\_, \_/x, \_ : q \to p$; $\_, \_/\_, \_ : p \to p$. Its in-condition is also $Q = \{q\}$, and its out-condition is $P = \{p\}$.

The empty seat $\mathcal{E}$ has left and right interfaces $X \times Y$. The graph $\mathbf{E}$ of the empty seat has one vertex e and one labelled edge $\_, \_/\_, \_ : e \to e$. Its in-condition is P and its out-condition is Q. The functions γ_0, γ_1 are uniquely defined.

The identity 1_X has left and right interface X. Its graph has one vertex $*$ and two labelled edges $\_/\_ : * \to *$ and $x/x : * \to *$. Its in- and out-conditions are the empty set $\emptyset$.

The child $\mathcal{C}$ has labelled graph as follows:

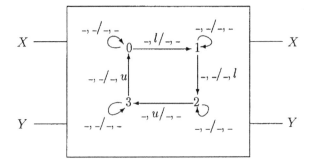

The states have the following interpretation: in state 0 the child has no forks; in state 1 it has a fork in its left hand; in state 2 it has both forks; in state 3 it has returned it left fork. The action l is to be interpreted as *locking a fork*, and the action u as *unlocking a fork*. The child's in-condition is P and its out-condition is Q. The function γ_0 takes p to 0; the function γ_1 takes q to 0.

The fork $\mathcal{F}$ has labelled graph as follows:

$$Y \longmapsto -/\text{-} \circlearrowright 1 \underset{u/\text{-}}{\overset{l/\text{-}}{\rightleftarrows}} 0 \underset{-/u}{\overset{-/l}{\rightleftarrows}} 2 \circlearrowright -/\text{-} \longmapsto Y$$

The fork's in-condition and out-condition are $\emptyset$. Its states are to be interpreted as follows: in state 0 the fork is free; in state 1 it is locked on the left; in state 2 it is locked on the right.

Let $\mathcal{S} = \mathsf{Cfb}_P(\mathcal{C} + \mathcal{R} + \mathcal{E} + \mathcal{L})$. This CP automaton has the following interpretation – it can either be a child (on a seat) or an empty seat. The transition elements $\mathcal{R}$ and $\mathcal{L}$ allow the seat to become occupied or vacated. Then Sofia's Birthday Party is given by the expression

$$\mathsf{Pfb}_{X \times Y}(\mathcal{S} \cdot (1_X \times \mathcal{F}) \cdot \mathcal{S} \cdot (1_X \times \mathcal{F}) \cdot \ldots \cdot \mathcal{S} \cdot (1_X \times \mathcal{F})).$$

This CP automaton has the behaviour as informally described above.

We can reobtain the classical Dining Philosopher problem as follows: modify the interfaces of $\mathcal{C}$ and $\mathcal{F}$ by composing with the projection $X \times Y \to Y$ to obtain new automata $\mathcal{C}'$ and $\mathcal{F}'$. Take all in- and out-conditions to be the empty set $\emptyset$. Then the Dining Philosopher (as formulated in [10]) is given by the expression

$$\mathsf{Pfb}_Y(\mathcal{C}' \cdot \mathcal{F}' \cdot \mathcal{C}' \cdot \mathcal{F}' \cdot \ldots \cdot \mathcal{C}' \cdot \mathcal{F}').$$

6   Conclusions

We have described an algebra whose operations reflect well the ideas behind the IWIM model of coordination. The normal communicating parallel activity of workers is expressed by the free and restricted products, whereas the changes in configuration are explained in terms of the restricted sum. Further using these operations we see that the manager process of the distributed sort algorithm discussed in [4] is a "polynomial" equation. We have also given an example of the mobility of processes using reconfiguration. The theory is compositional and has a strong mathematical basis, the details of which will appear elsewhere [11]. In categorical terms a CP automaton is a cospan between spans in the category of graphs, which fact can be seen as the origin of the operations of the algebra. There are in fact more operations than we have had space to describe here, including an extended sum, and a variety of special constants. Some idea of the extra operations can be found in [8], [9], [11].

References

1. F. Arbab, Coordination of massively concurrent activities, Technical Report CS–R9565, Centrum voor Wiskunde en Informatica, Amsterdam, The Netherlands, 1995, Available on-line at http://www.cwi.nl/ftp/CWIreports/IS/CS-R9565.ps.Z.
2. F. Arbab, The IWIM model for coordination of concurrent activities. In Paolo Ciancarini and Chris Hankin, editors, Coordination Languages and Models, volume 1061 of Lecture Notes in Computer Science, 34–56, Springer–Verlag, 1996.
3. F. Arbab, Manifold version 2: Language reference manual, Technical report, Centrum voor Wiskunde en Informatica, Amsterdam, The Netherlands, pages : 1–162, 1996, Available on-line at http://www.cwi.nl/ftp/manifold/refman.ps.Z .
4. F. Arbab, C. L. Blom, F. J. Burger, and C. T. H. Everaars, Reusable Coordination Modules for Massively Concurrent Applications, Software: Practice and Experience, vol. 28, No. 7: 703–735, 1998.
5. F. Arbab, What Do You Mean, Coordination?, March'98 Issue of the Bulletin of the Dutch Association for Theoretical Computer Science (NVTI)
6. A. Arnold, Finite transition systems, Prentice Hall, 1994.
7. M.M. Bonsangue, F. Arbab, J.W. de Bakker, J.J.M.M. Rutten, A. Scutellà, G. Zavattaro, A transition system semantics for the control-driven coordination language MANIFOLD, Technical Report SEN-R9829, Centrum voor Wiskunde en Informatica, Amsterdam, The Netherlands, 1998.
8. P. Katis, N. Sabadini, R.F.C. Walters, Bicategories of processes, Journal of Pure and Applied Algebra 115: 141–178, 1997.
9. P. Katis, N. Sabadini, R.F.C. Walters, Span(Graph): A categorical algebra of transition systems, Proceedings Algebraic Methodology and Software Technology, volume 1349 of Lecture Notes in Computer Science, 307–321, Springer Verlag, 1997.
10. P. Katis, N. Sabadini, R.F.C. Walters, On the algebra of systems with feedback and boundary, Rendiconti del Circolo Matematico di Palermo Serie II, Suppl. 63: 123-156, 2000.
11. P. Katis, N. Sabadini, R.F.C. Walters, An algebra of automata for reconfiguring networks of interacting components, manuscript.
12. R.F.C. Walters, Categories and Computer Science, Carslaw Publications 1991, Cambridge University Press, 1992.
13. W. Zielonka, Note on asynchronous automata, RAIRO, 1987.

GCCS: A Graphical Coordination Language for System Specification

Rance Cleaveland, Xiaoqun Du, and Scott A. Smolka

Department of Computer Science, SUNY at Stony Brook
Stony Brook, NY 11794–4400, USA
{rance,vicdu,sas}@cs.sunysb.edu

Abstract. We present GCCS, a graphical coordination language for hierarchical concurrent systems. GCCS, which is implemented in the Concurrency Factory design environment, represents a coordination model based on process algebra. Its coordination laws, given as a structural operational semantics, allow one to infer atomic system transitions on the basis of transitions taken by system components. We illustrate the language's utility by exhibiting a GCCS-coordinated specification of the Rether real-time ethernet protocol. The specification contains both graphical and textual components.

1 Introduction

As defined in [Cia96], a *coordination language* or *model* provides a framework for describing how independent "agents" may interact. A coordination model should therefore dictate a number of *coordination laws* describing how agents use the given coordination media (semaphores, monitors, channels, tuple spaces, etc.) to coordinate their activities.

In this paper, we present a coordination model based on *process algebra* whose coordination laws are given as a *structural operational semantics* [Plo81]. The process algebra we utilize for this purpose is called *Graphical Calculus of Communicating Systems* (GCCS), a graphical version of Milner's value-passing CCS [Mil89] for specifying hierarchical networks of communicating processes. The coordination media in our case consist of *channels*, and the corresponding coordination primitives are bi-party synchronous message passing. GCCS's operational semantics is given by a small collection of *semantic rules* that allow one to infer atomic system transitions on the basis of transitions taken by system components.

The main virtue of using process algebra as a coordination language is that *any programming language or design notation possessing a "compatible" operational semantics can, in principle, be incorporated into the resulting coordination framework.* Further, the presence of a formal operational semantics ensures that any system implemented using the coordination language may be simulated in a precise mathematical sense and formally verified, using, for example, equivalence and model checking. Moreover, the graphical and hierarchical nature of

A. Porto and G.-C. Roman (Eds.): COORDINATION 2000, LNCS 1906, pp. 284–298, 2000.

GCCS aids in the visual comprehension of the software architecture [S + 95] of the system under construction.

As a demonstration of these points, we have implemented a GCCS-based coordination framework in the Concurrency Factory design environment for concurrent and distributed systems [CGL + 94,CLSS96a,CLSS96b]. In that incarnation of the framework, subsystems may be specified in VPL, the Concurrency Factory's textual design notation, or in the subset of GCCS for graphically rendering communicating state machines. Both of these notations possess an underlying operational semantics based on the notion of transitions labeled by atomic actions, and are thus compatible with the operational semantics of GCCS.

The Concurrency Factory also provides facilities for automatically generating executable code from GCCS-based designs. To date we have implemented code generators for Java, Ada 95, and C. These code generators target a variety of execution platforms including those based on threads, RPC, and sockets. An important aspect of the Concurrency Factory's code generators is that code is produced for the entirety of the coordination layer of the submitted GCCS design, covering all aspects of interprocess synchronization and communication. At the process level, code is generated for constructs involving basic (sequential) flow of control and specified data structures. Place-holders are provided in the generated code for application-specific code not captured in the GCCS design.

The Concurrency Factory has been applied to a number of real-life case studies, including [DMN + 97,DSC99,DSSW99,DDR + 99]. The case study reported in [DMN + 97,DSC99]—involving the formal specification and verification of the Rether real-time software-based ethernet protocol for multimedia applications—in particular, makes substantial use of GCCS's coordination features. We thus use it here to illustrate our approach.

Traditional approaches to coordination deploy a coordination language during *coding* stages of system development; i.e. coordination languages have typically been programming languages as well. Some popular coordination languages of this nature include Linda [CG89], JavaSpaces [Sun98], and TSpaces [WMLF98]. GCCS, on the other hand, is intended primarily as a *design* language. For several reasons, however, this difference is not as large as it may first seem. First, as mentioned above, any language with a GCCS-compatible operational semantics can be incorporated into the GCCS coordination framework; thus, in principle, this includes programming languages (or some suitable subsets thereof). Secondly, it is possible to automatically generate executable code from GCCS coordinated designs, and this is the approach taken in the Concurrency Factory. A benefit of a design-oriented coordination model is that coordinated system descriptions may first be submitted to formal verification and simulation before being "compiled" into executable code, thereby affording system designers greater confidence in the final product.

In other related work, Bergstra and Klint [BK98] propose TOOLBUS, a software coordination architecture that uses scripts and pattern matching for describing the interaction among software components. The semantics of the scripts has been given in terms of the process algebra ACP. In [AG97] and [BCD99], architectural description languages with semantics based on process algebras have been proposed. Process algebraic techniques such as refinement and weak bisimulation equivalence are used to analyze architectural compatibility and architectural conformity of software systems.

Process algebra has also been used by Busi, Gorrieri, Zavattaro and co-workers as a semantic basis for a number of recently proposed coordination languages [BGZ98,BGZ00,BZ00,AdBB + 00], including Linda, JavaSpaces, TSpaces, and Manifold [AHS93]. This ground-breaking work allows one to clarify possible ambiguities in the definitions of these languages, discuss possible implementation choices, compare expressive power, and formally reason about programs written in these languages. In contrast, our approach uses process algebra and operational semantics *directly* as a coordination framework, rather than to define the semantics of independently proposed coordination languages. Moreover, any language equipped with a process-algebraic semantics becomes a candidate component-specification language for the GCCS framework, provided that the algebra's operational semantics are GCCS-compatible. Thus the coordination languages investigated by Gorrieri, Zavattaro, et al. are such candidates.

The rest of the paper is organized as follows. Section 2 gives an overview of the Concurrency Factory. Sections 3 and 4 describe the syntax and operational semantics of GCCS and VPL, respectively. Section 5 discusses some of the implementation issues surrounding GCCS as a coordination language. Section 6 presents the Rether example, while Section 7 gives our concluding remarks and future research directions.

2   The Concurrency Factory

The Concurrency Factory is an integrated toolset for specification, simulation, verification, and implementation of concurrent and distributed systems such as communication protocols and process control systems. The Factory uses process algebra as its underlying formal model of systems, and model checking and equivalence checking as its primary verification techniques. The goal of the project is to make process algebra and model checking both: (1) accessible to system engineers who might not be familiar with formal verification; and (2) applicable to the kinds of complex systems one is likely to encounter in real-life applications. Both considerations factored heavily into our design of the description languages. In support of (1), we wanted a graphical "architectural" language with constructs similar to the ones engineers use informally in the early design of a system. In support of (2), the notation needed to be modular and to support efficiently the manipulation of data.

These observations led to the inclusion of the following key features of the Concurrency Factory.

– A graphical editor and viewer supporting GCCS as a coordination language for hierarchically structured networks of communicating processes.

- A textual user interface for the VPL, a language based on Milner's CCS for describing systems of concurrent processes that communicate values. Like GCCS, VPL systems may be multi-layered or hierarchical.
- An interactive graphical simulator for GCCS that allows the user to witness GCCS-based interactions between coordinated subsystems, and to view these interactions at any level of the network hierarchy—simultaneously if so desired.
- A set of object interfaces for representing system specifications. Both GCCS specifications and compiled VPL programs have internal representations that, although quite different, share a high-level interface. Methods "at the interface" include a set of "semantic routines" that capture the operational semantics of these objects. The coordination mechanisms use these methods in order to calculate the interactions allowed between objects. The methods also provide a uniform interface to the Factory's verification and simulation routines.
- A suite of design and analysis routines that includes efficient model checkers for the modal mu-calculus, an expressive branching-time temporal logic, and a bisimulation checker.
- A graphical compiler that transforms GCCS and VPL specifications into executable Java or ADA 95 code.

The architecture of the Concurrency Factory is shown in Fig 1. The Factory is written in C++ and executes under X-Windows, using Tcl/Tk as the graphics engine, so that it is efficient, easily extendible, and highly portable.

3   Syntax and Semantics of GCCS

3.1   GCCS Syntax

GCCS contains two sublanguages: the *coordination layer* and the *process layer*. The coordination layer supports the definition of *systems*, where systems may be processes or *networks* of subsystems. Note that networks are hierarchical, as subsystems may themselves be networks, and that processes constitute the "leaves" of the hierarchy.

Within a network, subsystems may be topologically interconnected in the following manner. Each system possesses an *interface* defining the collection of *ports* the system can use can use to communicate with other systems. At the root-level of the hierarchy, a system's ports define its interface to the outside world. Ports are labeled and the communication actions that involve a given port are named in accordance with the port's label. A communication pathway between subsystems may then be formed by connecting ports of the systems to a common *bus*, the communication/coordination mechanism of GCCS. Connections between ports and buses are called *links*. Buses, like ports, may also be labeled, and communication actions occurring over ports linked to a labeled bus are renamed to the bus's label.

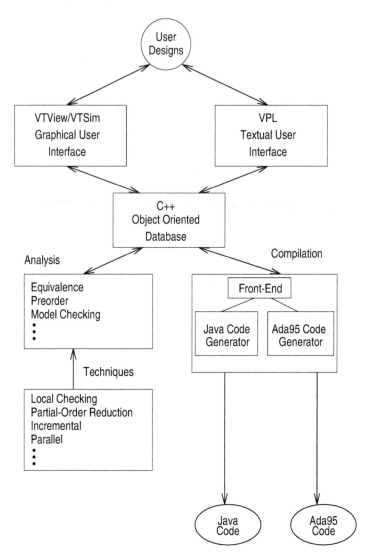

Fig. 1. The architecture of the Concurrency Factory.

Connections to buses may be multi-way, i.e. two or more systems may contain links to the same bus. However, communication over buses is bi-party and synchronous, meaning that any actual communication involves exactly two systems and requires a rendezvous. Besides its possible involvement in a synchronized communication, a communication action taken by a system over a particular port can be redirected to a port with a matching label one level higher in the system hierarchy.

The GCCS network appearing in the top middle panel of Figure 2 illustrates the above concepts. The example, corresponding to the aforementioned Rether protocol (discussed more fully in Section 6), involves a root system (Rether) composed of three subsystems: `adm_ctrl`, `band`, and `nodes`. `adm_ctrl` and `band` are processes (leaves) while `nodes` is a system whose coordination structure can be viewed by zooming in on its icon. As Figure 2 illustrates, interfaces are rendered graphically in GCCS as rectangles and ports are drawn as labeled blackened circles along rectangle perimeters. Line segments are used to link ports to buses.

The coordination-layer constructs of GCCS allow one to graphically depict the hierarchical coordination infrastructure of the specified system. The process layer of GCCS contains graphical constructs for specifying GCCS processes, the leaves of a GCCS system hierarchy. As described in Section 4, processes can also be specified textually using VPL. A GCCS process is essentially a communicating state machine or labeled transition system, consisting of states and state transitions. Each transition has a unique source state and target state, and is labeled by a communication action. As described above, communication actions are named in accordance with the label of the port over which they occur. A transition can also be labeled by τ, representing a CCS-like internal action [Mil89].

Also, as in CCS, communication actions are either input actions or output actions. Output actions are barred to distinguish them from input actions. Thus the action $\bar{a}$ represents an output action taken on behalf of a process over port a. Communication actually occurs in GCCS when an input action with a given name synchronizes with an output action of the same name. Thus, for instance, input action a can synchronize with output action $\bar{a}$. In "pure" GCCS, which for simplicity we focus on in this paper, communication is data-less, involving only the exchange of a signal (named a in the example). The version of GCCS currently implemented in the Concurrency Factory does support data exchange; the language has a type system consisting of bounded width integers together with record and array constructs, and ports and buses must have types associated with them. This support for data allows a seamless integration with VPL, which provides support for value passing between processes.

3.2   GCCS Semantics

The formal semantics of GCCS is based on labeled transitions systems. To define the semantics precisely we follow the approach used for other graphical languages such as Statecharts; we first introduce a term-language for GCCS and then define the semantics on these terms. We begin with a few preliminary definitions.

- $\mathcal{A}$ is an infinite set of *port names* not containing τ or ξ. $a, a', \ldots$ range over $\mathcal{A}$.
- $\mathcal{B} = \mathcal{A} \cup \{\xi\}$ is the set of *bus names*; ξ is the internal bus. $b, b', \ldots$ range over $\mathcal{B}$.
- $InputActions = \mathcal{A}$ is the set of *input actions*.
- $OutputActions = \{\bar{a} | a \in \mathcal{A}\}$ is the set of *output actions*. $\bar{a}, \bar{a'}, \ldots$ range over $OutputActions$, and $l, l', \ldots$ range over $InputActions \cup OutputActions$.

- $Act = InputActions \cup OutputActions \cup \{\tau\}$, where τ is an internal action, represents the set of actions. $\alpha, \beta, \ldots$ range over Act.
- $port : InputActions \cup OutputActions \rightarrow \mathcal{A}$ maps each non-τ action l to its associated port.

We now define the term language GCCS as follows.

- A *system* S is either a process or a network.
- A *process* is a tuple $\langle Q, \rightarrow, q_0, q \rangle$, where Q is a finite set of states, $\rightarrow \subseteq Q \times Act \times Q$ is a finite set of labeled transitions, $q_0 \in Q$ is the initial state, and $q \in Q$ is the current state. The set of processes is represented by $Proc$.
- A *network* is a tuple $\langle \overline{N}, B, L \rangle$ whose components have the following form.
    1. $\overline{N} = \langle \langle S_1, I_1 \rangle, \ldots, \langle S_n, I_n \rangle \rangle$ is a finite sequence of system/interface pairs, where each $I_i \subseteq \mathcal{A}$ is required to be finite. We use $|\overline{N}| = n$ to denote the length of $\overline{N}$.
    2. $B \subseteq \mathcal{B}$ is a finite set of buses.
    3. $L \subseteq \{1, \ldots, |\overline{N}|\} \times \mathcal{A} \times B$ is a finite set of links satisfying: for every $\langle i, a, b \rangle \in L$, $a \in I_i$, and for every $\langle i_1, a_1, b_1 \rangle$ and $\langle i_2, a_2, b_2 \rangle \in L$, if $i_1 = i_2$ and $a_1 = a_2$, then $b_1 = b_2$.

    We use Net to refer to the set of all networks.

The following auxiliary notations on networks will be useful in the sequel. Let $\mathcal{M} = \langle \overline{N}, B, L \rangle$, where $\overline{N} = \langle \langle S_1, I_1 \rangle, \ldots, \langle S_n, I_n \rangle \rangle$, be a network.

- $C(\mathcal{M}) = \{1, \ldots, n\}$ is the set of *component names* in $\mathcal{M}$.
- If $i \in C(\mathcal{M})$ then $S(\mathcal{M}, i) = S_i$ is the ith subsystem and $I(\mathcal{M}, i) = I_i$ is the ith interface.
- $B(\mathcal{M}) = B$ is the set of buses in $\mathcal{M}$.
- $L(\mathcal{M}) = L$ is the set of links in $\mathcal{M}$.
- Let S be a system, and let $i \in C(\mathcal{M})$. Then $\mathcal{M}[i := S]$ is the network obtained by replacing $S(\mathcal{M}, i)$ with S.

We now present the semantics of GCCS systems in the standard SOS style by giving a collection inference rules to define the transitions available to processes and networks. The resulting operational semantics essentially allows one to compile GCCS specifications into labeled transition systems. Each rule has one or more premises, a conclusion, and possible side conditions. The basic structure of a rule is as follows:

$$\frac{\text{Premise}}{\text{Conclusion}}[\text{Side Condition}]$$

There are five rules. The first determines the behavior of processes, while the rest are for networks.

1.

$$\frac{q \xrightarrow{l}_Q q'}{\langle Q, \rightarrow_Q, q_0, q \rangle \xrightarrow{l} \langle Q, \rightarrow_Q, q_0, q' \rangle}$$

This rule states that process transitions are also system transitions.

2.

$$\frac{S(\mathcal{M}, i) \xrightarrow{\tau} S'}{\mathcal{M} \xrightarrow{\tau} \mathcal{M}[i := S']}$$

This rule states that a network can execute a τ-transition if one of its subsystems can.

3.

$$\frac{S(\mathcal{M}, i) \xrightarrow{l} S'}{\mathcal{M} \xrightarrow{l} \mathcal{M}[i := S']} \left[\begin{array}{l} port(l) \in I(\mathcal{M}, i); \forall i \in C(\mathcal{M}), b \in B(\mathcal{M}), \\ \langle i, port(l), b \rangle \notin L(\mathcal{M}) \end{array} \right]$$

This rule states that a network can perform an input or output action provided that (1) one of its subsystems can perform such an action, (2) the action involves a port on the subsystem's interface, and (3) the port does not contain links to any buses.

4.

$$\frac{S(\mathcal{M}, i) \xrightarrow{l_1} S'}{\mathcal{M} \xrightarrow{l_2} \mathcal{M}[i := S']} [port(l_1) \in I(\mathcal{M}, i), \langle i, port(l_1), port(l_2) \rangle \in L(\mathcal{M})]$$

This rule states that a network can perform a relabeled input or output action l_2 if one of its subsystems can perform the action l_1 involving a port on its interface that is linked to a bus labeled by $port(l_2)$. Note that this rule implies that the bus in question cannot be internal (i.e. cannot be named "ξ"), since ξ is not in the range of $port$.

5.

$$\frac{S(\mathcal{M}, i) \xrightarrow{l_1} S'_i, S(\mathcal{M}, j) \xrightarrow{l_2} S'_j}{\mathcal{M} \xrightarrow{\tau} \mathcal{M}[i := S'_i][j := S'_j]} \left[\begin{array}{l} i \neq j; port(l_1) \in I(\mathcal{M}, i); port(l_2) \in I(\mathcal{M}, j); \\ \{l_1, l_2\} \cap InputActions \neq \emptyset; \\ \{l_1, l_2\} \cap OutputActions \neq \emptyset; \\ \exists b \in B(\mathcal{M}). \langle i, port(l_1), b \rangle \in L(\mathcal{M}), and \\ \langle j, port(l_2), b \rangle \in L(\mathcal{M}) \end{array} \right]$$

This rule describes a synchronization between two subsystems connected to a common bus b. For such a synchronization to occur, the actions involved must come from different subsystems, with one being an input and the other an output. They must also involve ports connected to the same bus.

Some comments about internal buses are in order. As mentioned above, Rule 4 can never be applied when the bus to which a port is connected is internal. Thus, internal buses provide a means of "forcing" synchronization: the only transitions involving an internal bus that can be inferred require the synchronization of two processes (Rule 5).

4   VPL

VPL is a textual language for specifying concurrent systems. Explicit linguistic support is provided for value passing and various control and data structures.

VPL-supported data types include integers of limited range as well as arrays and records.

VPL is one of the design notations currently incorporated into the GCCS coordination framework of the Concurrency Factory. As such, it can be used to specify leaf nodes in a GCCS system hierarchy. As in GCCS, however, a VPL specification is a tree-like hierarchy of subsystems, and a system is either a network or a process. So, a VPL program is only leaf-like in its position within the coordination hierarchy; in all other regards, it possesses full-fledged hierarchical structure.

A VPL network consists of a collection of systems running in parallel and communicating with each other through typed channels. VPL processes are at the leaves of the hierarchy. Each system, whether process or network, consists of a header, local declarations, and a body. The header specifies a unique name for the system and a list of "formal channels" (by analogy with formal parameters of procedures in programming languages). The names of the formal channels of a system can be used in the body of the system and represent events visible to an external observer.

Declarations local to a network include specifications of the subsystems of the network and channels for communication between subsystems that are to be hidden from the outside world. The body of a network is a parallel composition of its subsystems. A subsystem declared within a network can be used arbitrarily many times; each time a new copy of the subsystem is instantiated with actual channels substituted for the formal ones. Actual channels must match the formal ones introduced in the header and must be declared either as local channels or formal channels of the network immediately containing the subsystem.

Declarations local to a process consist of variable and procedure declarations. Procedure bodies, like process bodies, are sequences of statements. The basic statements of VPL are assignments of arithmetic or boolean expressions to variables, and input/output operations on channels. Complex statements include sequential composition, `if-then-else`, `while-do`, and nondeterministic choice in the form of the `select` statement. VPL's structural operational semantics is defined in [Tiw97] in a manner similar to the definition given above for GCCS. This semantics allows VPL system definitions to be treated semantically as labeled transition systems consisting of states and transitions, and therefore to be viewed as interchangeable at the abstract level with GCCS processes.

In the "pure" version of GCCS considered in this paper, VPL processes may not pass values to the GCCS layer. This capability is however realized in the version of GCCS implemented in the Concurrency Factory.

5   GCCS as a Coordination Language

Up to this point we have treated GCCS as a graphical description language for modeling systems that communicate synchronously. In this section we explain how GCCS in general, and more specifically the network layer of GCCS, indeed constitutes a coordination language.

Viewed as a language by itself, the network layer of GCCS provides constructs for assembling "communication architectures" with "holes" to be filled by processes. Until these holes are instantiated with processes, GCCS network structures cannot engage in execution steps; at a formal level, the semantic rules for networks all have premises that must be satisfied in order for network-level transitions to be inferred. However, once the "holes" in a network have been filled with component processes, the SOS rules for networks define how the transitions of these components may be combined into system-level transitions. Thus, at one level, the GCCS network layer enables "co-ordination structures" for GCCS processes to be constructed.

Of course, this line of reasoning does not justify viewing the network layer as a coordination language, since such languages must be capable of coordinating processes written in different notations. However, a careful analysis of the GCCS semantics, and of Rule 1 in particular, indicates that at a semantic level, the GCCS network layer does not depend on the specific syntactic form of processes beyond the syntax of action names. Consequently, *any* notation having a semantics given in terms of labeled transition systems with labels coming from the GCCS action set may be used to define entities to be used as processes. In addition, since the GCCS network constructs segregate "processes" from one another, local syntactic analyzers may be used to parse processes given in different notations, and simulators for the different notations may be yoked together inside a GCCS network simulator. We exploited these observations in our inclusion of VPL system definitions inside GCCS networks. VPL has its own independent tool support, including a compiler and a simulator. These tools are used by the GCCS coordination layer in assembling a heterogeneous system consisting of GCCS and VPL.

These observations also point to what is needed in order to include other system design notations within the GCCS coordination umbrella: the notation in question needs to have an operational semantics in terms of labeled transition systems, and the labels on the transitions need to be GCCS actions. Of course, it would in general be unrealistic to expect languages to have a semantics in terms of GCCS actions. However, existing specification languages for concurrent systems typically do have an operational semantics involving labeled transitions. To enable components written in such languages to be coordinated via GCCS, code would only need to be written for "translating", or "marshalling", the labels into GCCS actions. Such an enterprise would involve some subtlety, since the synchronization semantics of other languages differs from GCCS. However, the effort required is much smaller than for a full-fledged language reimplementation, and it would only need to be done once per language.[1]

---

[1] It also should be noted that in value-passing GCCS, values being exchanged would also require "marshalling". Such notions may be found in other coordination languages, and in CORBA in particular.

6 The Rether Case Study

In [DMN + 97,DSC99], we applied the Concurrency Factory to Rether, a software-based real-time ethernet protocol developed at SUNY Stony Brook [CV95]. We recount this case study here in order to illustrate GCCS's role as a coordination language. Rether was designed to provide guaranteed bandwidth and deterministic, periodic network access to multimedia applications over commodity ethernet hardware. It has been implemented in the FreeBSD 2.1.0 operating system, and is now being used to support the Stony Brook Video Server, a low-cost, ethernet LAN-based server providing real-time delivery of video to end-users from the server's disk subsystem.

Rether is a contention-free token bus protocol for the datalink layer of the ISO protocol stack. It is designed to run on top of a CSMA/CD physical layer. A network running the protocol normally operates in CSMA/CD mode, transparently switching to Rether mode when one or more nodes generate requests for real-time connections. An initialization protocol is used to coordinate the switch to Rether mode. Once in Rether mode, a token is used to control access to the medium: a node can transmit data only when it has the token.

Using GCCS as the coordination framework, we specified Rether in a combination of GCCS and VPL, and verified, using model checking, two essential properties of the protocol: Rether makes good on its bandwidth guarantees to real-time nodes without exposing non-real-time nodes to the possibility of starvation. Further details of the case study can be found in [DMN + 97,DSC99].

Figure 2, which contains a snapshot of the Concurrency Factory's graphical simulator in action, illustrates our GCCS/VPL encoding of Rether. It also illustrates how GCCS is utilized to coordinate systems written in completely different design notations. The center panel in the top half of the figure contains the GCCS network specification of the protocol, consisting of three subsystems, one for admissions control (adm_ctrl), one for bandwith monitoring (band), and one for the (four) LAN nodes that execute the protocol (nodes). Communication pathways between subsystems are formed by connecting a port of one subsystem to a port of another subsystem using a bus. For example, adm_ctrl communicates with nodes via bus4, which links port release of adm_ctrl with port release of nodes.

Ports in the network not connected to buses (such as start, cycle, rt0, and nt0) are for communication with the outside world, in this case, the user. The observable actions performed over these ports were used to encode the modal mu-calculus formulas we submitted to the Concurrency Factory's model checker during verification.

The other panels in the top half of Figure 2 capture some of the simulation facilities available in the Concurrency Factory, including a list of enabled transitions, a list of currently activated breakpoints (none in the example), and a history list. The list of enabled transitions indicates to the user which transitions can be executed next to continue the simulation. In this particular case, the last transition on the list (a τ-transition) is highlighted, and its execution

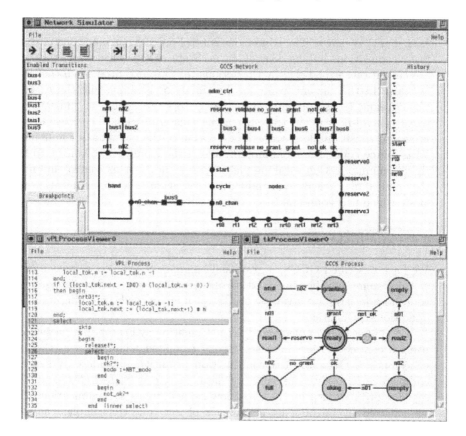

Fig. 2. A snapshot of Rether in the Concurrency Factory.

is now being simulated. The history list shows the sequence of transitions that have been executed so far during the simulation.

The simulation menu bar is also shown (top left corner, below File). The available options, from left to right, are Go-To-Next-State of simulation, Go-To-Previous-State of simulation, Jump-Back in history list, Jump-to-Beginning of history list, Execute-Until-Breakpoint, Set-Breakpoint, and Clear-Breakpoint. The simulator's pull-down File and Help menus are also depicted.

The lower-left panel of Figure 2 is a "process viewer" tool for VPL specifications, which allows a user to scroll up or down through the VPL source code of a specification. In the illustrated case, lines 113 through 135 of the VPL source code for a LAN node executing the Rether protocol are depicted, node number 0 to be specific. Lines 121 and 126 are highlighted by the simulator to indicate that the execution of the command `release!*` in line 125 is being simulated. The effect of this command is to output a signal over port `release`.

The lower-right panel is a process viewer for GCCS processes. It enables a user to pan through a GCCS graphical process specification. In the illustrated

case, the GCCS specification of the Rether protocol's admissions control process
(adm_ctrl) is shown. The admissions control process has nine control states and
twelve transitions linking control states. State ready is the start state.

Transitions are labeled by the actions that are executed when the transition
is taken. In the current example, the simulator is simulating the execution of
the release transition from state ready to state read2, as indicated by the
small control-flow token traveling along this transition. The execution of the
release transition along with the execution of the release!* command in the
VPL source code of node number 0, allows the simulator to convey to the user
that a communication is taking place between admissions control and node 0 so
that node 0 may release its bandwidth reservation. The communication medium
along which this communication occurs is bus4.

7   Conclusions

We have described GCCS, a graphical language for the coordination of hierarchical systems specified in a mixture of textual and graphical languages. GCCS's
coordination laws are given by the set of inference rules defining its structural
operational semantics.

GCCS has been implemented in the Concurrency Factory design environment
using a common object interface among component languages as the basis for
coordination. Currently the coordination primitives include only synchronous
communication of various types of data. Future work includes expanding the
set of coordination primitives to allow asynchronous communication. This can
be achieved by introducing a new bus object (one that implements message
queues) and extending the operational semantics of GCCS's coordination layer
accordingly.

We are also interested in bringing Statecharts [Har87] into the GCCS coordination framework. Recent work involving the authors [US94a,US94b,LBC99] on
process-algebraic/operational semantics for Statecharts represents a necessary
first step in this direction.

Acknowledgements The authors gratefully acknowledge the contributions of
Jayesh Gada, Sunil Jain, Phil Lewis, Brad Mott, Denis Roegel, Oleg Sokolsky,
Pranav Tiwari, Vikas Trehan, and Shipei Zhang, to the design and implementation of GCCS and the Concurrency Factory. They would also like to thank the
anonymous referee who brought references [AG97,BCD99] to their attention, and
Paul Klint for discussions regarding the ToolBus [BK98]. This research was supported in part by NSF grants CCR-9505562, CCR-9705998, and DMI-9961012.

References

AdBB + 00. F. Arbab, J.W. de Bakker, M.M. Bonsangue, J.J.M.M. Rutten, A.
Scutella, and G. Zavattaro. A transition system semantics for the control-
driven coordination language Manifold. *Theoretical Computer Science*,
2000. To appear.

AG97.   R. Allen and D. Garlan. A formal basis for architectural connection. *ACM Trans. on Software Engineering and Methodology.*, 6(3):213-249, 1997.

AHS93.   F. Arbab, I. Herman, and P. Spilling. An overview of Manifold and its implementation. ıConcurrency: Practice and Experience, 5(1):23-70, 1993.

BCD99.   M. Bernardo, P. Ciancarini, and L. Donatiello. Performance analysis of software architectures via a process algebraic description language. Technical Report UBLCS-99-20, University of Bologna, 1999.

BGZ98.   N. Busi, R. Gorrieri, and G. Zavattaro. A process algebraic view of Linda coordination primitives. *Theoretical Computer Science*, 192(2):167-199, February 1998.

BGZ00.   N. Busi, R. Gorrieri, and G. Zavattaro. Process calculi for coordination: From Linda to JavaSpaces. In *Proceedings of AMAST 2000, Lecture Notes in Computer Science*. Springer-Verlag, May 2000.

BK98.   J. A. Bergstra and P. Klint. The discrete time ToolBus - A software coordination architecture. *Science of Computer Programming*, 31:205-229, 1998.

BZ00.   N. Busi and G. Zavattaro. On the expressiveness of event notification in data-driven coordination languages. In *Proceedings of ESOP 2000, Lecture Notes in Computer Science*. Springer-Verlag, March 2000.

CG89.   N. Carriero and D. Gelernter. Linda in context. *Communications of the ACM*, 32(4):444-458, April 1989.

CGL + 94.   R. Cleaveland, J. N. Gada, P. M. Lewis, S. A. Smolka, O. Sokolsky, and S. Zhang. The Concurrency Factory: practical tools for specification, simulation, verification, and implementation of concurrent systems. In G.E. Blelloch, K.M. Chandy, and S. Jagannathan, editors, *Proceedings of DIMACS Workshop on Specification of Parallel Algorithms*, volume 18 of DIMACS Series in *Discrete Mathematics and Theoretical Computer Science*, pages 75-90, Princeton, NJ, May 1994. American Mathematical Society.

Cia96.   P. Ciancarini. Coordination models and languages as software integrators. *ACM Computing Surveys*, 28(2):300-302, June 1996.

CLSS96a.   R. Cleaveland, P. M. Lewis, S. A. Smolka, and O. Sokolsky. The Concurrency Factory: A development environment for concurrent systems. In R. Alur and T. A. Henzinger, editors, *Computer Aided Verification* (CAV '96), volume 1102 of *Lecture Notes in Computer Science*, pages 398-401, New Brunswick, New Jersey, July 1996. Springer-Verlag.

CLSS96b.   R. Cleaveland, P. M. Lewis, S. A. Smolka, and O. Sokolsky. The Concurrency Factory software development environment. In T. Margaria and B. Steffen, editors, *Proceedings of the Second International Workshop on Tools and Algorithms for the Construction and Analysis of Systems* (TACAS '96), Vol. 1055 of *Lecture Notes in Computer Science*. Springer-Verlag, 1996.

CV95.   T. Chiueh and C. Venkatramani. The design, implementation and evaluation of a software-based real-time ethernet protocol. In *Proceedings of ACM SIGCOMM '95*, pages 27-37, 1995.

DDR + 99.   Y. Dong, X. Du, Y. S. Ramakrishna, C. R. Ramakrishnan, I.V. Ramakrishnan, S. A. Smolka, O. Sokolsky, E. W. Stark, and D. S. Warren. Fighting livelock in the i-Protocol: A comparative study of verification tools. In *Tools and Algorithms for the Construction and Analysis of Algorithms (TACAS '99)*, Lecture Notes in Computer Science, Amsterdam, March 1999. Springer-Verlag.

DMN + 97. X. Du, K. T. McDonnel, E. Nanos, Y. S. Ramakrishna, and S. A. Smolka. Software design, specification, and veriffcation: Lessons learned from the Rether case study. In *Proceedings of the Sixth International Conference on Algebraic Methodology and Software Technology (AMAST'97)*, Sydney, Australia, December 1997. Springer-Verlag.

DSC99. X. Du, S. A. Smolka, and R. Cleaveland. Local model checking and protocol analysis. *Software Tools for Technology Transfer*, 2(3):219-241, November 1999.

DSSW99. Y. Dong, S. A. Smolka, E. Stark, and S. M. White. Practical considerations in protocol verification: The E-2C case study. In *Proceedings of the Fifth IEEE International Conference on Engineering of Complex Computer Systems (ICECCS '99)*. IEEE Computer Society Press, 1999.

Har87. D. Harel. Statecharts: A visual formalism for complex systems. *Science of Computer Programming*, 8:231-274, 1987.

LBC99. G. Lüttgen, M. von der Beeck, and R. Cleaveland. Statecharts via process algebra. In J.C.M. Baeten and S. Mauw, editors, *CONCUR '99*, volume 1664 of *Lecture Notes in Computer Science*, pages 399-414, Eindhoven, the Netherlands, August 1999. Springer-Verlag.

Mil89. R. Milner. *Communication and Concurrency*. International Series in Computer Science. Prentice Hall, 1989.

Plo81. G. D. Plotkin. A structural approach to operational semantics. Technical Report DAIMI FN-19, Computer Science Department, Aarhus University, 1981.

S + 95. M. Shaw et al. Abstractions for software architecture and tools to support them. *IEEE Trans. Software Engineering*, 21(4):314-335, April 1995.

Sun98. Sun Microsystems, Inc. *JavaSpaces Specifications*, 1998.

Tiw97. P. Tiwari. VPL-tool support for specification and verification of concurrent systems. Master's thesis, North Carolina State University, Raleigh, 1997.

US94a. A. C. Uselton and S. A. Smolka. A compositional semantics for Statecharts using labeled transition systems. In *Proceedings of CONCUR '94 – Fifth International Conference on Concurrency Theory*, Uppsala, Sweden, August 1994.

US94b. A. C. Uselton and S. A. Smolka. A process-algebraic semantics for Statecharts via state refinement. In *Proceedings of PROCOMET '94*. North Holland/Elsevier, 1994.

WMLF98. P. Wyckoff, S. W. McLaughry, T. J. Lehman, and D. A. Ford. TSpaces. *IBM Systems Journal*, 37(3), 1998.

A Timed Linda Language

Frank S. de Boer[1], Maurizio Gabbrielli[2], and Maria Chiara Meo[3]

[1] Universiteit Utrecht, frankb@cs.ruu.nl
[2] Università di Udine, gabbri@dimi.uniud.it
[3] Università di L'Aquila, meo@univaq.it

Abstract. We introduce a Timed Linda language (T-Linda) which is obtained by a natural timed interpretation of the usual constructs of the Linda model and by adding a simple primitive which allows one to specify time-outs. Parallel execution of processes follows the scheduling policy of interleaving, however maximal parallelism is assumed for actions depending on time. We define the operational semantics of T-Linda by means of a transition system (a denotational model is defined in [4]).

1 Introduction

Time critical features are rather important in the context of coordination of complex applications for open, distributed systems: In these systems often one has the need to express such timing constraints as upper limits on the wait for an event, that is time-outs, and fixed (bounded) duration for granting a service, so called leasing. In fact, JavaSpaces [13] and TSpaces [14], two coordination middlewares for distributed Java programming based on the Linda model [8], allow one to express similar timing constraints. Temporal aspects of concurrent computations have been extensively studied in many different formal settings, including timed process algebras, temporal logic (and its executable versions) and the concurrent synchronous languages ESTEREL, LUSTRE, SIGNAL and Statecharts. Timed extensions of concurrent constraint programming [11] (a programming paradigm quite similar to Linda) have also been recently investigated in [12,2].

In this paper we investigate (from a semantic perspective) a timed extension of Linda that we call T-Linda. We introduce directly a timed interpretation of the usual programming constructs of Linda by identifying a time-unit with the time needed for the execution of a basic Linda action (out, in and rd), and by interpreting action prefixing as the next-time operator. An explicit timing primitive is also introduced in order to allow for the specification of time-outs. The parallel operator of T-Linda is interpreted in terms of interleaving, as usual, however we assume maximal parallelism for actions depending on time. In other words, when two parallel processes both involve time critical actions, time passes for both of them. This approach is different from that one of [2], where maximal parallelism was assumed for any kind of action, and it is also different from that one studied in [5] (a detailed comparison is deferred to Section 3). We describe the operational semantics of our timed extension of Linda in terms of a transition system. We have defined also denotational semantics based on sequences of labelled pairs of multisets of tuples. However, due to space limitations, this model is not included in the present paper and can be found in [4].

A. Porto and G.-C. Roman (Eds.): COORDINATION 2000, LNCS 1906, pp. 299–304, 2000.

2   The Timed Linda Language

The basic idea underlying Linda [8] is that computation progresses via accumulation of information, represented in terms of tuples, in a global shared multiset called tuple space or store. Here we abstract from the specific nature of tuples and assume that these are elementary objects ranged over by $a, b, \ldots$. Information is produced and removed by the concurrent and asynchronous activity of several processes which can add a tuple a to the store by using the basic operation out(a). Dually, processes can also remove a tuple from the store by performing an in(a) operation and read a tuple from the store by means of a rd(a) operation. Differently from the case of out(a), both in(a) and rd(a) are blocking operations, that is, if a is not present in the store then the evaluation of in(a) and rd(a) is suspended, thus allowing one to express synchronization among different processes. In some dialects of Linda also a kind of if_then_else is present in the form of a construct rdp(a)?P_Q: If a is present in the store then the process P is evaluated, otherwise the computation proceed with the process Q (an analogous construct inp(a)?P_Q differs from the previous one only in that the tuple a, whenever present, is removed from the store). The $\parallel$ operator allows one to express parallel composition of two processes, non-determinism arises by introducing a *choice* operator $+$, and a notion of locality is obtained by introducing the process A $\setminus$ a which behaves like A, with a considered *local* to A.

When querying the store for some information which is not present (yet) a process will either suspend until the required information has arrived (in case of in(a) and rd(a) processes) or will take an alternative continuation (in case of rdp(a)?P_Q and inp(a)?P_Q). However, as previously mentioned, in many practical cases often one has the need to express time-outs, that is, one needs to specify that in case a given time bound is exceeded the wait is interrupted and an alternative action is taken.

In order to enrich *Linda* with such timing mechanisms, we assume the existence of a *discrete global clock* and assume that the basic actions out(a), in(a) and rd(a) take one time-unit. Computation evolves in steps of one time-unit, so called clock-cycles. We consider action prefixing as the syntactic marker which distinguishes a time instant from the next one. So out(a).P has now to be regarded as the process which updates the current store by adding a and then, at the *next* time instant, behaves like P. Analogously, if a is contained in the current store then the process in(a).P behaves like P at the next time instant, after having removed a from the store. If a is not present in the store at time t then the process in(a).P is suspended, i.e. at time $t + 1$ it is checked again whether the store contains a. The process rd(a).P behaves like in(a).P without removing information from the store.

The parallel construct is interpreted in terms of interleaving, as usual in many (timed) process algebras and in all the main Linda dialects. Maximal parallelism (which means that at each moment every enabled process of the system is activated) does not seem appropriate in this context, since competing requests for removing the same tuple should be scheduled. However, as we discuss later, maximal parallelism is assumed for time-elapsing, that is, time passes for all the activated components of the system.

Time-outs are modeled by introducing the construct rdp(a)$_t$?P_Q whose meaning is analogous to that one of the untimed version, with the difference that here one is allowed to wait t time units for the presence of the tuple a in the store and the subsequent evaluation of the process P; If this time limit is exceeded then the process Q is evaluated. Thus we end up with the following syntax.

Definition 1 (*Timed Linda* **Language**). *Assuming a given set of tuples* T, *with typical elements* $a, b \ldots$, *the syntax of the* Timed Linda *processes is given by the following grammar:*

$$P ::= \text{stop} \mid \text{out}(a).P \mid \text{in}(a).P \mid \text{rd}(a).P \mid \text{rdp}(a)_t?P\_P \mid$$
$$P \parallel P \mid P + P \mid P \setminus a \mid \text{recX}.P$$

In the previous definition we assume that only guarded forms of recursion are used, as usual.

2.1 Operational Semantics

The operational model of *T-Linda* can be formally described by a labeled transition system $T = (Conf, Label, \longrightarrow)$ where we assume that each transition step takes exactly one time-unit. Configurations (in) *Conf* are pairs consisting of a process and a multi-set of tuples (the tuple space, also called store). In the following $\uplus$ denotes the multisets union, while Label $= \{\tau, \sigma\}$ is the set of labels. We use labels to distinguish "real" computational steps performed by processes which have the control (label σ) from the transitions which model only the passing of time (label τ). So σ-actions are those performed by processes which modify the store (out, in), which perform a check on the store (rd, rdp$_t$) and it is a σ-action also that one corresponding to exceeding a time-out (rdp$_0$). On the other hand τ-actions are those performed by time-out processes (rdp$_t$) in case they have not the control. The transition relation $\longrightarrow \subseteq Conf \times Labels \times Conf$ is the least relation satisfying the rules R1-R14 in Table 1 and characterizes the (temporal) evolution of the system. So, $\langle P, m \rangle \stackrel{x}{\longrightarrow} \langle Q, m' \rangle$ with $x \in \{\sigma, \tau\}$ means that if at time t we have the process P and the store m, then at time $t + 1$ we have the process Q and the store m'. Let us now briefly discuss the rules in Table 1.

Rules **R1-R3** are self explanatory (notice that the evaluation of out(a), in(a) and read(a) takes one time unit and that, differently from the case of out(a), both in(a) and read(a) are blocking operations: In case the store does not contain a the computation is suspended).

The rules **R4-R7** show that the time-out process rdp(a)$_t$?P_Q behaves either as P or as Q depending on the presence of a in the tuple space in the next t time units: if $t > 0$ and a is present in the tuple space then P is evaluated (rule **R4**). If $t > 0$ and a is not present then the check for a is repeated at the next time instant and the value of the counter t is decreased (rule **R5**); Note that in this case we use the label σ, since a check on the store has been performed. As shown by rule **R6**, the counter can be decreased also by performing a τ-action: Intuitively this rule is used to model the situation in which, even though the evaluation of the time-out started already, another (parallel) process has the control. In this case, differently from the approach in [5], time continues to elapse (via τ-actions) also for the time-out process (see also the rules for the parallel operator). Rule **R7** shows that if the time-out is exceeded, i.e. the counter t has reached the value of 0, then the process rdp(a)$_t$?P_Q behaves as Q.

Rules **R8-R9** model the parallel composition operator in terms of *interleaving*, since only one basic σ-action is allowed for each transition (i.e. for each

Table 1. The transition system for *T-Linda* (symmetric rules omitted).

R1 $\langle \mathsf{out}(a).P, m \rangle \xrightarrow{\sigma} \langle P, m \uplus \{a\} \rangle$

R2 $\langle \mathsf{in}(a).P, m \uplus \{a\} \rangle \xrightarrow{\sigma} \langle P, m \rangle$

R3 $\langle \mathsf{rd}(a).P, m \uplus \{a\} \rangle \xrightarrow{\sigma} \langle P, m \uplus \{a\} \rangle$

R4 $\langle \mathsf{rdp}(a)_t?P\_Q, m \uplus \{a\} \rangle \xrightarrow{\sigma} \langle P, m \uplus \{a\} \rangle$ $t > 0$

R5 $\langle \mathsf{rdp}(a)_t?P\_Q, m \rangle \xrightarrow{\sigma} \langle \mathsf{rdp}(a)_{t-1}?P\_Q, m \rangle$ $t > 0$ and $a \notin m$

R6 $\langle \mathsf{rdp}(a)_t?P\_Q, m \rangle \xrightarrow{\tau} \langle \mathsf{rdp}(a)_{t-1}?P\_Q, m \rangle$ $t > 0$

R7 $\langle \mathsf{rdp}(a)_0?P\_Q, m \rangle \xrightarrow{\sigma} \langle Q, m \rangle$

R8 $\dfrac{\langle P, m \rangle \xrightarrow{x} \langle P', m' \rangle \quad \langle Q, m \rangle \xrightarrow{\tau} \langle Q', m \rangle \quad x \in \{\sigma, \tau\}}{\langle P \parallel Q, m \rangle \xrightarrow{x} \langle P' \parallel Q', m' \rangle}$

R9 $\dfrac{\langle P, m \rangle \xrightarrow{x} \langle P', m' \rangle \quad \langle Q, m \rangle \xrightarrow{\tau} \!\!\!\!\!/ \quad x \in \{\sigma, \tau\}}{\langle P \parallel Q, m \rangle \xrightarrow{x} \langle P' \parallel Q, m' \rangle}$

R10 $\dfrac{\langle P, m \rangle \xrightarrow{\sigma} \langle P', m' \rangle}{\langle P + Q, m \rangle \xrightarrow{\sigma} \langle P', m' \rangle}$

R11 $\dfrac{\langle P, m \rangle \xrightarrow{\tau} \langle P', m \rangle \quad \langle Q, m \rangle \xrightarrow{\tau} \langle Q', m \rangle}{\langle P + Q, m \rangle \xrightarrow{\tau} \langle P' + Q', m \rangle}$

R12 $\dfrac{\langle P, m \rangle \xrightarrow{\tau} \langle P', m \rangle \quad \langle Q, m \rangle \xrightarrow{\tau} \!\!\!\!\!/}{\langle P + Q, m \rangle \xrightarrow{\tau} \langle P' + Q, m \rangle}$

R13 $\dfrac{\langle P, (m \downarrow a) \uplus d \rangle \xrightarrow{x} \langle Q, m' \rangle \quad x \in \{\sigma, \tau\}}{\langle P^d \setminus a, m \rangle \xrightarrow{x} \langle Q^{m'\uparrow a} \setminus a, (m' \downarrow a) \uplus (m \uparrow a) \rangle}$

R14 $\dfrac{\langle P[\mathsf{recX}.P/X], m \rangle \xrightarrow{x} \langle P', m' \rangle \quad x \in \{\sigma, \tau\}}{\langle \mathsf{recX}.P, m \rangle \xrightarrow{x} \langle P', m' \rangle}$

---

unit of time). This means that the access to the shared resource consisting of the global tuple space is granted to one process a time. However, time passes for all the processes appearing in the $\parallel$ context at the external level, as shown by rule **R8**, since τ-actions are allowed together with σ-actions. On the other hand, a parallel component is allowed to proceed in isolation if (and only if) the other parallel component cannot perform a τ-action (rule **R9**). To summarize, we adopt maximal parallelism for time elapsing (i.e. τ-actions) and an inter-leaving model for basic computation steps (i.e. σ-actions)[1]. Rules **R10** – **R12**

---

[1] Easy modifications allow to consider more liberal assumptions such as different durations for basic actions, multiple read actions in parallel, starting of time elapsing when the time-out process is scheduled.

define the behavior of the choice operator. Here, differently from the usual cases, when performing τ-actions we do not select a branch in the choice (rules **R11** and **R12**) because these actions, as previously mentioned, denote only the passing of time. Analogously to the case of the parallel operator, a process P in a choice P + Q can locally advance its time (i.e. perform τ-actions) only if no other activated process in Q requires passing of time. As specified by rule **R13**, the process P \ a behaves like P, with a considered *local* to P, i.e. the information on a provided by the external tuple space is hided to P and, conversely, the information on a produced locally by P is hided the external world. To describe locality in rule **R13** the syntax has been extended by a process P^d \ a where d is a local tuple space of P containing information on a which is hidden in the external store. Initially the local store is empty, i.e. P \ a = $P^\emptyset$ \ a. In this rule we use also the following notation: Given a multiset m, we denote by $m \downarrow a$ the multiset obtained from m by deleting all the occurrences of the tuple a and we denote by $m \uparrow a$ the multiset consisting only of the occurrences in m of the tuple a. Rule **R14** treats the case of a recursive definition in the usual way [2].

Using such a transition system we can then define the following notion of observables which considers the input/output behavior of terminating computations, including the deadlocked ones: $\mathcal{O}_{io}(P) = \{\langle m, m' \rangle \mid \langle P, m \rangle \xrightarrow{\sigma}{}^*$ $\langle Q, m' \rangle \not\xrightarrow{\sigma}\}$ where P be a T-Linda process and $\xrightarrow{\sigma}{}^*$ denotes the reflexive and transitive closure of the relation $\xrightarrow{\sigma}$. Note that we consider only sequences of transition steps which do not involve τ-steps, as these do not correspond to actions on the store. It is easy to see that the operational semantics which associates to a process A its observables $\mathcal{O}_{io}(A)$ is not compositional. A compositional characterization of the operational semantics is given in [4] by using, so called, timed reactive sequences to represent *Linda* computations.

3   Related and Future Work

The definition of specific process calculi to reason formally about Linda coordination languages is quite recent [6,7] and only [5] considers formally temporal aspects of these languages.

The main difference between our approach and that one in [5] is in the interpretation of the time-out construct. While we assume that once the elapsing of time for a time-out has started it cannot be interrupted, this is not the case for the construct considered in [5], since according to the operational semantics given in the latter paper the following situation is possible: Given the process A ∥ rdp(a)$_t$?P_Q, the evaluation of the time-out starts, say at time $t' = 0$, and waits m time units for the presence of the tuple a in the tuple space (assuming $t - m > 0$); then, at time $t' = m$, the control pass to A, which starts performing (an unbound number of) out and in operations. Later on the control passes again to the time-out process and time starts again elapsing from $t' = m$, since A is assumed not to consume any time. The authors motivate this choice with the fact that this is what happens in JavaSpaces. On the theoretical level this means that, similarly to what happens in many timed process algebras (e.g. [3]), actions

---

[2] The relation $\longrightarrow$ described by the rules in Table 1 is well defined since the transition system it is strictly stratifiable (see [9]).

and terms of the language are partitioned into instantaneous and time consuming ones, and implicitly out and in actions are considered being instantaneous, since a global notion of time is considered[3]. To our opinion, in a Linda like setting out and in actions should not considered instantaneous, as these are the basic computational steps. For this reason we assumed that these operations take one time unit. This, together with the fact that elapsing of (global) time, once started, should not be interrupted, led us to the definition of the time-out that we discussed in the previous sections.

Future work includes an extension of our approach in order to take into account also preemption mechanisms and the study of temporal aspects in the context of Klaim, a language for mobile computing based on the Linda paradigm, since the implementation of this language include already a notion of time-out [1].

References

1. L Bettini, R. De Nicola, G.-L. Ferrari and R. Pugliese. Interactive Mobile Agents in X-Klaim. In *Proc. of the Seventh IEEE International Workshop on Enabling Technologies: Infrastructure for Collaborative Enterprises* (WETICE'98), pp.110-115, IEEE Computer Society, 1998.
2. F. S. de Boer, M. Gabbrielli, and M. C. Meo. A Timed Concurrent Constraint Language. *Information and Computation*, 2000. To appear.
3. P. Bremond-Gregoire and I. Lee. A Process Algebra of Communicating Shared Resources with Dense Time and Priorities. *Theoretical Computer Science* 189, 1997.
4. F. S. de Boer, M. Gabbrielli, and M. C. Meo. A denotational semantics for Timed Linda. Draft.
5. N. Busi, R. Gorrieri, and G. Zavattaro. Process Calculi for Coordination: from Linda to JavaSpaces. Proc. of 8-th International Conference on Algebraic Metodology and Software Technology. *Lecture Notes in Computer Science*. Springer-Verlag, 2000. To appear.
6. N. Busi, R. Gorrieri and G. Zavattaro. A Process Algebraic View of Linda Coordination Primitives. *Theoretical Computer Science*, 192(2):167-199, 1998.
7. R. De Nicola and R. Pugliese. Linda based Applicative and Imperative Process Algebras. To appear in *Theoretical Computer Science*, 2000.
8. D. Gelernter. Generative communication in Linda. *ACM Transcations on Programming Languages and Systems*, 70(1): 80-112, 1985.
9. J.F. Groote. Transition system specifications with negative premises. *Theoretical Computer Scince*, 118: 263-299, 1993.
10. M. Hennessy and T. Regan. A temporal process algebra. *Information and Computation*, 117: 221-239, 1995.
11. V.A. Saraswat, M. Rinard, and P. Panangaden. Semantic Foundation of Concurrent Constraint Programming. In *Proc. Eighteenth ACM Symposium on Principles of Programming Languages*, pages 333-353. ACM Press, 1991.
12. V.A. Saraswat, R. Jagadeesan, and V. Gupta Timed Default Concurrent Constraint Programming. *Journal of Symbolic Computation*, 22(5-6):475–520, 1996.
13. Sun Microsystem, Inc. JavaSpaces Specifications, 1998.
14. P. Wyckoff, S.W. McLaughry, T.J. Lehman, and D.A. Ford. TSpaces. *IBM Systems Journal*, 37(3), 1998.

---

[3] However, the authors in [5] consider also a possible local notion of time.

The LuCe Coordination Technology for MAS Design and Development on the Internet

Andrea Omicini, Enrico Denti, and Vladimiro Toschi

LIA, Laboratorio di Informatica Avanzata
DEIS - Università di Bologna
Viale Risorgimento, 2 40136 – Bologna, Italy
{edenti,aomicini,vtoschi}@deis.unibo.it

Abstract. Internet-based multi-agent systems call for new metaphors, abstractions, methodologies and *enabling technologies* specifically tailored to agent-oriented engineering. While *coordination models* define the framework to manage the space of agent interaction, ruling social behaviours and accomplishing social tasks, their impact on system design and development calls for an effective *coordination technology*. This paper presents LuCe, a coordination technology that integrates Java, Prolog and the notion of *logic tuple centre*, a programmable coordination medium, into a coherent framework. The power of the LuCe coordination technology is first discussed in general, then shown in the context of a simple yet significant system: a TicTacToe game among intelligent software agents and human players on the Internet.

1 Introduction

Multi-agent systems (MAS) are becoming an ubiquitous paradigm for building complex software applications, introducing in the AI field new issues coming from the Software Engineering area, such as the need for models and methodologies for MAS engineering, and the availability of *enabling technologies* [5]. This convergence results in a new research area, called *multi-agent system engineering* [9]. There, the emphasis is put on *task-oriented design*, where the global system goals are delegated to the responsibility of either individual agents (*individual tasks*) or agent societies (*social tasks*) [3,20,13].

While *coordination* deals in general with managing the interaction among components [16], in this context it addresses the issue of how agents interact: as agent architectures and languages [21] support the design and development of individual agents [14], *coordination models* [12,2,10,4,17,18,19] provide the metaphors and abstractions required to build agent societies [1]. In particular *coordination media*, which embed social rules as coordination laws, can work as the core for agent societies pursuing social tasks. However, coordination models alone cannot face the intrinsic complexity of building agent societies: the full exploitation of a coordination model for the design and development of multi-agent social behaviour requires a suitable *coordination system*, providing engineers with the enabling technology they need.

A. Porto and G.-C. Roman (Eds.): COORDINATION 2000, LNCS 1906, pp. 305–310, 2000.

This paper discusses how a *coordination technology* [1] like the LuCe (Logic Tuple Centres) coordination system can be exploited for the engineering of Internet-based MAS, exploiting the model's metaphors to provide ad-hoc development tools. As a case-study, we discuss a TicTacToe game among intelligent software agents and human players on the Internet, showing how the LuCe technology can effectively support the system design and development.

2   LuCe: Model and Technology

LuCe agents interact by exchanging *logic tuples* through a multiplicity of communication abstractions called *tuple centres*. The communication language is based on first-order logic: a tuple is a Prolog ground fact, any unitary Prolog clause is an admissible tuple template, and unification is the tuple matching mechanism. Agents perceive a LuCe tuple centre as a logic tuple space [11], which can be accessed through the typical Linda-like operations (out, in, rd, inp, rdp). Each tuple centre is uniquely identified by a ground Prolog term, and any ground term can be used to denote a tuple centre.

What makes a tuple centre different from a tuple space is the notion of *behaviour specification*, which defines how a tuple centre reacts to an incoming/outgoing communication event. From the agent's viewpoint, a tuple centre looks like a tuple space, and is accessed via the same interface: however, the tuple centre's behaviour in response to communication events is not fixed once and for all, but can be extended so as to embed the coordination laws into the coordination medium [6]. In particular, LuCe adopts the tuple centre model defined in [7], where the behaviour is defined in terms of *reactions* to communication events, expressed as first-order logic tuples, the *specification tuples*.

So, a logic tuple centre is conceptually structured in two parts: the *tuple space*, with ordinary communication tuples, and the *specification space*, with specification tuples. Agents can then be designed around their individual tasks, defining interaction protocols according to their own perception of the interaction space: tuple centres' coordination laws will take care of "gluing things together".

The clear distinction between the coordinating entities (tuple centres) and the coordinated entities (agents) naturally decouples individual and social tasks: the system social behaviour can then be changed just by changing the specification tuples. Moreover, the same coordination rules can be reused for other problems of the same class, applying the same behaviour specification to a different domain.

As far as technology is concerned, the LuCe system is built around three major ingredients: the Java technology (for the system development and the Web interface), Prolog, as the *lingua franca* for communication among heterogeneous Web agents, and tuple centre technology, exploited as the core of the LuCe system. In terms of development tools, since a tuple centre is characterised at any time by the set T of its tuples, the set W of its pending queries, and the set S of its reaction specifications, LuCe supplies a set of *Inspectors* to view, edit and control tuple centres from the data, the pending query and the specification viewpoints.

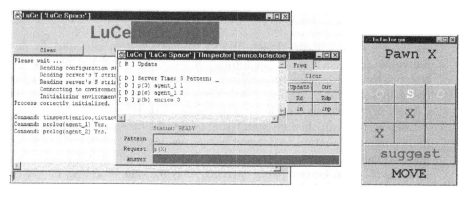

Fig. 1. A LuCe T Inspector in front of the LuCe console (left) and a GUI agent after asking for a suggestion (right)

The **T Inspector** is the tuple tracer/editor: as a tracer, it captures the state transitions of a tuple centre and shows the current state of the space T of tuples. As an editor, it allows the user to add, read or remove tuples via the standard communication primitives (*in, out, rd,* etc). Since user operations must be indistinguishable from agent ones, users cannot add or delete tuples directly: they can only perform communication operations via the proper buttons, so that any associated reactions are triggered. This is crucial to actually mimic agent's operations, so that tracing can be faithful. Other controls (see Fig. 1, centre) configure the tool's refresh frequency (how often the view should be updated, in terms of tuple centre transitions), and filtering options (which tuples to show).

The **W Inspector** is the pending query tracer, and works very much like the T Inspector: however, it provides users with the communication viewpoint in a *control-oriented* fashion, unlike the *data-oriented* fashion of the T Inspector.

The **S Inspector** is the specification editor: its purpose is to let users write reactions in a file, edit them, and reload the new specifications when done. So, no tuple space operations (*in, out, rd,* etc) are supported. Rather, it provides the user with buttons to *Consult, Edit, Update* and *Save* a specification set.

3   The Case Study: TicTacToe

The TicTacToe game is played on a grid of 3 × 3 cells by two players, namely circles (o) and crosses (x). Each player aims to put three pieces as to fill a line of the grid (vertically, horizontally or diagonally), while trying to prevent the other from doing the same. The application scenario is a Internet-based TicTacToe arena, where players can enter the game arena at any time, and must be ensured to find a game and an opponent – a human one, if available, or a software agent, if needed. Despite of its simplicity, the TicTacToe application features many of the typical issues of Internet-based multi-agent systems, yet it is simple enough to show the impact of the LuCe technology in a few pages.

3.1 Design by Tasks

As discussed in [14], the design of a multi-agent system can start by defining individual and social tasks: the former are to be delegated to single agents, the latter to the coordination media. Here, tasks include concurrently managing several games, enabling new players to enter a game (and always find an opponent), asking for suggestions, and leaving the game at their will.

The system can then be built using two agent categories: *GUI agents*, handling human interaction, and *expert agents*, owning the logic for playing, suggesting, and validating moves. More precisely, there will be one GUI agent (written in Java) for each human being currently playing, one expert agent (written in Prolog) for each game currently played, and a single *master agent* to start the multi-agent system and activate a new expert agent for every newly-created game. The `tictactoe` tuple centre stores game information and implements the desired coordination laws, bridging between the different domain representations.

3.2 Individual Tasks and Interaction Protocols

Once agents are assigned a task, their interaction protocols can be defined according to simple information-oriented criteria: which information is available / needed and when, how it is represented / accessed, etc. Given the uncoupling of agents induced by tuple-based coordination [12,8], each agent can be developed separately, using Inspectors to simulate the effects of the missing agents.

The Master Agent. The master agent's task consists of initialising the tuple centre and starting a new expert agent for every newly-created game. Initialisation is made by emitting an `init(TupleList)` tuple: it is the tuple centre's task to turn this into a set of single tuples. Then, the master starts repeatedly performing an `in(newGame(ID))` tuple, representing the need for the creation of a new TicTacToe game. Whenever such a tuple is found, the master agent activates a new expert agent for the newly-created game *ID*.

The Expert Agent. Each expert is dedicated to a single game: it validates human players' moves, plays in place of a human player (if needed), and suggests moves (if required). Since the logic for making and suggesting a move is the same, the expert actually needs to be able to perform only the first two tasks: turning its ability into a move or a suggestion is up to the coordination medium, in function of the current coordination state.

The expert agent is naturally written in Prolog. Basically, it repeatedly consumes `expertTask(+ID,-Task)` tuples, and performs the indicated *Task*. If *Task* is `validate(+GridS,+Role,+Move)`, the agent validates the *Move* and emits either an `invalid/2` or a `valid/4` tuple. If, instead, *Task* is `play(+GridS, +Role)`, the expert proposes a move according to the *GridS* status of game *ID*, emitting an `expertMove/5` tuple. Finally, if *Task* is `quit`, the expert just quits.

The GUI Agent. Each GUI agent represents a human player acting via an Internet browser. On startup, it tries to join the game arena by performing an `in(joinGame(-ID,-Role))` operation, getting its game *ID* and *Role*. Then, it starts capturing the game status in terms of a statusView(*ID* ,*Role* ,*GridS* , *Turn*) tuple, and displays it. *Turn* may be either *opponentTurn* or *yourTurn*: in the first case the agent just restarts its main loop, otherwise three commands are enabled: making a move, asking for a suggestion, and leaving the game.

The first two tasks cause an in(humanMove(*+ID* , *+Role* , *+Move* , *-OK*)) or an in(suggest(*+ID*, *+Role*, *-Move*)) operation to be performed, respectively: the returned tuple will contain either the validation by the expert agent (i.e., *OK* is true or false), or the proposed *Move*. The suggestion is shown as an 'S' on the GUI grid (Fig. 1, right). The intention of leaving the game, instead, just causes a leaveGame(*+ID*, *+Role*) tuple to be output, then the agent terminates.

3.3 Social Tasks

Tuple centres store the domain knowledge, mediate amongst the different agent's domain perceptions, and rule agent interaction so as to carry out the multi-agent system's social tasks. In the following, we just sketch the main related issues: for a deeper discussion and the full specification, we forward the reader to [15].

Domain Representation. The fundamental information concerns each game's status: as long as game *ID* is running, a gameStatus(*ID* ,*MoveNo* ,*GridS* ,*GameS* , *Next*) tuple represents the status *GameS* of game *ID* after move *MoveNo* has been performed, while waiting for the next move from player *Next* (x or o). The presence of a freeRole(*ID* ,*Role*) tuple indicates that no human player is playing as *Role* in game *ID*, which is therefore played by the expert agent. When the game ends, the gameStatus tuple is replaced by either a win(*ID* ,*Role* ,*MoveNo* , *GridS*) or a stalemate(*ID* ,*MoveNo* ,*GridS*) tuple, respectively.

Agent Perception. Each agent interaction protocol is designed around the agent's perception of the interaction space, and is independent both of the other agents' protocols and of the actual information representation in terms of tuples in tictactoe. For instance, GUI agents perceive the game status as statusView/4 tuples, though such tuples do not actually exist: they are dynamically produced in response to the agent's requests to consume them, according to tictactoe's coordination laws. In the development and test phases, this portion of the tictactoe behaviour specification may be tested via the S and T Inspectors, using their controls to simulate the actions of the missing agents.

Social Behaviour. The tuple centre embeds the social rules to drive agents' mutual interaction. For instance, a social behaviour is to ensure that any human player can always enter the game arena and find an opponent: no single agent could take care of this task, since master and expert agents have no human interface, while GUI agents are pure interface agents. This social behaviour is achieved by means of proper reactions, which intercept the in(joinGame(...)) operation, and exploit the freeRole tuple to produce the proper joinGame response – creating a new game if no freeRole exists.

All the other social tasks, including handling game end, validating and suggesting moves, enabling human players to enter and quit games transparently, are implemented analogously, as shown in [15].

References

1. P. Ciancarini. Coordination models and languages as software integrators. *ACM Computing Surveys*, 28(2):300–302, June 1996.
2. P. Ciancarini and C. Hankin, editors. *Coordination Languages and Models – Proc. of the 1st International Conference (COORDINATION'96)*, volume 1061 of *LNCS*, Cesena (I), 1996. Springer-Verlag.
3. P. Ciancarini, A. Omicini, and F. Zambonelli. Multiagent system engineering: the coordination viewpoint. In N. R. Jennings and Y. Lespérance, editors, *Intelligent Agents VI — Agent Theories, Architectures, and Languages*, volume 1767 of *LNAI*, pages 250–259. Springer-Verlag, 2000.
4. P. Ciancarini and A. L. Wolf, editors. *Coordination Languages and Models – Proceedings of the 3rd International Conference (COORDINATION'99)*, volume 1594 of *LNCS*, Amsterdam (NL), 1999. Springer-Verlag.
5. M. Cremonini, A. Omicini, and F. Zambonelli. Multi-agent systems on the Internet: Extending the scope of coordination towards security and topology. In *[9]*, pages 77–88, 1999.
6. E. Denti, A. Natali, and A. Omicini. Programmable coordination media. In *[10]*, pages 274–288, 1997.
7. E. Denti, A. Natali, and A. Omicini. On the expressive power of a language for programming coordination media. In *[17]*, pages 169–177, 1998.
8. E. Denti and A. Omicini. Designing multi-agent systems around a programmable communication abstraction. In J.-J. C. Meyer and P.-Y. Schobbens, editors, *Formal Models of Agents*, volume 1760 of *LNAI*, pages 90–102. Springer-Verlag, 1999.
9. F. J. Garijo and M. Boman, editors. *Multi-Agent Systems Engineering – Proc. of the 9th European Workshop on Modelling Autonoumous Agents in a Multi-Agent World (MAMAAW'99)*, volume 1647 of *LNAI*, Valencia (E), 1999. Springer-Verlag.
10. D. Garlan and D. Le Métayer, editors. *Coordination Languages and Models – Proceedings of the 2nd International Conference (COORDINATION'97)*, volume 1282 of *LNCS*, Berlin (D), 1997. Springer-Verlag.
11. D. Gelernter. Generative communication in Linda. *ACM Transactions on Programming Languages and Systems*, 7(1):80–112, January 1985.
12. D. Gelernter and N. Carriero. Coordination languages and their significance. *Communications of the ACM*, 35(2):97–107, February 1992.
13. F. Hattori, T. Ohguro, M. Yokoo, S. Matsubara, and S. Yoshida. Socialware: Multiagent systems for supporting network communities. *Comm. of the ACM*, 42(3):55–61, March 1999. Special Section on Multiagent Systems on the Net.
14. N. E. Jennings. Agent-oriented engineering. In *[9]*, pages 1–7, 1999. Invited talk.
15. LuCe home page. http://lia.deis.unibo.it/research/LuCe/.
16. T. Malone and K. Crowstone. The interdisciplinary study of coordination. *ACM Computing Surveys*, 26(1):87–119, 1994.
17. *Proc. of the 1998 ACM Symposium on Applied Computing (SAC'98)*, Atlanta (GA), 1998. ACM. Track on Coordination Models, Languages and Applications.
18. *Proc. of the 1999 ACM Symposium on Applied Computing (SAC'99)*, San Antonio (TX), 1999. ACM. Track on Coordination Models, Languages and Applications.
19. *Proc. of the 2000 ACM Symposium on Applied Computing (SAC 2000)*, Como (I), 2000. ACM. Track on Coordination Models, Languages and Applications.
20. M. P. Singh. Agent communication languages: Rethinking the principles. *IEEE Computer*, 31(12):55–61, December 1998.
21. M. Woolridge and N. R. Jennings. Intelligent agents: Theory and practice. *The Knowledge Engineering Review*, 10(2):115–152, 1995.

Scoped Coordination
in Open Distributed Systems

Iain Merrick and Alan Wood

University of York, United Kingdom
{im,wood}@cs.york.ac.uk

Abstract. This paper describes an efficient implementation of Scope, a coordination language for open distributed systems. We use distributed broadcasts for the IN primitive, which allows tuples to be placed on the most appropriate node and easily migrated. We test the performance of our reference implementation over a geographically-distributed network, and show how scopes can used to optimise the placement of tuples, minimising the effects of network latency and making full use of available bandwidth.

1 Introduction

This paper builds on work previously published in [8], where we proposed a coordination language based on 'scopes'. We will now show how this language, which we will refer to here as Scope, can be implemented efficiently in a distributed system. To back up our assertions, we also present some performance figures from our reference implementation. Due to space limitations, we do not discuss low-level details of our reference implementation in this paper.

1.1 Scope

Beginning with a minimal version of Linda [6], we replace tuplespaces with *scopes*, which can be regarded as sets of atomic names. We add some primitives to manipulate these sets: NEW creates a fresh name, and returns a singleton set containing that name; ADD performs a set union on two scopes, and SUB performs set difference. To test whether two scopes match, we test whether they have an element—an atomic name—in common. The null scope, which contains no names, does not match anything (including itself).

To summarise, Scope has the following primitive operations:

1. NEW: create a new scope, which does not match any other scope.
2. ADD(x,y): construct the scope $x + y$, which matches both x and y.
3. SUB(x,y): construct the scope $x - y$, which does not match y.
4. OUT(s,v): output the tuple (scope-value pair) (s, v).
5. IN(s,p): retrieve a tuple (s', v), where scope s' matches scope s and value v matches pattern p (in the normal Linda manner).

For a fuller explanation of this model, see [8].

A. Porto and G.-C. Roman (Eds.): COORDINATION 2000, LNCS 1906, pp. 311–316, 2000.
© Springer-Verlag Berlin Heidelberg 2000

1.2   Related Work

The growth of the Internet has sparked renewed interest in Linda as a coordination language for distributed computing, primarily in combination with the Java. (See [4] for an overview of this trend.) Such systems fall into two main categories: client-server systems, and mobile agent systems.

In **client-server** systems such as JavaSpaces [7] and TSpaces [5], a persistent server acts as a coordination medium for short-lived client processes. However, this centralisation can become a bottleneck, particularly in geographically distributed systems where a client may have a very poor connection to the server. In principle, this can be solved by distributing the server across several machines, but in practice this is difficult and rarely done. One of the few *working* distributed servers is WCL [11], which stores each tuplespace on a single node. Tuplespaces can be migrated to different machines at run-time, but no finer-grained migration is possible.

Mobile agent systems allow programs ('agents') to migrate around a persistent, distributed server. Agent-based coordination languages generally incorporate the concept of *location*, so that migration can be controlled by the programmer. Thus KLAIM [9] has 'localities', abstract locations which are mapped to physical locations by the kernel; H-KLAIM [1] and Bauhaus Linda [3] use hierarchical abstract locations; Lime [10] associates tuplespaces with agents rather than locations, merging the tuplespaces of agents at a given node into a single virtual tuplespace. However, we find that it is often inconvenient for the programmer to have to deal with explicit locations.

2   Implementing Scope

2.1   Tuple Placement and Migration

Scopes can overlap arbitrarily, so we cannot simply map them onto network nodes. Instead, we allow any tuple to be situated at any node of the network. This allows the OUT primitive to be implemented very cheaply: it simply places the newly-created tuple on our local node. (See figure 1.)

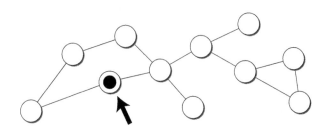

Fig. 1. OUT places a tuple in a node's local kernel space.

The IN primitive checks whether a matching tuple is held locally, then send a query to each of its neighbours. Each node which receives a query checks whether it has seen the query before, then whether it has a matching tuple; if not, it forwards the request onto its other neighbours. With a well-chosen topology, the request can be propagated through the network quickly and efficiently. (See figure 2.)

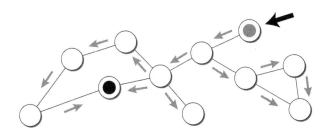

Fig. 2. IN broadcasts a query across the network.

If a node receives a query which matches a tuple it holds, it migrates the tuple onto whichever neighbouring node sent the query. This node in turn will pass the tuple 'against the arrows', and so on until it finally reaches the node which originally performed the IN. The tuple is then supplied to the user's program as the result of its IN call. (See figure 3.)

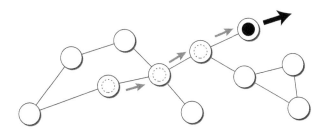

Fig. 3. Tuples migrate against the flow of an IN broadcast.

The NEW, ADD and SUB) primtives do not use the network at all: they simply manipulate sets of atomic names. Our implementation strategy has several other useful properties:

Locality—Each node only needs to know how to communicate with its neighbours; it need not even be aware of the existence of the remainder of the network. This is a desirable property for open systems.

Asynchrony—All messages passed between nodes are asynchronous, and ordering is unimportant. This allows us to avoid 'hand-shaking', which is particularly expensive in widely distributed systems.

Robustness—All messages are individually meaningful. A tuple is normally migrated in response to a query, but if there is no matching query the receiver will simply store the tuple in its local kernel space. This also means that tuples can be migrated at any time.

2.2   Cost Analysis

The use of a network-wide broadcast for each IN is less wasteful than it may seem. Note that in a geographically-distributed network, latency is often 100ms or more (noticeable even to humans), while bandwidth is usually only a bottleneck when sending large chunks of data. CPU cycles are almost always cheap and in plentiful supply.

When a query is broadcast, latency is only important if it delays the process which requires the result. It requires at least a round-trip journey for the result to filter back to the querying node, but the delays involved in forwarding unused queries are not important. These useless queries do use up bandwidth, but most queries are quite small; the response may be large, but it is not replicated or migrated unnecessarily.

Therefore, broadcasts need not significantly increase the cost of an IN. Note that they can be pruned in a tree-like topology. Moreover, the cost can be reduced drastically by pre-emptively migrating the tuple close to the node which will consume it; if the tuple is migrated onto the consuming node *before it is required*, the time spent blocking on the IN is essentially nil.

2.3   Example: A Notify Daemon

To demonstrate the expressiveness of our model, and explore the efficiency of our implementation, we will now show how to create a 'NOTIFY daemon' which emulates the NOTIFY primitive. Originally introduced in JavaSpaces[7], NOTIFY allows a process to install a callback function in tuplespace, which will be invoked when a specified event occurs. Its main use is to asynchronously notify a process when a new tuple arrives, by attaching a callback to OUT events. Busi and Zavattaro explore the expressiveness of this primitive in [2].

To emulate NOTIFY, we make available a well-known scope N which is used to look for new tuples. Processes ADD this scope to their own scopes if they wish their tuples to be 'notifiable'. This can be done immediately after each NEW; a wrapper function might be provided to do so automatically. Thus where a process would normally OUT a tuple in scope a, it now does so in $(a + N)$.

The NOTIFY daemon is a process which repeatedly tries to IN a tuple from the scope N. Having found one, it strips off the N with SUB and restores the modified tuple with OUT. It then consults its registry and passes a copy of the tuple to processes which registered an interest in tuples of that form. For a user process, then, 'calling NOTIFY' means registering oneself with the daemon process. Implementation of the registry is trivial.

This is not a perfect emulation of NOTIFY. JavaSpaces promises to invoke callbacks on *every* occurence of the relevant event, whereas our daemon might not get a chance to look at a new tuple before it is removed by another process. However, our scheme has the advantage of configurability: we can hide certain clients from NOTIFY, ask for notification of tuples which were created before we registered with the daemon, and so on. JavaSpaces' hard-coded NOTIFY does not permit such enhancements.

The daemon should be situated on some reasonably centralised node, so that its IN-OUT loop does not pull all the tuples out into the periphery of the network. Alternatively, we might employ several daemons at strategic locations, and enhance them with heuristics for optimising the distribution of tuples over the network.

3   Performance Analysis

To test our implementation, we loaded a server node with a large quantity of tuples, and on a remote node ran a process which retrieved multiple tuples with IN. We measured the time taken from just before the first IN (after the connection was established) until the return of the final IN. The server was situated in Scotland, and the client in the United States: at the time of testing, ping reported a round-trip time between the two machines of 210–220 milliseconds.

We measured the time taken to retrieve different quantities of tuples, in increments of 50, with both small (50 byte) and large (2KB) tuples. We also ran the program both with and without a scope-based optimisation: the tuples on the server were 'marked' with an extra scope, and an extra process on the client eagerly migrated tuples in this scope closer to the consumer. Note that we did not need to modify the consumer itself. Results are shown in figure 4.

The unoptimised program settled down into query-response handshaking, and was therefore limited by the 200ms latency. The optimised version successfully worked round this problem, running ten or fifteen times more quickly. Thus, our reference implementation can work efficiently in fairly realistic conditions,

| Number | Unoptimised | | Optimised | |
of tuples	Small tuples	Large tuples	Small tuples	Large tuples
50	11	37	1	4
100	22	71	2	6
150	33	107	4	9
200	44	142	7	10
250	54	178	16	13
300	65	208	11	14

Fig. 4. Time taken (in seconds) to retrieve a series of tuples over a slow connection.

and is capable of fully exploiting the available bandwidth. We think the results from this trivial program should scale to more substantial programs, but this has still to be verified.

4 Conclusion

We have presented a strategy for implementing Scope in an open distributed system, while preserving many of the advantages of closed-system Linda: users are presented with an intuitive location-free model; the kernel has a large degree of freedom in deciding which objects to place where, and when. A similar strategy might be used to implement a conventional Linda system, but we believe we have justified the addition of scopes in terms of both expressiveness (by emulating NOTIFY) and efficiency (by implementing an effective networking optimisation).

We plan to stengthen and extend our implementation to support a number of future projects, including optimisations along the lines discussed in section 3. We also intend to produce a set of formal semantics for the coordination model, having deliberately kept the model very simple to render it tractable to formal analysis. This would help bridge the gap between existing formal models and real-world implementations of Linda-like systems.

References

[1] L. Bettini, M. Loreti, and R. Pugliese. Structured nets in KLAIM. In *Proceedings of the 2000 ACM Symposium on Applied Computing*, pages 174–180. ACM, March 2000.

[2] N. Busi and G. Zavattaro. Event notification in data-driven coordination languages: Comparing the ordered and unordered interpretations. In *Proc. of the 2000 ACM Symposium on Applied Computing*, pages 233–239. ACM, March 2000.

[3] N. Carriero, D. Gelernter, and L. Zuck. Bauhaus Linda. In *Object-based models and languages for concurrent systems*, Lecture Notes in Computer Science. Springer-Verlag, 1995.

[4] P. Ciancarini, A. Omici, and F. Zambonelli. Coordination technologies for Internet agents. *Nordic Journal of Computing*, 6(3):215–240, 1999.

[5] D. Ford, T. Lehman, S. McLaughry, and P. Wyckoff. TSpaces. *IBM systems journal*, 37(3):454–474, Aug 1998.

[6] D. Gelernter. Generative communication in Linda. *ACM Transactions on Programming Language Systems*, 7(1):80–112, January 1985.

[7] Java Systems East. JavaSpace specification. Technical report, Sun Microsystems, June 1997.

[8] I. Merrick and A. Wood. Coordination with scopes. In *Proceedings of the 2000 ACM Symposium on Applied Computing*, pages 210–217. ACM, March 2000.

[9] R. D. Nicola, G. Ferrari, and R. Pugliese. KLAIM: a kernel language for agents interaction and mobility. *IEEE Trans. on Software Engineering*, 24(5):315–330, 1998.

[10] G. Picco, A. Murphy, and G. C. Roman. Lime: Linda meets mobility. Technical Report WUCS-98-21, Washington University, 1998.

[11] A. Rowstron. WCL: a co-ordination language for geographically distributed agents. *World Wide Web Journal*, 1(3):167–179, 1998.

Patterns for Coordination

L.F. Andrade[1], J.L. Fiadeiro[2,3*], J. Gouveia[1], A. Lopes[3], and M. Wermelinger[4]

[1] OBLOG Software S.A., Alameda António Sérgio 7 – 1 A,
2795 Linda-a-Velha, Portugal
{landrade,jgouveia}@oblog.pt

[2] Department of Computer Science, King's College London
Strand, London WC2R 2LS, UK
jose@fiadeiro.org

[3] Department of Informatics, Faculty of Sciences, University of Lisbon
Campo Grande, 1700 Lisboa, Portugal
mal@di.fc.ul.pt

[4] Dep. of Informatics, Fac. Sciences and Technology, New University of Lisbon
Quinta da Torre, 2825 Monte da Caparica, Portugal
mw@di.fct.unl.pt

1 Introduction

The separation between computation and coordination, as proposed by recent languages and models [7], has opened important new perspectives for supporting extendibility of systems, i.e. the possibility of adapting software systems to changes in requirements in an easy way. The evolutionary model that we have been developing is based on the representation of the more volatile aspects of the application domain like business rules as connectors whose purpose is to coordinate the interaction among core, more stable, components. The idea is that, in this way, evolution can be made to be compositional over the changes that occur in the application domain through the addition, deletion or substitution of connectors, without interfering with the services provided by the core objects of the system.

The applicability of this particular approach to evolution has been demonstrated in the field through the development of software systems in a number of domains using the OBLOG tool [www.oblog.com]. OBLOG provides a language and family of tools for supporting object-oriented development. One of the features that distinguish it from other products in the market is its collection of primitives for modelling the behavioural aspects of systems. These include the notion of *contract* [2], a semantic primitive corresponding to connectors as used in Software Architectures [1], which we brought into OO modelling as a means of supporting the coordination layer required by the approach that we described above.

Ideally, this method for evolving systems should be applicable regardless of the languages in which the core objects are programmed, thus allowing for the integration of third-party, closed components, like legacy systems. For such a general support to be possible, we need to abstract away from the specific coordination languages and

---

* On leave at (2) from (3) with the support of *Fundação para a Ciência e Tecnologia* and the *EPSRC*.

A. Porto and G.-C. Roman (Eds.): COORDINATION 2000, LNCS 1906, pp. 317-322, 2000.

models that have been proposed in the literature, universal principles that can be incorporated into a tool like OBLOG.

Our purpose in this paper is to relate progress that we have made so far into that endeavour. In section 2, we present a "mathematical pattern" that identifies essential mechanisms of coordination available in languages for parallel program design and architecture description. This pattern was used in [2] for giving semantics to contracts. In section 3, we present a design pattern that allows for such mechanisms to be implemented in platforms for component-based system development like CORBA, EJB and COM. This pattern was used for implementing contracts in OBLOG.

2   A Categorical Pattern for Coordination

Our mathematical approach to coordination was first outlined in [4]. It is based on the use of Category Theory as a means of formalising complex configurations of interconnected components, an approach that can be traced back to Goguen's work on General Systems Theory.   The basic motto of the categorical approach to systems is that morphisms can be used to express interaction between components, so that "given a category of widgets, the operation of putting a system of widgets together to form some super-widget corresponds to taking the colimit of the diagram of widgets that shows how to interconnect them" [5].

The specific application of this approach to coordination abstracts general principles from previous applications of categorical techniques to parallel program design centred on the notion of superposition [8]. In this approach, we assume that a notion of system (be it system specifications, models or designs) can be organised in a category SYS whose morphisms capture the relationship that exists between systems and their components (e.g. superposition). In this setting, we take the separation between coordination and computation to be materialised through a functor $int:SYS{\rightarrow}INT$ mapping the category of systems to a category of interfaces that represent the elements through which interconnections between system components can be established.

The fact that int "forgets" the computational aspects of systems, and that these do not play any role in the interconnections, is captured by the following properties:

> int is faithful;
> int lifts colimits;
> int has discrete structures.

The fact that int is faithful (injective over each hom-set), means that morphisms of systems cannot induce more relationships between systems than between their underlying interfaces. That is, by taking into consideration the computational part, we do not get additional observational power over the external behaviour of systems.

The second property means that, given any configuration diagram $dia:I{\rightarrow}SYS$ over systems and colimit $(int(S_i){\rightarrow}C)_{i:I}$ of $(dia;int)$, there exists a colimit $(S_i{\rightarrow}S)_{i:I}$ of dia such that $int(S_i{\rightarrow}S)=(int(S_i){\rightarrow}C)$. In other words, if we interconnect system components through a diagram, then any colimit of the underlying diagram of interfaces establishes an interface for which a computational part exists that captures the joint behaviour of the interconnected systems. This is a "correctness" result in the sense that it states that, by interconnecting the interfaces of systems, we are interconnecting the systems themselves.

The corresponding "completeness" result – that all interconnections can be established via interfaces – is given by the third property. The fact that *int* has discrete structures means that, for every interface $C:INT$ there exists a system $s(C):SYS$ such that, for every interface morphism $f:C \rightarrow int(S)$, there is a system morphism $g:s(C) \rightarrow S$ such that $int(g)=f$. That is to say, every interface C has a „realisation" (a discrete lift) as a system $s(C)$ in the sense that, using C to interconnect a component S, which is achieved through a morphism $f:C \rightarrow int(S)$, is tantamount to using $s(C)$ through any $g:s(C) \rightarrow S$ such that $int(g)=f$.

In this setting, interconnections are usually expressed through diagrams of the form

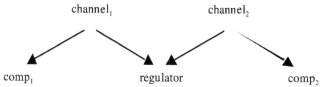

channel₁   channel₂

comp₁   regulator   comp₂

where the channels are of the form $s(C)$ for some interface C and the regulator is a component that superposes the coordination mechanisms that are required for regulating the interaction between the two components. See [2,3] for examples.

3   A Design Pattern for Coordination

The fact that a mathematical pattern exists for justifying our principle of supporting evolution through the superposition of connectors does not mean that it can be put into practice directly over the technology that is available today. In this section we show that, even if none of the standards for component-based software development that have emerged in the last few years (e.g. CORBA, EJB and COM) can provide a convenient and abstract way of supporting superposition as a first-class mechanism, an implementation can be given that is based on a design pattern that exploits some widely available properties of object-oriented programming languages such as polymorphism and subtyping.

Before we discuss the design pattern that we developed for coordination, we must point out that the level at which its "correctness" with respect to the mathematical pattern discussed in the previous section can be established is not a mathematical one. This is because neither the mathematical semantics nor mathematical abstractions of these platforms for component-based system development are available. Hence, we will argue for, rather than prove, its correctness. Furthermore, we did not take it as a task to "implement" the notions of object, morphism, colimit, etc. Instead, we have tried to make sure that the "spirit" of the mathematical solution was captured by the implementation pattern: we provide autonomous existence to interfaces, use these as a means for interconnecting programs, and ensure that interconnections are not lost by restricting them to the interfaces.

The class diagram below depicts the proposed pattern, based on well-known design patterns, namely the Proxy or Surrogate [6]. Its "correctness" relies on two main mechanisms. On the one hand, provision of a specific interface (*SubjectInterface*), as an abstract class, for every component. This interface is linked to the real program (*SubjectBody*) through a dynamically reconfigurable proxy reference. On the other hand, support for dynamic reconfiguration of the code executed upon requests for operations (including requests by *self* as in active objects), achieved through the proxy.

Reconfiguration of a predefined component (such as adapting the component for a specific use) or coordination of various components (such as behaviour synchronisation) is achieved by making the proxy reference a *polymorphic entity*. On the one hand, this proxy is provided with a *static type* at compile-time – the type with which this entity is declared (*ImplementationProxy*) – that complies with the interface of the component. On the other hand, the type of its values may vary at run-time through *Channel* as connectors are superposed or removed from the configuration of the system. These types, the ones that can be dynamically superposed, become the entity's *dynamic type* (dynamic binding).

The notion of dynamic binding means that, at run-time, such a proxy assumes different values of different types. However, when a request is made for services of the component, it is the dynamic binding mechanism of the underlying object-oriented language (e.g. C++, Java) that makes the choice of the operation implementation to execute (*SubjectBody* or *Channel*) based on the type to which the proxy belongs. Relying on this mechanism of later binding, the reconfiguration by superposition is implemented by (1) introducing the intended coordinated behaviour of the parties on *Regulator* objects, and (2) connecting them to the parties using the *Channel* objects as explained below.

In what follows, we explain, in more detail, the basic features of the pattern, starting with the participating classes.

SubjectInterface – as the name indicates, this is an abstract class (type) that defines the common interface of services provided by *ImplementationProxy* and *Subject*.

Subject – This is a concrete class that implements a broker maintaining a reference that lets the subject delegate received requests to the abstract implementation (*ImplementationProxy*) using the polymorphic entity proxy. At run-time, this entity may point to a *SubjectBody* if no regulator is active, or to the *Channel* that links the real subject to the regulators that coordinate its behaviour.

ImplementationProxy – This is an abstract class that defines the common interface of *SubjectBody* and *Channel*. The interface is inherited from *SubjectInterface* to guarantee that all these classes offer the same interface as *Subject* (the broker) with which clients of the real subject have to interact.

SubjectBody – This is the concrete domain class with the business logic that defines the real object that the broker represents. The concrete implementation of provided services is in this class.

Channel – This class maintains the interconnections between the real object (*SubjectBody*) and other components of the system. Adding or removing interconnections with the same real object does not require the creation of a new instance of this class but only of a new association with the new regulator and an instantiation link to the existing instance of *Channel*. This means that there is only one instance of this class associated with one instance of *SubjectBody*.

Regulator – This is an object that subsumes the coordination specified through the configuration diagrams defined in the previous section (colimit semantics); it is notified and takes decisions whenever a request is invoked on a real subject.

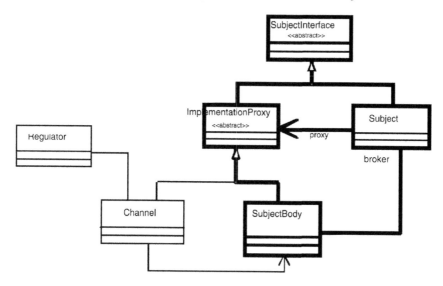

A typical execution of the pattern starts with a request for an operation of the object. Because clients interact with the real object via the broker, the call to any operation of the real object is handled by the broker *(Subject)*. The broker then uses the polymorphic entity proxy *(ImplementationProxy)* to delegate the execution on either the real object *SubjectBody*, or *Channel* if the real object is being coordinated. In the latter case, the *Channel* transfers the execution to the regulator which will then superpose whatever forms of coordination have been required.

Notice that superposing a new connector implies only modifications to the broker, making its proxy become a reference to the object that plays the role of channel. Doing only this minor modification, neither the code of clients nor the code of the broker and of the real object need to be modified in order to accommodate the new behaviour established by adding the connector.

4   Concluding Remarks

In this short paper, we outlined on-going work that explores some of the features made available by coordination models for supporting a discipline of system evolution that is compositional on the evolution of the application domain itself. The approach is based on the explicit identification, as first-class citizens, of the mechanisms that model business rules and other aspects of the application domain that require that the behaviour of its components be coordinated in order to achieve certain effects.

The solution that we found is based on a pattern that captures what in Software Architectures are called *connectors* [1] and implements what in Parallel Program Design is known as *superposition* [8]. In fact, our work consisted in abstracting from the concrete proposals that can be found in the literature, universal principles that capture the essence of these notions as far as their application to our evolutionary approach is concerned, and make it applicable to a wider range of languages and models.

This abstraction process was conducted in two directions. On the one hand, we searched for mathematical patterns that would capture the semantics of the coordination mechanisms that we wanted to make available in OBLOG. On the other hand, because the approach to evolution that we motivated above was developed in response to concrete needs for supporting development work in highly volatile business domains, we had to workout a way of making these coordination mechanisms available in concrete platforms for system development. As a result, a design pattern was developed that can make the proposed coordination mechanisms available over platforms for component-based system development like CORBA, EJB and COM. More specifically, the whole approach is supported by the OBLOG tool and has been tested in a variety of application domains. This design pattern was discussed in section 3. More examples are available in [2], where the notion of *contract* was proposed as an extension to the UML for representing connectors with the semantics discussed herein.

Further work is in progress, both in improving the evolutionary approach and its support through OBLOG, as well as in incorporating other associated mechanisms that we have developed over the proposed mathematical pattern. These include the mechanisms via which reconfiguration can be effectively performed dynamically [9].

References

1.   R.Allen and D.Garlan, "A Formal Basis for Architectural Connectors", *ACM TOSEM,* 6(3), 1997, 213-249.
2.   L.F.Andrade and J.L.Fiadeiro, "Interconnecting Objects via Contracts", in *UML'99 – Beyond the Standard*, R.France and B.Rumpe (eds), LNCS 1723, Springer Verlag 1999, 566-583.
3.   J.L.Fiadeiro and A.Lopes, "Semantics of Architectural Connectors", in *TAPSOFT'97*, LNCS 1214, Springer-Verlag 1997, 505-519.
4.   J.L.Fiadeiro and A.Lopes, "Algebraic Semantics of Coordination, or what is in a signature?", in *AMAST'98*, A.Haeberer (ed), Springer-Verlag 1999.
5.   J.Goguen, "A Categorical Manifesto", *Mathematical Structures in Computer Science* 1(1), 1991, 49-67.
6.   E.Gamma, R.Helm, R.Johnson and J.Vlissides, *Design Patterns: Elements of Reusable Object Oriented Software*, Addison-Wesley 1995.
7.   D.Gelernter and N.Carriero, "Coordination Languages and their Significance", *Communications ACM* 35, 2, pp. 97-107, 1992.
8.   S.Katz, "A Superimposition Control Construct for Distributed Systems", ACM TOPLAS 15(2), 1993, 337-356.
9.   M.Wermelinger and J.L.Fiadeiro, "Algebraic Software Architecture Reconfiguration" in *ESEC/FSE'90*, LNCS 1687, Springer-Verlag 1999, 393-409.

Coordination Models and Software Architectures in a Unified Software Development Process

Paola Inverardi[1] and Henry Muccini[1]

Dipartimento di Matematica
Universitá dell'Aquila
Via Vetoio, 1 - 67100 L'Aquila, Italy
e-mail{inverard, muccini}@univaq.it

Abstract. Coordination models and Software Architectures (SAs) have been recognized as valid tools to manage complex distributed systems. Coordination models and languages provide a specification level description of processes interaction, separating control issues from the computational concerns. Software Architectures provide a high level description of software components interactions designing applications as sets of autonomous, decoupled components. In this work we are going to present how Coordination models and SA can be linked together and how they can be integrated in a UML-based software development process ...

1 Introduction

In recent years, there has been a growing interest in software architectures (SAs) and coordination models. Although they play different roles in the software development life cycle strong similarities and analogies in concepts and finalities seem to hold [7]. SAs represent the first design step in which a complete system model is provided. They focus on the overall organization of a large software system (the glue) using abstractions of individual components and explicity modeling their interaction. Their description encompass both static and dynamic aspects of the system under design, from topology to inter-components communication descriptions. Coordination models instead, come in at a later development stage in order to provide a precise system specification. Their focus however is similar to SA since coordination models are specialized to describe process interaction in a concurrent environment abstracting away the details of computation and focusing on the interactions [3]. As a matter of fact at the SA description level, many important design choices related to the way components interact, are already taken. Thus (see Figure 1) SA level information can influence the static and dynamic structure of the implemented system and drive/constrain the coordination model specification.

In this work we are going to describe an extension to an our previous work [11] proposing a way to profitably and coherently relate these two system development phases. We cast our approach in a UML software development process [13] assuming that UML Diagrams can describe each step in the software development life-cycle [13,15,5,10]. Our approach allows us to use the SA model

A. Porto and G.-C. Roman (Eds.): COORDINATION 2000, LNCS 1906, pp. 323–328, 2000.

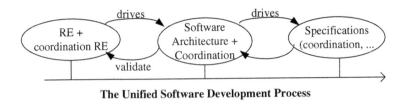

The Unified Software Development Process

Fig. 1. SA description drives Coordination models

to validate coordination requirements and to drive the generation of a correct (with respect to requirements) coordination model.

The paper is organized as follows: section 2 summarizes the generation of an analysis model starting from Use Cases; section 3 introduces software architectures. The approach is analyzed in section 4. Section 5 contains conclusions and future works.

The approach has been applied to the Teleservice and Remote Medical Care System (TRMCS) [4,11] case study, presented in the full version of this paper [12].

2   The Unified Software Development Process

A process defines *who* is doing *what, when* and *how* to reach a certain goal and serves as a guide for all participants in the software development. The Unified Process [13] is Use-Case driven, Architecture-Centric and, Iterative and Incremental. In this section we summarize only the process steps relevant to our approach: requirement capturing as Use Cases and Analysis model of Use Cases.

In the Unified Process, Use Cases drive the evolution of each development step. They capture functional requirements while Use Case Diagrams show how Use Cases are associated to Actors. *Use cases* represent a possible way of using the system while *actors* are who or what (humans or a subsystems) carry out use cases. Each user needs several different use cases, each representing the different ways he or she uses the system.

As a bridge between Requirements and Design Models an Analysis Model is generated to *realize* Use Cases. An Analysis model is a stereotyped [9] UML class diagram; it is composed of Analysis classes describing *how* a specific use case is realized in terms of "abstract" cooperating classes and associations between them. Analysis classes (in the following also simple called *classes*) always fit one of three basic stereotypes: **boundary, control** or **entity** (see Section 4). To create this model a set of use cases is selected and the analysis classes that participate in his realization are identified. Each class may participate and play roles in several use-case realizations.

So far, only the structure of objects implementing Use Cases has been found; nothing has been said on the interaction patterns. To understand how use cases are used by actors, Interaction Diagrams can be used. In particular, Collaboration Diagrams show how the focus control passes from object to object.

3   Software Architecture

Software architectures (SAs) represent the overall system structure by modeling individual components and their interactions. SAs support the formal modeling of a system allowing for both a topological (static) description and a behavioral (dynamic) one. The behavioral description provides means for an early in the life cycle validation of design choices, while the topological one can be used to carry on the development steps in a refinement (top-down) fashion, or to identify architectural components in a bottom-up fashion.

Thus, they naturally provide the right level of abstraction to express the logical coordination structure of complex distributed software.

Our approach assumes the existence of a formal definition of the Software Architecture encompassing both the static and the dynamic descriptions [8,1,14,6]. We assume that from an architectural description a Labelled Transition System (LTS) can be derived, whose node and arc labels represent respectively states and transitions relevant in the context of the SA dynamics. We also assume that states contain information about the single state of components and that labels on arcs denote relevant system state transitions. See [12] for the definitions.

The initial LTS state corresponds to the initial, static configuration of the system. Transition rules applied to the initial configuration define how the system dynamically evolves from its initial configuration, the label on an arc usually represents the event associated to the transition denoted by that arc. The set of final solutions represents the different possible states of the system in which the computation is considered to have completed. We also need the definition of a complete path: $p = S_0 \xrightarrow{l_1} S_1 \xrightarrow{l_2} S_2 \xrightarrow{l_3} \ldots \xrightarrow{l_n} S_n$. p is complete if S_0 is the initial state and S_n is a final one.

4   The Approach

Following the Unified Software Development Process [13] UML can be used to graphically depict the functional requirements and the high-level design of the system (as shown in Section 2).

In the following subsections we are going to identify how UML can be used to capture coordination policies at the Requirement level (Subsection 4.1), to understand how this information can be used to *drive* the SA description (Subsection 4.2) and how the SA can be used to *validate* Coordination requirements (Subsection 4.3). In Subsection 4.4 we briefly describe how the software architectural model can be subsequently used to *drive* a coordination model specification of the system and finally we summarize the approach (Figure 2).

4.1   UML Capturing Coordination

UML Interaction Diagram can be extracted on the Analysis model to represent possible execution scenarios [11]; each scenario represents one expected behavior

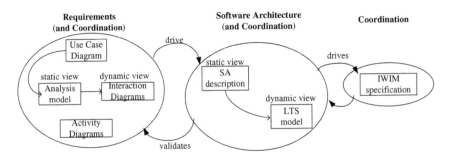

Fig. 2. From Requirements to Coordination models

(with respect to the coordination policies) and every scenario implicitly embodies the coordination policies. Interaction Diagrams can give information on the action sequencing but on how many processes are involved in the system, how they cooperate, how they synchronize. By the use of Activity Diagrams we can partially fix these problems putting in evidence how system functionalities can be grouped in several activities and how they can be sequenced. In the next Subsection we will show how the information captured in this first step can be propagated into the software architecture step.

4.2   From UML Diagrams to SA Model

We first need to identify the Components and the Connectors.

The Analysis model generated in section 2 can be a good starting point; each analysis class represents an abstract view of the system and is involved in conceptual relationships. Moreover, analysis classes always fit one of three basic stereotypes with the following semantics:

- boundary classes represent abstractions of windows, forms, communication interfaces;
- entity classes reflect logical data structure;
- control classes represent *coordination, sequencing, transactions and control of other objects*; they are used to encapsulate control related to a specific use case.

This model can be used to model the *topological* SA description but needs other information to describe the *dynamic interactions* architectural model: Activity Diagrams can be used for this goal. The underlying idea to generate an SA description from the Analysis model and the Activity Diagrams is the following:

- actors become components;
- control classes become *coordination* components; they will manage the coordination between several components and coordination components;
- each activity in the Activity Diagram has to be reflected in the SA; they can be used to specialize components or connectors.

4.3   Validating Interactions via SA Dynamic Model

Given the SA topological description, the software architect describes the system dynamics in terms of component and connectors. In our approach the SA dynamics is modeled by a Labelled Transition System (LTS). Each LTS complete path describes a possible execution scenario so that all LTS complete paths denote the set of all possible system behaviors. We can validate Analysis model Sequence Diagrams (SDs) by model checking them on the SA LTS. The main problem validating Analysis SDs and SA model is that they work on a different set of objects: Analysis model SDs objects are analysis level objects while SA objects are components.

Since we know how analysis objects are mapped to SA components (as briefly discussed in section 4.2) we can validate the SDs looking at objects that are in the two representations intersection.

4.4   From SA Model to IWIM Coordination Model

The IWIM [2] model for coordination is described by *processes, ports, channels* and *events*.

A *process* is a black box operating unit. It can be regarded as a *worker* process or a *manager* process. The first one can execute elaborations but it is not responsible for communication while the latter coordinates communications among worker and manager processes. A *port* is used for information exchange; each communicating process owns at least one port. A *channel* represents the interconnection between a producer process port to a consumer process port. There are five different alternatives for a channel; one is for synchronous communication while the others are useful for asynchronous one. *Events* are broadcast in the environment and could be picked up by a process.

SA items are comparable with IWIM items: SA components and IWIM processes are black box units; an SA component is the high level description of an IWIM process; the SA description is higher level since a single SA component can be realized by several IWIM processes. Following these considerations, it is amenable to realize a mapping between the SA description level to the Coordination:

- the SA coordination component (as defined in Section 4.2) becomes a manager process while others become worker process;
- the SA channel (and port) semantics is close to the IWIM model: each SA channel can be mapped in one of the five IWIM channels semantics;
- the IWIM events are comparable with transactions in the LTS model of SA dynamics.

The formalization of this mapping will be of interest for future works.

4.5   Summarizing the Approach

Here the steps followed by our approach are listed:

1. – Use Case Diagrams are captured from functional Requirements;
    – Use Cases are realized by the analysis classes;
    – interaction diagrams are extracted to describe the analysis model scenarios;
    – activity diagrams highlight system activities and synchronization;
2. using Analysis level objects and activity diagrams information, SA components and connectors can be selected and formally described;
3. – an LTS can be automatically generated (from the SA specification) to describe the system dynamics in terms of components interactions;
    – interaction diagrams and LTS can be compared for consistency checking;
    – an IWIM model construction can be driven by SA description.

References

1. Allen, R., Garlan, D.: A Formal Basis for Architectural Connection. *ACM Transactions on Software Engineering and Methodology*, 6(3):213–249, July 1997.
2. Arbab, F.: Coordination of massively concurrent activities. CWI Report CS-R9565 (1995).
3. Arbab, F.: What Do You Mean, Coordination? In the March '98 Issue of the *Bulletin of the Dutch Assoc. for Theor. Comp. Sc. (NVTI)*. Available at: <http://www.cwi.nl/ farhad/>.
4. Balsamo, S., Inverardi, P., Mangano, C., Russo, F.: Performance Evaluation of a Software Architecture: A Case Study. *IEEE Proc. IWSSD-9*, Japan (April 1998).
5. Booch, G.: Software Architecture and the UML. Slides available at <http://www.rational.com/uml/index.jtmpl>.
6. Compare, D., Inverardi, P., Wolf, A. L.: Uncovering Architectural Mismatch in Component Behavior. *Science of Computer Programming* (33)2 (1999) pp. 101-131.
7. Coordination '99: *Proc. 3rd Int'l Conf. on Coordination Languages and Models*, LNCS 1594, Springer Verlag, April 1999.
8. Darwin, an Architectural Description Language. Web site: <http://www-dse.doc.ic.ac.uk/research/darwin/darwin.html>.
9. Eriksson, H.E., Penker, M.: UML Toolkit. John Wiley & Sons (1998).
10. Hofmeister, C., Nord, R., Soni, D.: Applied Software Architecture. Addison-Wesley, (1999).
11. Inverardi, P., Muccini, H.: A Coordination Process Based on UML and a Software Architectural Description On *Proc. of the 2000 I.C. PDPTA*, session: Coordination Models, Languages, Systems and Applications, June 2000, Las Vegas, USA.
12. Inverardi, P., Muccini, H.: Coordination models and Software Architectures in a Unified Software Development Process On-line at: <http://univaq.it/~inverard>.
13. Jacobson, I., Booch, G., Rumbaugh, J.: The Unified Software Development Process. Addison Wesley, Object Technology Series (1999).
14. Luckham, D. C., Kenney, J. J., Augustin, L. M., Vera, J., Bryan, D., Mann, W.: Specification and Analysis of System Architecture Using Rapide. *IEEE TSE, Special Issue on Software Architecture*, 21 (4):336-355, April 1995.
15. Robbins, J.E., Medvidovic, N., Redmiles, D.F., Rosenblum, D.S.: Integrating Architecture Description Languages with a Standard Design Method. *Proc. 20th Int'l Conf. on Software Engineering* Apr. 1998, pp. 209-218.

Wilde: Supporting Change in Groupware

Stephen Barrett[1] and Brendan Tangney[1]

[1] Distributed Systems Group, Department of Computer Science, Trinity College Dublin, Ireland.
{Stephen.Barrett, Brendan.Tangney}@cs.tcd.ie

Abstract. An open systems approach for supporting groupware is advocated and an open systems middleware technology, called Wilde, is presented. Wilde is built on the principle of separating design from functional code. A distinguishing feature of Wilde is that it supports a design level paradigm that supports system redesign. A Wilde based systems can be redesigned after it has been deployed, and even as it executes. Wilde's implementation is discussed, and an example of its use with groupware is presented.

1   Introduction

Building Groupware is difficult. All but the most trivial examples are complex distributed multi-user systems [8]. In practice, accurately capturing the requirements of these systems is a substantial challenge [19][10]. For example, groupware users may seek to create ad-hoc collaborations using a number of different specialist standalone tools, not designed to integrate [6]. Video conferencing software is used across an intranet at one moment, and used across the Internet some time later. That the underlying platform quality differs and calls for very different system architectures is of no concern to the user [17]. The complexity and volatility of these kinds of requirements has limited the exploitation of groupware ideas in mainstream software systems [13].

Support systems, which take the form of middleware platforms, libraries and toolkits, and dedicated groupware languages, aim to simplify the development of groupware. There has been some success to date, but support remains limited. The typical solution offers functionally rich but inflexible support for a very narrow range of application types, or provides support that is generic but functionally limited [13].

We argue that groupware and groupware support systems must be far more adaptable if they are to deliver comprehensive and functional groupware support solutions [1]. Our premise is that actual integration and adaptation scenarios are too diverse to be consistently captured by any preconceived support system and that most groupware systems will inevitably have to be redesigned often over their lifetime.

Our approach is to support the redesign of software at an underlying level of programming paradigm, rather than at the level of service platforms or groupware toolkits. Our paradigm, called Wilde, is built on the principle of separating design from functional code. A distinguishing feature of Wilde is that it supports a design level view of system modification, and supports the redesign of executing systems. This is achieved via direct manipulation of a reified runtime design model, without

A. Porto and G.-C. Roman (Eds.): COORDINATION 2000, LNCS 1906, pp. 329-334, 2000.

the cost associated with traditional software maintenance cycles (i.e. recoding, recompiling and redeployment).

In the remainder of this paper, we explain the Wilde technology and provide a simple demonstration of its application to groupware. Finally, we comment briefly on related research in the area.

2   Wilde – Open Flexible Software

Wilde is a middleware runtime technology, implemented on Windows NT, which supports the construction of COM component based open systems [16]. Wilde applications are structured as re-configurable collections of autonomous collaborating components, which interact according to a design. This is specified in a simple declarative Architecture Description Language, called *Wildecard Description Language (WDL)*. Components are typically fine-grained functional system elements, such as buttons, windows and business objects, and are modelled as providers and consumers of typed services. The component type model is equivalent to, and compatible with that of industry standard component models such as COM [5] and the emerging CORBA Component Model (CCM) [18].

An application design specifies the types and number of components in the application, and how each component's service requirements are satisfied by other components. WDL provides a single modelling construct, called a 'wildcard'. The wildcard is used to describe abstract component types, and to describe abstract *compound components* as compositions of these types. Complex application designs are specified as recursive aggregations of compound components. In addition, WDL supports design specialisation via a multiple inheritance model, so supporting systems construction from existing reusable design patterns.

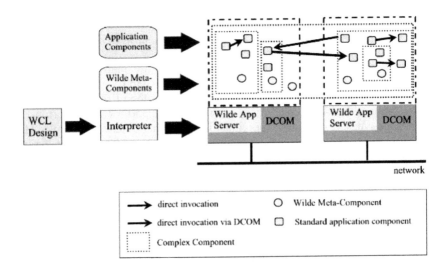

Fig. 1. Wilde Runtime Overview

Figure 1 illustrates a Wilde runtime system executing a Wilde based application over two nodes in a network. WDL designs are directly executed by Wilde's runtime system: there is no intermediate code generation stage. Given a WDL design and a set of appropriate components, the interpreter first parses and type checks the WDL design, and instantiates a meta-model to represent the application design. Following this, the interpreter directs the instantiation of application components and connects them to the meta-model. The meta-model is responsible for configuring application components, advising each component how its service requirements are provided, based on the role the component will play within the application. Thereafter, application components interact directly, without indirection through the meta-model. The resulting system is a network of components that communicate via the standard inter-component invocation model of the component technology.

Overall, the Wilde platform does not appreciably add to the overhead of standard component technologies. The meta-model does not impact meaningfully on the general execution of the application. Furthermore, the cost of interpreting WDL designs is negligible.

The runtime supports a structured system change mechanism via the typed transformation of an application design to another that is related across an inheritance hierarchy. The runtime compares the two designs and drives the modification of a system via the meta-model, which can be accessed and modified at runtime. Changes made to the model result in corresponding changes to the application proper. Components are added, removed, replaced, and service provision is redefined. In this way, Wilde provides a means for expressing both fine grained and substantial adaptations as variations in a system design in a type-safe and immediately executable form. We have implemented a range of groupware systems based on this approach. In the following section, we provide a brief illustrative example of the Wilde approach.

3   Wilde and Groupware

We consider here, a typical integration scenario in which a set of single-user applications must be integrated to support a collaborative session. One consideration among many is to integrate menu systems so that equivalent actions in each tool are tied and have potentially global effect across the collaborative system. We emphasise that, the appropriate integration strategy will be specific to the demands of the particular scenario [7]. For example, in a shared text-editor system that enforces a WYSIWIS synchronisation model, if one user selects a menu, all other users should perceive an equivalent action in their application. In a more sophisticated groupware system, the selection of a menu option might perhaps require a vote on the part of the participants before the action is performed. Another variant would allow interested parties subscribe to menu changes.

The Wilde approach to this and other integration problems is to consider them as adaptability problems that require the application to be redesigned. Consider a design for a single user text editor (with detail irrelevant to this discussion omitted) described below in WDL:

```
wildecard TextEditor {
components:
  GUI view;              // text editor has two components
  AppLogic al;
mappings:
  view.IMenu > al;       // al provides IMenu interface to view
}
```

This single-user system can be modified to support the sharing of menu selections so that it can be used as a component in a collaborative system. Of the many possible approaches, we illustrate here the salient points of adding a groupware menu system to each application to support voting. To do this we will redirect menu invocations to a proxy component added to each application, which filters these invocations based on the results of a vote it initiates amongst its peers. A straightforward method of doing this is to specialise the *TextEditorGUI* component of *TextEditor*, redefining it as a complex component, which includes a group menu proxy component for a group menu voting system (which intercedes in IMenu invocations) as follows:

```
wildecard GroupMenuGUI : private GUI {
required: IMenu, IMenuVote;
components: MenuProxy prxy;
mappings:
  GUI.IMenu > prxy;                 // IMenu provided to wrapped GUI  by prxy
  prxy.IMenu > GroupMenuGUI;        // prxy will pass on IMenu calls ...
  prxy.IMenuVote > GroupMenuGUI;    // assuming a successful vote
}
```

This new wildecard can now be used as a component in a shared text editor system. A simple free form shared text editor system is described below.

```
wildecard SharedTextEditor {
components:
  TextEditorComponent editor1;    // defined elsewhere as specialisation
  TextEditorComponent editor2;    // of TextEditor which redefines view type
  GroupMenuSystem gms;            //component for centralised menu system
mappings:
  editor1 <> editor2;            // maps all possible services
  editor1 <> gms; editor2 <> gms;
}
```

We have focused in this brief example on one small part of a full integration. Other aspects of the integration process are addressed in a similar manner. General adaptability problems (such as redesigning for variations in network quality) have equivalent solutions. In general, the range of transformations we can perform on a Wilde application are constrained only by the degree to which a systems functional code is decomposed into a set of components. The more fine-grained the component set is, the more open to redesign the system is. Wilde provides an appropriately high-level model for reasoning about redesign of such open systems. The original application designer is thus not required to guess how the application may be required to change in the future. By adhering to well understood principles of decomposition in the construction of a component based system, future flexibility is improved.

4   Related Work

Our application to groupware support is compatible with, but differs radically from, platform-based approaches [3], or toolkit based approaches [20]. We maintain that groupware and groupware support are best constructed using an appropriate underlying programming paradigm.

Many Linda oriented systems have been proposed in which components communicate anonymously via a tuple-space [4]. Event based and message-passing models offer similar de-coupling [14] [11]. However, as systems such as Olan [2], Darwin [15], and indeed our research shows, the necessary de-coupling of components is achievable within the context of procedural and object-oriented paradigms. This offers an advantage when constructing complex systems for which these paradigms are the most natural.

Our work is influenced by software composition research, examples of which include   [16] [12] [9]. Our work bears certain similarities to component based research systems such as Olan [2]. However, with Olan for example, design in our terms is fixed at compile-time. Flexibility associated with Olan is purely in terms of the numbers of components of fixed types and interaction a system might contain. In contrast, our approach supports the post compile-time redesign of applications constructed using an industry standard binary component technology.

5   Conclusions

Software domains such as Groupware are particularly challenging because it is very difficult to determine the exact requirements of such applications. A distinguishing feature of Wilde is that it provides a flexible design oriented paradigm with minimal overhead, allowing a system to be redesigned without recoding, and even as it executes. In supporting improved adaptability, Wilde provides a sound foundation on which more useful and responsive groupware can be constructed. As [13] points out, this is important if groupware is to be successful.

6   References

1. Stephen Barrett and Brendan Tangney, "Aspects Composing CSCW Applications," in OOIS (Object-Oriented Information Systems) '95, Springer-Verlag, Dec 1995.
2. L. Bellissard, S. Ben Atallah, A. Kerbrat and M. Riveill, "Component-based programming and application management with Olan," in Object based parallel and distributed computation, Frane-Japan worksho, OBPDC '95, J. Briot, J. Geib and A. Yonezaru (eds.), LNCS 1107, Springer Verlag, 1995.

3. Benford, S. and Mariani, J., eds, Requirements and metaphors of shared interaction. Lancaster University, Esprit Basic Research Report project 6225, D4.1., 1993.
4. R. Bjornson, N. Carriero, D. Gelernter, "From weaving threads to untangling the web: A view of coordination from Linda's perspective," in Proceedings of the second international conference on Coordination languages and Models, COORDINATION '97, Berlin Germany, Sep 1997, LNCS 1282,, Springer Verlag, 1997.
5. The Component Object Model Specification, Draft Version 0.9, October 24, 1995, Microsoft Corporation and Digital Equipment Corporation.
6. Cutkosky, M. R., Engelmore, R. S., Fikes, R. E., Genesereth, M. R., Gruber, T. R., Mark, W. S., Tenenbaum, J. M., And Weber, J. C. "PACT: An experiment in integrating concurrent engineering systems," IEEE Computer Magazine (Jan. 1993), 28-37.
7. Paul Dourish "Open implementation and flexibility in CSCW toolkits", PhD thesis, University College London, 1996.
8. C.A. Ellis, S.J. Gibbs, and R.L. Rein. "Groupware, some issues and experiences," Communications of the ACM, 34(1), January 1991.
9. Gelernter, D. and Carriero, N., "Coordination Languages and Their Significance," Comm. ACM, Vol. 35, No. 2, Feb. 1992, pp 97-107.
10. Greenberg, S., "Personalisable Groupware: Accommodating Individual Roles and Group Differences," in Proc. European Conference on Computer-Supported Co-operative Work CSCW'94, Amsterdam, Netherlands, pp. 17-32.
11. N. Haly, H. Minsky and V. Vingureanu, "Regulated coordination in open distributed systems," in Proceedings of the second international conference on Coordination languages and Models, COORDINATION '97, Berlin Germany, Sep 1997, LNCS 1282, Springer Verlag, 1997.
12. Helm, R., Holland, I.M. and Gangopadhyay, D., "Contracts: Specifying behavioural compositions in object-oriented," in Conf. On Object-Oriented Programming: Systems, Languages and Applications. European Conference on Object-Oriented Programming, pp. 169-180, ECOOP/OOPSLA, ACM Press, 1990.
13. G Henri ter Hofte, "Working apart together – foundations for component groupware", Telematica Instituut Fundamental Researh Series No. 001 (TI/FRS/001)
14. A. Holzbacher, M. Perin and M. Sudholt, "Modelling railway control systems using graph grammars: a case study," in Proceedings of the second international conference on Coordination languages and Models, COORDINATION '97, Berlin Germany, Sep 1997, LNCS 1282, Springer Verlag, 1997.
15. J. Kramer and J. Magee, "Darwin – Exposing the skeleton in the coordination closet," in Proceedings of the second international conference on Coordination languages and Models, COORDINATION '97, Berlin Germany, Sep 1997, LNCS 1282, Springer Verlag, 1997.
16. Oscar Nierstrasz, "Requirements for a composition language," in Proceedings of the ECOOP 94 workshop on Models and Languages for Coordination and Parallelism and Distribution, LNCS, Springer Verlag, 1995.
17. O'Grady, T., Flexible Data Sharing in a Groupware Toolkit. M.Sc. thesis, Department of Computer Science, University of Calgary, Calgary, Alberta, Canada. November 1996.
18. Object Management Group, "CORBA Components – Volume 1", December 1999.
19. W. Reinhard, J. Schweitzer and G. Volksen, "CSCW Tools: Concepts and Architectures", IEEE Computer, vol. 27, no. 5, May 1994.
20. Roseman, M. and Greenberg, S, "Building flexible groupware through open protocols," in Conf. On Office Information Systems, pp. 279-288, ACM, 1993.

On the Verification of Coordination[*]

Paul Dechering[1] and Izak van Langevelde[2]

[1] Hollandse Signaalapparaten B.V.
P.O. Box 42, 7550 GD Hengelo, The Netherlands
paul@dechering.net
[2] Centrum voor Wiskunde en Informatica
P.O. Box 94079, 1090 GB Amsterdam, The Netherlands
izak@cwi.nl

Abstract. Scenario-based verification is introduced as a technique to deal with the complexity of coordination languages, which feature both data manipulation and concurrency. The approach is exemplified by a verification study of the software architecture SPLICE that is used by Hollandse Signaalapparaten. A detailed specification of SPLICE, including the ETHERNET network that SPLICE is using, is written in the process-algebraic language μCRL and for a number of selected scenarios the transition system is automatically generated. For the resulting models, the properties of deadlock freeness, soundness, and weak completeness are automatically proven by model checking.

1 Introduction

Coordination languages are designed to facilitate the development of distributed systems by offering a coherent model of data and control through a clear-cut interface. However, it is far from obvious that the complex structure of distributed data and control, so nicely hidden from the coordination programmer, indeed constitutes the coherent model the programmer has in mind. It is exactly the combination of distributed data and distributed control which makes the verification of coordination a difficult problem.

In isolation, both data manipulation and distributed control have been subjected to verification studies. Classical theorem proving approaches [9] were already, at least theoretically speaking, suitable for proving properties of calculations in sequential programming languages. Furthermore, the study of concurrent systems made possible the verification of complex parallel systems, either through human theorem proving [11] or through semi-automated verification techniques like model-checking (see [4] for a recent overview). However, real-life systems readily exceed the capacities of the human theorem prover, and the role of data is a well-known cause of the infamous state space explosion. The combination of existing approaches to bridge the gap between data and concurrency is a research field of growing interest (for instance, see [12], where the integration

---

[*] Supported by ORKEST: "Onderzoek naar Randvoorwaarden voor de Konstruktie van Embedded SysTemen"

A. Porto and G.-C. Roman (Eds.): COORDINATION 2000, LNCS 1906, pp. 335–340, 2000.

of theorem proving and model checking is discussed), but to date the state of the art of verification falls short when it comes to realistic coordination.

This paper addresses the verification of coordination by proposing a verification technique that lies between model-checking and testing. The idea is to formally specify the coordination language, but instead of generating one all-embracing model, which would be astronomically large in size, if not infinite, to generate and verify models for specific situations. Each of these so-called *scenarios* represents one of the common situations the system may encounter. This way, each scenario covers a slice of the system's behaviour and by considering more and more scenarios the system can be covered more and more.

A test, based on a test case, considers one of the possible courses of actions the system may execute in this test case. In a concurrent system, with a high degree of non-determinism, even for one test case a large number of test runs might not reveal one of those rare error situations. A verification, based on one scenario, will consider all possible courses of actions the system can execute, including possibly rare error situations. So, the approach of verifying all possible variations in system behaviour in isolated test cases is more general than testing, which covers isolated traces of system behaviour in isolated test cases. On the other hand, it is less general than model checking, which covers all variations of system traces for all possible test cases.

The approach of *scenario-based verification* is exemplified with the coordination language SPLICE [1]. A detailed specification of SPLICE was written in μCRL [8], a language based on process algebra with data, and transition systems were generated using the native μCRL tool set. The actual analysis was supported by the CÆSAR/ALDÉBARAN tool set [7].

The paper is organised as follows. Section 2 introduces the coordination language SPLICE and Sect. 3 describes the approach of scenario-based verification using μCRL. Section 4 describes the properties to be verified and Sect. 5 presents the verification results. Finally, Sect. 6 evaluates the approach presented. The full report, including all specifications, of the research presented in this paper is [6].

2   An Overview of SPLICE

SPLICE (Subscription Paradigm for the Logical Interconnection of Concurrent Engines) was introduced as an architecture for *control systems* [1]. Non-functional requirements, e.g. a certain level of fault-tolerance, real-time constraints, adaptability, and concurrency, imposed on this type of systems make the development of control systems a complex matter, and the solution SPLICE offers to reduce this complexity is neatly tucked away behind its programming interface. Thus, SPLICE programmers can concentrate on the functional requirements.

The SPLICE kernel consists of a number of *agents* connected by a communication network. Each application running under the architecture is connected to an agent, which is responsible for the coordination with the other agents. A SPLICE system call by an application is processed by its agent, which typically sends requests over the network to the other agents, gathers responses and manages its local dataspace. Also, if one application does not respond anymore, it is replicated on another processor, making the system to some extent immune to processor and network failure. All this is implemented by the SPLICE agents, hidden away from the applications which just observe a stable and coherent environment of coordinated applications.

3   Scenario-Based Verification Using μCRL

The SPLICE architecture was specified in detail in μCRL [8], a language based on process algebra with data. The full specification takes up about 54 KB, which can be found in the full version of this paper [6]. The corresponding labelled transition system was generated using the μCRL tool set and fed into CÆSAR/ALDÉBARAN [7].

The CÆSAR/ALDÉBARAN tool set is used to further analyse the system generated. First, the system is *reduced modulo weak bisimulation*, which means that all non-observable actions, i.e. the interaction between SPLICE agents and the network, and all network activity, are abstracted away, finally resulting in a much smaller transition system. Then, this reduced system is subjected to model checking. This verification technique consists of checking whether properties, expressed as a theory in some temporal logic, are satisfied by a transition system, interpreted as a Kripke structure. The strong point of model checking as a verification technique is that it can be efficiently automated.

However, even for simple SPLICE applications, the size of the transition system generated already exceeds practical limits by several magnitudes, so somehow a restriction has to be imposed on the systems tested. The restriction that underlies the verification technique promoted in the current paper is to verify the application in certain well-defined situations or 'scenarios'. A scenario is a limited environment interacting with the application, for instance by reading and writing data, or by issueing application commands. Scenarios play the role in verification that is played by test cases in testing.

Summarising, scenario-based verification using μCRL consists of specifying both the SPLICE architecture and the scenarios in μCRL, to generate for each scenario the labelled transition system of this scenario and the architecture, and to reduce and model-check the resulting system, to verify the desired properties.

4   The Properties of SPLICE

The three properties of SPLICE studied in this paper are deadlock freeness, soundness, and completeness. The first speaks for itself, the second and third state that everything that can be read has been written and everything that is written can be read. However, generally the three properties do not hold.

SPLICE was designed to enable a high level of fault-tolerance, but in exceptional circumstances the system might break down. For instance, in the situation where one SPLICE component receives data at a higher rate than it can handle, an internal queue overflows and data is lost. The properties to be verified were weakened to apply to those situations where no exceptional disasters, flagged by 'panic' actions, happen.

Even with this restriction, completeness does not hold in its strong formulation (i.e. "all that is written can subsequently be read") for a number of reasons. First, it takes time for the record to be transferred over the network from the writer to the reader, so only eventually will the reader be able to access this record. Second, it is possible that the record is overwritten by another record with the same key, even if this second record was written before the first one. All that can be guaranteed is weak completeness.

deadlock freeness as long as no 'panic' or proper termination occurs the system is able to proceed with some action

correctness a record that is read was written in the past

weak completeness as long as no 'panic' occurs, it is *possible* that eventually a record can be read that was written and not overwritten by another record with the same key

These formulations are an informal rendering of the properties verified. The exact specification in temporal logic in the EVALUATOR [7] syntax is given in [6].

5 Experiments

For the verification of SPLICE itself, irrespective of any particular application, the scenarios must cover the characteristics of the architecture by making typical combinations of API calls. It goes without saying that the number of possible scenarios is huge, but to give an idea of the principle of scenario-based verification, a small number of scenarios consisting of simple combinations of read and write actions is used.

The scenarios that have been verified all consist of two applications, parameterised by: 1) the application reads any or each record that satisfies a query, or it does not read at all; 2) the application writes or not; 3) the application loops or not. The six scenarios are summarised in Table 1; the full specifications are presented in [6].

For each of the scenarios verified, the three properties of deadlock freeness, soundness, and weak completeness were proven to hold, which presents a modest support for the claim that these properties hold in general. This evidence needs to be strengthened by verifying more scenarios.

An indication of the cost of the scenario-based verification of SPLICE is presented in Table 1, which shows for each scenario the size of the transition system initially generated, the CPU time of the generation process, and the size of the system after reduction modulo weak bisimulation. Two features of these metrics catch the eye. First, transition system generation is expensive for SPLICE, even for the simple scenarios considered. Second, the reduction modulo weak bisimulation, that is abstracting from all internal behaviour, results in a transition system that is several orders of magnitude smaller. As such, Table 1 nicely

Table 1. The verified scenarios with the size of their transition systems and the CPU time to generate these (The experiments were performed on an 300 MHz MIPS R12000 processor)

scenario	application 1			application 2			generation metrics		
	reads	writes	loops	reads	writes	loops	# generated	# reduced	CPU time
1	any	yes	no	any	yes	no	846360	961	6h42m
2	each	yes	no	each	yes	no	554707	702	4h20m
3	any	no	yes	any	no	yes	477392	463	3h30m
4	each	no	yes	each	no	yes	474394	363	3h27m
5	any	yes	yes	any	yes	yes	4561900	3789	37h38m
6	each	yes	yes	each	yes	yes	4458013	2471	32h03m

supports the claim that SPLICE realises complex communications which can be abstracted from to a relative simple level. However, the size of the transition system initially generated appears to be a bottleneck in the analysis, since currently there is no way known to directly generate the smaller reduced system from the specification. A technique like on-the-fly model checking, used in SPIN [10], might bring relief, but it is not available in the current setting of the μCRL tool set.

6   Conclusions and Related Work

Scenario-based verification was introduced as a technique for the verification of coordination languages. The rationale of the technique is to benefit from the exactness of formal verification, while avoiding the state space explosion. The approach was exemplified by the verification of SPLICE using the process-algebraic language μCRL, the μCRL tool set, and the CÆSAR/ALDÉBARAN tool set.

Related approaches all focused at SPLICE at a more abstract level, not aiming at automated verification, and not including the detailed specification of the network used in this paper. An operational semantics is defined in [2] and a process-algebra for SPLICE is defined in [5]. However, the fact that these models are less detailed and not geared towards automated verification does not imply that they are inferior to the approach of the current paper. This is clear from [3], where manual theorem proving based on an abstract transition relation is used to establish equivalence results for a number of coordination models, including the one found in SPLICE. Conclusions at this level of generality cannot be drawn with a detailed model as is presented in this paper.

Scenario-based verification is limited in applicability in that the initial generation of transition systems is a true bottleneck. As was demonstrated in Sect. 5, the size of these increase quickly with the complexity of the scenarios, making the verification of more interesting scenarios impossible.

The strength of the approach, however, is that it facilitates the sound analysis of the key features of a coordination language, which is where both formal verification and testing fall short. For the former, any realistic model is too complex to be analysed formally, while the scope of the latter is limited to isolated system traces. Scenario-based verification is a golden middle.

References

1. M. Boasson. Control systems software. *IEEE Transactions on Automatic Control*, 38(7):1094–1106, July 1993.
2. M. M. Bonsangue, J. N. Kok, M. Boasson, and E. de Jong. A Software Architecture for Distributed Control Systems and its Transition System Semantics. In J. Carroll, G. Lamont, D. Oppenheim, K. George, and B. Bryant, editors, *Proceedings of the 1998 ACM Symposium on Applied Computing (SAC '98)*, pages 159 – 168. ACM press, Feb. 1998.
3. M. M. Bonsangue, J. N. Kok, and G. Zavattaro. Comparing software architectures for coordination languages. In P. Ciancarini and A. L. Wolf, editors, *Proceedings of Coordination '99*, volume 1594 of *Lecture Notes in Computer Science*, pages 150–165. Springer Verlag, 1999.
4. E. W. Clarke, O. Grumberg, and D. A. Peled. *Model Checking*. The MIT Press, 1999.
5. P. Dechering, R. Groenboom, E. de Jong, and J. Udding. Formalization of a Software Architecture for Embedded Systems: a Process Algebra for Splice. In *Proceedings of the Hawaiian International Conference on System Sciences (HICSS-32)*, Jan. 1999.
6. P. Dechering and I. A. van Langevelde. Towards automatic verification of SPLICE. Technical Report SEN-R0015, CWI, May 2000. Available from http://www.cwi.nl.
7. J.-C. Fernandez, H. Garavel, A. Kerbrat, R. Mateescu, L. Mounier, and M. Sighireanu. CADP (Cæsar/Aldébaran development package): A protocol validation and verification toolbox. In R. Alur and T. A. Henzinger, editors, *Proceedings of the 8th Conference on Computer-Aided Verification*, volume 1102 of *Lecture Notes in Computer Science*, pages 437–440. Springer Verlag, Aug. 1996.
8. J. F. Groote. The syntax and semantics of timed μCRL. Technical Report SEN-R9709, CWI, June 1997. Available from http://www.cwi.nl.
9. C. Hoare. An axiomatic approach to computer programming. *Commun. ACM*, 12(10):576–583, Oct. 1969.
10. G. J. Holzmann. *Design and Validation of Computer Protocols*. Prentice Hall, 1991.
11. Z. Manna and A. Pnueli. *Temporal Verifications of Reactive Systems – safety*. Springer Verlag, 1995.
12. S. Rajan, N. Shankar, and M. Srivar. An integration of model checking with automated proof checking. In P. Wolper, editor, *Proceedings of the 1995 workshop on Computer Aided Verification*, volume 939 of *Lecture Notes in Computer Science*, 1995.

Guaranteing Coherent Software Systems when Composing Coordinated Components[1]

Marisol Sánchez, José Luis Herrero, Juan Manuel Murillo, and Juan Hernández

Computer Science Department, University of Extremadura
Escuela Politécnica, Avda. de la Universidad s/n - 10.071 Cáceres. Spain
{marisol, jherrero, juanmamu, juanher}@unex.es

Abstract. Latest trends in coordination models and languages suggest that it must be supported the separated specification of and the dynamic change of coordination constraints. However, little attention has been paid to guaranteeing that, the application of a separately specified coordination pattern to a set of encapsulated objects, or changing the coordination constraints of a software system at run-time, will not produce semantic errors. These kinds of errors would produce an unpredictable system and, consequently, a lack of software quality. In this paper, a method of generating formal interpretable specifications for the reproduction of coordinated environments is presented. The benefits provided by this method are: (i) easy specification, verification and detection of inconsistencies when composing coordination and functional components, (ii) easy verification and detection of inconsistencies where coordination policies are changed dynamically and (iii) simulation of coordinated behaviors. The method is based on the use of the formal specification language Maude (as a simulation tool) and a coordination model. Although the paper adopts Coordinated Roles, it is also shown how the method can be adapted to other compositional coordination models.

1 Introduction

Day by day, compositional techniques are gaining more and more relevance in software engineering. Coordination models and languages promote this kind of techniques: last trends in this area [1][2] (to name a few) propose the separation of coordination constraints in components different from those to be coordinated. The final application is obtained combining the coordination and the functional components. However, little attention has been paid to subjects such as the way in which it can be guaranteed that the final behavior obtained in the composed application is semantically coherent, that is: (*i*) How can it be guaranteed that gluing together a coordination policy and a set of components (that have been coded separately) in an application will produce the expected behavior? and (*ii*) moreover, supposing that the expected behavior is produced, how can it be guaranteed that adding new coordination constraints to a running application or that changing the coordination constraints of such an application will not produce conflict with the current behavior?

---

[1] This work is supported by CICYT under contract TIC 99-1083-C02-02 and Junta de Extremadura under contract IPR98A041

A. Porto and G.-C. Roman (Eds.): COORDINATION 2000, LNCS 1906, pp. 341-346, 2000.

To ilustrate the problem that is faced in this paper (a extended version can be found at [7]), the simple case study presented in [1] will be used: a car park whose entrance is controlled by a ticket machine and a barrier. Both of them are controlled by active objects: a *Ticket_Machine* object that makes the machine produce a ticket on receiving the message *Give* and a *Barrier* object that makes the barrier rise on receiving the message *Elevate*. Both objects have been coded independently with their own synchronization constraints, but when they are put together in the car park application a coordination constraint must be imposed: the barrier cannot elevate if the ticket machine has not previously given a ticket. In [1] our research group proposed Coordinated Roles (*CR*) as a coordination model based on IWIM [2]. The case study can be solved with *CR* coding a coordinator component that simply serializes the execution of any pair of operations. Then, the programmer only has to: (*i*) create instances of the *Ticket_Machine* object, the *Barrier* object and the coordinator, (*ii*) make the binding between the *Give* method and the first operation of the coordinator and (*iii*) make the binding between the *Elevate* method and the second operation of the coordinator. However, as the three components have been coded separately, with no references between them, it cannot be anticipated whether the constraints imposed by the coordinator will or will not be coherent with the internal behavior of the objects (and their synchronization constraints). So, the final behavior of the application will be unpredictable. Moreover, even supposing that it has been demonstrated that the constraints of the coordinator are coherent with the behavior of the objects and, thus, that application works correctly, nothing can be anticipated if new coordination constraints are introduced or if the current coordination constraints are changed.

With the aim of avoiding this deficiency, a method of generating a formal interpretable specification is presented in this paper. This method allows not only the specification, verification and detection of inconsistencies when composing applications, but also the simulation of the global behavior of such applications. In addition, it also allows inconsistencies to be verified and detected when changing the coordination policies of an application at run-time. The method is based on the use of the formal specification language Maude [3] and a exogenous coordination model.

In section 2, the way in which Maude can be used to verify and simulate applications coordinated by means of *CR* is explained. Although the approach presented in this paper use *CR*, it is also outlined how the method can be adapted to any other exogenous coordination model In section 3 some related works are discussed. Finally, in section 4 the conclusions and future works are presented.

2   Verification and Simulation of Coordinated Environment

The approach presented in this work is based on the use of the formal specification language Maude. The method has two phases: the specification phase and the verification/simulation phase. At first, the functional and coordination components are formally specified in Maude. At the verification phase, the formal specification previously generated is executed by the Maude interpreter. Maude will verify the formal specification looking for inconsistencies or ambiguities. If the verification is successful, the execution will also provide a simulation of the coordinated system.

2.1 Formal Specifications with Maude

Maude is a formal language allowing the specification of modules that can be executed using an interpreter. It provides two different shells: Core and Full Maude. Core Maude provides the syntax of Maude. This syntax is defined by functional and system modules that define operations and algebraic equations that specify the semantic of such operations. System modules in addition define rewriting rules that obtain a new system configuration from a specific system configuration and set of operations. The second shell, Full Maude, subsumes all the functionality provided by Core Maude incorporating some new features: Object oriented modules definition and parameterized modules definition. As an example, figure 2 shows the object oriented modules corresponding to the ticket machine and the barrier.

```
(omod TICKET-MACHINE is   ...          (omod BARRIER is ...
  class tick-machine | action : Qid,     class barrier | action : Qid,
      total-requestE : MachineInt,           total-requestB : MachineInt,
      ACK-receivedE : MachineInt ,           ACK-receivedB : MachineInt .
      total-requestB : MachineInt,
      ACK-receivedB : MachineInt .        msg elevate : Oid -> Msg .
                                          ...
  msg give : Oid -> Msg .
  ...                                     crl[R1] : (elevate(B))
  crl[Give] : (give(M))                     < B : barrier | action : 'nil,
    < M : tick-machine | action : 'nil,              total-requestB : N,
              total-requestB : N ,                   ACK-receivedB : T >
              ACK-receivedB : T >       => < B : barrier | action : 'elevate,
  => < M : tick-machine | action : 'give,            ACK-receivedB : 0 >
              ACK-receivedB : 0 >       if N == T .
  if N == T .                           endom)
endom)
```

Fig. 2

2.2 Coordinators Definition in Maude

The coordinators from *CR* are defined in Maude using parameterized modules where the parameters will be theories. The theories provide the syntactic schema that the object modules to be coordinated must satisfy. The theory defining the abstract schemas for the barrier and the ticket machine is shown in figure 3. The theory specifies a schema that can be satisfied by any instance of a class (which receives the generic name *Object*) with one method and several attributes. The same theory can be used to define the abstract schemas for both the ticket machine and the barrier objects.

```
(oth OBJECT is
    ...
  class Object | element : Qid, total-requestE : MachineInt,
        ACK-receivedE : MachineInt , total-requestB : MachineInt,
        ACK-receivedB : MachineInt .
    msg Mobj : Oid -> Msg .
endoth)
```

Fig. 3

In order to perform their functions, coordinators from Coordinated Roles have to specify the different event notifications that must be requested to the coordinated objets adopting the roles. The different Event Notification Protocols of *CR* are specified in Maude using rewriting rules that inspect and modify some special attributes. Figure 4 shows the specification of the coordinator for the example.

```
(omod SERIALIZER[X :: OBJECT, Y :: OBJECT] is ...
  class serial[X, Y] | notificated : Bool, oper-executed? : Bool , list : QidList .
     ...
  crl [EoP1] :   < S : serial[X, Y] | notificated : false, oper-executed? : false >
              < M : Object.X | element : Q , ACK-receivedE : N >
           => < S : serial[X, Y] | notificated : true >
              < M : Object.X | ACK-receivedE :  N + 1 >  if Q =/= 'nil .
  crl [EoP2] :  < S : serial[X, Y] | notificated: true, oper-executed? : false >
              < M : Object.X | total-requestE : N, ACK-receivedE : T >
           => < S : serial[X, Y] |  oper-executed? : true >
              < M : Object.X | ACK-receivedE : 0 >  if N == T .
  rl [BoP] :  < B : Object.Y | element : 'nil , ACK-receivedB : N >
              < S : serial[X, Y] | oper-executed? : true , notificated : false >
           => < S : serial[X, Y] |  oper-executed? : false >
              < B : Object.Y |  ACK-receivedB : N + 1 > .
   ...
endom)
```

Fig. 4

The *SERIALIZER* module has two parameters of type *OBJECT* (the theory defined at the beginning of the section): *X* and *Y*. The purpose of this module is to serialize the execution of the operation *Mobj* of the objects *X* and *Y*. In order to achieve this, the *SERIALIZER* module will ask for the asynchronous notification of the EoP event of the operation *Mobj* of *X* and the synchronous notification of the BoP event of operation *Mobj* of *Y*. The execution of the operation *Mobj* of *Y* will only be allowed if a notification of the execution of the operation *Mobj* of *X* has previously been received. The rewriting rules *EoP1* and *EoP2* specify the protocol for the required asynchronous notification of the EoP event. When this event is notified the *SERIALIZER* module modifies the *operation-executed?* attribute. The protocol for the synchronous notification of the BoP event is specified by the rewriting rule *BoP*.

2.3 Composition Syntax in Maude

In *CR*, a composition syntax is used to make the binding between the objects to be coordinated and the roles declared by the coordinators. In Maude, a symmetrical binding is made between the object modules and the theories specified by the coordinators, using Views. In the figure 5, the *Ticket-dispatch* view makes the binding between the *Object* class and the features of the *OBJECT* theory with the *ticket_m* class and the features of *TICKET-MACHINE* object module. Similarly, the *Barrier* view makes the binding between the class and features of the *OBJECT* theory with the *barrier* class and the features of *BARRIER* object module.

The use of views and theories is the mechanism that establishes the binding between coordinated modules and coordinator modules. On the one hand this makes the coordination pattern perfectly reusable whilst on the other hand, the coordinated modules do not need to know when another module is added to the configuration.

```
(view Ticket-dispatch from OBJECT      (view Barrier from OBJECT to
         to TICKET-MACHINE is                        BARRIER is
   class Object to tick-machine .         class Object to barrier .
   attr element . Object to action .      attr element . Object to action
     ...                                     ...
   msg Mobj to give .                     msg Mobj to elevate .
endv)                                   endv)
```

Fig. 5

```
(omod EXAMPLE1 is protecting SERIALIZER[Ticket-dispatch , Barrier] .
 op init : -> Configuration ...
 eq init = < 'S : serial[Ticket-dispatch , Barrier] |  notificated : false ,
                                        oper-executed? : false , list : nil >
       < 'B : barrier | action : 'nil , total-requestB : 1 , ACK-receivedB : 0 >
       < 'M : tick-machine | action : 'nil , total-requestE : 1 ,
                  ACK-receivedE : 0 , total-requestB : 0 , ACK-receivedB : 0 >
         (give ('M) give ('M) elevate ('B) elevate('B) give ('M) ...
 endom)
```

Fig. 6

2.4 Launching the Application

The module *EXAMPLE1* (figure 6) shows the specification of an application using the *ticket-machine* and *barrier* objects and a *serial* coordinator object. *EXAMPLE1* defines the operation *init*. This operation defines an initial configuration of a system and a set of operations to be executed by such a system.

The Maude interpreter will execute the *init* operation of *EXAMPLE1*. Firstly, Maude will verify automatically the global specification of the system. And secondly, the execution of the system operations will be simulated. By changing the set of operation, the behavior of the system in several situations can be simulated. If the system is not correctly implemented, Maude would return an error and no operations would be performed. The power of the interpreter was decisive in the choice of Maude as a formal tool for the specification of coordinated systems.

2.5 Adapting the Method in Order to Use Other Exogenous Coordination Models

The approach presented has shown how Maude can be used to specify, verify and simulate coordinated applications coded using *CR*. The same approach can be adapted to any other exogenous coordination model, observing some general rules. Functional and coordination components are represented by specification modules. In particular, specification modules representing coordination components are parameterized, in which the parameters represent the coordinated components. The use of theories will allows the coordinators to access the features of coordinated components without making explicit reference to them. So, the reusability of the coordinator modules is guaranteed. The views will be used to make the binding between the coordinator parameters and the components to be coordinated. Finally, in order for the coordination constraints to be implemented, rewriting rules are used in the specification modules which correspond to coordinator components.

3   Related Works

Although this work has chosen Maude as formal language, there are other algebraic specification languages like OBJ3 and CafeOBJ[4] that could be adopted. However, Maude has some additional features like reflective capabilities and the Metalevel. These allow new modules with new operations to be defined and become integral to Maude. Such features have already proven fruitfull in our research.

In [5] the problem that is faced in this paper is also detected. This work highlights the critical challenge faced by software developers when trying to ascertain whether system components are correctly integrated. To provide a solution, both a specification method based on CHAM formalism and an algorithm to check the system properties are proposed. The method is mainly focused on early detection of deadlock situations.

The work presented in [6] must also be mentioned. In this work, active systems are specified using LOTOS and SDL. The goal is to generate prototypes of Java programs from specification modules. As is explained in the next section our research group has automatic code generation as a common goal.

4   Conclusions and Future Works

This paper has clarified how Maude can be used to generate formal specifications of coordinated applications in which coordination code is separated of coordinated components. The formal specifications in Maude can be interpreted, verified, and simulated. This allows the programmer to know whether, applying a coordination pattern to a set of functional components will produce coherent behavior.

We believe that coordination and its separated specification must be supported also at the design stage, integrating the necessary tools into UML to support the correct design of the coordination constraint. Such coordination constraints will be automatically translated to a specification in Maude to be verified. Finally, using the Metalevel and the reflective capabilities of Maude, a code generator will be developed to produce Java and Coordinated Roles code from the specification modules.

References

1. J.M. Murillo, J. Hernández, F. Sánchez, L.A. Álvarez. Coordinated Roles: Promoting Reusability of Coordinated Active Objects using Event Notification Protocols. *Third International conference Coordination'99*. LNCS 1594. Springer-Verlag. 1999.
2. F. Arbab. The IWIM Model for Coordination of Concurrent Activities. *First International conference Coordination'96*. LNCS 1061. Springer-Verlag. 1996.
3. M. Clavel, S. Eker, P. Lincoln, and J. Meseguer. Principles of Maude. *1st Intl. Workshop on Rewriting Logic and its Applications*, Electronic Notes in Theoretical Computer Science, Elsevier Sciences, 1996.
4. R. Diaconescu and K. Futatsugi CafeOBJ Report, Volume 6 of AMAST series in Computing, World Scientific, 1998.
5. P. Inverardi, A. Wolf and D. Yankelevich. Checking Assumptions in Component Dynamics at the Architectural Level. *2nd.International conference Coordination'97*. LNCS 1282. Springer-Verlag. 1997.
6. P. Poizat, C. Choppy and J. Royer. From Informal Requirements to COOP: a Concurrent Automata Aproach. *FM'99 - World Congress on Formal Methods in the Development of Computing Systems*, Toulouse, France. LNCS 1709. Springer-Verlag. 1999.
7. M. Sánchez, J. Herrero, J. M. Murillo. Behaviour Simulation in Cooperating Environments. *Technical Report TR-7/2000. Department of Computer Science. University of Extremadura.* http://webepcc.unex.es/marisol/TR7-2000.ps.gz

Coordination-Based Design
of Distributed Systems

Joost N. Kok[1] and Kaisa Sere[2]

[1] Leiden Institute of Advanced Computer Science, Leiden University
P.O.Box 9512, 2300 RA Leiden, The Netherlands
joost@liacs.nl
[2] Turku Centre for Computer Science, Åbo Akademi University
Lemminkäisenkatu 14A, 20520 Turku, Finland
kaisa.sere@abo.fi

Abstract. We present a component-based formal approach to the design of distributed systems based on the coordination of the interaction and of the flow of control using graphical notation, refinement and guarded composition.

1 Introduction

The need to integrate graphical notations like UML [2] with formal development methods has been recognised by several researchers [4,5]. In this paper we show how visual diagrams have direct conterparts in the formal description technique, the action systems, that we use.

The *action system* formalism [1] is a state based approach to distributed computing. The two main development techniques used on action systems are *refinement* and *guarded composition*. We propose a dynamic version of guarded composition in which objects can restrict other objects in their execution by imposing an additional guard on them. The guarded composition is a powerful mechanism for the coordination of the flow of control.

We focus on coordination and study the interaction between components. We show that by first giving a high-level visual specification to the coordination architecture makes the communication media explicit into the component structure at the level of the action system specification. Hence, we can formally develop and reason about the communication component in the same manner as we develop and reason about other components in a distributed system. The advantage we get is that for instance communication protocols between components can be stepwise developed within the refinement calculus from abstract components modelling coordination focusing on these components and not anymore as a side product of developing the functional aspects of the system. Moreover, one can envisage a clear separation between coordination and other components in initial stages of the design, followed by mixing these components in later stages using correctness-preserving refinement steps.

A. Porto and G.-C. Roman (Eds.): COORDINATION 2000, LNCS 1906, pp. 347–352, 2000.

2   OO-Action Systems

We give a brief overview of the OO-Action Systems. For more details consult [3]. A *class* C is a statement of the form

$$C = \|[\quad \textbf{attr} \quad y^* := y0 \; ; \; x := x0$$
$$\textbf{obj} \quad n$$
$$\textbf{meth} \; m_1 = M_1 \; ; \; \cdots \; ; \; m_h = M_h$$
$$\textbf{do} \; O \; \textbf{od}$$
$$\|]$$

A class consists of four declaration sections. In the attribute declaration the *shared attributes* in the list y, marked with an asterisk $*$, describe the variables to be shared among all active objects. The *local attributes* in the list x describe variables that are local to an object instance of the class. The list n of *object variables* describes a special kind of variables local to an object instance of the class. They contain names of objects and are used for calling methods of other objects. We assume that the lists x, y and n are pairwise disjoint. A *method* $m_i = M_i$ describes a procedure of an object instance of the class. The *class body* **do** O **od** is a description of the actions O to be executed repeatedly when the object instance of the class is activated.

An *OO-action system* OO consists of a finite set of classes $OO = \{C_1, ..., C_n\}$ such that the shared attributes declared in each C_i are distinct and actions in each C_i or bodies of methods declared in each C_i do not contain *new* statements referring to class names not used by classes in OO.

There are some classes in OO, marked with an asterisk $*$. Execution starts by the creation of one object instance of each of these classes. Each object, when created, chooses enabled actions and executes them. Actions within an object operating on disjoint sets of local and shared attributes, and object variables can be executed in parallel. They can also create other objects by executing new-statements. Actions of different active objects can be executed in parallel if they are operating on disjoint sets of shared attributes. Objects interact by means of the shared attributes and by executing methods of other objects.

Consider two classes A and B in an OO-action system $C = \{... A, B, ...\}$. The *guarded composition*, denoted $g_1 \rightarrow A \| g_2 \rightarrow B$, of the two classes is an OO-action system $C' = \{... g_1 \rightarrow A, g_2 \rightarrow B, ...\}$, where every action of an object from class A (B) is guarded by the boolean expression g_1 (g_2) on the attributes of the classes in an OO-action system. Hence, an action in an object instance from class A (B) can be enabled only in a state where g_1 (g_2) evaluates to true.

The guarded composition on classes can be lifted to the level of OO-action systems. Consider two OO-action systems, $\mathcal{A}$ and $\mathcal{B}$, where the global attributes and methods of the two systems all have distinct names. We define the guarded composition $g_1 \rightarrow \mathcal{A} \| g_2 \rightarrow \mathcal{B}$ of $\mathcal{A}$ and $\mathcal{B}$, where g_1 and g_2 are boolean expressions on the attributes of the OO-action systems, to be the OO-action system which in its set of classes contains the union of the classes of both OO-action systems. Thus, guarded composition of OO-action systems will combine the state spaces of the two components. The method declarations and the actions in the composition consist of the method declarations and actions in the original systems. The actions of $\mathcal{A}$ and $\mathcal{B}$ are, however, guarded by the boolean expressions g_1, g_2, respectively. In order to have a *dynamic* version of the guarded composition on the level of objects, the following statement is added to the language: *expression.restrict(boolean expression)*. Here the first expression should deliver either a reference to an object or a class name. When this statement is executed, the left expression is evaluated and when the first expression delivers an object name, then this object will be restricted by having an additional guard, which is given by the boolean expression. Note that this boolean expression can access the local and global attributes and objects of the object executing it, and only the global attributes and objects of the object that will be restricted. In case that the first expression gives a class name, then all instances of this class (already existing or newly created ones) will have the same additional guard given by the boolean expression.

3 Coordination of OO-Action Systems

Let A and B be two components (classes or OO-action systems) in a guarded composition $A \parallel B$ (when the guards are equivalent to *true*, then we often omit them). Communication between the two components is modelled via a tuple space. A tuple is added into the tuple space by calling the *add* method associated with the tuple space. A tuple is removed with a call to the *rem* method. The presence of *tuple* in the tuple space is checked by a call to the *exists* method. Hence, the components A and B call these methods when interacting with the tuple space. This results in the class diagram in Fig. 1 where the methods are located in the tuple space and the components have a relationship with this. Hence, we have identified the coordination pattern on the level of classes.

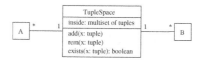

Fig. 1. The tuple space

The tuple space translates into a class $\mathcal{T}$ without any actions, but with three methods corresponding to the three methods given in the class diagram. The attribute *inside* models the contents of the tuple space.

$$\mathcal{T} = \lVert \begin{array}{ll} \textbf{attr} & inside : multiset\ of\ tuples \\ \textbf{meth} & add(x : tuple) = (inside : = inside \cup \{x\}) \\ & rem(x : tuple) = (inside : = inside - \{x\}) \\ & exists(x : tuple) = (x \in inside) \end{array}$$
$$\rVert$$

The overall functionality of the system $\{T, A, B\}$ is given by the guarded composition $T \parallel A \parallel B$ as all the systems are represented in the class diagram of Fig. 1. Observe that A and B will have object variables refering to T. The guarded composition $T \parallel A \parallel \forall x : tuple.\neg exists(x) \rightarrow B$ will coordinate the work so that the an action in a B class is activated only when there are no tuples in a tuple space.

The *pipe* is an other communication media used in some pipe-and-filter coordination models [6]. It models a FIFO queue.

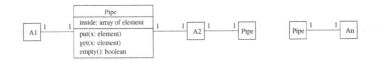

Fig. 2. A pipe

Also the pipe is a class, here called $\mathcal{P}$, without any actions. It has three methods corresponding to the three global procedures, *put, get, empty*, given in the class diagram. The attribute *inside* models the contents of the pipe.

$$\mathcal{P} = \ [\![\quad \textbf{attr} \quad inside : array \ of \ element$$
$$\textbf{meth} \quad put(x : element) = (inside : = inside \cdot \langle x \rangle)$$
$$get(x : element) =$$
$$(x, inside : = head(inside), tail(inside))$$
$$empty() = (inside = \langle \ \rangle)$$
$$]\!]$$

As we have now clarified the component structure and the access methods for the communication media, we can start developing implementations for the components or add new components in the system as will be demonstrated below in our example. We can, for instance, give more structure to the tuple space or the pipe. We can also add autonomous functionality and intelligence to the communication component. This development work is done within the refinement calculus framework. In our case all the refinement work can be carried out in the standard refinement calculus framework without the need to develop any new calculi.

4   A Train System

We give an example of the stepwise development of a coordinated system using dynamic guarded composition.

Let us start by introducing the problem: we have a (possibly infinite) railway track divided into blocks. There is a number of trains that have to run over this track. All the trains start at the first block. We develop the system in the OO-action system formalism. Then we want to coordinate the behavior by imposing constraints on the behaviour.

$$\mathcal{T}rain = \Vert[\;\; \mathbf{obj} \;\; block^*$$
$$\mathbf{do} \quad block.next \neq nil \rightarrow$$
$$block.leave(); \; block := block.next; \; block.enter()$$
$$\mathbf{od}$$
$$]\Vert$$

$$\mathcal{B}lock = \Vert[\;\; \mathbf{attr} \quad number := 0 \qquad \#\# \; number \; of \; trains \; in \; block$$
$$\mathbf{obj} \quad next^* := nil$$
$$\mathbf{meth} \;\; enter = (number := number + 1)$$
$$leave = (number := number - 1)$$
$$]\Vert : enter, leave$$

$$\mathcal{R}wc^* = \Vert[\;\; \mathbf{obj} \;\; firstblock := new(Block); lastblock := firstblock;$$
$$\mathbf{do} \quad new(Train).block = firstblock \qquad \#\# \; create \; new \; train$$
$$\| \quad lastblock.next := new(Block); \; lastblock := lastblock.next$$
$$\mathbf{od}$$
$$]\Vert$$

First we introduce that each block has a maximum number of trains that can be accomodated in it. This number may vary from block to block. Second, trains are divided into two classes: fast and slow trains. If there are fast and a slow trains in the same block, then only the fast trains can move and the slow trains should be suspended until the fast trains have left the block.

For the first restriction we replace the Block class by

$$\mathcal{C} = \Vert[\;\; \mathbf{attr} \quad number := 0, max :\in \{1, 2, \ldots\}, b := true$$
$$\mathbf{obj} \quad next^* := nil$$
$$\mathbf{meth} \;\; enter = (number := number + 1)$$
$$leave = (number := number - 1)$$
$$\mathbf{do} \quad b \rightarrow Train.restrict(Train.block.next = self \wedge number \geq max);$$
$$b := false$$
$$\mathbf{od}$$
$$]\Vert : enter, leave$$

Here max is the maximal number of trains in the block. The restriction says that a train is not allowed to enter a block if the block is full (the block restricts the trains).

For the second step we replace the $\mathcal{T}rain$ class by (A slow train is restricted by a fast train if both are in the same block)

$$\mathcal{T}rain = \Vert[\;\; \mathbf{attr} \;\; kind^* :\in \{slow, fast\}, b := true$$
$$\mathbf{obj} \;\; block^*$$
$$\mathbf{do} \quad kind :\in \{slow, fast\}$$
$$\| \quad block.next \neq nil \rightarrow$$
$$block.leave(); \; block := block.next; \; block.enter()$$
$$\| \quad b \rightarrow Train.restrict(Train.block = self.block$$
$$\wedge Train.kind = slow \wedge self.kind = fast);$$
$$b := false$$
$$\mathbf{od}$$
$$]\Vert$$

5   Conclusions

We have studied the use of graphical notations in the design of coordination aspects of software architectures. The added value we gained is the fact that architectural details of the communication media between components in a distributed object-based system, become components of their own rights. Hence, they can be developed and further refined in isolation. The diagrams play a vital role in our approach as they (1) force the designer to focus on the interaction between various components and (2) expose the component structure more explicitly than what a mere action system specification would do. The coordination aspects were also studied via the guarded composition operator. The dynamic notion of guarded composition seems to work well and is a natural way to add constraints to OO-action systems.

References

1. R. J. R. Back and K. Sere. Stepwise refinement of action systems. *Structured Programming*, 12:17–30, 1991.
2. G. Booch, J. Rumbaugh, and I. Jacobson. *The Unified Modeling Language User Guide*. Addison-Wesley, October 1998.
3. M. M. Bonsangue, J. N. Kok, and K. Sere. Developing object-based distributed system. In *Formal Methods for Open Object-based Distributed Systems (FMOODS'99)*, Florence, Italy, February 1999. Kluver Academic Publishers.
4. R. Breu, U. Hinkel, C. Hofmann, C. Klein, B. Paech, B. Rumpe, V. Thurner. Towards a Formalization of the Unified Modeling Language. In *Proceedings of ECOOP'97*. Jyväskylä, Finland, June 1997. Lecture Notes in Computer Science 1241. Springer Verlag.
5. R. Kneuper. Limits of Formal Methods. *Formal Aspects of Computing* 9(4): 379-394, Springer Verlag 1997.
6. J. Philipps and B. Rumpe. Refinement of pipe-and-filter architectures. In Proc. of *FM'99 – Formal Methods*, Volume 1, Toulouse, France, 1999, volume 1708 of *Lecture Notes in Computer Science*. Springer–Verlag, 1999.

Author Index

Lecture Notes in Computer Science

For information about Vols. 1–1825
please contact your bookseller or Springer-Verlag

Vol. 1865: K.R. Apt, A.C. Kakas, E. Monfroy, F. Rossi (Eds.), New Trends Constraints. Proceedings, 1999. X, 339 pages. 2000. (Subseries LNAI).

Vol. 1866: J. Cussens, A. Frisch (Eds.), Inductive Logic Programming. Proceedings, 2000. X, 265 pages. 2000. (Subseries LNAI).

Vol. 1867: B. Ganter, G.W. Mineau (Eds.), Conceptual Structures: Logical, Linguistic, and Computational Issues. Proceedings, 2000. XI, 569 pages. 2000. (Subseries LNAI).

Vol. 1868: P. Koopman, C. Clack (Eds.), Implementation of Functional Languages. Proceedings, 1999. IX, 199 pages. 2000.

Vol. 1869: M. Aagaard, J. Harrison (Eds.), Theorem Proving in Higher Order Logics. Proceedings, 2000. IX, 535 pages. 2000.

Vol. 1872: J. van Leeuwen, O. Watanabe, M. Hagiya, P.D. Mosses, T. Ito (Eds.), Theoretical Computer Science. Proceedings, 2000. XV, 630 pages. 2000.

Vol. 1873: M. Ibrahim, J. Küng, N. Revell (Eds.), Database and Expert Systems Applications. Proceedings, 2000. XIX, 1005 pages. 2000.

Vol. 1874: Y. Kambayashi, M. Mohania, A M. Tjoa (Eds.), Data Warehousing and Knowledge Discovery. Proceedings, 2000. XII, 438 pages. 2000.

Vol. 1875: K. Bauknecht, S.K. Madria, G. Pernul (Eds.), Electronic Commerce and Web Technologies. Proceedings, 2000. XII, 488 pages. 2000.

Vol. 1876: F. J. Ferri, J.M. Iñesta, A. Amin, P. Pudil (Eds.), Advances in Pattern Recognition. Proceedings, 2000. XVIII, 901 pages. 2000.

Vol. 1877: C. Palamidessi (Ed.), CONCUR 2000 – Concurrency Theory. Proceedings, 2000. XI, 612 pages. 2000.

Vol. 1878: J.P. Bowen, S. Dunne, A. Galloway, S. King (Eds.), ZB 2000: Formal Specification and Development in Z and B. Proceedings, 2000. XIV, 511 pages. 2000.

Vol. 1879: M. Paterson (Ed.), Algorithms – ESA 2000. Proceedings, 2000. IX, 450 pages. 2000.

Vol. 1880: M. Bellare (Ed.), Advances in Cryptology – CRYPTO 2000. Proceedings, 2000. XI, 545 pages. 2000.

Vol. 1881: C. Zhang, V.-W. Soo (Eds.), Design and Applications of Intelligent Agents. Proceedings, 2000. X, 183 pages. 2000. (Subseries LNAI).

Vol. 1882: D. Kotz, F. Mattern (Eds.), Agent Systems, Mobile Agents, and Applications. Proceedings, 2000. XII, 275 pages. 2000.

Vol. 1883: B. Triggs, A. Zisserman, R. Szeliski (Eds.), Vision Algorithms: Theory and Practice. Proceedings, 1999. X, 383 pages. 2000.

Vol. 1884: J. Štuller, J. Pokorný, B. Thalheim, Y. Masunaga (Eds.), Current Issues in Databases and Information Systems. Proceedings, 2000. XIII, 396 pages. 2000.

Vol. 1885: K. Havelund, J. Penix, W. Visser (Eds.), SPIN Model Checking and Software Verification. Proceedings, 2000. X, 343 pages. 2000.

Vol. 1886: R. Mizoguchi, J. Slaney /Eds.), PRICAI 2000: Topics in Artificial Intelligence. Proceedings, 2000. XX, 835 pages. 2000. (Subseries LNAI).

Vol. 1888: G. Sommer, Y.Y. Zeevi (Eds.), Algebraic Frames for the Perception-Action Cycle. Proceedings, 2000. X, 349 pages. 2000.

Vol. 1889: M. Anderson, P. Cheng, V. Haarslev (Eds.), Theory and Application of Diagrams. Proceedings, 2000. XII, 504 pages. 2000. (Subseries LNAI).

Vol. 1890: C Linnhoff-Popien, H.-G. Hegering (Eds.), Trends in Distributed Systems: Towards a Universal Service Market. Proceedings, 2000. XI, 341 pages. 2000.

Vol. 1891: A.L. Oliveira (Ed.), Grammatical Inference: Algorithms and Applications. Proceedings, 2000. VIII, 313 pages. 2000. (Subseries LNAI).

Vol. 1892: P. Brusilovsky, O. Stock, C. Strapparava (Eds.), Adaptive Hypermedia and Adaptive Web-Based Systems. Proceedings, 2000. XIII, 422 pages. 2000.

Vol. 1893: M. Nielsen, B. Rovan (Eds.), Mathematical Foundations of Computer Science 2000. Proceedings, 2000. XIII, 710 pages. 2000.

Vol. 1895: F. Cuppens, Y. Deswarte, D. Gollmann, M. Waidner (Eds.), Computer Security – ESORICS 2000. Proceedings, 2000. X, 325 pages. 2000.

Vol. 1896: R. W. Hartenstein, H. Grünbacher (Eds.), Field-Programmable Logic and Applications. Proceedings, 2000. XVII, 856 pages. 2000.

Vol. 1897: J. Gutknecht, W. Weck (Eds.), Modular Programming Languages. Proceedings, 2000. XII, 299 pages. 2000.

Vol. 1898: E. Blanzieri, L. Portinale (Eds.), Advances in Case-Based Reasoning. Proceedings, 2000. XII, 530 pages. 2000. (Subseries LNAI).

Vol. 1899: H.-H. Nagel, F.J. Perales López (Eds.), Articulated Motion and Deformable Objects. Proceedings, 2000. X, 183 pages. 2000.

Vol. 1900: A. Bode, T. Ludwig, W. Karl, R. Wismüller (Eds.), Euro-Par 2000 Parallel Processing. Proceedings, 2000. XXXV, 1368 pages. 2000.

Vol. 1901: O. Etzion, P. Scheuermann (Eds.), Cooperative Information Systems. Proceedings, 2000. XI, 336 pages. 2000.

Vol. 1902: P. Sojka, I. Kopeček, K. Pala (Eds.), Text, Speech and Dialogue. Proceedings, 2000. XIII, 463 pages. 2000. (Subseries LNAI).

Vol. 1906: A. Porto, G.-C. Roman (Eds.), Coordination Languages and Models. Proceedings, 2000. IX, 353 pages. 2000.

Vol. 1912: Y. Gurevich, P.W. Kutter, M. Odersky, L. Thiele (Eds.), Abstract State Machines. Proceedings, 2000. X, 381 pages. 2000.

Vol. 1913: K. Jansen, S. Khuller (Eds.), Approximation Algorithms for Combinatorial Optimization. Proceedings, 2000. IX, 275 pages. 2000.

Vol. 1923: J. Borbinha, T. Baker (Eds.), Research and Advanced Technology for Digital Libraries. Proceedings, 2000. XVII, 513 pages. 2000.

Vol. 1924: W. Taha (Ed.), Semantics, Applications, and Implementation of Program Generation. Proceedings, 2000. VIII, 231 pages. 2000.

Vol. 1926: M. Joseph (Ed.), Formal Techniques in Real-Time and Fault-Tolerant Systems. Proceedings, 2000. X, 305 pages. 2000.